LOGOS AND SOPHIA

SOCIETY OF BIBLICAL LITERATURE

DISSERTATION SERIES
David L. Petersen, Old Testament Editor
Pheme Perkins, New Testament Editor

Number 134

LOGOS AND SOPHIA
The Rhetorical Situation
of 1 Corinthians
by
Stephen M. Pogoloff

Stephen M. Pogoloff

LOGOS AND SOPHIA
The Rhetorical Situation of 1 Corinthians

Scholars Press
Atlanta, Georgia

LOGOS AND SOPHIA
The Rhetorical Situation of 1 Corinthians

Stephen M. Pogoloff

Ph.D., 1990
Duke University

Advisor:
D. Moody Smith

Library of Congress Cataloging in Publication Data
Pogoloff, Stephen M.
Logos and sophia: the rhetorical situation of 1 Corinthians/
Stephen M. Pogoloff.
p. cm. — (Dissertation series; no. 134)
Originally presented as the author's thesis (Ph.D.)—Duke University, 1990.
Includes bibliographical references.
ISBN 1-55540-784-6 (alk. paper). — ISBN 1-55540-783-8 (pbk.: alk. paper)
1. Bible. N.T. Corinthians, 1st, I-IV—Criticism, interpretation, etc. 2. Rhetoric in the Bible. I. Title. II. Series: Dissertation series (Society of Biblical Literature); no. 134.
BS2675.2.P69 1992
227'.2066—dc20 92-34962
CIP

Printed in the United States of America
on acid-free paper

ACKNOWLEDGMENTS

This dissertation is in many ways the fruit of the teaching of my professors. The contributions of Dr. George Kennedy in the areas of methodology and the history of rhetoric are obvious, and this work would never even have been envisioned if not for his inspiration. I must also thank Dr. Dan O. Via for his challenging teaching in the area of hermeneutics, the marks of which can be found throughout the dissertation. In the area of social history, Dr. Dale Martin has offered invaluable assistance. And for the encouragement to question orthodox exegesis of 1 Cor., and to pursue the following alternative, I thank my supervisor, Dr. D. Moody Smith.

I also wish to thank those who have taught me in the area of New Testament in the past: John Koenig, J. Louis Martyn, Raymond Brown, A.E. Harvey, George Caird, and especially Arthur Moore.

Also deserving great thanks are those who have made this effort financially possible, and whose moral support has been just as valuable. This includes many groups, churches and individuals, among whom I especially wish to thank The Episcopal Church Foundation and Robin and Marianne Anker-Peterson.

Most of all, I thank my family, and especially my wife Christina, for graciously tolerating my foolish desire to learn more.

TABLE OF CONTENTS

ABBREVIATIONS

All abbreviations for journals and reference works are standard, as found in:

Joseph A. Fitzmeyer. *An Introductory Bibliography for the Study of Scripture*, revised edition. Rome: Biblical Institute Press, 1981.

or

Leland G. Alkire, Jr., ed. *Periodical Title Abbreviations*, 5th edition. Detroit: Gale Research Co., 1986.

Abbreviations for classical works are also standard, as found in:

The Oxford Classical Dictionary, 2nd edition. Oxford: Clarendon, 1970.

or

Henry George Liddell and Robert Scott, *A Greek- English Lexicon*, 9th edition, revised by Henry Stuart Jones. Oxford: Clarendon: 1940.

or

Konrad Ziegler and Walther Sontheimer, eds. *Der Kleine Pauly*, Vol. I. Stuttgart: Alfred Druckenmüller, 1964.

INTRODUCTION

How are we to understand the first four chapters of 1 Corinthians? Critics generally attempt to answer this question by painstakingly reconstructing the historical situation. However, "full as the Corinthian letters are of valuable raw material, it is no easy task to win from them a clear account of what was going on in the Corinthian church of the 50s of the first century."[1] This difficulty is evident in the great variety of proposed reconstructions, especially of the "σοφία" ("wisdom") so prominent in the opening chapters. Despite this variety of reconstructions which to some extent lead to conflicting interpretations, the following study attempts a fresh reading of these chapters. I believe this is possible because of three currents in present NT scholarship. As we shall see, these currents are interrelated in a major shift in interpretive stance.

Foremost among these currents is a rediscovery of and renewed appreciation for ancient rhetoric. Traditionally, NT critics have argued that the world of the NT was at best tangentially connected to the world of rhetoric. However, the traditional view is based on several assumptions which are now changing. First, classicists and now NT scholars are increasingly recognizing that ancient rhetoric was a far cry from our notions of "mere rhetoric." We have mistakenly understood it as narrowly concerned with style, or as no more than a dry collection of rules, or as the reserve of an educated elite. Rather, it affected virtually all Greco-Roman culture, and was intertwined with values on nearly every level of society. This rhetorical culture shaped all communications, and thus most communities and social movements, including early Christianity.

---

[1]C.K. Barrett, *Essays on Paul* (Philadelphia: The Westminster Press, 1982), 1.

Also contributing to NT scholarship's recovery of rhetoric are the rapidly changing assumptions about social barriers in the ancient world. Just as rhetoric has been moved closer to early Christian communities by under-standing it as a wide cultural force rather than just an elitist one, so have Christian communities been moved out of their narrowly lower class and at times exclusively Palestinian vs. Hellenistic or Jewish vs. Gentile environments. No longer are the early Christian documents viewed as non-literary; no longer can we view Paul or any other first-century Jew as isolated from Hellenistic culture. Thus, we must take into account the dominating role of rhetoric in the Greco-Roman world when we interpret any NT document.

The second current which allows a fresh look at 1 Cor. is the renewed interest in social factors in under standing NT texts. These factors are helping us to further "embody" doctrinal discussions in their social dimensions, discussions which have at times been treated in a somewhat "docetic" manner.[2]

The third current is radical change in hermeneutical theory. From every quarter, the value, meaning, or even possibility of historical reconstruction has been challenged. From these challenges have arisen various alter-native interpretive strategies. Frequently, these strategies are non- or even anti-historical, and tend toward purely literary readings. The insights of such proposals are provocative, yet counter-intuitive, since the meanings of the texts seem in some sense historically grounded. Between non- or anti-historical literary approaches and traditional historical criticism stands rhetorical criticism. While still a young and unsettled approach, rhetorical criticism allows the interpreter to read the texts as both literary and historical. The point of intersection between the two is the rhetorical, rather than the historical, situation.

Together, these currents allow a revised understanding of the situation Paul addresses in 1 Cor. 1-4. Paul's previously enigmatic references to rhetoric begin to make sense. By focusing on the rhetorical situation, we can avoid many of the blind alleys which have tempted critics when they have tried to determine what "actually"

---

[2]Robin Scroggs, "The Sociological Interpretation of the New Testament: The Present State of Research," *NTS* 26 (1980), 165-166.

happened rather than the meaning of Paul's rhetoric. The social constraints of Paul's rhetorical situation can help us see that we need not assume that Paul is addressing only doctrinal disagreements between himself and the Corinthians or between Corinthian factions.

This assumption led many scholars to countless yet fruitless and now largely abandoned attempts to discern the doctrinal differences among the groups of 1:12.[3] It also lies behind the two main hypotheses of what Paul means by "worldly wisdom": the older view that Paul was confronting the ideas of Greco-Roman philosophy, or the more recent one that he was confronting "gnostic" religious doctrines. In other words, scholars have tended to assume that ideas foreign to the gospel invaded the community, and these ideas caused divisions, whether between factions, between Paul and the Corinthians, or between Paul and other opponents. Paul is then seen as exclusively concerned with doctrine, asking the Corinthians to substitute his ideas for theirs.

However, study of later chapters of 1 Cor. has convinced many critics that Paul's rhetoric is more pastoral response to social realties than abstract doctrine.[4] If we extend these insights to the opening chapters, we may find social and cultural factors which enflesh Paul's language. In those chapters, we will be able to follow Paul's leads about rhetoric, divisiveness, social status, and boasting.

---

[3]For a summary of these attempts, see J.C. Hurd, *The Origin of First Corinthians* (New York: Seabury, 1965), 80-117.

[4]Especially Gerd Theissen, *The Social Setting of Pauline Christianity* (Philadelphia: Fortress, 1982).

PART I

RHETORIC AND RHETORICAL CRITICISM

CHAPTER I

RHETORIC REDIVIVUS

When Paul writes to the Corinthians that his κήρυγμά was not ἐν σοφίᾳ λόγου (1:17), not καθ' ὑπεροχὴν λόγου ἢ σοφίας (2:1), not ἐν πειθοῖς σοφίας λόγοις (2:4), nor ἐν σοφίᾳ ἀνθρώπων (2:5), any urban Hellenistic reader would have taken his disclaimers to refer to rhetorical practice. Thus Bauer translates the first phrase as "cleverness in speaking."[1]

Even some of the greatest critics of the relevance of ancient rhetoric must give it some place. For example, Schmithals admits that όυκ ἐν σοφίᾳ λόγου (1:17) probably means "not in wise discourse. . . . Similarly, in 2:4 . . . Paul sets himself against the rhetorically elaborated eloquence which the Hellenist treasured in the highest measure and regarded as a necessary precondition for any genuine education. Perhaps some in Corinth had denied, not altogether incorrectly, that the apostle had this education."[2]

Why, if Schmithals and others agree that Paul explicitly names rhetoric as his subject, do they so quickly dismiss it and move on to search for some other kind of wisdom? I believe they did so partly because in their inherited intellectual environment, they misunderstood rhetoric as mere form. In a second, related move, some critics conflated rhetorical "form" and philosophical "content," which many

---

[1]BAGD, 759.

[2]Walter Schmithals, *Gnosticism in Corinth: An Investigation of the Letters to the Corinthians*, trans. J.E. Steely (Nashville: Abingdon, 1971), 142.

then dismissed in favor of other "contents." The remainder of this chapter sketches the loss and recovery of rhetoric as more than mere form, while the second chapter examines the question of form and content in the light of our renewed understanding of ancient rhetoric.

The recovery of rhetoric, we shall see, involves more than simple historical information. It is tied to a major shift in world-view. This post-positivist or anti-foundational world-view can lead us to reformulate interpretation itself as a rhetorical enterprise. A methodology for such an interpretive stance is discussed in Chapter 3. Using this methodology, a new reading of the situation to which Paul responded in 1 Cor. 1-4 will be offered in Part II.

Rhetoric as Mere Form

Schmithals goes on to argue that Paul must mean more by "wisdom" than mere rhetoric:

> When Paul rejects this wisdom, he means not only the form of the matter but its content as well. . . . The σοφός, the γραμματεύς, and συζητητής of 1:20 are not first of all brilliant orators but representatives of a quite different wisdom, for Paul a wisdom of this world, to which he counters not with a foolish oratory, but with the foolishness of the cross. . . . Thus the apostle is engaged in a polemic against the wisdom in form and content. . . . Thus the content of the Corinthian preaching was in some way a doctrine of knowledge, so that on the basis of wisdom in form and content some actually felt superior to the preaching of Paul.[3]

This same concept of rhetoric as mere form appears repeatedly in the views of other scholars. They normally assume that so far as σοφία λόγου refers to rhetoric, it means "cultivating expression at the expense of matter . . . the gift of the mere rhetorician."[4] This

---

[3]Ibid., 142-143.

[4]Archibald Robertson and Alfred Plummer, *A Critical and Exegetical Commentary on the First Epistle of St. Paul to the Corinthians*, 2nd ed. (Edinburgh: T.&T. Clark, 1914), 5. See also page 15: "Preaching was St. Paul's great work, but his aim was not that of the professional rhetorician. Here he rejects the standard by which an age of rhetoric judged a speaker. The Corinthians were judging by externals."

typically leads to the assumption that Paul is speaking of two *different* meanings of σοφία within the same or closely related passages. For example, Horsley asserts that "in 1 Corinthians 1-4 Paul reacts against *two* aspects of *sophia*: wisdom as speech as well as wisdom as the means of salvation."[5] *Mere form*, it is argued, cannot be all that is at stake in Paul's mighty defense of ὁ λόγος τοῦ σταυροῦ. Rather, it is argued, some *content* is at stake, so Paul must have two meanings of σοφία in mind: one, a wise content espoused by some or all of the Corinthians (perhaps with one or more outside opponents), the other no more than a clever way of expressing this content. The race is then on to find this elusive content.

Perhaps most persuasive in this regard has been Ulrich Wilckens. He points out that in 1:17 Paul sets σοφία against the cross, "but when he does this, can it simply be a question in this antithesis of a contrary *form* of the proclamation, must it not be a question at the same time of far more, namely a substantial contrast in view of the *content* of the proclamation?"[6] (emphasis mine)

Wilckens and Schmithals go on to define this content as gnostic,[7] but others using this same reasoning see other contents.

---

[5]Richard A. Horsley, "Wisdom of Words and Words of Wisdom in Corinth," *CBQ* 39 (1977), 224.

[6]Ulrich Wilckens, *Weisheit und Torheit* (Tübingen: J.C.B. Mohr, 1959), 20; cf. passim, "σοφία," *TDNT* 7, 522: "This is not traditional Greek rhetoric. . . . The attack on σοφία λόγου is not so much on the form of speech as on the content." See also Hans Dieter Betz, *Der Apostel Paulus und die sokratische Tradition: Eine exegetische Untersuchung zu seiner "Apologie" 2 Korinther 10-13*, (Tübingen: J.C.B. Mohr, 1972), 59: Betz argues, against Käsemann and Schmithals, that in 2 Cor. 10:10 and 11:6, λόγος does not refer to spontaneous pneumatic speech. Rather, λόγος and γνῶσις are two sides of the same content: λόγος is γνῶσις come to expression. In other words, Betz says, λόγος is the form of speech, γνῶσις its content. For support, Betz offers a 3rd century B.C.E. Cynic letter, which argues that the worth of an argument is not in speech, but in γνῶμαι which can be brought to expression in various speeches. Betz comes close to hitting the mark when he identifies Paul's reference to rhetoric. But his bifurcation of content as knowledge and speech as expression leads him to translate 2 Cor. 11:6 as "even if I am unskilled in expressing myself in words, I still know what I want to say." We would come closer to the mark by avoiding such bifurcation, thus understanding Paul to say, "even if I am not a professional orator, I am not ignorant." On this verse, see further, pp. 214-221.

[7]Similarly, C. K. Barrett, *A Commentary on the First Epistle to the Corinthians*, 2nd edition (New York: Harper & Row, 1968), 49, 55, concludes that σοφία in

For example, Fee follows the traditional argument that the wise content is Hellenistic philosophy. He admits that Paul is clearly referring to rhetoric in 1:17 and 2:1-5 so he appears puzzled to find in 2:6-16

> a surprising turn toward the content of the preaching, not its manner or effect. . . . The other contrast, the question of form and manner, between preaching in such a way as "to distinguish myself in logos and sophia" (2:1) and "with a demonstration of the Spirit's power" (2:5), is a real one and must be spoken to. But the more urgent concern is between sophia itself and the message of the cross.[8]

Again and again we find scholars underestimating the importance of the meaning of σοφία λόγου as rhetoric because they understand rhetoric as no more than mere form. But can form and content be separated so neatly? If we examine the "rhetoric" to which Paul refers, we will find the answer to be not as straightforward as NT scholars seem to have assumed.

The Recovery of Rhetoric

Greco-Roman rhetoric, in theory, education, and practice, was concerned with the complete act of communication. It started not with a ready-made content; rather, it started with the character of the speaker and his education, moved through methods to discover the

---

1:17 means "rhetorical skill" yet perceives Paul as confronting a σοφία in 1:19 which in content is "akin to gnosticism."

[8]Gordon Fee, *The First Epistle to the Corinthians* (Grand Rapids: Eerdmans, 1987), 65-66. Fee clearly distinguishes wise rhetorical form and wise content: p. 9 ("As to the form of wisdom, [the Corinthians] were particularly repelled by his lack of the rhetorical skills that ordinarily accompanied sophia") and p. 49 (The Corinthians may have thought of apostles as itinerant philosophers, "many of whom were sophists--more concerned with polished oration than with significant content.") For similar distinctions in addition to the above, see Johannes Weiss, *Der erste Korintherbrief* (Göttingen: Vanderhoeck & Ruprecht, 1910), 23; C. F.Georg Heinrici, *Das erste Sendschrieben des Apostel Paulus an die Korinthier* (Berlin: Wilhelm Hertz, 1880), 11; Timothy H. Lim, "Not in Persuasive Words of Wisdom, but in the Demonstration of the Spirit and Power," *NovT* 29 (1987), 149.

content and shape of the argument and the nature of the audience, and then to the style and method of presentation appropriate to the situation. But by the nineteenth century, "rhetoric" meant only stylistic ornamentation with figures of speech. We have inherited much of our understanding of rhetoric from this truncated form.

> A modern text-book of rhetoric deals largely with style—choice of words, figures of speech, formation of sentences, arrangement of paragraphs. . . . An ancient Rhetoric . . . is concerned with matter as well as with style. Invention, or the discovery of ideas and subject matter, was the first and perhaps the most important section of any formal treatise on rhetoric.[9]

Even classicists tended to undervalue rhetoric until a renewal of interest in recent decades. Earlier scholars sometimes lacked a thorough understanding of the development of rhetoric and its place in classical society. This deficiency often led to a one-sided view of rhetoric as an arid and inflexible system of rules, as restricted to concern with ornamentation, or as influencing only a small segment of society. The renewal among classicists is now influencing many NT critics.[10] Yet,

---

[9]H. M. Hubbell, introduction to Cicero, *De Inventione*, LCL (Cambridge, Mass.: Harvard University Press, 1949; London, William Heinemann, 1949), ix. cf. Paul Ricoeur, *The Rule of Metaphor*, trans. Robert Caerny with Kathleen McGloughlin and John Costello (Toronto: University of Toronto Press, 1977), 9-10: Aristotle's *Rhetoric* focuses on the invention of arguments and proofs, which "constitutes the principal axis of rhetoric. . . . (This theory of argumentation by itself takes up two thirds of the treatise). . . . Rhetoric died when the penchant for classifying figures of speech completely supplanted the philosophical sensibility that animated the vast empire of rhetoric."

[10]The renewed appreciation and understanding of rhetoric appears most prominently in several works by Hans Dieter Betz, especially *Galatians: A Commentary on Paul's Letter to the Churches in Galatia* (Philadelphia: Fortress, 1979). For other examples, see Philip L. Shuler, *A Genre for the Gospels: The Biographical Character of Matthew* (Philadelphia, Fortress, 1982); Michael Brinsmead, *Galatians—Dialogical Response to Opponents* (Chico, CA: Scholars' Press, 1982); Christopher Forbes, "Comparison, Self-Praise, and Irony: Paul's Boasting and the Conventions of Hellenistic Rhetoric," *NTS* 32:1 (January, 1986): 1-30; S. H. Travis, "Paul's Boasting in II Corinthians 10-12," *Studia Evangelica* 6 (1973): 527-32; Lawrence Welborn, "A Conciliatory Principle in I Corinthians 4:6," *NovT* 29:4 (1987): 320-346; Joop Smit, "The Letter of Paul to the Galatians: A Deliberative Speech," *NTS* 35:1 (1/89) 1-26; for further references see Duane F. Watson "The New Testament and Greco-Roman Rhetoric: A Bibliography,"

> to many biblical scholars rhetoric probably means style, and they may envision . . . [rhetorical criticism] as a discussion of figures of speech and metaphors not unlike that already to be found in many literary studies of the Scriptures. The identification of rhetoric with style . . . is a common phenomenon in the history of the study of rhetoric, but represents a limitation and to some extent a distortion of the discipline of rhetoric as understood and taught in antiquity. . . . Rhetoric is that quality in discourse by which a speaker or writer seeks to accomplish his purposes.[11]

Walter Ong notes the same discrepancy between modern and past views of rhetoric, pointing out that many today still see rhetoric as

> verbal profusion calculated to manipulate an audience, an operation whose aims are suspect and whose typical procedures are mostly trivializing. Yet in centuries past rhetoric was commonly used in the West to refer to one of the most consequential and serious of all academic subjects and of all human activities. As the art of persuasion, the art of producing genuine conviction in an audience, rhetoric affected the entire range of human action as nothing else in theory or in practice quite did. . . . The study of rhetoric required engagement in the totality of human affairs, in politics and other decision making fields, in real life.[12]

JETS 31:4 (12/88) 465-472.

However, even the recent enthusiasm for "rhetorical criticism" as a new method often tends to be a socio-literary, not an historical, discipline; i.e., critics restrict themselves to modern theories of rhetoric. For example, Raymond Humphries, *Paul's Rhetoric of Argumentation in I Corinthians 1-4* (Ann Arbor: University Microfilms, 1980) and Karl Plank, *Paul and the Irony of Affliction* (Atlanta: Scholars Press, 1987). Another good example is Vernon Robbins' *Jesus the Teacher: A Socio-Rhetorical Interpretation of Mark* (Philadelphia: Fortress, 1984). Though Robbins leads the reader to believe that the he aims to recover the rhetoric of Mark's Hellenistic readers, he relies almost entirely on modern rhetorical theories, especially those of Kenneth Burke, and barely touches on ancient rhetorical practice.

[11]George A. Kennedy, *New Testament Interpretation through Rhetorical Criticism* (Chapel Hill: The University of North Carolina Press, 1984), 3.

[12]Walter J. Ong, forward to *The Present State of Scholarship in Historical and Contemporary Rhetoric*, ed. Winifred Bryan Horner (Columbia & London: University of Missouri Press, 1983), 1.

This same misperception of rhetoric eventually led academic communities to reject it entirely by the end of the nineteenth century.[13] This "scholarly contempt," can be traced back into the nineteenth century Germany,[14] of particular importance to biblical scholarship. Thus, it is not surprising that biblical scholars generally shared this anti-rhetorical intellectual climate. This contempt was not often addressed by the only American students of rhetoric in speech and communication departments because, except for preaching, these scholars rarely ventured into theology.[15] Not until the interdisciplinary efforts of such scholars as Judge, Betz and Kennedy did NT

---

[13]Samuel Ijsselling, *Rhetoric and Philosophy in Conflict: An Historical Survey*, trans. Paul Dunphy (The Hague: Martinus Nijhoff, 1976), 1-2: "The word "rhetoric" received a pejorative meaning, suggesting the use of underhanded tricks, fraud and deceit, or the stringing together of hollow words, hackneyed expressions and mere platitudes. To be rhetorical was to be bombastic." In the same vein, see Chaim Perelman, *The New Rhetoric and the Humanities: Essays on Rhetoric and Its Applications* (Boston: D. Reidel, 1979), 1-5: "For those of us who have been educated at a time when rhetoric has ceased to play an essential part in education, the idea of rhetoric has been definitely associated with the 'flowers of rhetoric'—the name used for the figures of style with their learned and incomprehensible names. . . . In the Western tradition, 'rhetoric' has frequently been identified with verbalism and an empty, unnatural, stilted mode of expression . . . ostentatious and artificial discourse. . . . Aristotle would have disagreed with this conception of rhetoric as an ornamental art. . . . For Aristotle, rhetoric is a practical discipline that aims, not at producing a work of art, but at exerting through speech a persuasive action on an audience." Cf. idem, "Rhetoric," *The New Encyclopedia Britannica*, 15th ed., vol. 26 (Chicago: Encyclopaedia Britannica, 1988), 806: "Well into the 20th century, 'elocution' [style] in popular speech meant florid delivery and 'rhetoric,' because of its principal concern with oratory, meant purple prose. In academic circles, 'rhetoric' referred largely to principles of 'belles lettres' until 'belletristic' became a pejorative; then 'rhetoric' in a host of college 'composition' courses referred to less philosophically troublesome principles of paragraph development and thematic arrangement. cf. idem, "Address at Ohio State University" in *Practical Reasoning in Human Affairs: Studies in Honor of Chaim Perelman*, ed. James L. Golden and Joseph J. Pilotta (Dordrecht, Holland: D. Reidel, 1986), 2; Ricoeur, *Metaphor*, 9.

[14]James L. Kinneavy, "Contemporary Rhetoric," in *The Present State of Scholarship in Historical and Contemporary Rhetoric*, ed. Winifred Bryan Horner (Columbia: University of Missouri Press, 1983), 167-170; cf. M.L. Clarke, *Rhetoric at Rome: A Historical Survey* (London: Cohen & West, 1953), *v*.

[15]James L. Kinneavy, *Greek Rhetorical Origins of Christian Faith: An Inquiry* (New York: Oxford University Press, 1987), 25.

scholars begin to revise perceptions of the relationship of NT texts to classical rhetoric.

Like Betz and Kennedy with NT texts, James Muilenburg has led a group of Hebrew Scripture scholars in applying rhetorical analysis to biblical texts. Muilenburg limits himself to stylistic aspects of rhetoric, but even this circumscribed move is pressed upon him by the limitations of form criticism, including the illegitimacy of separating form and content:

> Form and content are inextricably related. They form an integral whole. The two are one. Exclusive attention to the *Gattung* may actually obscure the thought and intention of the writer or speaker. . . . It is the creative synthesis of the particular formulation of the pericope with the content that makes it the distinctive composition that it is. . . . A responsible and proper articulation of the words in their linguistic patterns and in their precise formulations will reveal to us the texture and fabric of the writer's thought, not only what it is that he thinks, but as he thinks it.[16]

Muilenburg, Betz, and a growing number of other scholars have recognized the falsity of the common view of rhetoric as no more than stylistic packaging designed to manipulate an audience, a falsity born of many centuries of intellectual history. Given the strength and longevity of this history and the philosophical rationale behind it, we should not be surprised to find that commentators on 1 Cor. still tend to operate with a view of rhetoric as mere form.

Of course, this view of rhetoric goes far beyond discussions of 1 Cor. We find the consensus NT critical view of less than thirty years ago in the article on "Rhetoric and Oratory" by F.C. Grant in the *Interpreter's Dictionary of the Bible*. Grant asserts that all the writers of the NT were more or less insulated from rhetorical influence not only by their predominantly lower class status, but by their "Semitic, biblical, Greco-Jewish" reaction against the corruption of rhetoric, which never raised itself above "a conjurer's bag of tricks for amazing the hearers or persuading the court." Grant argues that it was the victory of this kind of rhetoric over the grander vision of Isocrates which "came to be looked upon as the crown and climax of education, and the proof of both its value and its validity." Grant

---

[16]James Muilenburg, "Form Criticism and Beyond," *JBL* 88 (1969), 5-7.

takes Paul's disclaimers in 1 Cor. at face value: Paul "positively rejected the artful literary and rhetorical devices of the 'wise in this age.'"[17] Grant sees Paul's rejection of rhetoric as corroborating the general lack of coincidence between the worlds of the NT and rhetoric. So we can confidently say, "Paul was no Greek rhetorician." Further, the only influence of rhetoric upon Paul was "the popular Cynic-Stoic 'diatribe', the speech in the market place which these street preachers of ethical and political philosophy used in their efforts to improve mankind."[18]

Today, Grant's views may still represent those of many critics, but a new consensus is clearly emerging. At the forefront of this new consensus is Hans Dieter Betz, who recognizes that the relationship of the NT, especially the Pauline corpus, to "rhetoric is experiencing a revival after decades of silence. Although sometimes advocated as a 'new' approach, the subject is really as old as the New Testament itself."[19] Betz traces the recognition of Paul's rhetorical skills back to Augustine and through Erasmus, Melanchthon, Luther, Calvin, Grotius, and into the 19th century. But then in the late 19th century, the *Zeitgeist* changed. "The monumental work by Eduard Norden, *Die antike Kunstprosa*, published in 1898, clearly helped to put a stop to this sort of research. Norden acted as if he had been appointed to protect the territory of classicists from the intrusions of New Testament scholars." He fiercely attacked such scholars as Carl Friedrich Georg Heinrici (1844-1915) who had used classical Greek and Roman sources to analyze Paul's rhetoric. Heinrici and others reacted in defense, and "Norden retracted much of what he had said" in an appendix to the second volume of *Die antike Kunstprosa*, "but it appears that few New Testament scholars paid attention to this appendix, so that Norden's verdict continued to impress the theologi-

---

[17]F.C. Grant, "Rhetoric and Oratory," *IDB* 4, 76-77.

[18]Ibid., 76. Without giving him credit, Grant here acknowledges the influence of Rudolf Bultmann's dissertation, *Der Stil der paulinischen Predigt und die kynisch-stoische Diatribe* (Göttingen: Vandenhoeck & Reprecht, 1910), which established the only influence of rhetoric on the NT texts widely recognized in the twentieth century.

[19]Hans Dieter Betz, "The Problem of Rhetoric and Theology according to the Apostle Paul,"in *L'Apôtre Paul. Personalité Style et Conception du Ministère*, ed. A. Vanhoye, *Bibliotheca Ephemeridum Theologicarum Loveniensium* (Leuven: University Press, 1986), 16-17.

cal world." In the early twentieth century, Betz continues, "denouncing rhetoric became fashionable." But in our time, the subject of rhetoric is of interest because of "several changes in the intellectual orientation and the state of scientific research . . . [including] new interest in rhetoric . . . in the fields of the humanities, in philosophy and classics."[20]

This interest in rhetoric includes a renewed appreciation of the universal value of the analytical tools of classical rhetoric, especially as laid down by Aristotle. These tools, as reinterpreted in the "new rhetoric" of such theorists as Chaim Perelman and Kenneth Burke, have been appropriated by virtually every discipline which deals with communication, including the literary analysis of biblical texts. But of more immediate significance for historical study of the NT is the reawakened study of Greco-Roman rhetoric by classicists and historians. One important indication of the changed climate is the formation of the International Society for the History of Rhetoric, which issued the first scholarly journal for the study of the history of rhetoric (*Rhetorica*) in 1983. But these are recent changes; if historians and classicists had under-valued the importance of rhetoric in understanding Greco-Roman culture, we should not be surprised that NT critics shared their views.

NT criticism was cut off from classical rhetoric not only by the general intellectual climate but also by factors internal to NT criticism. Here we must note the pervasive influence of Adolf Deissmann, who concurred that the NT documents as a whole are non-literary, and that their world is therefore removed from literary culture. Deissmann's judgment was clearly tied not only to his romantic view of the lower classes[21], but also to a negative assessment of the rhetorical culture of the elite:

> The New Testament was not a product of the colorless refinement of an upper class. On the contrary, it was, humanly speaking, a product

[20]Ibid., 19-20.

[21]Deissmann's romanticism is widely noted: e.g., Stanley K. Stowers, *Letter Writing in Greco-Roman Antiquity*, (Philadelphia: Westminster Press, 1986), 18-19; John H. Schütz, introduction to *The Social Setting of Pauline Christianity: Essays on Corinth by Gerd Theissen*, ed. and trans. John H. Schütz (Philadelphia: Fortress, 1982); Abraham Malherbe, *Social Aspects of Early Christianity*, 2nd edition (Philadelphia: Fortress, 1983), 32.

> of the force that came unimpaired, and strengthened by the Divine Presence, from the lower class. This reason alone enabled it to become the Book of all mankind .... The New Testament has become the Book of the People because it began by being the Book of the People.[22]

Deissmann's arguments are at once literary and social. By comparing NT texts with papyri, he distinguished between literary epistles and non-literary letters and classed Paul's writings with the latter. "There can be no doubt of the unliterary character of Paul's letters."[23] By the same evidence he also concluded: "By its social structure Primitive Christianity points unequivocally to the lower and middle classes."[24] 1 Cor. 1:26-31 is an especially important piece of evidence, "one of the most important testimonies . . . that Primitive Christianity gives of itself. . . . [It is] a movement of the lower classes."[25]

But Deissmann's views of social class, which prevailed until recently, have now fallen to a new consensus.[26] And the once

---

[22]Gustav Adolf Deissmann, *Paul: A Study in Social and Religious History*, 2nd ed., trans. W. Wilson (London: Hodder & Stoughton, 1926) 144-145.

[23]Ibid., 12; see also 27-52.

[24]Note Deissmann's inclusion of the "middle class" here. Clearly, he does not so much wish to emphasize the lowness of social location as the great distance from the upper class (and the literature of the upper class which scholars had hitherto used for comparison). Even in modern revisions upward, few scholars wish to include the minute upper class, but only to allow for a cross-section of the rest of society. Since it is notoriously difficult to classify the middle ground between the upper and lower extremes of Greco-Roman society, the disagreement between Deissmann and more recent scholars may be less than usually perceived.

[25]Gustav Adolf Deissmann, *Light From the Ancient East: The New Testament Illustrated by Recently Discovered Texts of the Graeco-Roman World*, 4th ed., trans L. Strachan (New York: George A. Doran, 1927), 7-9.

[26]e.g., E. A. Judge, *The Social Pattern of Christian Groups in the First Century* (London: Tyndale, 1960); idem, "The Early Christians as a Scholastic Community", *JRH* 1 (1960-61), 125-137; Malherbe, *Social Aspects*; Robert M. Grant, *Early Christianity and Society: Seven Studies* (New York, Harper & Row, 1977); Gerd Theissen, *The Social Setting of Pauline Christianity*, (Philadelphia: Fortress, 1982); Wayne Meeks, *The First Urban Christians: The Social World of the Apostle Paul* (New Haven and London: Yale University Press, 1983). One of the surest signs of the strength of this consensus can be found in John G. Gager's *Kingdom and Community: The Social World of Early Christianity* (Englewood Cliffs, NJ: Prentice-Hall, 1975), 95: Though Gager's theoretical framework depends on

dominant position of his literary views have also been so modified as to become almost unrecognizable. The *koine* of the NT texts is not, as Deissmann argued, entirely unliterary. Rather, "in the last 50 years, . . . there has been general agreement that the literary aspects of NT Greek have been overly minimized. Research continues to be presented which shows many points of contact between this [NT Greek] and that written by both classical and contemporary literary authors, not only in vocabulary, but also in morphology and syntax."[27]

Further, Deissmann's distinction between literary epistles and non-literary occasional letters, though still somewhat useful, is highly misleading. Extensive research comparing Pauline letters with Hellenistic epistolary conventions has revealed that although Paul transforms those conventions, the general framework from which he departs is still evident, especially in his openings and closings.[28] The relationships in the bodies of the letters are less clear, but research has already revealed some of them[29] and precisely in this area numerous rhetorical analyses are now bearing the greatest fruit.

---

understanding Christianity as arising from a group of people who sensed themselves as deprived, he nuances this theory by appeal to *relative* deprivation, which "destroys the romantic image of early Christians as nothing but a collection of country yokels and impoverished slaves."

[27]James W. Voelz, "The Language of the New Testament," *ANRW* 2.25.2 (1984), 928.

[28]John L. White, *Light from Ancient Letters* (Fortress: Philadelphia, 1986); idem, "New Testament Epistolary Literature in the Framework of Ancient Epistolography," *ANRW* 2.25.2, (1984), 1739-42; for a pioneering and still useful study, see Paul Schubert, *Form and Function of the Pauline Thanksgivings* (Berlin: Töpelmann, 1939); cf. David E. Aune, *The New Testament in its Literary Environment* (Philadelphia: Westminster Press, 1987), 12: "Paul's letters were written in a popular form of literary Greek using Hellenistic arguments styles and forms." See also Stowers, *Letter Writing*, 19-20: "Deissmann's antithesis between the natural and the conventional was typical of nineteenth- and early twentieth-century Romanticism. . . . Now, however, theorists of literature and culture are widely agreed that there is a conventional dimension to all intelligible human behavior. Thus Deissmann's dictum that 'the letter is a piece of life, the epistle is a product of literary art' (*Light from the Ancient East*, p. 230) is a misguided contrast. All letters are literature in the very broadest sense. Even the common papyrus letters follow highly stylized letter-writing conventions."

[29]e.g., Bultmann, *Stil*; Stanley Kent Stowers, *The Diatribe and Paul's Letter to the Romans* (Chico, CA: Scholars Press, 1981); Betz, *Galatians*; Brinsmead, *Galatians—Dialogical Response to Opponents* (Chico, CA: Scholars' Press, 1982.

Also contributing to the distance between "literary works" and NT texts was the rise of form criticism. In an enormously influential article, K. L. Schmidt argued that the gospels belong to *Kleinliteratur* as distinct from *Hochliteratur*. The former is the anonymous product of folk transmission, while the latter is the self-conscious work of an author who employs literary style.[30] Schmidt's arguments, along with those of other form critics,[31] corroborated the growing evidence that NT communities and writers were isolated from Hellenistic literary activity.

However, in recent years, this sharp division between *Hochliteratur* and *Kleinliteratur* has been widely recognized as an overstatement. Schmidt was persuasive partly because most extant ancient literature was composed and preserved by the upper classes, producing the illusion that the NT texts are in a class by themselves.[32] In contrast,

> recent studies have made it increasingly apparent that the antithetical categories of *Hochliteratur* and *Kleinliteratur* have value only as ideal types as opposite ends of a complex spectrum of linguistic and literary styles and levels. The pyramidal character of ancient society had an impact on literary culture as well as on other aspects of social and cultural life. The literary conventions and styles of the upper classes percolated down to lower levels, and they occur in attenuated forms in popular literature.[33]

Furthermore, the shape of gospel criticism has changed dramatically since the time of the early form critics. Redaction criticism and

---

[30]K.L. Schmidt, "Die Stellung der Evangelien in der allgemeinen Literaturgeschichte," *Eucharistarion: Studien zur Religion und Literatur des Alten und Neuen Testaments Hermann Gunkel zum 60 Geburtstag*, 2 Teil, ed. Hans Schmidt (Göttingen: Vandenhoeck und Ruprecht, 1923), 50-134.

[31]e.g., Martin Dibelius, *From Tradition to Gospel* (New York: Doubleday, 1966), 1-2; Rudolf Bultmann, *History of the Synoptic Tradition*, trans. John Marsh (New York: Harper & Row, 1963), 371-373.

[32]In fact, Schmidt (84-114) could find no ancient examples of *Kleinliteratur*, and so employed parallels from the middle ages and later.

[33]Aune, *Literary Environment*, 12; cf. Shuler, 7, 11: "In effect, [Schmidt's] position precludes comparisons with almost all literature of the period of the gospels because no examples of *Kleinliteratur* are available. . . . No doubt the ancient world did produce 'high' and 'low' forms of literature, but it also, doubtless, produced a great deal which would lie somewhere in between."

narrative literary criticism[34] have virtually overcome the older views of the gospel writers as noncreative collectors of anonymous traditions.[35] In fact, several studies have persuaded an increasing number of scholars that the gospels are generically related to Hellenistic biographies.[36]

Another factor which steered early twentieth century NT critics away from the relevance of rhetoric was the renewed interest in eschatology. The discovery of pervasive, profound, and distinctly Jewish eschatological notions throughout the NT moved that world very far from the previously assumed philosophical and ethical one of classical culture. But today, even the strictly Jewish world can no longer be viewed as isolated from Hellenistic culture.[37] And if true of the Jewish milieu, it is even more true of the more gentile milieu of Pauline Christianity.

This has been underlined by E. A. Judge, whose important work has helped reestablish the Greco-Roman social milieu of the NT. Judge readily admits that scholars of the 18th and 19th centuries were wrong to identify the NT texts too closely with the classical tradition, and 20th century history of religions scholars too closely with Hellenistic ideas. But

---

[34]e.g., Norman R. Petersen, *Literary Criticism for New Testament Critics* (Philadelphia: Fortress, 1978); David M. Rhoads and Donald Michie, *Mark as Story: An Introduction to the Narrative of a Gospel* (Philadelphia: Fortress, 1982); Jack Dean Kingsbury, *The Christology of Mark's Gospel* (Philadelphia: Fortress, 1983); R. Alan Culpepper: *Anatomy of the Fourth Gospel: A Study in Literary Design* (Philadelphia: Fortress, 1983).

[35]Graham Stanton specifically points to redaction criticism as breaking down the distinction between *Hochliteratur* and *Kleinliteratur*: G. L. Stanton, *Jesus of Nazareth in New Testament Preaching* (Cambridge: University Press, 1974), 125.

[36]Stanton; Shuler; Vernon Robbins, *Jesus the Teacher*; Aune, *Literary Environment*, 27-36, 43-45; Charles H. Talbert, *What is a Gospel?: The Genre of the Canonical Gospels* (Philadelphia, Fortress, 1977); Martin Hengel, *Acts and the History of Earliest Christianity* (Philadelphia: Fortress, 1979), 12-45.

[37]e.g., Martin Hengel, *Judaism & Hellenism: Studies in Their Encounter in Palestine During the Hellenistic Period*, trans. J. Bowden (Philadelphia: Fortress, 1974); idem, *Jews, Greeks, and Barbarians: Aspects of the Hellenization of Judaism in the Pre-Christian Period*, trans. J. Bowden (Philadelphia: Fortress, 1980). Many neo-orthodox scholars perceived Judaism and Christianity as isolated from the pagan world; to the neo-orthodox theologian, the eschatological vision equals a lack of interest in the present world, and a concomitant refusal to partake of the forms of this world.

> the fact remains that it was written in Greek if not by rhetorically literate Greeks at least partly for them. . . . Such is the subtlety of the lost rhetorical art, that until we have it back under control we can hardly think we know how to read passages which both by style and content belong to Paul's struggle with rhetorically trained opponents for the support of his rhetorically fastidious converts.[38]

Before interest in rhetoric revived, the last major scholar to recognize the general relevance of rhetoric to NT texts was Johannes Weiss. Weiss died before he could undertake his sweeping survey of the subject, but not before influencing his student Rudolf Bultmann to apply ancient rhetorical analogies to the NT. In his dissertation, Bultmann demonstrated that Paul employed a highly developed type of rhetoric (the diatribe) in his letter to the Romans. Yet Bultmann also maintained that Paul's letters displayed the lowest level of literary and rhetorical culture,[39] for "the diatribe was seen [at that time] as a form designed for use by ignorant and vulgar Cynics in their preaching to the uneducated masses."[40] But just as Deissmann's arguments of social level have fallen to a new consensus, scholarly judgments of the low social level of the diatribe have been revised upwards. The diatribe is not popular public street preaching, but a form developed for private teaching in the philosophical schools, in which a teacher poses and responds to real or hypothetical questions.[41] Furthermore, just as one can easily suspect Deissmann of romantic ulterior motives, one also suspects that Bultmann hoped to find a literary form (popular preaching) which would corroborate his view of the primacy of proclamation over theology. Nevertheless, Bultmann's work has properly become a fixture in critical orthodoxy. Ironically, it was also the last major work of its kind for decades.

In those decades, scholars rarely employed rhetorical criteria. When they did, they almost always restricted themselves to figures of speech. This "fragmentation" of rhetoric is still "tenaciously endur-

---

[38]E.A. Judge, "Paul's Boasting in Relation to Contemporary Professional Practice," *ABR* 16 (1968) 46-48.

[39]Bultmann, *Stil*, 2-3.

[40]Stowers, *Diatribe*, 17.

[41]Ibid., 263.

ing."[42] Both Humphries and Wuellner point to Conzelmann's commentary on 1 Cor. as typical of this tendency.[43] Thus, one can go through the whole commentary and have the impression that the only influences of rhetorical theory and practice were figures drawn from the popular diatribe as described by Bultmann.[44]

The same limitation of rhetoric to style seems to be generally true of the work of Hebrew Scripture scholars, even though they have been quicker to appeal to rhetorical analysis. Thus, Gitay appreciates previous rhetorical studies of the Hebrew Scriptures, which "are concerned with rhetoric as effective speech, and which, therefore, analyze material according to rhetoric's pragmatic goal—the appeal to the audience. Nevertheless, these studies confine themselves primarily to only one aspect of the rhetorical discipline, which is style." In particular,

> Muilenburg's definition and use of the term rhetoric does not understand rhetoric as the art of persuasion. That is to say, both Muilenburg and his followers are concerned with style as a functional device for determining the literary unit and its structure, but their analysis is not oriented towards rhetoric as the pragmatic art of persuasion.[45]

Against this view of rhetoric as no more than style stand Kennedy, Gitay, Humphries, and others who call for a rhetorical criticism which embraces more than style, a criticism which takes into account all aspects of the text, including the rhetorical situation and the argument.[46]

---

[42]Wilhelm Wuellner, "Where is Rhetorical Criticism Taking Us?", *CBQ* 49 (1987) 450. See also Kennedy, *NT Interpretation*, 3.

[43]Humphries, 32; Wilhelm Wuellner, "Greek Rhetoric and Pauline Argumentation," *Early Christian Literature and the Classical Intellectual Tradition*, ed. W. Schoedel & R. Wilken, (Paris: Editions Beauchesne, 1979).

[44]Hans Conzelmann, *1 Corinthians*, trans. James W. Leitch, (Philadelphia: Fortress, 1975), especially p. 5.

[45]Yegoshua Gitay, *Prophecy and Persuasion: A Study of Isaiah 40-48*, Forum Theologiae Linguisticae, no. 14, ed. Erhardt Güttgemanns (Bonn: Linguistica Biblica, 1981), 27.

[46]Kennedy, *NT Interpretation*, 12; Humphries, *Paul's Rhetoric of Argumentation*, 37. Cf. Wuellner, "Where," 451-452: "The theorists in the Muilenberg School failed to realize how much the prevailing theories of rhetoric were victims of that 'rhetoric restrained,' i.e., victims of the fateful reduction of rhetoric to

Yet even in these calls for "rhetorical criticism" of the biblical texts, the role of ancient rhetoric is not always clear because of confusion between historical and philosophical issues, "old" rhetoric and "new" rhetoric. "New" rhetoric is the product of scholarship which recognizes that virtually all speech is rhetorical (i.e. persuasive, not just descriptive) and therefore open to analysis in the categories developed by the Greeks. Thus, even if the rhetoric to be analyzed had not been conceptualized by the culture in which it was written (e.g., from the Hebrew canon), the Greek categories can provide universal concepts for such analysis. This recognition has produced new rhetorical theories which largely embrace but also criticize and augment the "old" or classical theories. Particularly since the terminology often overlaps, and "new" rhetoric often refers to the ancient as well as modern sources as authorities, references to "rhetorical criticism" can often be confusing.[47]

This confusion stems from a difficulty inherent in rhetorical criticism: if a text is rhetorical regardless of the writer's exposure to rhetorical theory, then the task of assessing the influence of ancient rhetoric upon an ancient writer becomes more difficult. The historical and universal aspects of rhetorical theory are thus closely related yet distinct.

But the distinction is sometimes glossed over by scholars, thus adding to the confusion. Thus, Wuellner wants to refute the "sustained opposition to the idea that Paul's method of arguing was self-consciously Greek", yet has "advocated . . . not simply a revival of classical rhetoric for modern students, but incorporated the efforts of what is known as 'the new rhetoric'."[48] Humphries is far clearer in his intent: he uses only "new" rhetoric to analyze 1 Cor. 1-4. He argues that it is relevant because any speaker or writer is operating rhetorically if he or she has the desire and opportunity to persuade an audience, whether his or her skill is from natural ability, imitation,

---

stylistics, and of stylistics in turn to the rhetorical tropes or figures. Reduced to concerns of style, with the artistry of textual disposition and textual structure, rhetorical criticism has become indistinguishable from literary criticism."

[47]For brief sketches of the confused situation of rhetorical criticism, see Wuellner, "Where," esp. 450-454, and C. Clifton Black, "Rhetorical Criticism and Biblical Interpretation," *ExpTim* 100 (1989), 252-258.

[48]Wuellner, "Greek Rhetoric," 178, 188.

or extensive schooling. Yet as soon as Humprhries makes this assertion, he supports it with a footnoted quotation which describes not the philosophical, but the *historical* justification for the influence of ancient rhetoric upon the writers of the NT.[49]

Even Kennedy, who generally keeps these issues distinct, at times fails to do so. The primary goal of his method is historical: to read the NT texts as they would be read by an early Christian, for "even those without formal education necessarily developed cultural preconceptions about appropriate discourse." Thus rhetorical analysis of the NT is historically justified. It is also philosophically justified since rhetoric is a universal phenomenon. But when Kennedy finds only a philosophical justification (e.g., for preconceptual Jewish rhetoric), he asserts that "we have little choice but to employ the concepts and terms of the Greeks."[50] But whether the "concepts and terms of the Greeks" are adequate is a question that properly belongs to "new" rhetoric. In practice, Kennedy resorts to new concepts when "old" rhetoric is inadequate.[51]

We do in fact have some choice, and many limit themselves strictly to modern rhetorical theories.[52] But if we wish to uncover the historical connections of Greco-Roman rhetoric and NT texts, the matter is more complex. This complexity is caused not only by the overlapping historical and universal roles of rhetoric, but also because

---

[49]Humphries, 14; the note cites J.P. Pritchard, *A Literary Approach to the New Testament* (Norman: University of Oklahoma, 1972), 10-13. Despite Pritchard's promise to analyze the texts in accordance with ancient rhetoric, his understanding is limited to figures. For a more widely known application of rhetorical theory which fails to carefully distinguish between modern and ancient aspects, see Robbins, *Jesus the Teacher*.

[50]Kennedy, *NT Interpretation*, 5, 10-11. Certainly, Kennedy's confidence in the wisdom of Aristotle is well founded, as Ijsselling, *Rhetoric and Philosophy in Conflict*, 33, confirms: Aristotle's "tract on rhetoric has been extremely important for a possible rhetorical analysis and critical reading of literary, scientific and philosophical texts." But, as Wuellner points out ("Where," 463), "The discipline of rhetorical criticism will emerge as a 'dynamic process,' not as a system, least of all that of a neo-Aristotelian or neo-Ciceronian system."

[51]Kennedy, *NT Interpretation:* e.g. rhetorical unit, 33; exigence, 34-35; religious rhetoric, 6.

[52]One excellent example of the fruitfulness of "bracketing" historical questions can be found in Karl Andrews Plank, *Paul and the Irony of Affliction*, (Atlanta: Scholars Press, 1987).

ancient theory is not always adequate to analyze or explain the forces which shaped actual rhetorical practice. Betz, in his commentary on Galatians, tries to circumvent this complexity by limiting himself to ancient rhetorical theory. Thus, he employs the strict generic categories so loved by writers of handbooks, especially those of late antiquity. But Betz seems to oversimplify the situation, for "Greco-Roman literary composition often departed from the prescriptions of ancient literary and rhetorical theory. . . . Ancient theory, valuable as it is, must not be allowed to impede the understanding of actual texts."[53]

This inadequacy of Betz's methodology has been addressed by his student M. Mitchell, who adds the study of the forms of actual texts to her investigation of the form of 1 Cor. This allows Mitchell greater flexibility than Betz in his recent works, and her argument that 1 Cor. is predominantly deliberative is persuasive. However, Mitchell still fails to recognize the limitations of a purely historical rhetorical methodology. She insists that "the modern 'New Rhetoric' . . . should not be confused or intertwined with historical arguments about Paul's rhetoric in the light of the Greco-Roman rhetorical tradition."[54] However, her two terms, "confused" and "intertwined" are not equivalent. "Confusion," as I have pointed out above, should be avoided. However, the scholar who distinguishes between "old" and "new" rhetoric may still "intertwine" them. In fact, the modern critic often must "intertwine" them, since ancient rhetorical theories are simply inadequate for certain hermeneutical tasks.

The ancient theories are inadequate partly because they detach theory from practice. But the reason they do this is more important: theirs is an inductive abstraction from real situations. They recognized that real speeches were situational. Thus, as we shall see, the rhetoricians taught their students to depart from theoretical, standard forms according to the dictates of actual situations. Mitchell assumes

---

[53]Aune, *Literary Environment*, 206-208; cf. Kennedy, *NT Interpretation*, 144-152, and Smit, "The Letter of Paul to the Galatians". By adhering too rigidly to his perceptions of ancient rhetorical categories, Betz has misperceived Paul's rhetoric as judicial rather than deliberative with judicial elements.

[54]Margaret Mary Mitchell, *Paul and the Rhetoric of Reconciliation: An Exegetical Investigation of the Language and Composition of 1 Corinthians*, unpublished Ph.D. Dissertation, University of Chicago Divinity School, 1989.

that by comparing forms which functioned in generally similar ways (politically) we can deduce the function of Paul's rhetoric. However, formal similarities can easily mislead; we need only think of Fish's famous text, "Is there a text in this class?" to recognize that form in situation, not form alone, determines meaning. Such insights are modern and philosophical, yet we cannot avoid "intertwining" them with ancient rhetoric if rhetorical criticism is to aid meaningful readings.

Thus, when Kennedy and others import modern theories to augment ancient ones, they are justified; but they should also clarify their rationale for importing modern theories and carefully distinguish between modern and ancient. In this work, I shall rely predominantly on classical rhetorical theory, but also bolster this with some modern theory in the manner of Kennedy. I hope I do so in a way that avoids both confusing admixture and illegitimate historical purism.

In any case, these criticisms of rhetorical criticism do not detract from its fundamental significance. The advent of rhetorical criticism strongly indicates the new environment which invites new interpretations.

Rhetoric and Anti-Foundationalism

The long-held view of rhetoric as mere form stems in part from historical criticism's faith in rational or empirical epistemologies. This approach has distorted our views of rhetoric, both historical and contemporary. In particular, historicist modes of exegesis have often sought to find the "core" (content) of the theology of biblical texts by removing the socio-linguistic "peel" (form).[55] Such "docetic" meth-

---

[55]e.g., note the comments of Elisabeth Schüssler Fiorenza, *The Book of Revelation: Justice and Judgement* (Philadelphia: Fortress, 1985), 3, 23, 184: In the 18th century, scholars "advocated a sharp distinction between literary form and theological content" in Revelation. "This dichotomy . . . which reduces apocalyptic imagery to a mere container or cloak of timeless essences and propositional truth, has ever since marred the discussion of apocalyptic literature." Instead, "apocalyptic language is not just the container or form for the Christian communities' faith experience but it is constitutive of it." In place of form/content dichotomies, Fiorenza refers to the "form-content configuration

odologies have all too often falsified the unity of thought, expression, and socio-historical situation of texts and their interpretation. This seems to be the case in the history of criticism of the opening chapters of 1 Cor., where scholars have attempted to isolate some ideological controversy without complete justice to the situation. Once we understand rhetoric as part of a whole system of socially related modes of perceiving reality, we are less tempted to resort to such "onion peeling" tactics.

In contrast to modernist epistemologies, we increasingly see a move to anti-foundational linguistic hermeneutics. Anti-foundational hermeneutics assume that we find meaning, including understanding texts and constructing histories, only within socio-linguistic worlds. Such hermeneutics, especially as persuasively developed by Gadamer in *Truth and Method*,[56] are familiar to many NT critics. Gadamer knocks the foundations out from under Enlightenment positivist epistemologies, and replaces them with community- and tradition-based linguistic modes of understanding, rooted in rhetorical theory.[57] He asserts

> The instrumentalist devaluation of language that we find in modern times makes it possible for 'language' as such, i.e. its form, separated from all content, to become an independent object of attention. . . . Does this take account of [language's] unique quality, which is that language embraces everything—myth, art, law, etc.?[58]

Eagleton summarizes the changing intellectual landscape:

> The hallmark of the 'linguistic revolution' of the twentieth century, from Saussure and Wittgenstein to contemporary literary theory, is the recognition that meaning is not simply something 'expressed' or 'reflected' in language. . . . It is not as though we have meanings, or experiences, which we then proceed to cloak with words; we can only have the meanings and experiences in the first place because we have a language to have them in. What this suggests, moreover, is that our experience as individuals is social to its roots; for there can be no

(*Gestalt*)."

[56]Hans-Georg Gadamer, *Truth and Method* (New York: Crossroad, 1984).

[57]Idem, "Rhetoric, Hermeneutics and the Critique of Ideology," in *The Hermeneutics Reader*, ed. Kurt Mueller-Vollmer (New York: Continuum, 1989).

[58]idem, *Truth and Method*, 365. Cf. Joel C. Weinsheimer, *Gadamer's Hermeneutics: A Reading of Truth and Method*, (New Haven: Yale, 1985), 233-34.

> such thing as a private language, and to imagine a language is to imagine a whole form of social life.[59]

Perhaps most articulate in this area is Stanley Fish, especially in his recent collection of essays, *Doing What Comes Naturally*:

> Anti-foundationalism asserts [that] all . . . entities and values, along with the procedures by which they are identified and marshaled, will be inextricable from the social and historical circumstances in which they do their work, . . . [They are] functions of the local, the historical, the contingent, the variable, and the rhetorical. . . .
>
> Such, at any rate, is the anti-foundationalist argument, which has been made in a variety of ways in a variety of disciplines: in philosophy by Richard Rorty, Hilary Putnam, W.V. Quine; in anthropology by Clifford Geertz and Victor Turner; in history by Hayden White; in sociology by the entire tradition of the sociology of knowledge and more recently by the ethnomethodologists; in hermeneutics by Heidegger, Gadamer, and Derrida; in the general sciences of man by Foucault; in the history of science by Thomas Kuhn; in the history of art by Michael Fried; in legal theory by Philip Bobbot and Sanford Levinson; in literary theory by Barbara Herrnstein Smith, Walter Michaels, Steven Knapp, John Fekete, Jonathan Culler, Terry Eagleton, Frank Lentricchia, Jane Tompkins, Stanley Fish, and on and on. Obviously it is not an isolated argument; in fact, today one could say that it is the *going* argument. And yet, it would be *too much* to say that foundationalist argument lies in ruins. It is in fact remarkably resilient and resourceful in the face of attacks against it.[60]

To witness the continuing strength of foundationalism, one need only attend a conference of Biblical scholars. There, the dream lives on of liberating biblical interpretation from the bonds of tradition and dogma so its true meaning might be "objectively" determined by finding some irreducible "content" knowable apart from the situatedness of the Bible's communities. But "foundationalist theory fails, lies in ruins, because it is from the very first implicated in everything it claims to transcend."[61]

---

[59]Terry Eagleton, *Literary Theory: An Introduction* (Minneapolis: University of Minnesota, 1983), 60.

[60]Stanley Fish, *Doing What Comes Naturally: Change, Rhetoric, and the Practice of Theory in Literary and Legal Studies* (Durham: Duke University, 1989), 344-45.

[61]Ibid., 345.

Thus, epistemology itself is rhetorical by nature, since the axioms of rational thought are not rationally demonstrable but are held only by persuasion.[62]

> Contemporary philosophies . . . have understood that the choice of a linguistic form is neither purely arbitrary nor simply a carbon copy of reality. The reasons that induce us to prefer one conception of experience, one analogy, to another, are a function of our vision of the world. The form is not separable from the content; language is not a veil which one need only discard or render transparent in order to perceive the real as such; it is inextricably bound up with a point of view, with the taking of a position.[63]

Foundationalists often argue that anti-foundationalism leads to "a nightmare vision in which a liberated self goes its unconstrained way believing and doing whatever it likes."[64] In fact, some extreme anti-foundationalists do argue for such individual autonomy.[65] But this

> is a misreading of anti-foundationalism at one of its most crucial points, the insistence on situatedness. A situated self is a self whose every operation is a function of the conventional possibilities built into this or that context. Rather than unmooring the subject, . . . anti-foundationalism reveals the subject to be always and already tethered by the local or community norms and standards that constitute it and enable its rational acts. Such a subject . . . cannot be free . . . to originate its own set of isolated beliefs without systematic constraints.[66]

As we shall see in Chapter 3, the idea of situational restraints is both central and fruitful for rhetorical criticism. For rhetoric is above all situational, contextual, and tethered to *sensus communis*. This situated, rather than ultimate, quality of rhetoric disturbed the philosophers.

---

[62]Ernesto Grassi, *Rhetoric as Philosophy: The Humanist Tradition*, trans. John Michael Krois and Azizeh Azodi (University Park: Pennsylvania State University, 1980), 18-34.

[63]Perelman, *The New Rhetoric and the Humanities*, 45.

[64]Fish, *Doing What Comes Naturally*, 346.

[65]e.g., Richard E. Vatz, "The Myth of the Rhetorical Situation," *Ph&Rh* 6 (1973), 154-161. See below, pp. 103-104.

[66]Fish, *Doing What Comes Naturally*, 346.

> Indeed, another word for anti-foundationalism *is* rhetoric, and one could say without too much exaggeration that modern anti-foundationalism is old sophism writ analytic. The rehabilitation by anti-foundationalism of the claims of situation, history, politics, and convention in opposition to the more commonly successful claims of logic, brute fact empiricism, the natural, and the necessary marks one more chapter in the long history of the quarrel between philosophy and rhetoric.[67]

As a child of the Enlightenment, modern biblical criticism has been firmly in the camp of rational and empirical epistemologies. Its prejudice against rhetoric in both method and in its importance in the ancient world has been, as we have said, a matter of more than misinformation.

> What is at stake . . . is a difference in worldviews. . . . In the philosopher's vision of the world rhetoric (and representation in general) is merely the (disposable) form by which a prior and substantial content is conveyed; but in the world of *homo rhetoricus* rhetoric is *both* form and content, the manner of presentation and what is presented.[68]

In an anti-foundational world then, language is inseparable from meaning, and rhetorical form is inseparable from content. As Ricoeur argues, any reality is linguistically constituted, created by communally shared metaphors. "Discourse, whether scientific or poetic, is metaphorical in the sense that it never describes reality directly, but provides a heuristic fiction to enable us to see reality in a new way, but only as a secondary reference."[69] Perelman comments, "Those who, with Paul Ricoeur, acknowledge the place in philosophy of metaphoric truths which . . . propose a restructuring of reality . . . cannot deny the importance of rhetorical techniques in making one metaphor prevail over another." For this reason, even "adornment" with figures of speech, when used properly, cannot be separated from content, for a figure leads to a change in perspective.

---

[67]Ibid., 347.

[68]Ibid., 483.

[69]Paul Ricoeur, *Interpretation Theory: Discourse and the Surplus of Meaning* (Fort Worth: Texas Christian University, 1976), 66-68.

> If we think of figures as ornaments added on to the content of discourse, we see only the rhetorical technique of style—flowery, empty, ridiculous ostentation. But since a single and perfectly adequate way to describe reality does not exist, any other way cannot be seen only as a falsification or deformity; the separation between the form and content of discourse cannot be realized in as simple a way as classical thought imagined it.[70]

In this new philosophical climate, not just Fish and Gadamer, but many other anti-foundationalist thinkers, such as Ricoeur, Grassi, Ijsselling, and Perelman frequently appeal to classical rhetoric. As Fiorenza points out, "discourse theory and reader-response criticism as well as the insight into the linguisticality and rhetorical character of all historiography represent a contemporary revival of ancient rhetoric."[71]

We might say that the Enlightenment was a digression from which we are now recovering. As Enlightenment rationalism turned from Renaissance humanism, rhetoric declined. In particular, Descartes excludes from philosophy the "probable" knowledge of poetry, rhetoric, politics and history in favor of the "critical" philosophy of valid demonstration based on rational proof.[72] "Descartes' work was seen as the beginning of modern thought. . . . Hence rhetoric, *sensus communis*, and every form of poetic expression were rejected as not belonging to philosophy."[73] Such rationalism separated "form and content, the latter alone being thought worthy of a philosopher's attention."[74]

Even before Descartes, Ramus merged analytical and dialectical reasoning into one field of rational argument, while rhetoric was limited to the eloquent and ornate use of language. Following Ramus' lead, his friend, Omer Talon, published in 1572 "the first systematic rhetoric limited to the study of figures. . . . In this way

[70]Perelman, *The Realm of Rhetoric*, 7, 39.

[71]Elisabeth Schüssler Fiorenza, "Rhetorical Situation and Historical Reconstruction in 1 Corinthians," *NTS* 33 (1987), 386.

[72]Grassi, *Rhetoric as Philosophy*, 37-39.

[73]Ibid., 3.

[74]Perelman, *The New Rhetoric and the Humanities*, 28.

classical rhetoric came into being—this rhetoric of figures which led progressively from the degeneration to the death of rhetoric."[75]

As we pointed out above, Enlightenment attacks on rhetoric were nothing new. Both Descartes and Bacon

> were explicitly hostile to rhetoric, but in this respect, they were not the first . . . and by no means the last. One can even say that the whole of modern philosophy and especially modern science are characterized by a negative attitude with regard to rhetoric. . . . It seems as if it had been affirmed on the side of rhetoric that philosophy and rhetoric had grown apart and had nothing to do with each other. Rhetoric would then only be a matter of expression or formulation with no relation to truth. Expression is thus conceived as a purely external affair while thought is internal. . . . This is probably connected with a fundamental dualism that is characteristic of modern times, namely the dualism between internal and external, thinking and speaking, thought and expression, body and soul, or philosophy and rhetoric. Both Bacon and Descartes stand at the origin of this dualism.[76]

As heirs of the Enlightenment, modern thinkers have generally rejected rhetoric, considering it dangerous, deceptive, and radically opposed to scientific arguments. "There is a search for the naked truth or the bare facts, while any embellishment is nothing but words and irrelevant to the matter itself."[77]

Thus, Grassi writes of the changes that came with the Enlightenment:

> Over the centuries, under the aspect of the relationship between content and form, the thesis was again and again developed that images and rhetoric were to be appreciated primarily from outside, for pedagogical reasons, that is, as aids to "alleviate" the "severity" and "dryness" of rational language. To resort to images and metaphors, to the full set of implements proper to rhetoric and artistic language, in this sense, merely serves to make it "easier" to absorb rational truth. Therefore rhetoric generally was assigned a formal function, whereas philosophy, as *episteme*, as rational knowledge, was to supply the true, factual content. . . . But . . . the original . . . assertions have in their structure a belief, a figurative, imaginative character, so that every original speech is in its aim illuminating and persuading. In this

---

[75]idem, *The Realm of Rhetoric*, 3-4.

[76]Ijsselling, 66-67.

[77]Ibid, 67.

original speech evidently it is impossible to separate content and form.[78]

If form and content are inseparable in every kind of discourse, even in a subject as abstract and impersonal as philosophy, this is even more clearly the case for the kinds of discourse employed by Paul and his communities: discourses about community beliefs, authority, and ethics. Such discourses are at the opposite end of Kovesi's spectrum from those in which form and content may be more easily distinguished. At one end of the spectrum are modes of discourse in which form and content are related only by strict definitions. At this extreme stands geometrical language, whose form is unambiguously determined by its definition. Geometrical language is thus completely impersonal and non-rhetorical. But for these reasons, geometrical language is unlike most other language. At the other extreme stands moral language, for the content of an action becomes moral only when it is put into the form of moral discourse. Kovesi demonstrates this by pointing out that various actions grouped together under a single moral form such as "inadvertent" have no empirical similarity. Thus moral language, in which "we want to avoid or promote something, excuse or blame people for certain happenings or acts" receives its meaning perhaps more from its form than from its content.[79] Such discourse thus gives meaning to otherwise disconnected contents through rhetorical means (i.e., the persuasive appeal to *sensus communis*). For this reason, when discourses are rhetorical, attempts to analyze content apart from form will inevitably distort meaning. For such discourse, we must see

> that the material and formal elements of a notion are inseparable. . . . Without the formal element there is just no sense in selecting, out of many others, those features of a thing or an act that constitute it that thing or act. . . . Decisions and attitudes, insights, wants, needs, aspirations and standards . . . are part and parcel of our notions. . . . Evaluation is not an icing on a cake of hard facts. . . . There is a point in bringing certain features and aspects of actions and situations together as being relevant, and by removing this point, by removing

---

[78]Grassi, *Rhetoric as Philosophy*, 80, 26-27.

[79]Julius Kovesi, *Moral Notions* (London: Routledge & Kegan Paul, 1967) 9-16.

> the 'evaluative element', we are not left with the same facts minus evaluation.[80]

Just as philosophers increasingly recognize the indissoluble dialectic of language and reality, form and content, so too do literary critics. Enormously influential in this regard has been Booth's *The Rhetoric of Fiction*, which marked the turn from Platonic or realist criticism to a recognition of the integrity of the text's own "world." Booth comments:

> Regardless of how we conceive the core of any literary work, will it be entirely freed of a rhetorical dimension? On the contrary, at the very moment of initial conception, at the instant when James exclaims to himself, "Here is my subject," a rhetorical aspect is contained within the conception: the subject is thought of as *something that can be made public*, something that can be made into a communicated work. . . .
>
> The notion of firmly constituted natural objects inducing natural responses came into literature originally in emulation of the nineteenth-century scientist, dealing dispassionately, objectively, with concrete reality. It was never as fruitful an idea in literature as it was in science. Now that the scientists have given up the claim that they are seeking one single formulation of a firmly constituted reality, unaffected by the limitations and interests of the observer, perhaps we should once again pack up our bags and follow after. Undifferentiated reality is never given to men in a "natural," unadorned form. . . . Thus, every literary "fact"—even the most unadorned picture of some universal aspect of human experience—is highly charged by the meanings of the author, whatever his pretensions to objectivity.
>
> What this means is that any story will be unintelligible unless it includes, however subtly, the amount of telling necessary not only to make us aware of the value system which gives it its meaning, but, more important, to make us willing to accept that value system, at least temporarily.[81]

If we are to render Paul's "telling" intelligible, we must be willing to accept the value system of the ancient world, a value system which appears bizarre to scientistic approaches but familiar to anti-foundational ones. In such a rendering, we may begin to understand Paul's references to rhetorical speech as encompassing both form and

---

[80]Ibid., 23-25.

[81]Wayne C. Booth, *The Rhetoric of Fiction*, 2nd ed. (Chicago: University of Chicago, 1983), 104-105, 112.

content. In the following chapter, we will look more closely at the role of rhetoric in Paul's first century Greco-Roman social world, a world in which rhetoric was appreciated as more than mere form.

CHAPTER II

FORM AND CONTENT IN CLASSICAL RHETORIC

Ancient rhetorical theory included a highly developed analysis of effective communication which went far beyond mere style or form. In classical rhetoric, one begins not with style, but with "invention", in which one collects the arguments appropriate to the situation. Then in "arrangement" the orator decides the order in which he will present these arguments to maximize their effectiveness. Only then is style considered, only a part of which includes figures (though in late antiquity an increasingly large part as fascination with "ornamentation" increased).

However, the academic prejudice against rhetoric as mere form is not entirely unfounded, for rhetorical theory and practice sometimes were little more than that. From its beginnings in ancient Greece, rhetoric was often accused of being no more than an outward form of persuasion with no concern for truthful content. One of the most famous of these accusations was leveled by Plato when he wrote "as self-adornment is to gymnastic, so is sophistry to legislation; and as cookery is to medicine, so is rhetoric to justice."[1] In other words, while gymnastic is an art (τέχνη) which aims to improve the body, self-adornment is a merely a thing learned by experience (ἐμπειρία) or a knack (τριβή) which "deceives men by

[1]Pl. *Grg.* 465c.

forms and colors, polish and dress . . . assuming an extraneous beauty." Rhetoricians and sophists, then, have no more concern for real justice when they plead in courts or in the assembly than do cooks or cosmeticians for real medical health or physical beauty. They are mere flatterers who tickle the ears of the hearers with the frivolous things they want to hear, rather than feeding them with the truth they need to hear.

These complaints were often repeated by later critics of rhetoric. The comparison with cosmetics, the accusation of flattery, and the summary accusation of making the worse appear the better all became philosophical *topoi*.

Relying on these comments, modern scholars often take these charges as Plato's last word on the subject; but that is not really true. The *Gorgias* is the beginning not only of a tradition of philosophical criticism of rhetoric, but also of an acceptance of its necessity. The question for philosophy becomes not whether rhetorical expression should be eschewed in favor of philosophical content, but what kind of rhetoric is philosophically acceptable. Plato concludes "that rhetoric is to be used for this one purpose always, of pointing to what is just . . ."[2] He raises the question of

> how rhetoric is to be linked to the Good Life. The aim of true rhetoric, we may be sure, is nothing other than improvement and education; the only proper use of persuasion is to make us better. But are we, then, incapable of making a true use of rhetoric ourselves until we have been improved by its offices? What happens in the meantime, until the desired conversion has been effected? Here, Plato might say, is the place for Socrates. This is the value of great and wise men: we must listen to them, the mouthpieces of true rhetoric, until we are in a position to think and speak for ourselves. Once we have become capable of wise and prudent action, we may enter politics or whatever profession of wisdom we choose.[3]

Much of the *Gorgias* is tongue in cheek: while Socrates rails against the sophist Gorgias and his students, he tacitly admits that philosophy itself is rhetorical. For example, Socrates distinguishes

---

[2]Ibid., 527c.

[3]W. C. Helmbold, Introduction to *Gorgias*, The Library of Liberal Arts (Indianapolis: Bobbs-Merrill, 1952), vii. See also Pl. *Grg.* 500b-d, 503-4, 515c, 517a.

dialectic, in which philosophers seek the truth through dialogues of brief questions and answers, and rhetoric, which persuades the ignorant through long monologues.[4] For this reason, he asks Gorgias and Polus to refrain from long discourses.[5] But then he ironically admits,

> It may, indeed, be absurd of me, when I do not allow you to make long speeches, to have extended mine to so considerable a length. However, I can fairly claim indulgence: for when I spoke briefly you did not understand me; you were unable to make any use of the answer I gave you, but required a full exposition.[6]

Thus, the philosopher must adapt his rhetoric to the nature of his audience, a tacit acceptance of a fundamental rhetorical principle. In fact, the whole dialogue is a "brilliant and successful" use of rhetoric,[7] an irony often noted by the rhetoricians.[8]

In the *Phaedrus*, Plato develops his idea of a philosophically acceptable rhetoric. "The ideal rhetoric proposed by Socrates . . . is itself not unlike the ideal sought by the Sophists in general, Isocrates in particular. . . . It sought a union of verbal skills with learning and wisdom."[9] There, Socrates admits that philosophy and rhetoric need each other, for without the help of the art of speaking, "the knowledge of the truth does not give the art of persuasion,"[10] yet "he who knows not the truth, but pursues opinions, will, it seems, attain an art of speech which is ridiculous, and not an art at all."[11] Rather, "if the speech is to be good, must not the mind of the speaker know the

---

[4]Pl. *Grg.* 447c, 454e-455a, 459a.

[5]Ibid., 449b, 461c-462a.

[6]Ibid., 465e-466a. See also 519d-e.

[7]Helmbold *viii.* Also George A. Kennedy, *Classical Rhetoric and Its Christian and Secular Tradition from Ancient to Modern Times* (Chapel Hill: The University of North Carolina Press, 1980), 50: Socrates has a "'rhetoric' of his own; he attains his purposes through valid argument, but also by irony, by subtly appealing to the better instincts in men, and elsewhere also by a mystical pathos."

[8]e.g., Cic. *De Or.* 1.47; cf. Quint. 5.7.28.

[9]Perelman, "Rhetoric," 805.

[10]Pl. *Phdr.* 260d.

[11]Ibid., 262c. Plato is also attacking opinion (δόξα) as inferior to knowledge (ἐπιστήμη).

truth about the matters of which he is to speak?"[12] In other words, the quality of rhetorical form is tied to the truth of its content. Further, if rhetoric is to be effective, it must know how to organize its content. Those who are concerned only with "brachylogies and figurative speech" and other matters of mere technique do not possess the true art of persuasion, but only preliminaries to the persuasive organization of the whole argument.[13]

Furthermore, the rhetorician needs philosophical analysis of persons, for he must know how to shape the argument to the audience: "A man . . . must understand the nature of the soul, must find out the class of speech adapted to each nature, and must arrange and adorn his discourse accordingly."[14] But the same connection of word and soul also, conversely, makes philosophical truth dependent on rhetorical expression. Philosophy aims to raise the soul above passion so it can remember the eternal truths;[15] but to achieve this end, the teacher of philosophy must tailor his speech to the soul of the pupil. For this reason, Plato elevates oratory above written treatises since a written work cannot be questioned, or explain itself, or defend itself: "It knows not to whom to speak or not to speak." But oratory, "the living, breathing word of him who knows, . . . written with intelligence (ἐπιστήμη) in the mind of the learner, . . . is able to defend itself and knows to whom it should speak." The philosopher "employs the dialectic method and plants and sows in a fitting soul intelligent words which are not fruitless, but yield seed from which there spring up in other minds other words capable of continuing the process for ever." Thus philosophical rhetoric is necessary "to speak by the method of art, . . . either for purposes of instruction or of persuasion."[16]

Plato's approach to rhetoric opened the way for Aristotle to develop his teacher's ideals. In his *Rhetoric*, we again find both form and content as the proper domain of rhetoric: "Rhetoric is useful, because the true and the just are naturally superior to their opposites,

[12]Ibid., 259e; cf. 277b.

[13]Ibid., 269a-c.

[14]Ibid., 277b-c.; cf. 271.

[15]Ibid., 249.

[16]Ibid., 275e-277c.

so that, if decisions are improperly made, they must owe their defeat to their own advocates; which is reprehensible. . . . Generally speaking, that which is true and better is naturally always easier to prove and more likely to persuade." In fact, Aristotle gives most of his attention to the contents of an argument, whether "inartistic" (i.e., supplied to the orator from without, such as evidence or witnesses) or "artistic" (i.e., arguments which must be discovered or "invented" by the orator). Among the artistic arguments are not only those that rely on the character of the speaker (*ethos*) or the emotions of the audience (*pathos*), but also those that rely on the logic of the speech itself (*logos*): "Persuasion is produced by the speech itself (τῶν λόγων), when we establish the true or apparently true from the means of persuasion applicable to each individual subject." Thus, like dialectic, rhetoric is a faculty of furnishing arguments (λόγοι), or, more precisely, "the faculty of discovering the possible means of persuasion in reference to any subject."[17] Thus, although Aristotle treated rhetoric narrowly as a theoretical rather than a productive art, he clearly envisioned that in the actual production of speeches the orator deliberates on his subject matter in a manner similar to the philosopher in dialectic.

Aristotle had considerable influence on later rhetorical teaching, but the Hellenistic rhetoric encountered by Paul is far more the heir of Isocrates (436-338 B.C.), the contemporary of Plato. Several years before Plato founded the Academy, Isocrates opened his school in Athens and ran it successfully for more than fifty years. Isocrates brought together and developed the various strands of Hellenic rhetoric (technical, sophistic, and philosophical) in his educational system. Successors to Isocrates' school flourished and became the basis of most education of the Hellenistic world and eventually of Rome as well.[18] This widespread dominance of rhetoric in Hellenis-

---

[17]Arist. *Rh.* 1355a-1356a.

[18]H. I. Marrou, *A History of Education in Antiquity*, trans. George Lamb, (New York: Sheed & Ward, 1956), 95-96; Donald Lemen Clark, *Rhetoric in Greco-Roman Education* (New York: Columbia University Press, 1957), 59-60; Kennedy, *Classical Rhetoric*, 34-35, 89; Clarke, *Rhetoric at Rome*, 10-11, 37.

tic *paideia* (in both senses of education and culture) means that we can reconstruct that culture with a certain degree of confidence.[19]

In Isocrates, we find a consistent concern for the unity of form and content. He accepted Plato's criticisms of the danger of a purely technical rhetoric (one concerned merely with the techniques of persuasive form and not content) or sophistic rhetoric (one concerned with content, but not the truth of that content). He attacks those sophists who "have no interest whatever in the truth, but . . . promise to make their students such clever orators that they will not overlook any of the possibilities which a subject affords."[20] Such men not only deceive by lies in their speeches, but they are generally dishonest.[21] Isocrates defends himself against the common charge of making the worse appear the better, "the kind of eloquence which enables people to gain their own advantage contrary to justice"[22] Since the true art of oratory is concerned with persuading of the truth of its content, it aims to discover all its resources, wisely applied to each situation: i.e., invention, arrangement, and style, not just the mechanical application of rules. This approach to oratory demands exhaustive education, including the study of philosophy, as well as a high moral character.[23]

Thus, Isocrates established the ideal of the morally fit and liberally educated orator. He sees truth, goodness, and eloquence cooperating: "Honest men . . . do not remain fixed in opinions which they have formed unjustly, but are in quest of the truth and are ready to be convinced by those who plead a just cause."[24]

---

[19]By "culture," I mean the dominant integrated pattern of values, social forms, and linguistic and literary norms of Greco-Roman society. I take for granted that this *paideia* varied even among the upper classes, and that its relevance decreased as we move down the social scale. Yet its strength was such that all lived within its world- defining power, even if with weaker articulation among οἱ πολλοί. However, we must also be sensitive to differences where we can detect them.

[20]Isoc. *Against the Sophists* 9. Norlin comments (LCL, n. b): "Their interest was not in the triumph of justice but in making 'the worse reason appear the better.'"

[21]Ibid., 7.

[22]Isoc. *Antidosis* 89.

[23]Isoc. *Against the Sophists* 10-21.

[24]Isoc. *Antidosis* 170.

This ideal required an educational system that would provide the broad knowledge necessary for the complete orator. Unlike earlier sophists who claimed that anyone, even the most ignorant and poorly educated, could be taught to be persuasive, Isocrates held that the student must first of all have natural ability, for he must have not only a good voice and self-assurance but also "a mind which is capable of finding out and learning the truth and of working hard and remembering what it learns."[25] Without such qualities and the added lessons of practical experience, education can improve but not perfect a speaker or writer.[26] For this reason, only a few of Isocrates' pupils actually became professional orators or teachers of oratory; the rest retired into private life (ἰδιώτης).[27] Yet Isocrates claims that his method of sophistic education allowed even those who prefer to live in private to become more gracious in social intercourse, keener judges of discourses and more prudent counselors than most.[28] It has this effect because it is a training of the intellect (τήν τῆς φρονήσεως ἄσκησιν), so that our minds are "made more serviceable through education."[29] The establishment of this educational model was so universal that four centuries later in Rome, the Elder Seneca still testifies that "you can easily pass from this art [eloquence] to all others; it equips even those whom it does not train for its own ends. . . . The practice of declamation will help you in those pursuits to which you are whole-heartedly devoted."[30]

Isocrates summarizes his aim as cultivating the ability "to think and speak well" (φρονεῖν εὖ καὶ λέγειν).[31] Thinking and speaking are not two activities which can be separated, but are always united:

> There is no institution devised by man which the power of speech has not helped us to establish. . . . The power to speak well is taken as the surest index of a sound understanding, and discourse which is true and lawful and just is the outward image of a good and faithful soul. With this faculty we both contend against others on matters which are

---

[25]Ibid., 189.

[26]Ibid., 192; cf. idem, *Against the Sophists* 15.

[27]Ibid., 201.

[28]Ibid., 204.

[29]Ibid., 209-14; cf. 271, 275, 277.

[30]Sen. *Contr.* 2.pr.3-4.

[31]Ibid., 244.

> open to dispute and seek light for ourselves on things which are unknown; for the same arguments which we use in persuading others when we speak in public, we employ when we deliberate in our own thoughts; and, while we call eloquent those who are able to speak before a crowd, we regard as sage those who most skillfully debate their problems in their own minds. . . . None of the things which are done with intelligence take place without the help of speech.[32]

When we jump from Isocrates to first century Corinth, we follow not a straight line, but a wide diffusion of Isocrates' ideals and methods which made rhetorical teaching and practice increasingly uniform throughout the Hellenistic world. Although the major Greek texts of the period are not extant, the Romans in large measure relied on the Greek teachers.[33] Their writings reveal a fairly consistent picture of the same ideals of *paideia*, changed only by the peculiar values of Roman public and political life: the production of the educated, cultured, civicly minded individual who could speak persuasively by dint of his wisdom–i.e., his character, knowledge, understanding, education, and practical ability to use the language. Since Corinth lay on the cusp of Greek and Roman culture, we can assume both the traditional strength of Greek rhetorical teaching and the direct influence of its Roman heirs.

The anonymous *Rhetorica ad Herennium*, written about 80 B.C.E., "reflects Hellenistic rhetorical teaching. Our author, however, gives us a Greek art in Latin dress, combining a Roman spirit with Greek doctrine."[34] Though the work is strictly a technical manual, even here we find the same emphasis on both content and form. While "it is true that copiousness and facility in expression bear abundant fruit," it does so only "if controlled by proper knowledge." Such knowledge must include all matters of public speech, including

---

[32]Isoc. *Nicocles* 6-9.

[33]Clarke, *Rhetoric at Rome*, 11, 36: "The Greeks were to conquer here as elsewhere, and Roman rhetoric was to become little more than an adaptation of Greek rhetoric. . . . [Roman rhetoric] bears all the marks of its Greek origin. It was the creation of the Greek intellect. . . . On the whole the Romans took to it with surprising readiness. From its first introduction to the end of Roman civilization it was part of the intellectual background of the educated Roman."

[34]Harry Caplan, introduction to *[Cicero] Ad C. Herennium: De Ratione Decendi (Rhetorica ad Herennium)* (Cambridge, Mass.: Harvard University Press, 1954; London: William Heinemann, 1954), vii.

law and public policy. Thus, the first faculty a speaker should possess is invention, "the devising of matter, true or plausible [*veri similis*, i.e., probable or realistic], that would make the case convincing."[35]

Far from seeing ornamented language as the essence of persuasion, *Ad Herennium* emphasizes those parts of a discourse which are most strongly determined by content: the narration of facts and the proof and refutation. The narration should be brief and clear so the facts are easy to follow, and it must be verisimilar, for often even "the truth cannot gain credence otherwise."[36] In the proof and refutation, the orator argues how the facts should be evaluated. It is here that the orator's art is most critical: "The entire hope of victory and the entire method of persuasion rest on proof and refutation, for when we have submitted our arguments and destroyed those of the opposition, we have, of course, completely fulfilled the speaker's function."[37] The speaker's function is not simply to dress up a predetermined content, but to learn about the general subject, research the relevant facts, analyze how these facts are related to one another and to general knowledge, and present these findings to an audience in a way that will persuade them to accept the speaker's argument and point of view.

Like the author of *Ad Herennium*, the great Roman orator Cicero (106-43 B.C.E.) resisted the accusation that rhetoric was concerned with only form or style. Carrying forward the ideals of Isocrates, he aimed to synthesize all wisdom in the education of the orator:

> I hold that eloquence is dependent upon the trained skill of highly educated men. . . . A knowledge of very many matters must be grasped, without which oratory is but an empty and ridiculous swirl of verbiage. . . . No man can be an orator complete in all points of merit, who has not attained a knowledge of all important subjects and

---

[35] Rhet. Her. 1.1.1-1.2.3. The modern reader may be disturbed by the rhetoricians' acceptance of probable rather than true arguments. But this appeal to what seems to be true is basic to all argument, whether we recognize it or not (see above, pp. 39-40).

[36] Ibid., 1.9.14-16.

[37] Ibid., 1.9.19.

> arts. . . . Unless there is such knowledge, there must be something empty and almost childish in the utterance.[38]

Ideally, "the genuine orator must have investigated and heard and read and discussed and handled and debated the whole of the contents of the life of mankind, inasmuch as that is the field of the orator's activity, the subject matter (*subiecta materies*) of his study."[39] As Judge observes, "since the sophists were in fact as disposed to take an interest in what they talked about, the ancient distinction between those who cared only about words and those who cared about ideas breaks down."[40]

Similarly, Cicero asserts that "eloquence consists of language and thought [*sententia*]."[41] Thus, he explicitly opposed separating form and content, for they are

> things that cannot really stand apart. Every speech consists of matter [*res*] and words [*verba*], and the words cannot fall into place if you remove the matter, nor can the matter have clarity if you withdraw the words. . . . The half-educated . . . find it easier to deal with matters that they cannot grasp in their entirety if they split them up and take them piecemeal, and who separate words from thoughts [*sententiae*] as one might sever body (*corpus*) from mind [*animus*]—and neither process can take place without disaster. . . . [But] it is impossible to achieve an ornate style without first procuring ideas and putting them into shape, and at the same time . . . no idea can possess distinction without lucidity of style.[42]

---

[38]Cic. *De Or.* 1.2.5, 1.5.17, 1.6.20.

[39]Ibid., 3.15.54.

[40]E.A. Judge, "The Early Christians as a Scholastic Community," *JRH* 1 (1960-61), 126.

[41]Cic. *opt. gen.* 2.4.

[42]Cic. *De. Or.* 3.5.19, 24. See also 1.11.48-51: "For excellence in speaking cannot be made manifest unless the speaker fully comprehends the matter he speaks about (*de quibus dicit, percepta sint*). . . . Style, if the underlying subject-matter (*res*) be not comprehended and mastered by the speaker, must inevitably be of no account or even become the sport of universal derision. For what so effectually proclaims the madman as the hollow thundering of words—be they never so choice and resplendent—which have no thought or knowledge behind them?" Also 1.4.63: "Neither can anyone be eloquent upon a subject that is unknown to him, nor if he knows it perfectly and does not know how to shape and polish his style, can he speak fluently even upon that which he does know."

Cicero inspired Quintilian (40-95 C.E.), the greatest ancient writer on education. Quintilian greatly admired Cicero as one who fulfilled the ideals of liberal rhetorical education. In general, "it is surely the orator who will have the greatest mastery of all such departments of knowledge and the greatest power to express it in words."[43] That is, the education of the orator encompasses the whole depository of culture. Quintilian accurately describes secondary education under the *grammaticus* as studying poets and "every kind of writer," as well as music, astronomy, and philosophy. These subjects are necessary if one is to speak eloquently. "Unless the foundations of oratory are well and truly laid by the teaching of literature, the superstructure will collapse. The study of literature is a necessity for boys . . . and the sole branch of study which has more solid substance than display."[44] In this vein, Quintilian defines rhetoric as "the science of speaking well" in every sense, i.e., "to think and speak rightly," "persuading men to do what ought to be done."[45] As Ijselling comments, "one had to learn to speak about all there was to say and to know."[46]

Like Cicero, Quintilian opposes the notion that form and content are separable. Instead, he asserts, nothing is alien to the art of speech. For Quintilian, *res* (content) and *verba* (form) are fundamentally united:[47]

> As to the material of oratory, some have asserted that it is speech (*oratione*). . . . If . . . we interpret 'speech' as indicating the words

---

[43]Quint. 1.pr.17.

[44]Ibid., 1.4.4; cf. 1.10.1-8. In 1.10.34-39, Quintilian argues that geometry is helpful in preparing for rhetorical training because "geometry arrives at its conclusions from definite premises, and by arguing from what is certain proves what was previously uncertain. Is not this just what we do in speaking?" Geometry uses the syllogism, "but even the orator will sometimes, though rarely, prove his point by formal logic. For, if necessary, he will use the syllogism, and he will certainly make use of the enthymeme which is a rhetorical form of syllogism."

[45]Ibid., 2.15.34-35.

[46]Ijsselling, 10.

[47]Grassi, *Rhetoric as Philosophy*, 47-51. In addition to Quintilian's explicit statements, Grassi points to his concern with stasis theory as illustrating his conviction that rhetoric's province covers all content, not just form, since questions of stasis apply to every human activity.

> (*verba*) themselves, they can do nothing unless they are related to facts. . . . For my own part, and I have authority to support me, I hold that the material of rhetoric is composed of everything (*omnes res*) that may be placed before it as a subject for speech.[48]

Quintilian admits that rhetoricians' main concern is properly style, and it is style alone which distinguishes the true orator from the merely informed. Yet such a concern for style can never be isolated from the concern for content:

> I would have the orator, while careful in his choice of words, be even more concerned about his subject matter. For, as a rule, the best words are essentially suggested by the subject matter and are discovered by their own intrinsic light. . . . Eloquence . . . if only her whole body be sound, will never think it her duty to polish her nails and tire her hair.[49]

We see, then, that the leading theorists of rhetoric treated their subject as concerned with far more than the ornaments of style. However, their statements are apologetic and polemical, confronting those (especially philosophers) who would accuse rhetoric of concern with mere appearances. For this reason, we might be tempted to dismiss their apologies as irrelevant to the reality of Paul's Corinth. However, the unity of form and content they espoused was, in large measure, lived out in the wider rhetorical culture.

Rhetoric and Culture

Greeks had long held the spoken or written word to be the locus of what is at once most valued and capable of transmission, i.e., *paideia* (education and culture). Since most Hellenistic peoples could be Greek only through language and culture, they particularly valued the *paideia* acquired in the rhetorical schools. Thus, through rhetorical education and the general use of speech, the culture itself became rhetorical.

---

[48]Quint. 2.21.1-4.

[49]Ibid., 8.pr.13-22.

In fact, rhetorical education "must be placed at the very centre of any genuine picture" of Hellenistic civilization.[50] It transformed a variety of far flung cultures into a world with a shared culture. As Isocrates wrote,

> Beautiful and artistic speech . . . is the work of an intelligent mind. . . . [Athens] knew that whether men have been liberally educated from their earliest years . . . is made manifest most of all by their speech, and that this has proved itself to be the surest sign of culture [παιδεύσις] in every one of us, and that those that are skilled in speech are not only men of power in their own cities but are also held in honour in other states. And so far has our city distanced the rest of mankind in thought and in speech that her pupils have become the teachers of the rest of the world; and she has brought it about that the name "Hellenes" suggests no longer a race but an intelligence, and that the title "Hellenes" is applied rather to those who share our culture [παιδεύσις] than to those who share a common blood.[51]

What Isocrates proclaimed of his day was even more true of later centuries: Hellenism was a "civilization of paideia."[52] In Judge's assessment, "the historian of the ancient world . . . could hardly exaggerate the importance of rhetoric in shaping antiquity's own understanding of itself."[53]

Rhetoric did far more than train orators; it gave the only introduction possible to a variety of literary and cultural pursuits: the reading and writing of poems, letters, histories, dialogues, philosophical essays, and all other arts of discourse and in fact any public occupation. "Thus in the Greco-Roman schools education was almost exclusively education in rhetoric, which the ancients considered an adequate preparation for the life of free men."[54]

---

[50]Marrou, 97.

[51]Isoc. *Paneg.* 48-50.

[52]Hengel, *Judaism and Hellenism*, Vol I, 65.

[53]Judge, "Paul's Boasting," 42.

[54]Donald Lemen Clark, *Rhetoric in Greco-Roman Education* (New York: Columbia University, 1957), 65; cf. Kinneavy, *Rhetorical Origins*, 20: "The concept of rhetoric . . . dominated the schooling of the time in Greek and Roman education, and it was conspicuous in Jewish schools also. It was an honorific concept, much more complex than just a combination of intellectual and emotional appeals."

> For the Greeks "ρητορική τέχνη" was a real art, exalted above the rest, having no equivalent in other area of Greek civilization. It flourished both from the practical viewpoint in that it was carefully cultivated and from the theoretical viewpoint in that it was much reflected upon. . . . Learning to speak held a very particular place in Greek "paideia", that is, education and culture. Rhetoric was not just one of the many subjects to be learnt at school but by far the most important and to a certain extent the only subject.[55]

When we picture ancient education and culture we often make the mistake of thinking of it as primarily philosophical. But "Plato had been defeated; posterity had not accepted his educational ideals. The victor, generally speaking, was Isocrates, and Isocrates became the educator first of Greece and then of the whole ancient world."[56] Although philosophy competed for students on the tertiary educational level, on the whole it was a minority counter-culture "for an intellectual elite prepared to make the necessary effort. It meant breaking with the usual culture, whose general tone was literary, rhetorical and aesthetic."[57] Even under the Principate, when opportunities for public speech declined, parents who paid for their children's education did not have "much time for philosophy. Rhetoric was what everybody wanted."[58]

Rhetoric's influence extended far beyond the upper class. Except for specialized "trade schools" for slaves and lower class free in large urban centers[59], virtually all education, including the learning of "letters" (roughly, age 7 to 12) and "grammar" (13-17), as well as "rhetoric" (up to age 20 or even higher) was viewed as a continuum which aimed to produce the complete eloquent individual. Even if one's economic status limited a student to only part of this progression, that part would communicate a certain amount of rhetorical and literary theory and practice.

In the study of "letters," the student aimed to master reading and writing. Texts and anthologies, often quite advanced, were read

---

[55]Ijsselling, 10; cf. Marrou, 99-101, 204-205.

[56]Marrou, 194; cf. Ijsselling, 16.

[57]Ibid, 206.

[58]M. Winterbottom, "Introduction," *The Elder Seneca: Declamations*, trans. M. Winterbottom, LCL (Cambridge: Harvard, 1974), *ix*.

[59]Robert A. Kaster, "Notes on 'Primary' and 'Secondary' Schools in Late Antiquity," *TAPA* 113 (1983), 323-346.

aloud (in the manner of all ancients, a practice which helped erase the distinction between written and oral literature). Thus, literary education had already begun, and the sense of appropriateness of one's own communications was shaped by hearing, copying, and memorizing approved texts.[60] This level of education was almost universal, often including slaves. Outside the three special settings of the "trade schools," the primary schools taught by the γραμματιστής, or home bound instruction for upper class children, the "letters" were often taught by the rhetorically trained γραμματικός,[61] thus exposing even young children to a rhetorical teacher.

In the study of "grammar," the γραμματικός prepared his students for advanced instruction by the ῥήτωρ. This included an elaborate study of classical poets and other writers, including orators. In addition, the students were drilled in the προγυμνάσματα, exercises which would become building blocks of rhetorical practice.[62] "It is

---

[60]Stanley F. Bonner, *Education in Ancient Rome: From the elder Cato to the younger Pliny* (Berkeley and Los Angeles: University of California Press; 1977), 172-179. "The lines which were set for practice in writing were specially selected because they contained some useful observation on life or conduct, some exhortation or warning, which might with advantage be remembered in later years." Maxims (γνῶμαι, *sententiae*), like the example quoted by Paul, "bad company ruins good morals" (1 Cor. 15.33) were particularly useful in this regard. "These maxims had to be learned by heart, and it is not surprising that pupils acquired a very considerable stock of them, and that authors in later life sometimes recalled a *sententia* which took them back to the lessons of the primary school." Primary students also read longer works: Greeks read Homer, Romans probably read fables.

[61]As a socially and economically low-status group, teachers are a good example of the fallacy of oversimpli- fying the social level of rhetoric's influence. In fact, many *grammatici* were slaves; see Clarence A. Forbes, "The Education and Training of Slaves in Antiquity," TAPA 86 (1955), 326, 339-340, 344; Forbes cites Cicero, *De officiis* (1.42.151): "The professions such as medicine, architecture, and teaching of the liberal arts, which either involve a higher learning or are utilitarian to no small degree, are honorable for those to whose social status they are suited." cf. Sen *Contr.* 2.pr.5: "The rhetorician Blandus, . . . [was] the first Roman knight to teach in Rome. Before his time, the teaching of the most noble subjects was restricted to freedmen, and by a quite unsatisfactory custom it was accounted disgraceful to teach what it was honorable to learn." For a good discussion of multidimensional social stratification and status inconsis- tency, see Meeks, *The First Urban Christians*, 22-23, 53-55.

[62]Quint. 2.1.3 complains that "subjects which once formed the first stages of rhetoric have come to form the final stages of a literary education, and boys who are ripe for more advanced study are kept back in the inferior school and

clear to any student of the Roman educational system that preparation for public speaking was the chief preoccupation of teachers, parents, and pupils alike, and that education was accordingly mainly linguistic and literary in its earlier stages, and predominantly oratorical and legal in its more advanced form."[63]

Thus, rhetoric influenced the entire culture through education, literature, values, and uniformity across time and space. It also influenced the culture through the constant presence of a variety of orators. Declamations (practice speeches on imaginary or historical subjects which were the mainstay of tertiary teaching and learning) became an end in themselves and a source of public entertainment. The rhetorician would declaim not only to impress tuition paying parents who visited the school; he would also declaim before large and cultivated audiences, even going on lecture tours to exhibit his rhetorical virtuosity. Enthusiastic audiences in the provincial cities would pay to hear these speeches. Even when a student finished his training and entered a non-rhetorical profession, or a ῥήτωρ retired, he would continue to compose and perhaps deliver declamations.[64] In the Imperial age, the Roman

> school has thrown open its doors and become something like a theatre. The stage is held by the rhetorician, no longer a pedantic theorist and now rather a star performer. . . . The declamation in fact became a social occasion. . . . The professors . . . entertained the

---

practice rhetoric under the direction of teachers of literature (*grammaticus*). Thus we get the absurd result that a boy is not regarded as fit to go on to the schools of declamation till he knows how to declaim." Quintilian is credible here since he is frustrated by a reality which departs from his ideal. Many scholars conclude that the γραμματικός had usurped part of the role of the ῥήτωρ by the middle of the first century B.C.E. See Malherbe, *Social Aspects*, 56; Clark, 63; Kennedy, *NT Interpretation*, 5; Marrou, 160-1, 173; Bonner, *Education*, 252. Against this consensus, Forbes ("Comparison, Self-Praise, and Irony," 7) asserts that the προγυμνάσματα were not taught by the γραμματικός until the end of the first century C.E. Judge ("Paul's Boasting," 44) also insists that rhetoric was learned only at the tertiary stage, and so "formed a peculiarly conspicuous social dividing line between those who belonged to the leisured circles for whom such education is possible and those who could only afford the common literacy necessary to earn one's living."

[63]S. F. Bonner, *Roman Declamation in the Late Republic and Early Empire* (Liverpool: University Press, 1949), vi.

[64]Clark, 216; Marrou, 204.

general public with their performances. Sometimes the pupil was to be heard declaiming with his masters, imitating and outdoing them. . . . Sometimes too, adults who were not professional teachers would revisit the schools and join in the declamations. . . . Indiscriminate applause was the rule in the schools. The listeners would jump from their seats at the end of each period and rush forward with excited cries. *Sententia* of the master rhetoricians would be passed round, learnt by heart and repeated.[65]

By the second century C.E., public declamations were delivered throughout the empire in temples, theaters, council chambers, and "sometimes specially built lecture halls . . . [which] could be large and splendid. . . . Audiences could be large, perhaps a thousand or more."[66]

Besides the declamations of professional rhetors, a large conglomeration of popular preachers (e.g. Cynics) and others were constantly attempting to get the ear of a public who appreciated a good speech.

Nothing is more characteristic of Hellenistic civilization than this category that included wandering poets, artists, philosophers, rhetors, and specialists in hygiene, who went from city to city, from one end of the Greek world to the other, armed with fine speeches and sure of an enthusiastic reception. The lecture became the most vital form of literature. . . . Hellenistic culture was above all things a rhetorical culture, and its typical literary form was the public lecture.[67]

This widespread influence of rhetoric is summed up by Aune:

Elevated literary forms and styles were not locked away in the libraries and salons of the rich and educated, they were on public display. During the first and second centuries A.D., public performances by rhetoricians were in great demand, and they . . . received wealth and prestige along with fame. Listening to the public recitation of literary works was also a popular form of entertainment. All levels of the population of the Roman world were exposed to the variety of structures and styles found in the rhetoric, literature, and art that were on public display throughout the Empire.[68]

---

[65]Clarke, *Rhetoric at Rome*, 85-86, 97.

[66]D. A. Russell, *Greek Declamation* (Cambridge: University Press, 1983), 76.

[67]Marrou, 187, 195.

[68]Aune, *Literary Environment*, 12-13.

For yet one more reason, rhetoric profoundly shaped ancient culture: rhetoric tended to shift its focus from oral to written literature. During the Hellenistic period, rhetoric still focused primarily upon oral and civic applications, but rhetoricians increasingly used it to analyze and compose written texts, including letters.[69]

For all these reasons, "the rhetorical theory of the schools found its immediate application in almost every form of oral and written communication."[70] "A great many things in the Greek and Latin authors that escape us or astonish us explain themselves quite easily when they are seen against this educational background."[71]

One of the things that begins to explain itself is Paul's references to σοφία λόγου. In the Greco-Roman milieu of Corinth, one who was described as speaking ἐν σοφίᾳ λόγου would have been understood to be an educated, cultured individual who could speak to a group about a subject in a manner which persuaded them by evidence and argument presented in a suitable style (see Chapter Four). Such speech communicated not just the subject matter, but also explicitly or implicitly communicated the character and authority (*ethos*) of the speaker. This *ethos* was, as we shall see, intimately tied to issues of social status, boasting, and rivalries. A description of one who spoke ἐν σοφίᾳ λόγου would not have been understood merely as one who took up some content and polished it with style. "Although Paul shows no sign of finding primary or secondary education a source of problems, there are very clear indications that he had thrown himself into a total confrontation with those who espoused the reigning values of higher education."[72]

---

[69]Kennedy, *Classical Rhetoric*, 5. Cf. Theon *Prog.* 2.138-143: "Practice in the exercises is absolutely necessary, not only for those who intend to be orators, but also if someone wants to be a poet or prose-writer, or if he wants to acquire facility with some other form of writing. For these exercises are, so to speak, the foundation stones for every form of writing (λόγων)."

[70]Kennedy, *NT Interpretation*, 10.

[71]Marrou, 197.

[72]Judge, "Reaction," 11.

Philosophical Content in Rhetorical Form?

We have seen that exegetes see σοφία λόγου as referring primarily to something other than rhetoric because they have misunderstood rhetoric as mere form. But they have also turned away from rhetoric for another closely related reason. Since they viewed rhetoric as mere form, they have also assumed that if a mere rhetorician were deemed wise, he would normally have been offering a particular content dressed up in rhetorical language: philosophical wisdom. The models for such "rhetorical-philosophical" speech often come from the "Second Sophistic," which is well documented for the second century C.E. and later.

This tendency has been noted by Horsley:

> With all the interest in Gnosticism and Wisdom-Christology, . . . *sophia* as eloquent speech has been somewhat neglected. With the exception of the older works by Weiss, commentaries have devoted very little attention to the motif of speech in 1:17; 2:1-4, 13; 4:19-20. The one major and influential study which has dealt more extensively with wisdom as eloquent speech, that of Johannes Munck, lumps the eloquence together with wisdom as the means (and content) of salvation. . . . Thus when eloquence has been discerned as an important element in the Corinthian situation, it has been understood primarily in terms of the rhetoric of popular Hellenistic philosophy. New Testament scholarship is thus in the anomalous position of finding that the one aspect of *sophia* in Corinth represents Jewish wisdom speculation or a kind of proto-Gnosticism, while the other aspect of *sophia*, persuasive speech, is wisdom like that of Greek philosophy.[73]

As Munck himself puts it, argues that Paul refers to "a mixture of philosophy and sophistry, typical of that age"[74]. Like Munck, Weiss argued that the σοφία λόγου of 1 Cor. was philosophical-

[73]Horsley, "Wisdom," 224-25.

[74]Johannes Munck, *Paul and the Salvation of Mankind* (London, SCM Press, 1959), 153. Similarly, R. Grant ("The Wisdom of the Corinthians," 52) argues that the Corinthians see themselves as Stoic wise men who "may have regarded themselves as proficient in rhetoric because of their wisdom." Fee (65) points to the current philosophical milieu as emphasizing both "human understanding and rhetorical skill." Robertson & Plummer, *Commentary on First Corinthians*, 29, describe the eloquence of the rhetorician as "a beautiful philosophy."

rhetorical wisdom. Weiss began by distinguishing Paul's terms according to a form/content dichotomy, asserting that λόγος refers to the eloquence of form, and σοφία refers to the wisdom of content. The meaning of the expression must then be either external rhetorical devices or a rational, dialectical, philosophical way of knowledge. But Weiss also argued that for Paul rhetoric and dialectical argument are so closely related that "it makes little difference whether σοφία λόγου is understood as eloquence which conforms to the thought of wisdom or as a wisdom which is joined with eloquence." Yet "σοφία . . . is the chief idea; we translate: 'not in wisdom, so that I would set out the proclamation with proofs from the arsenal of worldly wisdom, which I would express with the devices of rhetoric.'"[75]

This interpretation of σοφία λόγου as philosophical speech in rhetorical dress gives those who dismiss rhetoric even more ammunition. Leading the way here is Ulrich Wilckens. As we saw above, Wilckens dismisses rhetoric because he views it as mere form. But he also dismisses it because he assumes that anyone who argues for rhetorical form must also argue for philosophical content. Wilckens correctly points out that we have little evidence of philosophical ambitions in Corinth. If we can reject philosophical content, he argues, then we can reject its rhetorical partner.[76]

Wilckens's arguments have not persuaded all, but there does appear to be a consensus, as summed up by Davis:

> Some have regarded the evidence and the respect for wisdom at Corinth as products of an over-admiration among the members of the community for the ideas, and especially the eloquence associated with Hellenistic philosophy and rhetoric. Serious consideration of this suggestion, however, has persuaded most that the proposal does not do complete justice to the totality and variety of the terminology that appears to have been in use at Corinth.[77]

---

[75]Weiss, *Der erste Korintherbrief*, 23 (translation mine).

[76]Wilckens *Weisheit*, 1-3; cf. idem, "Σοφια," 522: "It seems that in this section the Christian preacher is opposing any philosophical or rhetorical presentation of the Gospel according to the standards of Greek philosophy. . . . His opponents are Gnostics, not Greek philosophers. . . . This is not traditional Greek rhetoric. . . . There is no evidence in the epistles that Paul was educated in one of the Greek philosophical schools."

[77]James A. Davis, *Wisdom and Spirit: An Investigation of 1 Corinthians 1:18-3:20 against the Background of Jewish Sapiential Traditions in the*

However, this marriage of philosophy and rhetoric does not really match what we know of the first century C.E. Certainly the two overlapped, but more often they conflicted and competed socially and verbally. Socially, both philosophers and rhetoricians aimed to educate Greco-Roman youth, and thus to provide the norms for culture. This competition fueled fierce verbal attacks and counter-attacks which frequently borrowed their *topoi* from arguments between the sophists and Plato. This verbal exchange heated up in the 2nd century B.C.E. and continued into and well beyond the first century C.E.[78] Throughout Greco-Roman times, the two hostile cultures "fiercely disputed each other's right to exist."[79] As rhetoric won this battle, it became the dominant educational and social force, and philosophy often found itself in a reactionary position.

The two approaches to education and life deeply affected each other, as outlined above. Yet never did philosophy become rhetoric or vice-versa, for their approaches were radically different. Rhetoric could so easily dominate the culture because it simply reflected the culture back to itself: the values which are found to be persuasive (including the value placed upon the mastery of language) were simply codified and mastered. Philosophy, on the other hand, always aimed to evaluate cultural norms by its own lights before accepting or rejecting them. Philosophers taught and even developed rhetorical theory, but only as a subject to scrutinize and employ for the sake of philosophical truth.

For this reason, though the Stoics led other schools in teaching rhetoric, their own rhetoric was easily criticized. Cicero is grateful to the Stoics

> for being the only one of all the schools that has pronounced eloquence to be a virtue and a form of wisdom. But clearly there is

---

Greco-Roman Period (Lanham, Md: University Press of America, 1984), 4. Cf. Birger Albert Pearson, *The Pneumatikos-Psychikos Terminology in 1 Corinthians: A Study in the Theology of the Corinthian Opponents of Paul and its Relation to Gnosticism*, SBL Dissertation Series 12 (Missoula: SBL, 1973), 30, 102.

[78]George Kennedy, *The Art of Persuasion in Greece* (Princeton: Princeton University Press, 1963); idem, *Classical Rhetoric*, 89.

[79]Marrou, 210-211; cf. Hans Dieter Betz, *Der Apostel Paulus und die sokratische Tradition: Eine exegetische Untersuchung zu seiner "Apologie" 2 Korinther 10-13* (Tübingen: J.C.B. Mohr, 1972) 15-18, 60-66.

> something in them that is quite out of keeping with the orator whom we are depicting. . . . Even the style of their discourse, though possibly subtle and undoubtedly penetrating, yet for an orator is bald, unfamiliar, jarring on the ear of the public, devoid of clarity, fullness, and spirit, while at the same time of a character that makes it quite impossible to employ in public speaking; for the Stoics hold a different view of good and bad from all their fellow-citizens or rather from all other nations, and give a different meaning to "honor," "disgrace," "reward," "punishment,"—whether correctly or otherwise does not concern us now, but if we were to adopt their terminology, we should never be able to express our meaning intelligibly about anything.[80]

As Cicero recognizes here, rhetoric triumphed over philosophy partly because it recognized that all human concerns, including knowledge, character, and justice, are the subject of language.[81] Rhetoric became the "queen of the arts," and so included philosophy in its curriculum. But philosophy could not turn the tables on rhetoric; it could not "regard language as just one more subject of reflection. Language is rather a transcendental *conditio sine qua non* of every philosophy."[82] As Ricoeur puts it,

> rhetoric is philosophy's oldest enemy and its oldest ally. 'Its oldest enemy' because it is always possible for the art of 'saying it well' to lay aside all concern for 'speaking the truth'. . . . But philosophy was never in a position either to destroy rhetoric or to absorb it. Philosophy did not create the arenas—tribunal, political assembly, public contest—in which oratory holds sway, nor can philosophy undertake to suppress them. Philosophical discourse is itself just one discourse among others.[83]

Just as the philosophers did not become rhetors, the rhetors did not become philosophers. To rhetoric, philosophy was an important subject, but only as one cultural aspect among many. "No matter how important philosophy may be for Cicero, it is merely one of the areas

---

[80]Cic. *De Or.* 3.18.65-66; Cf. idem, *Fin.* 3.1.3, 4.3.4.: The Stoics "affect an exceedingly subtle or rather crabbed style of argument; and if the Greeks find it so, even more must we. . . . [Such rhetoric] may convince the intellect, but cannot convert the heart."

[81]See above, pp. 62-64.

[82]Ijsselling, 19.

[83]Ricoeur, *Rule*, 10-11.

with which the orator must be thoroughly acquainted. . . . In Cicero's view philosophy is an acquisition of culture which one can appropriate."[84]

Cicero admitted that oratory alone, without the aid of (Stoic) philosophy for ethical values, is useless and even harmful. Yet wisdom has no practical value if it is mute and voiceless. Early in his career, Cicero conjectured that wisdom and eloquence had become unnaturally separated through the shrewd devices of lesser orators; their undeserved power of eloquence caused its bad reputation. But wise, noble, ethical men ought to study oratory or the evils of lesser tongues will prevail.[85]

Later in his career, Cicero blamed the disputes on the philosophers, viewing philosophers as more concerned with abstract thought than the virtues of citizenship. He argues that Greeks originally called wisdom [*sapientia*] "this method of attaining and expressing thought . . . this faculty of speaking" by which they "imparted education both in right conduct and in good speech." But philosophers, having too much leisure time, became overly interested in unnecessary matters, "and have spent the whole of their time and their lives in the sciences that were invented for the purpose of molding the minds of the young on the lines of culture [*humanitas*] and virtue."[86] As a result of the unnatural separation of rhetoric and philosophy, we have the "undoubtedly absurd and unprofitable and reprehensible severance between the tongue and the brain, leading to our having one set of professors to teach us to think and another to teach us to speak."[87] "The philosophers looked down on eloquence and the orators on wisdom, and never touched anything

---

[84]Ijsselling, 35. Cf. Clarke, *Rhetoric at Rome*, 55-56, 123: To Cicero, philosophy "means little more than having something to say. . . . The philosophy of his orator consists in knowing about philosophy, and philosophy is only one of the things he must know about. . . . Quintilian . . . did not care for philosophers, and though he admits the oratorical uses of philosophy, he does so grudgingly."

[85]Cic. *Inv. Rhet.* 1.1.1-1.5.6; idem, *De Or.* 3.14.55: "The stronger this faculty is, the more necessary it is for it to be combined with integrity and supreme wisdom [*prudentia*], and if we bestow fluency of speech on persons devoid of those virtues, we shall not have made orators of them but shall have put weapons into the hands of madmen."

[86]Cic. *De Or.* 3.14.57-58.

[87]Ibid., 3.16.61.

from the side of the other except what this group borrowed from that one, or that one from this; whereas they would have drawn from the common supply indifferently if they had been willing to remain in the partnership of early days."[88]

Like Cicero, *Ad Herrenium*,[89] and Theon,[90] Quintilian also argues that the orator should study philosophy, but again only as one among many subjects in a liberal education. Quintilian adopts the arguments of Isocrates and Cicero that the orator must be of good character; this ideal orator's ethical understanding in fact qualifies *him* as the true philosopher. Philosophy should not exist as a separate vocation, for "who short of being an utter villain, does not speak of justice, equity and virtue?"[91] In fact, Quintilian accepts Plato's criticisms of rhetoric and explicitly incorporates them. He interprets Plato's attitudes much as I have outlined above, a reading which stands out among the rhetoricians since they usually treat Plato as merely condemning rhetoric.[92] In the *Gorgias,*

> Plato does not regard rhetoric as an evil, but holds that true rhetoric is impossible for any save a just and good man. In the *Phaedrus* he makes it even clearer that the complete attainment of this art is impossible without the knowledge of justice, an opinion in which I heartily concur.[93]

Thus, the orator must study philosophy, but only among the other subjects for advanced study. The student will read philosophy, but also poetry, history, classics, and law. And in addition to such reading, the student will also write and speak.[94] Again following Cicero, he stresses that philosophy is especially important for morally shaping the rhetorician. Yet "it is desirable that we should not

---

[88]Ibid., 3.19.72.

[89]*Rh. Her.* 1.1.1.

[90]Theon *Prog.* 1.1-7.

[91]Quint. 1.pr.16.

[92]In this, the rhetoricians are not alone. As Quintilian wrote (2.15.24), "the majority, content with reading a few passages from the *Gorgias* of Plato, unskillfully excerpted by earlier writers, refrain from studying that dialogue and the remainder of Plato's writings, and thereby fall into serious error."

[93]Ibid., 2.15.24-31.

[94]Ibid., 10.1, 12.2-3.

restrict our study to the precepts of philosophy alone."[95] Further, "this exhortation of mine must not be taken to mean that I wish the orator to be a philosopher, since there is no other way of life that is further removed from the duties of a statesman and the tasks of an orator." On the contrary, he views philosophers as idle, pretentious men who have cut themselves off from public service to indulge in esoteric discussions which serve no practical use. An orator "should be a wise man (*sapientem*) in the Roman sense, that is, one who reveals himself as a true statesman . . . in the actual practice and experience of life."[96] Such values were widespread, as illustrated by Tacitus, who writes that Agricola was saved from a lack of moderation by his mother's *prudentia*, for he "was inclined to drink more deeply of philosophy than is permitted to a Roman senator."[97]

Quintilian's version of the division of philosophy and rhetoric, like that of the early Cicero, blamed orators of low character. But as rhetoric was crippled by cutting itself off from philosophy, so philosophy was crippled by the same separation:

> As soon as speaking became a means of livelihood and the practice of making an evil use of the blessing of eloquence came into vogue, those who had a reputation for eloquence ceased to study moral philosophy, and ethics, thus abandoned by the orators, became the prey of weaker intellects. . . . In our own day the name of philosopher has too often been the mask for the worst vices. For their attempt has not been to win the name of philosopher by virtue and the earnest search for wisdom; instead they have sought to disguise the depravity of their characters by the assumption of a stern and austere mien accompanied by the wearing of a garb differing from that of their fellow men.[98]

To some extent, the barriers between philosophy and rhetoric were transcended. Sophisticated teachers like Cicero and Quintilian could claim to be the true philosophers; a normal rhetorical education included some philosophy; a small proportion of privileged students studied in both rhetorical and philosophical schools;[99] and

---

[95]Ibid., 12.2.29.

[96]Ibid., 12.2.7.

[97]Tac. *Agr.* 4.

[98]Quint. 1.pr.13-15.

[99]Bonner, 86.

the practical success of rhetoric led most philosophical schools to teach it. But even these areas of overlap were incomplete: philosophical rhetoric was often rendered ineffective by its own dogma; much rhetorical teaching was far less sophisticated than that of Cicero and Quintilian, remaining more narrowly concerned with the techniques of persuasion; and much rhetorical practice was concerned only with success. Such masters of manipulation continually attracted criticism from philosophers, while the counter-cultural verbal and behavioral rhetoric of the philosophers continued to attract the disdain of the success-oriented rhetors. In the Imperial period, rhetoric was particularly open to attack. Since opportunities for meaningful public address were greatly curtailed, rhetorical display was often reduced to showpieces, and Stoic philosophers claimed it had lost its content and become empty playing with style.[100]

Moreover, no matter how much the two found common ground, they remained distinct and competitive subcultures. Thus, in the late first or early second century C.E., the Stoic philosopher Epictetus readily admits the value of rhetoric as a God-given faculty necessary to teach and learn moral principles. But rhetoric becomes a trap when one elevates it beyond this role as a utilitarian handmaiden to philosophy. When thus elevated, Epictetus dismisses it with traditional philosophical *topoi*: "This faculty of speech and of the adornment of language, if it really is a separate faculty, what else does it do, when discourse arises about some topic, but ornament and compose the words, as hairdressers do the hair?"[101]

These subcultural conflicts are particularly evident in the differences between the normal social rôles of rhetoricians and philosophers. For our purposes, this aspect is perhaps the most important. Rhetoricians tended to be men of influence, power, culture, and status. Philosophers often criticized and sometimes eschewed these very things. These contrasts are brought out in the two types of figures idealized in Greco-Roman biographies: "public men (good citizens) who lived within and often controlled the

---

[100]Perelman, *The New Rhetoric and the Humanities*, 5.

[101]Epictetus *Discourse* 2.23.

structures of society, and philosophers who lived outside those structures."[102]

Quintilian clearly communicates his cultured prejudices against philosophy. He complains that those who claim to be philosophers are

> The victims of a more arrogant form of sloth; they assume a stern air and let their beard grow, and, as though despising the precepts of oratory, sit for a while in the schools of the philosophers, that, by an assumption of a severe mien before the public gaze and by an affected contempt of others they may assert their moral superiority, while leading a life of debauchery at home. For philosophy may be counterfeited, but eloquence never.[103]

These social dimensions of Quintilian's attitudes are noted by Ijsselling:

> One should keep in mind that Quintilianus was a typical representative of the established order, being a well-known teacher at a recognized educational institution and being extremely erudite, well read, and highly civilized: he was a man of culture who esteemed his culture most highly. Anyone despising or at all critical of civilization was regarded by him as hypocritical, eccentric, naive and hardly practical. Hence he would have nothing to do with the critics of his society, in the firm conviction that *paideia* i.e. education and culture, is a question of adaptation and the formation of the elite. All who neither wish nor are able to conform, and all those who are uneducated, remain on the edge of society, making no real contribution to true humanity. [It is] important . . . to realize that rhetoric in ancient times was held in high esteem and that the orator was an extraordinarily powerful man.[104]

Quintilian's attitude arose not only from his own social rôle, but, as Clarke points out, from the changing rôle of the philosopher, who

> had been half-professor, half-preacher; now he was wholly a preacher. And he demanded a whole-hearted allegiance, and was apt to dismiss literature and culture as frivolous distractions. . . . Quintilian, the tutor of Domitian's adopted sons, the man whose ideal was the *Romanus sapiens*, the good citizen capable of playing his part in

---

[102]Aune, *Literary Environment*, 33.

[103]Quint. 12.3.12.

[104]Ijsselling, 10.

public affairs, would not be likely to feel much sympathy with those whose outlook was so remote from his own.[105]

These tirades of Quintilian against the philosophers mark "a certain climax" in the conflict between rhetoric and philosophy.[106] When we remember that this climax occurred in the first century C.E., we must be especially cautious about any close linkage between rhetoric and philosophy in Paul's Corinth.

However, the situation was not so simple, since neither philosophy nor rhetoric stayed in the worlds of their schools. In particular, philosophy became "popular," and it is to this popular philosophy that those who wish to marry it to rhetoric as Paul's σοφία λόγου often wish to appeal. But just what do we mean by "popular philosophy"? If we are referring, for example, to the Stoicism which became popular with the Roman aristocracy, then we can indeed find examples among rhetors (including Cicero); but the cultural wisdom of these rhetors was never limited to philosophy. If we mean the eclectic ideas which became so widely held that they could be found on the lips of virtually any urban person, then certainly the rhetors were wise in this sense. "Specialization in one school, even what we would call competence in any, belonged to pedants, not to gentlemen. . . . Most richer men, from Petronius' egregious Trimalchio to senators of older wealth and cultivation, seem to have picked up at least a smattering of the chief terms of dispute."[107] But even such diffused, confused, and diluted philosophy hardly constituted the major concern of oratory. On the contrary, though rhetoricians considered themselves competent to speak on any subject including ethics, their major interests were usually issues of courts, politics, history, law, literature, and honor. If, on the other hand, "popular philosophy" refers to wandering street preachers of eclectic philosophy, then we might question just how "wise" (cultured) the rhetoric of such men would have been perceived.

However, we do find "philosopher-rhetors" in Philostratus's descriptions of the Second Sophistic. These sophists of the second and third century C.E. provide the model for those, especially Munck,

---

[105]Clarke, *Rhetoric at Rome*, 113.

[106]Ijsselling, 39.

[107]MacMullen, *Enemies*, 48.

who wish to speak of the easy marriage of popular philosophy and rhetoric in Paul's day.

During the Second Sophistic, "it was, in fact, possible for the professions of philosopher and rhetor to be conflated and confused."[108] The title of sophist seems
to have been given to anyone whose virtuoso rhetoric gave him a big public reputation. Thus, we find not only philosophers who deserved the additional title of sophist, but doctors, grammarians, physicians, and certainly lawyers.[109] Further, one man might combine more than just philosophy with rhetoric. For example, the sophist Galen's primary interest was medicine, but he was also a philosopher and rhetor. Some sophists were philosophers, most were not, according to the basic classification of Philostratus.

But this fusion of philosophy and rhetoric cannot be easily translated into Paul's Corinth for several reasons: 1) Even Philostratus can find no more than eight examples of philosophical sophists between the fourth century B.C.E. and his own time.[110] 2) The Second Sophistic postdates Paul's Corinth by a century; we have no evidence that sophists who styled themselves as philosophers were present in Corinth, much less that the later sophism had become a normal social rôle.[111] 3) Even during the heydey of the Second

---

[108]G.W. Bowersock, *Greek Sophists in the Roman Empire* (Oxford: Clarendon, 1969), 12. Philostratus is supported by inscriptions giving both titles to a single man.

[109]Ibid., 13-15. In fact (34, 36), doctors seem to have gained their elevated status as sophists before philosophers did. Under Vespasian, an inscription recording the immunity of teachers links the παιδευταί who were grammatici and rhetors, with the ἰατροί, and this conjunction persisted throughout the subsequent immunity legislation. In Hadrian's edict, we find rhetors, doctors, and now philosophers conjoined; Pius also conjoins them, but does not grant philosophers immunity.

[110]George Kennedy, *The Art of Rhetoric in the Roman World: 300 B.C. - A.D. 300*, Vol. II of *A History of Rhetoric* (Princeton: Princeton University Press, 1972), 558.

[111]Bowersock, 9-10: "Even Philostratus is hard put to think of any other representatives after Aeschines before the reign of Nero. . . . the plain fact is that the Second Sophistic . . . was a distinctive growth of the high empire, and it would not have been a senseless man who called it new." However, the Second Sophistic did grow out of the rôles of earlier cultured sophists and rhetors who often had careers in politics and diplomacy. It was new "because in the second century a type, long in existence, became so widely diffused and enjoyed such

Sophistic, the social roles of philosopher and sophist were still clearly distinguished, even if overlapping.[112] These distinctions continued tendencies of Hellenistic culture. Sophists, whether philosophers or not, upheld cultural values, and the culture rewarded them with status, power, and money. Philosophers who were not sophists often stood against the culture and offered an alternative to it. Such counter-cultural philosophers were often held in low esteem by those who upheld the status quo. 4) Those sophists who did use school or popular philosophy as the subject of their speeches were again only continuing a previous tendency: a rhetor considered himself able to speak on any subject. In fact, the theme of the declamations of the later sophists was often chosen by someone in the audience.[113] We have no evidence that in Paul's Corinth one whose speech was considered wise would *necessarily* have been expected to speak philosophically; he might speak on any subject appreciated by his audience, such as the value of healthy food or exercise or religion.

---

unprecedented authority."

[112]Philostr. *VS* 484, though describing philosopher- rhetors, still insists that the combination was an anomaly: though "the philosophers who expounded their theories with ease and fluency . . . were not actually sophists, they seemed to be so, and hence came to be so called;" cf. 479-480. Bowersock, 11: "Of a genuine rivalry between philosophers and rhetors there can be no doubt . . . for philosophy and rhetoric constituted the two principal parts of higher education. Their practitioners competed with each other for the allegiance of the young." Cf. Wilmer Cave Wright, Introduction, *Philostratus and Eunapius: The Lives of the Sophists* trans. Wilmer Cave Wright, LCL (Cambridge, Mass.: Harvard University Press, 1927; London: William Heinemann, 1968), x, xiv, xv, xviii, who sharply distinguishes between sophists and philosophers in the Second Sophistic: "When Philostratus speaks of [Julia Domna's] circle of mathematicians and philosophers, it must be remembered that the former were certainly astrologers . . . and that the latter were nearly all sophists." Though Philostratus gives a "hurried and perfunctory review of the philosophers who were so eloquent that they were entitled to a place among the sophists," he goes on to the "genuine sophists. . . . Though the sophists often show jealousy of the philosophers, philosophy without eloquence was nowhere. . . . In short, every form of literary composition was subservient to rhetoric, and the sophists whom Plato perhaps hoped to discountenance with a definition were now the representatives of Hellenic culture. 'Hellene' had become a technical term for a student of rhetoric in the schools."

[113]Kennedy, *Rhetoric in the Roman World*, 560, referring to Philostr. *VS* 1.529.

The differences between perceptions of social rôles of philosophers and rhetors is clearly expressed by Dio Chrysostom. Though Dio was rhetorically trained and was like sophists in other regards, after his conversion to philosophy he placed himself in the socratic tradition, contrasting it with sophistic ignorance and devices.[114] As a philosopher, he satirized the popular image of his rôle. Philosophers, he writes, are commonly suspected of privately mocking ordinary people as "unenlightened" and

> pitiable creatures, beginning, in fact, with those who are reputed to be rich and prosperous, persons whom these mockers themselves envy and believe to be little different from the gods in felicity; furthermore, they suspect that these philosophers disparage and ridicule them as being extravagant in eating and drinking, as wanting a soft bed to sleep on and the company of young women and boys whenever they repose, and plenty of money, and to be admired and looked up to by the mob, things which they believe to be more important and better than anything else. Because of this suspicion they of course dislike those who do not admire or prize the same things as they do and do not hold the same opinion about the things of chief importance. Therefore they seize for themselves the initiative in reviling and jeering at the philosophers as being luckless and foolish, knowing that if they succeed in showing that the philosophers are senseless and daft they will at the same time also prove themselves to be prudent and sensible.

Dio defends his role as philosopher, claiming that the philosopher, unlike the sophist, aims "to admonish [others] and put them to the test and not to flatter or to spare any one of them, but on the contrary, [aims] to reprove them to the best of his ability by his words and to show what sort of persons they are."[115]

Similarly, Horace mocks the impracticality of the Stoic wise man, who claims worldly titles of success ("wise," "rich," "ruler"). Yet "mischievous boys pluck at your beard, and unless you keep them off with your staff, you are jostled by the crowd that surround you, while

[114]Dio Chrys. *Or.* 12.1-16. Cf. Betz, *Apostel*, 66; Kennedy, *Rhetoric in the Roman World*, 568: "The effect of exile . . . was to convince Dio that the rewards of life which he had been pursuing, power, wealth, fame, and pleasure, were idle and to turn him in the direction of moral philosophy. Though he scorns sophistry, he never rejects eloquence and he continues to make use of oratorical forms."

[115]Dio Chrys. *Or.* 72.7-16.

you, poor wretch, snarl and burst with rage, O mightiest of mighty."[116]

Such views of philosophers were so common, MacMullen assembled the following montage from a variety of ancient writers:

> Those of the rougher sort appeared in every part of the empire from Italy eastward, in one of the commonest of literary clichés: identified by their long hair, beards, bare feet and grimy rags, their wallets, staffs, and knapsacks; by their supercilious bearing, paraded morals, scowling abuse and rodomontade against all men and classes; shameless they seemed, and half-educated, vulgar, jesting; beggars for money, beggars for attention, parasites on patrons, or petitioners at the door, clustered at temples or street corners, in cities and army camps; loudmouthed shouters of moral saws driven to a life of sham by poverty, Cynics, Stoics, "philosophers," all alike. . . . Even the worst frauds could make a living off some village, if they did not stay too long. Clever men could impose on a more important and discriminating audience, in Rome, for example. . . . The gains of philosophy were made only at the price of recurrent disillusionment.[117]

If philosophy and rhetoric still competed so strongly in a later age that tended to merge them, surely this was even more true in Paul's Corinth. When Paul refers to one who speaks ἐν σοφίᾳ λόγου, we must allow the possibility that he meant a cultured rhetor who could speak on any subject. If Wilckens is right that no philosophical disputes are evident, this does not rule out wise cultured speech of some other kind.

Thus, we must allow for the possibility that rhetoric is the primary reference of σοφία λόγου. Our renewed understanding of ancient rhetoric within today's changed intellectual landscape substantiates our suspicion that scholars were premature when they confidently rejected the relevance of "mere form." Clearly, the issue deserves to be reopened.

Judge has ably summed up the situation:

> Philosophy in particular should be set in relation to St. Paul as a phenomenon of education and society. In what way did philosophical ideas generally circulate amongst cultivated people? The formal

[116]Hor. *Sat.* 1.3.124-136.

[117]MacMullen, *Enemies*, 59-60.

> tradition of the great classical schools is not the answer to this question. Philosophy in that strict discipline was a matter for only a very few—those with the special interest and ample leisure required to devote years of adult life to such training. Nor does the answer lie in the notorious activities of the Cynic street preachers. They were far too conspicuous and vulgar to do anything but repel people from the well-established circles in which Paul moved. But there must have been some form of intellectual intercourse behind the closed doors of educated people. When Paul withdrew from the synagogue in one city after another he must have carried on his activities under the umbrella of some accepted social convention or institution which made such meetings easy. It does little to help answer this question to examine Paul's enterprise in the light of subsequent ecclesiastical practice, or that of the mystery cults. In these cases we are dealing with religious procedures, in which order and ceremony, decorum and restraint were of the essence of the matter. But Paul belongs to a society of vigorous talk and argument about behaviour and ideas, carried on through privately organised meetings. If we knew more about the antecedents of the sophistic movement that flourished in the second century, we might come closer to the social setting of Paul's mission.[118]

Once I have sketched an appropriate methodology, I aim to help us understand Paul's letter in the light of precisely these antecedents.

[118]Judge, "Classical Society," 32.

CHAPTER III

SITUATIONAL RHETORIC

In the first two chapters, we asked why, if NT critics agree that Paul is referring to rhetoric in 1 Cor. 1:16, 2:1, and 2:4, have they dismissed it as the key to understanding these chapters? We have found that the reason may lie in perceptions of rhetoric which are now rapidly changing. New perceptions lead to new interpretations, since "no reader confronts a text innocently, but always understands it from some perspective which shapes and organizes the perception of its meaning."[1]

The time is ripe, then, to re-evaluate these chapters in the light of our renewed understanding of rhetoric. But this understanding cannot be separated from the rest of the "linguistic revolution." That is, we can no longer take a simple approach to historical reconstruction, as if we were somehow exempt from the subjectivity of socio-linguistic worlds, or as if the meaning of a text lies in the ashes of the past. But these challenges to historical criticism do not mean we must turn away from history. Instead, rhetorical criticism offers a paradigm for integrating the various interpretive strategies which now sometimes compete.

This paradigm has been noted by E. Schüssler Fiorenza in a main paper presented at the General Meeting of SNTS in 1986. She argues that rhetorical criticism's concept of the rhetorical situation can integrate the historical, literary, hermeneutical/pastoral, and social world approaches. Rhetorical criticism is particularly appropriate for

---

[1]Karl Plank, *Paul and the Irony of Affliction* (Atlanta: Scholars Press, 1987), 62-63.

the NT texts because they were produced in a culture in which rhetoric defined public discourse, including that of Paul. Moreover, it is a form "of literary criticism that explores the particular historical uses of language in specific social political situations." In fact, we are seeing "a contemporary revival of ancient rhetorics" in "discourse theory and reader-response criticism as well as the insight into the linguisticality and the rhetorical character of all historiography."[2]

Rhetoric and Poetics

Despite the shared poetic and rhetorical nature of all writing and reading, Fiorenza also emphasizes the difference between works which are written (or read) as predominantly poetic or rhetorical. "The poetic work attempts to create and to organize imaginative experience." But "unlike poetic works, actual speeches, homilies, or letters are a direct response to a specific historical-political situation and problem." Fiorenza borrows her concept of rhetorical situation from Bitzer, who draws similar distinctions based on audience: "The poetic audience consists of persons capable of participating in aesthetic experiences induced by the poetry. But the rhetorical audience must be capable of serving as mediator of the change which the discourse functions to produce" and thus shares a real historical situation with the author.[3]

Employing this distinction, Fiorenza argues that although interpretation of 1 Cor. begins with the insights of reader-response criticism, it should aim not so much to employ aesthetic criteria as to "move from the 'world of the text' of Paul to the actual world of the Corinthian community" (while still recognizing that the "actual world"

---

[2]Fiorenza, "Situation," 386. Cf. Jane P. Tomkins, "An Introduction to Reader-Response Criticism," in *Reader- Response Criticism: From Formalism to Post-Structuralism*, ed. Jane P. Tompkins (Baltimore: Johns Hopkins, 1987) xxv: "The assertion that all discourse is 'interested' amounts to a reinsertion of literature into the stream of ordinary discourse. . . . [The reader-response critics] assert that meaning is a consequence of being in a particular situation in the world. The net result of this epistemological revolution is to repoliticize literature and literary criticism. . . . This view of language . . . is not unlike that of the Greek rhetoricians."

[3]Lloyd F. Bitzer, "The Rhetorical Situation," *Ph&Rh* 1, 8.

is itself "narrative laden and can only be constituted as a 'sub-text' to Paul's text.") "Since many things are presupposed, left out, or unexplained in a speech/letter, the audience must in the process of reading 'supply' the missing information in line with the rhetorical directives of the [implied] speaker/writer."[4]

Bitzer and Fiorenza distinguish sharply between poetic and rhetorical discourse for the purpose of analysis, but such types of discourse rarely exist in pure form: any text read as poetic can also be read as persuasive and socially situated, just as texts which function rhetorically do so partly through the power of poetic worlds. Every text can be read as *both* poetic and rhetorical.

Rhetoric and Poetics . . . readily become confused, because there is a large area which they share in common. Also, although some works lend themselves more readily to treatment in terms of Rhetoric than in terms of Poetics, or vice versa, even a work of pure science can be shown to have some Rhetorical or Poetic ingredients.[5]

At least since Booth's *The Rhetoric of Fiction*, the rhetorical dimensions of fictitious narratives have been apparent. Conversely, rhetorical situations are partly poetic fictions. This insight is the focus of the debate over the "reality" of rhetorical situations, a debate which mirrors other contemporary discussions about reality. Nearly all participants in these debates now agree that even the most scientific or rhetorical discourse "creates and organizes imaginative experience," to borrow Fiorenza's description of poetic texts. Fiorenza's "concrete historical situation" of a rhetorical text, a category she draws from Bitzer, has been challenged, most strongly by Vatz. Vatz writes that descriptions of situations

> only inform us as to the phenomenological perspective of the speaker. . . . No situation can have a nature independent of the perception of its interpreter or independent of the rhetoric with which he chooses to characterize it. . . . As Edelman states, "language does not mirror an objective 'reality' but rather creates it by organizing

---

[4]Fiorenza, "Situation," 387-89.

[5]Kenneth Burke, "Rhetoric and Poetics," in *Language as Symbolic Action* (Berkeley: University of California), 302; cf. Fiorenza, *Revelation*, 187.

meaningful perceptions abstracted from a complex, bewildering world."[6]

Vatz collapses fictive and historical into a single category without distinction. For example, he asserts that "no one understands or understood the 'situation' in Vietnam, because there never was a discrete situation." Yet when we go beyond Vatz's individualist view of fictive worlds to recognize the communal nature of rhetoric, we do find discrete situations. For example, though Vatz quotes Edelman at length, he overlooks Edelman's frequent references to "groups of people" who establish situations "by a process of mutual agreement upon significant symbols." In his own formulations, Vatz always speaks of the rhetor as an autonomous individual.

For these reasons, few have been satisfied with Vatz's reformulation of the nature of rhetorical discourse and situation. However, his article generated a lengthy debate which has helped clarify the issue. Most important is an article by Patton, who points out that "the role of perceptions does not reduce the situational approach to mere relativism. . . . The perceptions cannot be merely matters of personal preference or speculation if they are to be constitutive of genuinely rhetorical discourse." Instead, these phenomenological objects are shaped within the dialectic between speaker and audience, critic and implied author—a dialectic through which social perceptions are born.[7]

---

[6]Vatz, 154-161, citing Murray Edelman, *Politics as Symbolic Action* (Chicago: Markham, 1971), 66.

[7]John H. Patton, "Causation and Creativity in Rhetorical Situations: Distinctions and Implications," *QJS* 65 (1979), 36-55. See also Scott Consigny, "Rhetoric and Its Situations," *Philosophy and Rhetoric* 7:3 (1974), 175-186; Arthur B. Miller, "Rhetorical Exigence," *Ph&Rh* 5:2, 111-118; Alan Brinton, "Situation in the Theory of Rhetoric", *Philosophy and Rhetoric* 14:4 (1981), 234-248; Philip K. Tomkins, John H. Patton, Lloyd F. Bitzer, "The Forum," *QJS* 66 (1980), 85-93. Fiorenza (*Revelation*, 188) recognizes this communal nature of rhetorical realties as a key to rhetorical versus poetic reference: "Whereas the poetic image can employ a full range of meaning and often contains a complex bundle of meanings which can be contradictory if they are reduced to their ideational equivalents, rhetorical symbols are related to each other within the structure of a work in terms of the ideas, values, or goals of the author, which must be at least partially shared with the audience."

Rhetorical and Literary Criticism

Fiorenza's paradigm for integrating methods is similar to that of Norman Petersen, one of the few NT critics who has seriously attempted "to integrate contemporary literary and sociological capabilities into the traditional philological base of the historical critical method."[8] Similar to Fiorenza's distinction between poetic and rhetorical texts, Petersen distinguishes between stories and letters. Both have narrative (showing) and discursive (telling) aspects. In stories, the narrative aspect dominates the discursive. But in letters, discourse, "speaking to someone, subordinates the story and its narrative world to the presentation of the message. . . . In narratives, the message is in the story. In letters, the story is in the message"[9]

Since discursive texts have implicit narratives, they can be read with the insights of literary criticism. While most literary critics claim that their methods are not intended to replace, but only supplement historical criticism, these claims usually lack any suggestion of how the two might be related.[10] This gap Petersen attempts to fill in a way much like Fiorenza:

Readers are caught up in the story, and the world in which we move while captive is that of the story, its narrative world, the world of events and relations to which the story refers. On the other hand . . . in order to comprehend the actors' actions we must understand the sociological facts governing their actions, namely, the symbolic forms and social arrangements. The original readers . . . probably understood the story as they read the letter or heard it read. But we, coming from other houses, as it were, are confronted with critical problems. We have to *re*construct the symbolic forms and social arrangements of which their world was constructed.[11]

---

[8]Petersen, *Rediscovering Paul,* ix.

[9]Petersen, *Rediscovering Paul,* 9.

[10]For a clear example of the difficulties literary critics encounter when they try to integrate literary and historical readings, see Rhoads and Michie, comparing the final chapter with the introduction by Reynolds Price.

[11]Ibid., 4.

In his study of Philemon, Petersen attempts to address these critical problems with the aid of social anthropology and the sociology of knowledge, since "we know enough about fathers, children, brothers, sisters, masters, and slaves to follow what Paul is saying."[12] Even if we agree with this bold assessment of the state of research into ancient social categories and value systems, Petersen implies that a reader who constructs a narrative will want to know such things. The reader will want to know them because they are part of the structure of any discourse.

> A society is a shared way of behavior. We cannot get far in understanding a society before decoding the ways its members communicate their wants and needs to one another, and in order to do that, we must first understand the ways in which these persons see and define themselves and the world in which they live. In this sense, language is the central and primary problem in social studies, although by language I mean far more than mere grammar, syntax, and vocabulary. What I mean is the sum total of ways in which the members of a society symbolize or categorize their experience so that they may give it order and form and thereby manipulate it and also deal with their fellows who share this experience with them. Language, then, includes not only words but gestures, facial expressions, clothing, and even household furnishings—in short, total symbolic behavior. Those with a common language share common values and perceptions and thus form a moral group, a kind of church.[13]

Our task as readers, then, includes imaginatively entering the alien socio-linguistic world of the text.

> The reader of a narrative is therefore like an anthropologist to the extent that both are participant observers in other worlds. . . . [Both] must suspend both belief and disbelief in these worlds in order to comprehend life as it is lived in them. Both the reader and the anthropologist "learn" these worlds by attending to the things referred to and done in them, to how they are referred to and done, and why. . . . Both literary critics and anthropologists are concerned with the meanings of the actors' behavior within the actors' world of meanings.[14]

---

[12]Ibid., 23.

[13]T. O. Beidelman, *The Kaguru: A Matrilineal People of East Africa* (New York: Holt, Rinehart and Winston, 1971), 30, quoted in Petersen, *Rediscovering Paul*, 19.

[14]Petersen, *Rediscovering Paul*, 20.

While this task is in one sense discrete, it also implies the further task of examining related narrative worlds—those of other Pauline letters, other texts, and finally "the total amount of information available from all 'informants' in a closed social and cultural situation. . . . Ultimately the fullest understanding can only be attained by attending to them all in their interrelatedness."[15]

In his study of Philemon, Petersen focuses only on the worlds of the letter and of the Pauline corpus. But even so, he assumes "that Paul has borrowed the role names of master, slave, father, child, sons, brothers, and sisters from the kinship and master-slave institutions in the world outside the church." Similarly, "Because Paul assumes that the addressees of his letter share these categories with him, we can assume that they represent the ways in which members of one society 'see and define themselves in the world in which they live' (Beidelman)."[16] Thus, Petersen's approach is implicitly rhetorical, since he argues that the reader who constructs the narrative world of a discursive text will inquire about the communicative norms in the surrounding culture which constrain the perceptions and discourse of the implied author and addressees.

At the same time that Petersen integrates historical and literary worlds, he carefully avoids locating the meaning of a text in historical reconstruction. History cannot be an autonomous source of meaning; rather, it is yet one more narrative construction, one written by an historian who is dependent on his or her own rhetorical situation. There are no "bare facts" to which one can appeal. Narrative constructions of history are important to contextualize other narratives. But to interpret Paul's letters, we construct not the narrative of history, but the narrative world of Paul.[17]

Rhetorical Situation

The reader of discourse consciously or unconsciously constructs an implied narrative which makes sense of that discourse. From a

---

[15]Ibid., 21.
[16]Ibid., 22-24.
[17]Ibid., 10-14.

rhetorical perspective, that narrative describes the rhetorical situation—that to which the author is responding. The concept of rhetorical situation first entered rhetorical scholarship through an article by Lloyd Bitzer, who argues that the situation that provokes rhetorical response profoundly shapes that response. Bitzer analyzes those constituents of a situation which both prompt and constrain the rhetoric of a speaker or writer. He defines rhetorical discourse as that which "functions ultimately to produce action or change. [Such a] discourse comes into existence because of some specific condition or situation which invites utterance." The situation is constituted by an exigence ("an imperfection marked by urgency"), an audience, and constraints inherent in the situation. The speaker or writer "finds himself obliged to speak at a given moment . . . to respond appropriately to the situation."

The audience is not just any group of hearers or readers, but those "who are capable of being influenced by discourse and of being mediators of change."[18] This audience orientation of rhetorical criticism is one feature that offers the critic particular insight. For example, we will ask later why Paul refers to a Jewish scribe (1:20) in the midst of a discussion of Greek wisdom. This question escapes many commentators, even those who are thoroughly convinced of the gentile nature of Paul's audience; for when the text is simply read as the thought of Paul and not as addressing a particular audience, his easy mixture of Jewish and Gentile images poses no problem.

Besides exigence and audience, a rhetorical situation is characterized by a set of constraints. These can be "persons, events, objects or relations . . . [which] have the power to constrain decision and action needed to modify the exigence. Standard sources of constraint include beliefs, attitudes, documents, facts, traditions, images, interests, motives and the like."[19] The orator can be the source of some of these constraints, since he brings his own beliefs, values, etc. to the situation. These constraints are analogous to the historical constraints described by A.E. Harvey in *Jesus and the Constraints of History*.[20]

---

[18]Bitzer, "Situation," 4-8.

[19]Ibid., 8.

[20]A. E. Harvey, *Jesus and the Constraints of History* (Philadelphia: Westmin-

In Bitzer's view, rhetorical situations are "located in reality, are objective and publicly observable historical facts in the world we experience, are therefore available for scrutiny by an observer or critic who attends to them." Rhetorical situations differ from "contrived" or "spurious situations in which the existence or alleged existence of constituents is the result of error or ignorance, and from fantasy in which exigence, audience, and constraints may all be the imaginary objects of a mind at play."[21] As has been noted above, Bitzer overstates his case, since absolute distinctions between fact and fiction are hermeneutically naive. Yet the distinction, while only a matter of degree, is still an important one. Poetic writers and readers construct a world which is relatively independent of publicly observable worlds. Rhetorical speakers and audiences construct a world which is presumed to be recognizable to its implied intended readers.

In the case of Hellenistic texts, the role of rhetoric is doubled: it functions in the general way described by Bitzer, and, as Kennedy points out, is also a constraint in those ancient situations influenced by its Greco-Roman formulations.[22] For this reason, analysis of these texts in *classical* rhetorical categories can lead toward the goal of "reading the Bible as it would be read by an early Christian, by an inhabitant of the Greek-speaking world in which rhetoric was the core subject of formal education and in which even those without formal education necessarily developed cultural preconceptions about appropriate discourse."[23] Further, as we shall see, rhetoric was a constraint in a third sense in 1 Cor. 1-4, since the social role of rhetors and rhetoric became an explicit issue.

The Situation of the Reader

The concept of rhetorical situation not only helps us construct an implied context, but also offers a bridge between that context and

---

ster, 1982); see Kennedy, *NT Interpretation*, 160.

[21]Bitzer, "Situation," 11.

[22]Kennedy, *NT Interpretation*, 160.

[23]Ibid., 5, 34-36.

the situation of the modern reader. As reader-response critics persuasively argue, a text is actualized and its world created only in the act of reading.[24] As Wayne Booth points out, a reader constructs an implied author and reader who are not the same as the actual author and reader. The implied author is that dynamic "core of norms and choices" which the reader constructs as the source of the point of view of the text. The implied reader is the self which the implied author imposes upon the actual reader, a self who must enter the implied author's normative world if the reader is to understand the text.[25]

However, this need not lead to a view of interpretation as ahistorical. As Booth argues, neither the implied author nor reader is a fiction divorced from the actual author or reader. They are distinguished from the actual writer and reader not by a dichotomy of fact and fiction, but by the phenomenology of writing and reading. The Paul we meet in his letters is not the same as the historical Paul, for in his letters we encounter only the self he presents as relevant to a given rhetorical situation. We do not encounter the Paul who cursed when his knife slipped, the sleeping Paul, or the Paul who must wait in line to pay his taxes. But the reader of the Pauline letters does construct a Paul that he or she believes represents relevant aspects of the historical Paul, who, for example, passionately believes in the importance of the crucifixion and resurrection of Christ. The implied reader is likewise the self who can, at least temporarily, share these convictions. As Plank puts it, Paul's language "discloses deep convictions, engages his readers in their sense of self, and creates a unity with the message it would express."[26]

Furthermore, the reader who focuses on the rhetorical dimension of a text shares that dimension with the implied author and implied intended (i.e., the presumed original) reader. A text which functioned rhetorically in the original situation will continue so if the reader interprets it as addressing his or her attitudes or actions within

---

[24]See Jane P. Tompkins, ed., *Reader-Response Criticism: From Formalism to Post-Structuralism*, (Baltimore: Johns Hopkins, 1980).

[25]Booth, 70-76, 137-138.

[26]Plank, 1.

the new situation. But the situation is not entirely new; rather, it is related to the original situation in the following way:

> Many [rhetorical] situations grow to maturity and are resolved; others disintegrate. A few situations persist because the exigences are deeply embedded in the human condition. War and peace, triumph and tragedy, slavery and freedom, life and death, guilt and innocence—such universal or archetypal exigences are ever present and account for situations perpetually forming. When a speaker responds to one of these he may speak to a double but complementary situation: first, to the persisting situation; . . . second, to a situation generated in a particular place and time by some specific threat to freedom. Milton's *Areopagitica* was a rhetorical response to a particular threat to freedom during his own time. However, for us and for people of all time his work is a classic response to the universal situation.[27]

"This is why it is possible to have a body of truly *rhetorical* literature."[28] Thus, rhetorical situation helps explain the phenomena of canon and Gadamer's notion of classical texts.

> What we call 'classical' is something retrieved from the vicissitudes of changing time and its changing taste. . . . It is a consciousness of something enduring, of significance that cannot be lost and is independent of all the circumstances of time, in which we call something 'classical'—a kind of timeless present that is contemporaneous with every other age.[29]

The meaning of canonical texts, of Bitzer's universally rhetorical literature and of Gadamer's classical literature are actualized in the present, but remain moored in the past. This helps explain why the meaning of the text for the modern reader includes but is not limited to historical-critical work. Gadamer points out that the "timelessness" of the classical

---

[27]Lloyd F. Bitzer, "Functional Communication: A Situational Perspective," in *Rhetoric in Transition: Studies in the Nature and Uses of Rhetoric*, ed. E.E. White (University Park: Pennsylvania State University, 1980), 35-36; note Bitzer's use of the word "classical," a key term for Gadamer's similar understanding. See also idem, "The Rhetorical Situation," 10, 13.

[28]Bitzer, "Rhetorical Situation," 13.

[29]Gadamer, *Truth and Method*, 256.

> does not exclude the fact that works regarded as classical present tasks of historical understanding to a developed historical consciousness that is aware of the historical distance. It is . . . the aim of the historical consciousness to . . . know [the classical work] as an historical phenomenon that can be understood solely in terms of its own time. But this understanding will always be more than the mere historical construction of the past 'world' to which the work belongs. Our understanding will always include consciousness of our belonging to that world. And correlative to this is the fact that the work belongs to our world.[30]

Similarly, Bitzer argues for the present as the full rhetorical situation for the text, but also implies that relocating it in history will affect the reader's construction of its meaning: "Imagine for a moment the Gettysburg Address entirely separated from its situation and existing for us independent of any rhetorical context: as a discourse which does not 'fit' any rhetorical situation, it becomes either poetry or declamation, without rhetorical significance."[31] Even without reference to history, we still possess a rhetorical situation, for the "features" of the "Gettysburg situation" which "persist" provide a new context. But without the context of historical discourse, the difference between a rhetorical and a poetic text diminishes greatly. In fact, Bitzer recognizes that it is the *context* in which a work is placed that shapes the meaning: "We should note that the fictive rhetorical discourse within a play or novel may become genuinely rhetorical outside its fictive context—if there is a real situation for which the discourse is a rhetorical response."[32]

Fiction is effective precisely because its narratives are so loosely tethered to the narratives of history. On the other hand, even a poetic reading does not isolate the reader from the historical author's response to his or her situation. Rather, the reader seeks to fulfill the intentions of the author for his "intended reader, . . . for the

---

[30]Ibid., 258.

[31]Bitzer, "Rhetorical Situation," 10; cf. Kenneth Burke, "Rhetoric and Poetics," in *Language as Symbolic Action: Essays on Life Literature, and Method* (Berkeley and Los Angeles: University of California Press, 1968), 296: "Though Demosthenes was definitely a rhetorician at the time he wrote, his persuasiveness becomes more like sheer literary appeal, once the occasions on which he spoke cease to be felt as immediately burning issues."

[32]Bitzer, "Rhetorical Situation," 11.

efforts of readers are always efforts to discern and therefore to realize (in the sense of becoming) an author's intention."[33] In fact,

> One cannot understand an utterance without *at the same time* hearing or reading it as the utterance of someone with more or less specific concerns, interests, and desires, someone with an intention. . . . This of, course, does not mean that intention anchors interpretation in the sense that it stands outside and guides the process; intention like anything else is an interpretive fact; that is, it must be construed; it is just that it is impossible *not* to construe it and therefore impossible to oppose it either to the production or the determination of meaning.[34]

This is particularly apparent when texts are read as rhetorical; the implied author bids the reader to construct a world recognizable to the intended audience. The only question, then, is whether that world will be relatively naive or relatively informed by historical discourse.

Rhetorical situation, then, allows us to "move from the 'world of the text' of Paul to the . . . world of the Corinthian community"[35] without ever leaving the world of the reader. We may take for granted that 1 Cor. was originally received as rhetorical. It is universally judged to be an actual letter by Paul to a community of Christians in Corinth. Any letter is rhetorical, but especially this one: even his opponents consider it "weighty and strong." Furthermore, Paul intends his words to be performative: "what we say when absent we do when present" (2 Cor 10:10-11), a connection of word to praxis he makes clear as he begins the body of the letter itself ("I appeal to you brethren, that you . . . ": 1 Cor. 1:10). If the letter had not been at least provocative and/or persuasive, it is difficult to imagine why the Corinthians would have preserved it. And in the centuries since, it has continued to function rhetorically for the millions of readers in the stream of tradition. Thus, when we analyze it as a rhetorical work addressed to a rhetorical situation, we are moving within a well established community of interpretation.

---

[33]Fish, "Interpreting the *Variorum*," 174.

[34]Idem, *Doing What Comes Naturally*, 100.

[35]Fiorenza, "Situation," 388.

Rhetorical Situation as Publicly Observable

Since we are interpreting 1 Cor. 1-4 as rhetorical, we may assume that Paul's reading of the situation in Corinth must overlap that of the Corinthians themselves. For this reason, we need no longer entertain suggestions that Paul and the Corinthians perceived contradictory situations. As Patton points out, such contradictory perceptions are possible, but they would disable the rhetorical function of the work by disconnecting the audience from the speaker.

Differing perceptions originate, according to Bitzer, either in diverging assessments of factual conditions, or in relating these facts differently to some interest. By factual conditions he means "any set of things, events, relations, ideas, meanings—anything physical or mental—whose existence is (or is thought to be) independent of one's personal subjectivity."[36] Several critics have had difficulty understanding how Bitzer could view ideas or meanings as "independent of subjectivity" but he asserts only that they are, in a given community, considered to be subject to evidential challenge. Thus, an idea such as "Christ crucified is foolishness to the gentiles" is factual and objective because it could be challenged or established to the satisfaction of community members by interviewing gentile neighbors.

Such external or internal factual conditions are related to an interest, i.e., an ethical evaluation of the factual situation which judges it to be an exigence calling for a discursive response. Rhetorical discourse can take place only to the extent that speaker and audience share perceptions both of factual conditions and the exigence as one possible interpretation of those facts.

When these constraints on rhetorical discourse are ignored, critics sometimes invent a Paul whose discourse could not have communicated with the Corinthians. For example, Wilckens suggests that Paul misunderstood the slogans of 1:12 to mean that the Corinthians championed the apostles as sources of division, while the Corinthians perceived the same slogans as sources not of divisions but of unity (because the separate champions had united them through

[36]Bitzer, "Functional Communication," 28.

baptism into Christ).[37] Similarly, Schmithals argues that Paul encountered Gnostics in Corinth, didn't know they were Gnostics, and naively adopted their mythical language to present his Gospel. The Gnostics in turn understood Paul's use of the myth in their own sense, thinking Paul was a Gnostic. Neither party understood what the other was saying.[38] Again, Schmithals speculates that Paul, through ignorance, is addressing an unreal situation in 1 Cor.: "i.e., he is as yet unaware of the presence of the 'superlative apostles'."[39]

Each of these suggestions sketches a situation in which Paul and the Corinthians perceive different factual conditions. Such 'double-blind' situations are standard fodder for *situation* comedies: Lucy, referring to the baby, "little Ricky," tells Ethel that there's a new love in her life. Desi overhears and thinks she has a boyfriend. So Desi tries to make Lucy jealous by leaving out a love note to his "girl-friend." Lucy finds it and thinks its written to her and so writes a note to her "secret lover", which Ricky finds and misinterprets, and so forth.

The comedy ends when the characters encounter the realities of the situation and the desire for community compels them to communicate by correcting their diverging perceptions of factual conditions. Likewise, Wilckens's and Schmithals's reconstructions of misinformed communication would have led the Corinthians either to: 1) correct Paul and to evaluate 1 Cor. as comical and unworthy of preservation (contra 2 Cor. 10:10), or 2) apathetically allow a lack of communication, since they desire no further community with Paul. Instead, as 2 Cor. shows, the communication continued without any evidence of factual correction. The Corinthians treated Paul's letters as having rhetorical power, even if the nature of his rhetoric was a problem for some.

This constraint of situation has been noticed by Scroggs in his criticism of Wilckens's theory:

> Despite the carefulness with which Wilckens has worked, his conclusions reduce the first two chapters to an argument which would have been completely incoherent to the Corinthians. . . . The

---

[37]Wilckens, *Weisheit*, 16.
[38]Schmithals, 70.
[39]Ibid., 114.

> question cannot be by-passed: on what grounds would these contrasts [between Paul's kerygma and his wisdom and the wisdom of the Corinthians] make sense to the Corinthians? Manifestly only if they could understand *something* at least of their own position in what Paul says about them, and *something* of the difference between themselves and Paul in what the apostle says about his own position. In Wilckens's interpretation neither of these would have been possible, and the chapters could only appear to them as complete nonsense. If Paul writes and preaches in terms of his audience, as he claims he does [2 Cor 1:3] Wilckens's view is already difficult.

Furthermore, 2 Cor. 10:10, with their judgement that his letters are "weighty and strong," shows that "the Corinthians understood him well enough."[40]

Thus, the reader is constrained to construct a situation which was recognizable to both Paul and his Corinthians. Yet even as the reader moves toward Paul's narrative of that situation, it is certainly not the same narrative that a historian might write. In the first place, it will always remain a subtext constructed from within the reader's world for the narrow purpose of interpreting the text[41] (though it may have value for other interpretations and for wider historical reconstruction). Furthermore, the situation is constructed from within the implied author's world. Even the implied audience is a construction of writer and reader.

The rhetorical situation, then, is not the same as the historical situation. This is not because the historical situation is more "objective". "Objective history" has always been difficult on practical grounds; it has become philosophically indefensible and hermeneutically bankrupt. Rather, history is an attempt to interpret the past in a way that integrates disparate phenomena into a single meaningful narrative. My purpose is to interpret not the past but a *text* received from the past.[42] In constructing the rhetorical situation, the reader

---

[40]Robin Scroggs, "Paul: *Sophos* and *Pneumatikos*," *NTS* 14 (1967), 33-4; n. 1.

[41]e.g., Kennedy, *NT Interpretation*, 40: "In Chapter 4 Matthew provides information about the *rhetorical situation* which he wishes readers to envision."

[42]cf. Wuellner, "Where," 463: "Like the linguistic criticism advocated by R. Fowler, the emerging new rhetorical criticism regards 'the texts it studies not as isolated and timeless artifacts [(*Wuellner:*) or revelation of timeless truths], but as products of a time of writing *and* [emphasis Wuellner's] of a time of reading." Wuellner quotes R. Fowler, *Linguistic Criticism* (Oxford: Oxford University, 1986), 178.

searches for a narrative which will make sense of the particular concerns addressed by the author who inhabits a world which is more alien to us than it was to his original audience. The socio-linguistic "facts" which they took for granted we must reconstruct. For this reason, philological and social historical research are invaluable aids, but they are not the source of meaning. That can come only in the world of the reader. Thus, situational rhetorical criticism offers a mediating position between historical and literary criticism, in which the "world" of the text is neither fiction nor fact, but a value laden interpretation of a situation shared by reader, implied author, and implied intended reader. Further, the reader's interpretation is constrained by the community he shares not only with author and original recipients, but with tradition and with present communities of readers, primarily the communities of the academy and the church.

A Functional Approach to Rhetorical Criticism

The value of constructing the rhetorical situation of the Pauline epistles has become increasingly, if only implicitly, clear to NT scholars. Rather than viewing the texts as abstract theological statements, critics increasingly understand Paul's letters as pastoral responses to particular situations. The constraints of these situations and their effect upon Pauline discourse have provided one of the main avenues of advance for Pauline scholarship in recent years.[43]

The methodology for the remainder of this study, then, will be a rhetorical one in which I attempt to write a narrative of the rhetorical situation. Like any hermeneutical circle, the method itself is dynamic rather than linear, since each element influences the others. Thus, the rhetorical situation can be considered only while simultaneously discerning Paul's rhetorical response to that situation, as well as listening for the meaning of that response in my/our own situation.[44]

---

[43]e.g., the notion of "contingency" in J. Christian Beker, *Paul the Apostle: The Triumph of God in Life and Thought* (Philadelphia: Fortress, 1984).

[44]These are Kennedy's next stages after identifying the rhetorical situation: Kennedy, *NT Interpretation*, 37-38.

However, some things are best considered before others. Since I have identified situational rhetoric as the locus in which reader and text, author and audience meet, I also follow Bitzer's understanding of rhetoric as primarily functional: "Situational rhetoric commences not with attention to speaker intention and artistry, nor with focus on language resources, the argumentation process, or natural psychological processes; rather it commences with the critical relation between persons and environment and the process of interaction leading to harmonious adjustment."[45] For these reasons, Kennedy commends determining the rhetorical situation as the second step of his method of rhetorical criticism. This step follows the delimitation of the rhetorical unit,[46] but is prior to the examination of the arrangement of arguments. These formal features can then be analyzed to see how they "work together—or fail to do so—to some unified purpose in meeting the rhetorical situation, . . . to define their function in context." In this way, we can avoid those errors made by critics who focus on form without sufficient attention to situation.[47]

A good example of such an error can be found in an important article by L. L. Welborn. Welborn also attempts to determine the rhetorical situation of 1 Cor. 1-4, and his conclusions are very close to mine. However, as he is sketching that situation, he identifies *form* as the key to function in a way that distorts his argument. He notes that "through all the attempts to arrive at the origin of" the "party cries" in 1:12,

> their *form* has never been investigated. If one seeks the formal derivation of these expressions, one is always led back to the realm of politics. . . . Ancient political parties . . . are named after the *individuals* whose interests they served. . . . A declaration of allegiance to a party so personal in organization could take no form

[45]Bitzer, "Functional Communication," 25.

[46]I have assumed but not argued that 1 Cor. 1-4 is a rhetorical unit, since "scholars are virtually unanimous in regarding . . . 1:10 - 4:21 as a discrete section of the letter, a section which treats the problem of Corinthian factions. . . . The παρακαλῶ sentences in 1:10 and 4:16 are regarded as forming an *inclusio*. . . . 4:17-21 . . . appropriately conclude this section." (M. Mitchell, 287-8; even Mitchell, who insists on focusing on the entire letter as a rhetorical unit, admits that "as a discrete proof section" it has a "function.")

[47]Kennedy, *NT Interpretation*, 33-38; cf. A.H. Snyman, "Style and the Rhetorical Situation of Romans 8:31-39," *NTS* 34 (1988), 218-231.

other than that which it is given in 1 Cor 1:12—"I am of Paul!" "But I, of Apollos!"[48]

Attracted by this formal parallel, Welborn fails to notice the obvious *differences* in Paul's situation which dictate different functions for similar forms. Political factions (by which Welborn means explicit competitions for power) "constellated around a few men of noble houses who contended for power. . . . Political parties thus took the form of groups of clients and personal adherents pledged to particular leaders."[49] While I agree that the Corinthians factions partook of this social norm, the Corinthian slogans function differently. The Corinthian slogans champion *teachers*, not political leaders. If the formal parallels held, the slogans would be something like "I am of Stephanus!" "But I, of Chloe!"

When we find formal parallels, we must be careful to seek how the author has adapted or even combined them with others to address a particular situation. Welborn certainly succeeds in illustrating the political "aspects" or "dimension"[50] of the situation in Corinth, and his insights flow from the key he finds in the formal parallels. But he fails to notice differences in the situations addressed by these similar forms. Like the historians of religion's small pond of religious parallels, the political pond in which he is fishing is too small.

Very similar to Welborn's argument is the recent dissertation of M. Mitchell. She too wishes to find the rhetorical situation to which

---

[48]L.L. Welborn, "On the Discord in Corinth: 1 Corinthians 1-4 and Ancient Politics," *JBL* 106 (1987), 90. However, even these formal parallels have been questioned; see M. Mitchell, 114-116.

[49]Ibid., 91-92. However, Welborn also wants to attribute political divisions to economic divisions. For this, he relies on the confrontation of oligarchic and democratic political rhetorics. In this, he overlooks the distinction between, on the one hand, these anachronistic rhetorics of class struggle and, on the other, the political realities of Roman times. As Judge points out, "political competition was not conducted between economic strata, horizontally organized, but between vertically organized social hierarchies. The fact that one party is labelled 'popular' and another 'aristocratic' must not be allowed to obscure the fact that all such factions rest equally upon the client structure of the community, and are designed to serve the ends of noble patrons associated through their various *amicitiae*." Judge, "Early Christians," 5-7.

[50]Ibid., 86, 107.

Paul responds. But her method is strictly formal. She finds numerous parallels throughout the letter to the "vocabulary and topoi used in political rhetoric to combat factionalism" and assumes that this demands the conclusion that "dissension is at issue throughout all 16 chapters." But this assumption is seriously flawed. First, one would have to demonstrate that these terms and topoi were used *exclusively* for such purposes. Second, one would have to demonstrate that such terms were not in this case used in a new, metaphorical sense. For example, Paul uses slavery manumission terms and *topoi*, but this does not show that slavery rather than salvation was the issue he addressed. Since all situations are discreet, all discourse is in a sense metaphorical. Thus, the particular situation must be sought.

Similar problems appear in Bünker's formal analysis of 1 Cor. 1:10-4:21 and 1 Cor. 15. Bünker finds formal parallels with judicial rhetoric[51] of a style that indicates that it is aimed at the few higher status, better educated Corinthians.[52] However, as Fiorenza points out, Paul cannot be aiming to convict the higher status Christians, since he in 16:15-18 urges the Corinthians to be subject to Stephanus and other high status patrons and leaders. Thus, "the overall genre of 1 Corinthians is not judicial or forensic. Rather, it appears that the genre of 1 Corinthians is best understood as 'largely deliberative although it contains some judicial passages.'"[53] (It also has an epideictic passage in the "subtle" introduction of 1:4-9.[54]) As I shall argue below, I agree with Bünker that Paul aims much of his rhetoric at the higher status Corinthians, but it is not to convict them, but to alter their attitudes and behaviors. Bünker's very general observations are headed in the right direction, but are unfocused because he emphasizes form over function.

This has been brought out in an article by M. Jordan on philosophical protreptic. Jordan seeks to find the genre of protreptic or parenesis in the ordinary sense of "a certain combination of form,

---

[51]M. Bünker, *Briefformular und rhetorische Disposition im 1 Korintherbrief*, Göttinger theologische Arbeiten 28, ed. Georg Strecker (Göttingen: Vandenhoeck & Ruprecht, 1983), 50-51.

[52]Ibid., 17-18, 52-53.

[53]Fiorenza, "Situation," 392-93, quoting Kennedy, *NT Interpretation*, 87; cf. M. Mitchell, 17-89, who argues that the entire letter is deliberative.

[54]*Rh. Her.* 1.7.11; Cic. *Inv. Rhet.* 1.18.26.

diction, and subject-matter." He finds, however, great variation in these areas. He concludes that these works are unified not by form, diction, and subject matter, but by

> the "rhetorical situation" of protreptic. While each philosophic author may diagnose the hearer's needs differently, and so prescribe a different pedagogy, each author confronts a hearer whose choice is the target of many other persuasions. The unity of philosophic protreptic . . . would seem to lie in this "exigence," in the hearer's moment of choice between ways of life. . . . Protreptics are just those works that aim to bring about the firm choice of a lived way to wisdom—however different the form of those works and their notions of wisdom might be.[55]

Genre as Situational

By emphasizing function over form, situational rhetoric differs from some other types of rhetorical criticism, those which see form as the key to understanding the rhetoric encountered in the text. In situational rhetoric, form, particularly genre, is subsumed to situation as one of its many constraints. That is, the situation constrains the author to employ one or more generic forms. In some situations this constraint will be stronger than in others. As Bitzer argues,

> From day to day, year to year, comparable situations occur, prompting comparable responses; hence rhetorical forms are born and a special vocabulary, grammar, and style are established. . . . A form of discourse is not only established but comes to have a power of its own—the tradition itself tends to function as a constraint upon any new response in the form.[56]

This argument has been developed in an important article by K. Jamieson. Like Bitzer, Jamieson asserts that "genres are shaped in response to a rhetor's perception of the expectations of the audience and the demands of the situation" so that even without generic traditions, the situation will shape the rhetoric in predictable ways. In some situations more than others, antecedent rhetorical forms

---

[55]Mark D. Jordan, "Ancient Philosophic Protreptic and the Problem of Persuasive Genres," *Rhetorica* 4 1986, 309-333.

[56]Bitzer, "Rhetorical Situation," 13.

shape the perception of the proper response. How then do we determine whether situation or genre is more dominant?

> Some rhetors are more constrained by genre than others because of their sense of the presentness of the past. An institutional spokesman who draws his perceptions of his role from the traditions of the institution itself tends, for example, to feel generic constraints more acutely than does the rhetor not tied to a tradition-bound institution. Because a long-lived institution initiates a great body of rhetoric, a set of standardized forms for its rhetoric tends to evolve. . . . The rhetor cannot avoid the play of traditional forms on encapsulation of his message; the audience and the critic within that audience cannot avoid generic classification in perceiving and evaluating the critical object.

Jamieson emphasizes that even when generic constraints are strong, "genres should not be viewed as static forms but as evolving phenomena. . . . While traditional genres may color rhetoric they do not ossify it. Rhetors perpetually modify genres. New genres do emerge."[57]

This argument nuances the emphasis on situation or function over form by helping us discern the variable weight of generic forms in different situations. We must judge the relative strength of the generic tradition in the particular situation we are attempting to reconstruct. In some situations, form will be a dominant constraint and will demand greater attention; in others, function.

NT texts are not at either extreme of Jamieson's spectrum. On the one hand, as I argued in the first two chapters, they cannot be properly evaluated when isolated from their rhetorical culture. Thus, the generic constraints of that culture, as well as those of Jewish tradition and developing Christian tradition (e.g., the "forms" of form criticism) must be taken into account. On the other hand, the early Christian community was relatively free of institutional expectations. As Aune points out, one must avoid "the fallacy of holistic comparison" when analyzing complex and developing generic relationships. This is particularly true when considering Hellenistic Jewish or early Christian literature, since "*adaptation,* not wholesale borrowing, was

[57]Kathleen M. Hall Jamieson, "Generic Constraints and the Rhetorical Situation," *Ph&Rh* 6 (1973), 162-170.

the rule." This flexibility is even more apparent in the letter form of many early Christian texts

> since it exhibits more variety and flexibility than any other literary form.
>
> . . . Early Christian letters tend to resist rigid classification, either in the three main types of oratory or in terms of the many categories listed by the epistolary theorists. Most early Christian letters are multifunctional and have a 'mixed' character. . . . Attempts to classify one or another of Paul's letters as *either* judicial *or* epideictic (or one of their subtypes) runs the risk of imposing external categories on Paul and thereby obscuring the real purpose and structure of his letters.[58]

Recognizing the relative generic freedom enjoyed by the NT writers, Wuellner observes that "there has been a gradual shift from the traditional occupation with literary genre and with historical situation toward a concern with the argumentation and rhetorical situation."[59] Kennedy, agrees that "in general, identification of genre is not a crucial factor in understanding how rhetoric actually works in units of the New Testament."[60]

Unfortunately, these insights have not been sufficiently appreciated. Too much rhetorical criticism employs the ancient handbooks as if they offered rigid generic formulas. Even the most basic division into judicial, deliberative, and epideictic

> is a little too neat. Aristotle and the rhetorical theorists who succeeded him did not inductively analyze *actual* speeches, but rather prescribed how ideal speeches *ought* to be constructed. While that does not mean that there was no overlap between theory and practice, it does suggest that actual speeches could be more complex and eclectic that the rhetorical handbooks might suggest.[61]

---

[58]Aune, *Literary Environment*, 46, 159, 203.

[59]Wuellner, "Greek Rhetoric", 19.

[60]Kennedy, *NT Criticism,* 33.

[61]Aune, *Literary Environment*, 199; however, Aune oversimplifies the situation by ignoring the primarily descriptive role of rhetoric. In fact, the rhetors often *did* analyze actual speeches.

Clarke points out that "school rules were seldom followed exactly by a mature orator." From his analysis of Cicero's speeches, Clarke concludes that they

> were real speeches, and any study of them which does not take into account the conditions under which they were delivered and the purposes which they were intended to serve will miss the mark. The rhetorical analyses found in older editions give the impression that Cicero constructed his speeches solely after the formulae of the rhetorical schools and without any reference to the practices of the Roman courts, the exigences of debate and the immediate political situation. In fact Ciceronian oratory owed more to such factors as these than to the rules of the textbooks.[62]

What Cicero practiced, Quintilian explicitly advises, when he downgrades the importance of rhetorical theory in favor of the dictates of circumstance.[63]

If highly stylized speeches in the stable and tradition-bound situations of courtroom, assembly, and funerals retained such flexibility, the letter form was even more flexible. Thus, Stowers's classification of ancient letters, which follows the epistolary theorists, allows "enormous flexibility."[64] It "views letters *functionally*, i.e., in terms of the actions that people intended to perform through them."[65] As Humphries notes, "the generic constraints of the Greek common literary letter were subordinate to the demands of argumentation."[66]

---

[62]Clarke, *Rhetoric at Rome*, 62-63, 108.

[63]Quint. 2.13.

[64]Stowers, *Letter Writing*, 51-173. He notes (52) that "the classification of letter types according to the three species of rhetoric only partially works." Further, (53) the writer composes "according to generic patterns, which must fit the circumstances of the author's particular situation in writing." Thus, (56) the ancient classifications of letters were "according to typical actions performed in corresponding social contexts and occasions. The types in the handbooks give a sample, in barest outline, of form and language that is appropriate to the logic of the social code in a particular instance. The author, then, could elaborate, combine and adapt this ideal according to the occasion in view, his purpose and his literary abilities."

[65]Aune, *Literary Environment*, 162.

[66]Humphries, 5.

Even the classification that Stowers adopts from epistolary theorists developed late. In the first century C.E., the application of rhetorical theory to letter writing was, on the whole, quite general.[67] Moreover, despite our new perceptions of Christian communities as higher on the social scale and of rhetoric as having a broader influence across social lines, the Christian communities do not appear to have been populated by the highly literate class for whom proper form was most important. Rather, as Aune puts it, the generic expectations "percolated down" from the top.

Thus, Paul was constrained by formal expectations, but not as strongly as other ancient writers in other situations. Rather than begin with form, then, we do best to begin with rhetorical situation. This task is the focus of the remainder of this dissertation. To the extent that my argument is persuasive, it will put us in a better position to assess how Paul marshals the formal arrangements within his constraints. From there the critic can complete the circle by returning to the situation of the modern reader to evaluate the continuing rhetorical function of the text. Yet the completed circle is not the end of interpretation either, for this rhetorical unit has been artificially isolated from the rest of the letter. Further, it can be recontextualized in the whole of the Pauline corpus, into the canon, and into further worlds of understanding and praxis.

But every project must be limited. This one focuses on the rhetorical situation addressed by Paul in his opening chapters to the Corinthians.

---

[67]Abraham J. Malherbe, *Ancient Epistolary Theorists* (Atlanta: Scholars' Press, 1988), 3.

PART II

THE RHETORICAL SITUATION OF 1 CORINTHIANS 1-4

CHAPTER FOUR

Οὐκ ἐν Σοφίᾳ Λόγου

Exigence

"Paul makes no secret of the particular exigence which has invited his response in 1 Cor. 1-4: Chloe's people [τῶν Χλόης] have arrived with news of ἔριδες in the Corinthian church"[1] (1:11). These divisions are to Paul a serious "imperfection marked by urgency" and the ostensive occasion for his letter. In these ἔιδες (rivalries, or wordy disputations[2]), each of the Corinthians claims particular allegiance to Paul, or Apollos, perhaps also to Cephas, or Christ, each setting his claims over against those of his fellow Christians (1:12). This report is alarming to Paul because such divisions transgress the unity of Christ: "μεμέρισται ὁ Χριστός;" (1:13; also 3:1-3, 11:17-22, 12:12-27, etc.). But it is not immediately clear why these particular divisions are treated so negatively.

Paul's reaction is puzzling because under the right circumstances, he seems to condone the existence of factions. He often set himself and his co-workers against other Christian teachers with whom he disagreed; if anyone teaches a gospel which fundamentally disagrees with Paul's, he is to be ἀνάθεμα (Gal. 1:6-9, 2:11, 5:10-12, 6:12-13;

---

[1]Welborn "A Conciliatory Principle," 342; cf. Humphries, 30; Wilckens, 5, recognizes, despite his primary interest in the content of Corinthian wisdom, that the most burning issue for Paul is the danger to unity presented by the appearance of quarrels between groups.

[2]LSJ 689.

Phil. 3:2; 2 Cor. 11:4, 13-15). An apostle of the gospel can never submit to any human authority for the sake of unity (Gal 2:5-6). Similarly, Paul instructs the Corinthians not to associate or eat with a brother the community has judged too sinful (1 Cor. 5:11). Presumably, if the Corinthians had been divided over whether to follow Paul or some other teacher with whom he fundamentally disagreed or whom he considered offensively sinful, Paul would commend those who said "I am of Paul" and rebuke the false teachers, their teaching, and those who followed them.

Rather than be guided by these indications, scholars for many years turned to divisions over doctrine familiar in their reading of Galatians, and assumed that the divisions of 1 Cor. 1:12 meant doctrinal wrangling among the groups. Although many still argue for such reconstructions,[3] such approaches are increasingly criticized on several grounds.

First, they fail to recognize that the smoke of divisions do not necessarily imply the fire of doctrine.

> Until now, scholars have directed their attention almost singularly to the theological position of Paul's detractors, arguing negatively from his responses to their supposed theology and identity. We must not take it for granted, though, that a reaction in theological terms indicates that the detractors held a different theological or philosophical viewpoint. It may point to a social situation.[4]

The social and ethical nature of the situation becomes clear when we compare various references to divisions. In 1 Cor. 11:19, Paul refers to divisions at the dinners, this time using the word αἱρέσεις as a synonym for the σχίσματα he mentions in the previous

---

[3]e.g., Gerhard Sellin, "Das 'Geheimnis' der Weisheit und das Rätsel der 'Christuspartei' (au 1 Kor 1-4)," *ZNW* 73 (1982), 69-96, argues the popular position that Apollos was Paul's theological rival; Victor Hasler, "Das Evangelium Des Paulus in Korinth. Erwagungen Zur Hermeneutik," *NTS* 30 (1984), 109-129, who argues that Paul competed with Apollos and Cephas; Gerd Luedemann, *The Opposition to Paul in Jewish Christianity*, trans. M. Eugene Boring (Minneapolis: Fortress, 1989), 65-80, argues that the Cephas party is the locus of an anti-Pauline Jewish Christianity (but rejecting the Manson/Barrett thesis of legalism among the "strong"). For a summary of earlier attempts, see Hurd, *Origin*, 97-105.

[4]Marshall, ix.

verse. He also uses αἱρέσεις in 1:10 to describe the divisions of 1:12, and again in 12:25 as opposing his ideal of unity in the church. Though the divisions in each case are different, his rhetoric opposing them is very similar. Concerning the αἱρέσεις at dinner in ch. 11, Simon notes

> that in the oldest Christian writings the term *hairesis* does not necessarily have the sense of doctrinal deviation. In addition to 1 Cor 11:19 *hairesis* appears in the catalogue of vices in Gal 5:20 alongside of διχοστασίαι (dissensions). . . . The cause of these divisions is not necessarily to be found in points of doctrine: it may be simply a matter of personal rivalries and matters of prestige and honor.[5]

Second, Paul does not criticize the other teachers. Rather, he insists that he and the other apostles are united (3:22-4:1).[6] Paul particularly emphasizes the good relationship between himself and Apollos as a model for the church (3:5-9; 3:22-4:1; 4:6; 16:12).[7] Those who begin with the assumption of doctrinal differences must rely on special pleading, such as that Paul 'protests too much' about this unity and so betrays his objection to the teaching of Apollos.[8] But Paul's rhetoric does not communicate such a hidden agenda, even diplomatically. Such an extremely subtle tactic would be very unlike the Paul we know from his other letters, a Paul who was far from diplomatic in confronting those he considered competitive teachers with false doctrines. If anything, he moved in the opposite direction, condemning through hyperbole.

Third, if Paul opposes the other teachers, then not only would we would expect him to criticize Apollos and/or Cephas, but to positively identify with the Pauline group which is faithful to his teachings. But we hear him doing the exact opposite: he is *more*

---

[5]Marcel Simon, "From Greek Hairesis to Christian Heresy," in *Early Christian Literature and the Classical Intellectual Tradition*, ed. William Schoedel and Robert L. Wilken, Théologie Historique 53 (Paris: Éditions Beauchesne, 1979), 109.

[6]Schmithals, 202; Frederick Willem Grosheide, *Commentary on the First Epistle to the Corinthians* (Grand Rapids: Eerdmans, 1953), 37.

[7]F. F. Bruce, "Apollos in the New Testament," *Ekklesiastikos Pharos* 57 (1975), 354-55. Wilckens, *Weisheit*, 11; Welborn, "A Conciliatory Principle, 326; Fee, 48, 55-56.

[8]Horsley, "Wisdom of Words," 231.

critical of the group which claims allegiance to him than of any other group. His first reaction to the slogans, after his rhetorical question, "Is Christ divided?" is to criticize those who use his name to set themselves apart from others (1:13). Again in 3:4-9 and 4:6, Paul focuses his criticism on those of Apollos and himself, each time emphasizing the over-arching unity in God enjoyed by the two teachers. "St. Paul has no partiality for those who claim himself, nor any respect for those who claim Christ, as their special leader. Indeed, he seems to condemn these two classes with special severity. . . . All four are alike wrong."[9]

This point is so persuasive that it led Nils Dahl to abandon the thesis he had proposed in a now famous article. Dahl had argued that Paul is defending his authority against those who would prefer the teaching of Apollos or Cephas. But Dahl now recognizes that "to call the section 'apologetic' is to downplay the degree to which Paul is critical of his own adherents as well as of those of his opponents." Instead, the chapter contains "apologetic elements."[10] Despite Dahl's retraction, his thesis is widely cited as axiomatic.

Even more telling than the criticism he levels at the group which says 'I am of Paul' is the audience he consistently addresses: the entire church, or at least representatives of all the groups.[11] Even when he turns to one group (those of Paul), his point applies to all the groups. As Grosheide comments,

> Paul does not say in I Cor. 1 that the members of the church with their slogans adhered to a definite doctrine, i.e., a false doctrine. The apostle does not combat a false doctrine in I Corinthians. . . . The tone in I Corinthians is quite different from that in Galatians . . . where Paul opposes the Judaizers. The one thing we find here is that each Corinthian has his slogan. No other difference is mentioned but these slogans. All are exhorted to unity. Nobody is right. And when in the following chapters Paul reprimands several sins it is not one group but the whole church which is reprimanded. Therefore we conclude that there was no essential or doctrinal difference between the four groups.[12]

---

[9]Robertson & Plummer, 11.

[10]N.A. Dahl, "Paul and the Church at Corinth According to 1 Cor. 1:10-4:21," in *Studies in Paul* (Minneapolis: Augsburg, 1977), 61, n. 50.

[11]Wilckens, *Weisheit*, 1, fn 2 and 5, fn 1; Fee, 6, 47.

[12]Grosheide, 37.

Similarly, Munck comments,

> Paul is not arguing in chs. 1-4 against false doctrine. . . . There is no dogmatic controversy in the first four chapters. . . . Paul is not arguing against the individual factions and their false teachers . . . since the Corinthians' shortcomings in respect of their bickerings are regarded in this section as primarily ethical failures.[13]

Yet another problem with identifying the exigence as theological battles among the groups of 1:12 rather than as ethical dimensions of division itself is the apparent disappearance of these groups as a concern after the first four chapters. This makes it very difficult to read the letter as addressing the same divisions throughout.[14] Occasionally commentators have argued that we do hear of certain groups later, e.g., that the "Christ party" reappears in 1 Cor. 8 as "the strong" who have knowledge and in 2 Cor. 10:7 as those who are confident they are of Christ;[15] but such arguments no longer garner much support. More persuasive is the supposition that Paul is concerned with various kinds of divisive and boastful behaviors and attitudes in the church; the slogans are just one symptom of the deeper ethical problem. This problem reappears most prominently in the divisive use of the χαρισμάτα (12:12-27 and 13:4-6), but also in the discussions of litigation (6:1-8) and the Lord's Supper (10:17-18; 11:17-22, 33-34). As Welborn comments,

> What threatened the survival of the community of chosen people was not seductive gnostic theology or infectious Judaistic propaganda, but the possibility that its adherents might "behave like ordinary men" (3:3). . . . It is no longer necessary to argue against the position that the conflict which evoked 1 Corinthians 1-4 was essentially theological in character. The attempt to identify the parties with the views and practices condemned elsewhere in the epistle, as if the parties

---

[13]Munck, 152.

[14]Munck, 139; Schmithals, 203; Fee, 5; Hurd, 96. A few critics appeal to this factor as evidence for chapters 1-4 being a separate letter (e.g., Sellin, "Geheimnis," 72), but most critics would agree with Kümmel that "the assumption of a secondary compilation of I Corinthians is to be rejected as extremely improbable." (*Introduction*, 278)

[15]e.g., Schmithals, 199.

> represented different positions in a dogmatic controversy, has collapsed under its own weight.[16]

Hurd concludes that

> I Corinthians apparently was addressed by Paul to a single, more or less unified, opposing point of view. . . . What does the oral information [of 1:12] mean? Perhaps it is not too harsh a judgement to say that more often than not the answer which scholars have given to this question has been determined more by what each scholar has brought to I Corinthians than by what he has learned from this letter. To seek, for example, the nature and source of the superior knowledge and wisdom of the Corinthians leads the scholar away from I Corinthians down various paths of investigation affording a variety of answers.[17]

Historians of religion may wish to move away from 1 Cor.,[18] but interpreters aim to explore its world. In that world, Paul is addressing an exigence of the ethical dimensions of division, not doctrinal divergence. But we still must ask just why this division is so alarming to Paul.

---

[16]Welborn, "Discord," 88. Cf. Helmut Koester, "*GNOMAI DIAPHOROI*: The Origin and Nature of Diversification in the History of Early Christianity," in *Trajectories through Early Christianity*, ed. James M. Robinson and Helmut Koester (Philadelphia: Fortress, 1971), 149: "There were no theological parties in Corinth. Apollos (Acts 18:24), a Jew from Alexandria, may have contributed to the rise of such boasting in wisdom, when he instructed the church at Corinth after Paul's departure. Paul, however, had no theological or personal quarrel with Apollos." Cf. idem, "Ulrich Wilckens: *Weisheit und Torheit*," *Gnomon* 33 (1961), 591. Contra Dennis Ronald MacDonald, *There is no Male and Female: The Fate of a Dominical Saying in Paul and Gnosticism*, Harvard Dissertations in Religion, 20 (Philadelphia: Fortress, 1987), 66, who refers to this same page in Koester, incorrectly claiming that Koester argues that Apollos and Paul were antagonists. MacDonald also insists that Pearson views Paul and Apollos as antagonists, but Pearson (18) only makes the same point as Koester: since Apollos was educated in Alexandrian exegetical principles, we have yet one *more* route through which Hellenistic Jewish mystical speculation *might* have entered Corinth, in addition to the synagogue and Paul himself.

[17]Hurd, 107.

[18]As Judge ("Classical Studies," 23) comments, "The History of Religions School confined itself to the supposed traffic of ideas within the history of religions, as though that were essentially where the phenomenon of the New Testament belonged. . . . It tried to explain too much in terms of too few ideas brought in from too far away."

The Constraint of Wisdom

The teachers Paul mentions, himself and Apollos (1:12; 3:4-6, 22; 4:6), perhaps also Cephas or his emissaries (1:12, 3:22), or even Christ (if some claim to be taught by Christ alone, 1:12, 3:23), Paul views as basically agreeing with him. But this reading of the text raises a particular problem. Paul quickly moves from the immediate exigence of divisions to the theme of wisdom. What constraints might there be in the situation that would motivate Paul to address the divisions as a phenomenon of wisdom and as a threat to the theology of the cross?[19]

The latter point is particularly puzzling. Generally, it has been solved by assuming that the Corinthians boasted of a wisdom whose theological *content* somehow denied Paul's theology of the cross. Frequently, this theological content has been seen as an a pneumatic enthusiasm with an over-realized eschatology in which the Corinthians focus on their present participation in the reign of God. But, as Scroggs points out, "Paul nowhere in these verses [1:18-2:5] explicitly argues a theological issue. In so far the older view that rhetoric is an issue must still be given its right."[20]

Scroggs finds the issue of rhetoric compelling here because while Paul makes no theological argument, he does refer specifically and repeatedly to rhetoric. After Paul raises the exigence of divisions in 1:10-12, he quickly moves, after a digression about baptism in 1:14-16, to the issue of proclamation and wisdom in 1:17: "Christ sent me to proclaim the gospel, but not in cleverness of speech, lest the cross of Christ be emptied (ἀπέστειλέν με Χριστὸς εὐαγγελίζεσθαι, οὐκ ἐν σοφίᾳ λόγου, ἵνα μὴ κενωθῇ ὁ σταυρὸς τοῦ Χριστοῦ)." The issues of the cross, proclamation, wisdom, boasting, and division remain major themes for the rest of chapters 1-4. The reader is constrained to relate all these factors when constructing a narrative of the rhetorical situation.

---

[19]Sellin, "'Geheimnis,'" 69.

[20]Scroggs, "ΣΟΦΟΣ," 33-55.

Baptism

Despite the clear connection of rhetoric and wisdom, many commentators assume that baptism is a major theme while rhetoric is a minor one. But Paul does not connect baptism and wisdom, only baptism and division.[21] Even then, it is only one of three rhetorical questions he employs to point out the absurdity of the Corinthian slogans. These questions, when taken with the slogans, form a chiasm (Paul/Christ, Christ/Paul). Those whose slogan comes last, "ἐγὼ Χριστοῦ," Paul asks μεμέρισται ὁ Χριστος; Those whose slogan comes first, "ἐγὼ Παύλου," Paul asks two ironic questions, emphasizing his particular displeasure in the use of his own name for the purposes of division: μὴ Παῦλος ἐσταυρώθη ὑπὲρ ὑμῶν, ἢ εἰς τὸ ὄνομα Παύλος ἐβαπτίσθητε;

Employing several rhetorical devices, Paul emphasizes that all the slogans and questions of 1:12-13 are about a single theme. Strong figures in 1:12 emphasize that though the champions are different for each group, Paul's criticism is the same: the *repetitio* (repetition of words)[22] of "ἐγὼ [δε]," the *paranomasia* (similarity sounds of words) of the initial Π/Απ and K/X sounds,[23] and the ὁμοιόπτωτον (words in similar cases even if the endings vary)[24] of Παύλου, Ἀπολλῶ, Κηθᾶ, Χριστοῦ. 1:12 is then tied to 1:13 by the chiasm pointed out above. This continuous theme of divisions is emphasized in 1:13 through parallel rhetorical questions.[25] This parallelism is a form of amplifi-

[21]Robert Walter Funk, *Language, Hermeneutic, and the Word of God* (New York: Harper & Row, 1966), 277: Baptism is secondary and peripheral to Paul's main concern of unity based on Christ's crucifixion. Baptism is not taken up again after 1:16, while crucifixion "dominates the remainder of the discussion (through 4:21)."

[22]Quint. 9.1.33, 9.3.28-30; *Rhet. her.* 9.28.38, who uses the term "reduplication" (ἀναδίπλωσις): "Reduplication is the repetition of one or more words for the purpose of Amplification. . . . The reiteration of the same word makes a deep impression upon the hearer."

[23]Quint. 9.3.66-80; *Rhet. Her.* 4.22.31; Humphries, 60.

[24]*Rhet. Her.* 4.20.28.

[25]On rhetorical questions, see Quint. 9.2.7: "a question involves a figure when it is employed not to get information, but to emphasize our point; cf. *Rhet. her.* 4.15.22.

cation called *accumulation*,[26] enhanced by the *paranomasia* of the repeated "μ" of μεμέρισται and μή, and "Παυλ" of Παῦλος and Παύλου.

Thus, Paul's rhetoric does not move to a new argument about baptism, but is tied together in support of a single point: rivalries are not acceptable. Baptism serves as a supporting example, a παράδειγμα, "the citing of something done or said in the past, along with the definite naming of the doer or author."[27] Aristotle recommends using examples after enthymemes (rhetorical syllogisms in which one of the premises is implicit), so that they will sound like evidence rather than the basis of induction, which is rarely suitable to rhetorical speeches.[28] This is just what Paul has done. In 1:10-13 comes the enthymeme:

Premise:	There should be no σχισμάτα among Christians.
Implied premise:	Rivalries inevitably lead to σχισμάτα.
Conclusion:	There should be no rivalries among Christians.

Then in 1:14-16 comes the example of Paul's baptismal activity, complete with historical detail. If the reader misreads it as information for inductive analysis (as do some modern critics), he must conclude that only those few people baptized by Paul should be "of Paul." In that case, Paul's further barbs aimed at the Pauline group are puzzling. So too is his failure to mention baptism again until 10:2 and 15:29, and then again, only as examples supporting other points. Instead, Paul's rhetoric about baptism sounds, in Hellenistic ears, as evidence supporting his contention that he should not be a source of disunity.

---

[26]Quint. 8.4.26-7 supplies an example of accumulation of series of rhetorical questions, all with the same reference: "What was that sword of yours doing, Tubero, the sword you drew on the field of Pharsalus? Against whose body did you aim its point? What meant those arms you bore? Whither were your thoughts, your eyes, your hand, your fiery courage directed on that day? What passion, what desires were yours?"

[27]*Rhet. her.* 4.49.62, especially Caplan's note *a*; Quint. 5.11.1-2.

[28]Arist. *Rh.* 2.20 (1394a).

Yet a number of commentators argue that Paul is reacting to the Corinthians' claims of mystical relationships with their baptizers.[29] Wilckens in this way explains how the Corinthians could be united and yet at the same time champion different teachers. He argues that the Corinthians see themselves as united in Christ, but still attached to their baptizers as their particular bearers of salvation.[30] But, as Koester points out, this explanation makes little sense when one observes not only the lack of attention to baptism after this point, but also that it cannot be a criticism of the "Christ party," nor of the Pauline group (unless it has only a few members). Furthermore, Wilckens can maintain his view only by having Paul and the Corinthians agree (without understanding that they are agreeing) that the community ought not be divided, that no one is baptized in the name of Paul, and that the whole community belongs to Christ.[31]

If we are to avoid falling into the same trap, we must listen to Paul's rhetoric. When we do, the situation has very little to do with baptism. Thus, we should not appeal to Paul's aside in 1:13-16 for the key, but to the whole of the section, with an eye to the whole of the letter.

Wise Speech

When we hear the letter in a linear, oral fashion,[32] we notice a sudden shift in 1:17. The οὐ γὰρ . . . ἀλλὰ formula alerts the audience of a shift from the example of baptism to the subjects of Paul's preaching, wisdom of speech, and the cross of Christ. Thus, the exigence of division gives way to constraints upon how Paul interprets that exigence.

---

[29]e.g., Richard Horsley, "Spiritual Marriage with Sophia," *Vigiliae Christianae* 33 (1979), 47. Cf. James M. Robinson, "Kerygma and History in the New Testament," in *Trajectories through Early Christianity*, ed. James M. Robinson and Helmut Koester, (Philadelphia: Fortress, 1971), 33.

[30]Wilckens, *Weisheit*, 16-17.

[31]Koester, "Wilckens," 591; cf. Funk, *Language*, 290.

[32]On reading NT and other ancient texts in this way, see Kennedy, *NT Interpretation*, 5-6; Paul J. Achtemeier, "*Omne Verbum Sonat:* The New Testament and the Oral Environment of Late Western Antiquity," *JBL* 109 (1990), 3-27.

The reader is then faced with the question of how these three constraints relate to each other and to the exigence. But this question depends on how we understand the phrase "σοφία λόγου".[33] Both words are extremely common with extensive semantic ranges, thus allowing the great variety of interpretations offered by modern exegetes. But one meaning stands out among the others as the most common and least specialized or esoteric: "sophisticated speech."

The original meaning of σοφία, "*cleverness* or *skill* in handicraft and art," continued throughout antiquity. It could also mean "*skill* in matters of common life, *sound judgement, intelligence, practical wisdom,* etc., . . . *cunning shrewdness,* . . . *learning.*" Less frequently, it meant "*speculative wisdom,*" including knowledge of divine matters, or "*natural philosophy.*" Finally for readers of the LXX it meant that wisdom which is of, from, or directed toward God, or even God's Spirit.[34]

It is important to note that the ordinary usage of σοφία suggested nothing of philosophical or religious speculation. Quite the contrary, σοφία was a matter of learning applied to *practical* accomplishment.

> The word generally means any deeper insight into the relationship of a matter to the business of life. Thus the seven competent wise men are the statesman, the judge, the legislator, the thinker, the inventor, and the writer; above all they knew how to counsel in practical questions of life. Their entire knowledge and wisdom of all these areas encompassed the idea of σοφία, but it must be practically applicable.[35]

---

[33]"Scholars have found the transition to this section abrupt and the point at issue perplexing. The role of this section [1:17-2:5] in Paul's advice on factions depends upon the content of 'wisdom' (σοφία) against which Paul polemicizes." Welborn, "Discord," 101.

[34]LSJ, 1621-22.

[35]PW, s.v. "Sophia," (my translation); cf. Ulrich Wilckens, "Σοφία," 467-470. Wilckens recognizes that for the earlier sophists, wisdom was "the power of clever speech [which] subjects the world to the sophist," and may thus be taught. But he errs when he asserts that the sophists were "publicly rejected," and σοφία came to refer only to philosophical ideas and qualities. Following only the philosophical tradition, he loses the rhetorical culture flowing from Isocrates, the common error outlined above in Chapter 2.

This is the sense in which Aristotle, for example uses the word: "Since it is most pleasant to command, it is also pleasant to be regarded as wise (σοφός)."[36]

Λόγος has so many common meanings that it is impractical to list them here. These meanings overlap those of σοφία in three significant aspects. First, λόγος, in its more specialized philosophical usage, means "reason" or "philosophical dialogue"; combining this with σοφία as "philosophy" suggests dialectical reason as a possible meaning of σοφία λόγου. This has been a popular alternative throughout the history of exegesis, and it fits well theologically with much of what Paul says in the rest of the chapter. Secondly, λόγος in both Jewish and Greek (especially Stoic) speculative thought sometimes refers to the word or wisdom of God. Since σοφία can also mean speculative or divine wisdom and is explicitly related to λόγος in Stoic thought, σοφία λόγου has been taken to mean mystical speculation, and this meaning has provided many reconstructions in this century.

Despite the appeal of these first two intersections of the semantic fields of σοφία and λόγος, the third intersection is so compelling that few commentators can avoid taking it into account.[37] That third aspect includes one of the most common, everyday meanings of λόγος as "speech." From the papyri we can gather that λόγος developed from its ordinary sense of "word" or "saying" to its developed meaning as "speech in progress."[38] Thus, in both koine and literary texts, λόγος was commonly understood to mean speech. In particular, it was used to mean a "*speech* delivered in court, assembly, etc.";[39] in other words, it meant the product of *rhetoric*. In this sense, then, σοφία λόγου would mean clever or skilled or educated or rhetorically sophisticated speech. This

basic significance of education as a cultural boundary marker is clearly registered by Paul. When he says in Rom 1:14, "I am under obligation to both Greeks and barbarians," he refers to the classic distinction made by Greeks between those who shared their *paideia*

---

[36]Arist. *Rh*. 1.11.27 (1371b).

[37]See above, p. 5.

[38]MM, 379.

[39]LSJ, 1058.

> and those who could not speak Greek at all. Similarly, when he speaks in the same sentence of "the wise" and the "foolish," he refers to the distinction within Greek culture between those who were highly educated and those who were not.[40]

This meaning of σοφία λόγου as cultured speech fits the immediate context best, since Paul is referring to his manner of proclamation. Thus, BAGD translates the phrase as "cleverness in speaking."[41] "The σοφία which Paul fears will undermine the community is nothing other than rhetoric."[42]

Combining these two words in a single context was natural enough in a world where the accomplished or "wise" man was expected to be eloquent. Thus, Isocrates points out that παιδεία cannot quickly make a student "more accomplished in speech" (σοφωτέρους ἐν τοῖς λόγοις) than those who have the advantage over them both in years and experience, for it takes far longer than a year to make them "capable and accomplished rhetors (ἀγαθοὺς και τελέους ῥήτορας, cf. 1 Cor. 2:6)."[43]

Isocrates's use of σοφός to describe a rhetor is a natural one, yet it is somewhat unusual from the pens of the rhetoricians because of their polemical situation vis-a-vis the philosophers. One of the great struggles among philosophers (especially between Stoics and Cynics) was what constituted the truly wise person. Rhetoricians, as we shall see, asserted their own claims in this regard. But they had to be careful in their claims, as Plutarch's criticisms demonstrate:

> While men resent the writers and speakers who assume the epithet "wise" (τῆς σοφίας), they are delighted with those who say that they love wisdom (τοῖς φιλοσοφεῖν) or are advancing in merit, or put forward some other such moderate and inoffensive claim. Whereas the rhetorical sophists (ῥητορικοὶ σοφισταὶ) who at their displays of eloquence accept from the audience the cries of "how divine" and "spoken like a god" lose even such commendation as "fairly said" (μετρίως) and "spoken as becomes a man" (ἀνθρωπίνως).[44]

---

[40]Judge, "Reaction," 70.

[41]BAGD, 759.

[42]Welborn, "Discord," 102; idem, "Conciliatory," 339. Cf. Bünker, 77; Lim, 146-47.

[43]Isoc. *Antidosis* 199-200. Note that the primary meaning of ἀγαθός is "well-born" (LSJ, 4).

[44]Plutarch, *De se ipsum citra invidiam laudando*, 12 (*Mor.* 543E-F).

In this polemical situation, rhetoricians tend to grant the word σοφία to philosophy while simultaneously claiming that only the orator can be truly wise (and, therefore, philosophy should never have been separated from oratory).[45] In common usage more removed from this polemic, σοφία continued to be used to describe those with particular practical skill or cleverness.

This ordinary understanding of "wise speech" is brought into focus by the popularity of references to Homer's Nestor throughout antiquity in both Greek and Latin.[46] Homer describes Nestor as an articulate public speaker (λιγὺς ἀγορητής) from whose mouth flowed speech sweeter than honey.[47] Many subsequent writers echo this verse, including the rhetoricians.[48] Particularly significant for our purposes is the epigram recorded in the *Palatine Anthology*, which uses σοφία and a cognate of λόγος to describe Nestor's skill (γλώσσης ἡδυλόγου σοφίῃ) by which he won the highest prize among mortals.[49] The popular honey metaphor for sweetness of speech is picked up by Plutarch, when he writes that the honey bee is σοφή because it "flatters" (κολακεύω) with the sweetness of its honey.[50] Plutarch's reference to wise speech is thus doubly clear, since flattery was a common accusation thrown against rhetoricians and sophists, especially by philosophers; this tradition is clearly reflected in 1 Thess. 2:5 (ἐν λόγῳ κολακείας).

The ordinary understanding of σοφία is particularly brought out by its frequent conjunction with δεινός, "clever or skillful." When conjoined, the two words form an apt description of cultured speech, and orators in particular were described as possessing δεινότης.[51] For example, Diodorus Siculus, writing a few years before Paul, describes Gorgias ὁ ῥήτωρ, admired for his τέχνη ῥητορική, as

---

[45]See above, pp. 83-87.

[46]A. Otto, *Die Sprichwo|rter und sprichwo|rtlichen Redensarten der Ro|mer: gesammelt und erkla|rt* (Leipzig: Teubner, 1890), 216-17, 242.

[47]Hom. *Il.* 1.248-9.

[48]*Rh. Her.* 4.33.44.

[49]*Anth. Pal.* 159.

[50]Plut. *De Amore Prolis*, *Mor.* 494A.

[51]LSJ 374-75.

surpassing his contemporaries δεινότητι λόγου.[52] As we shall see, those with σοφόι or δεινόι λόγοι were often accorded such honor.

Wisdom and Social Status

As we have already begun to see, when σοφία and λόγος are combined in ancient usage, they frequently imply far more than just technical skill at language. Rather, they imply a whole world of social status related to speech. For example, one common antonym of σοφός is φαῦλος, which when used "in point of education or accomplishments," means not just bad or inferior, but "*low* in rank, *common, mean.*"[53]

Thus, σοφία tends to describe educated or cultured characteristics of persons of high social standing. This is born out by the tradition of the Seven Wise Men mentioned above. Although the list varied somewhat in both length and the identities of some of the men, it was a popular one throughout antiquity. Many of their sayings circulated in and beyond Paul's time as pithy *sententia* or σοφόι, "sage remarks."[54]

MacMullen remarks on the exclusive importance of eloquence for upper class persons:

> The one art in which cultivated people commonly expressed their cultivation, from the fifth century B.C. to the fifth century A.D. [is one] we no longer practice nor value, and tend to ignore. That was *eloquentia*. For a thousand years it remained at the heart of classical civilization, placing its heroes upon embassies, rostrums, richly endowed chairs, and the platforms of special theaters; at last, as statues, upon pedestals in the Roman forum itself. All other arts [painting, drawing, sculpture, architecture, and drama] save poetry were left to slaves or to the lower classes. . . .
>
> This art . . . engaged the idle hours of an aristocracy forever dabbling or pretending to dabble or seriously learned in literature. . . . They could see a relation almost hidden from us between their

---

[52]Diod. Sic. 12.53.2.

[53]LSJ 1920.

[54]Plut. *Conv. sept. sap.*, *Mor.* 160E.

politics and what we would call their culture, and defended it as an extension of their freedom.[55]

All of this we see reflected in Plutarch's "Dinner of the Seven Wise Men." Plutarch places the supper at the home of one of the wise men, Periander, the ruler of Corinth (c. 600 B.C.). Periander was included among the wise apparently because of his great worldly success in developing Corinthian arts, crafts, industry, commerce, and building.[56] In his portrayal of Periander, Plutarch displays the wisdom (practical cleverness) valued in the Corinth of Paul's time; for if Periander was celebrated throughout the ancient world as a paradigmatic wise man, he was likewise celebrated in his own city, which Plutarch knew well only a short time after Paul. That city was still well known for its practical accomplishments in commerce, banking, transportation, and industry.

In Plutarch's account, σοφία is consistently used in the sense of cultured cleverness. Thus the wise are able to solve riddles, are held in esteem, and are the friends of kings who need their practical advice.[57] Such σοφία, in typical fashion, is also called δεινότης.[58] Though the wise claim a democratic ideal, they are perceived as always aiming for honor.[59] An indication of the honor due them is that people should have faith (πιστευτέον) in their wisdom.[60] The degree of honor was such that winning the competition in witty conversation could even overcome lowly birth.[61] This conjunction of wise speech and social status is brought out by the typical use of φαῦλος as an antonym for σοφία.[62]

The wisdom described in Plutarch's account covers a great variety of subjects. The cultured discourse of the dinner guests includes not only riddles, but politics, religion, home life, polite

---

[55]Ramsey MacMullen, *Enemies of the Roman Order* (Cambridge: Harvard, 1966), 15.

[56]Plut. *Conv. sept. sap.*, *Mor.* 148C.

[57]Ibid., 146F-147C.

[58]Ibid., 148D, 159C.

[59]Ibid., 149B.

[60]Ibid., 164D.

[61]Ibid., 151B-E.

[62]Ibid., 158A-B.

behavior, possessions, story-telling, and even diet. In the discussion of diet, we find a list of this and other "wise" things about which Hesiod wrote: "the daily course of life, mixing wine, the great value of water, bathing, women, the proper time for intercourse, and the way in which infants should sit." The diet in question is adopted by Solon; the "wise" nature even of this subject is so clear that it is assumed that he must have been convinced by some sophistical argument (σοφιζόμενος).[63] In describing this widely varied wisdom as the property of the sophist, Plutarch indicates the growing social role of such sophists as purveyors of virtually any subject considered useful or fashionable by their cultured consumers. Even Homer becomes a σοφώτατος,[64] a description which in late antiquity increasingly became a title of lawyers and professors,[65] i.e., sophists who were socially and financially enriched by their speech.

Another place we find the conjunction of wise speech and social status is popular Stoicism. The teaching of orthodox Stoics is reported by Cicero in *De Finibus Bonorum et Malorum*, "the only systematic account surviving from antiquity of those rules of life which divided the allegiance of thoughtful men during the centuries when the old religions had lost their hold and Christianity had not yet emerged."[66] According to Cicero, the Stoics taught that the "wise man" (the ideal *sapiens*) is alone truly rich and a king.[67] The Stoics' use of such words as "rich" and "king" was metaphorical (though, given their own upper class station, hardly accidental or insignificant). At the same time, they held that a "wise man" would often enjoy many worldly benefits as "preferred indifferents," including money, sound senses, good health, and good fame (εὐδοξία):[68] "All wise men at all times enjoy a happy, perfect, fortunate, . . . praiseworthy, . . . honourable, . . . esteemed" life. The wise man will be a "lofty, distinguished, magnanimous and truly brave man."[69] Thus, Stoic ethics, unlike

---

[63]Ibid., 158B.

[64]Ibid., 164D.

[65]LSJ, 1622.

[66]H. Rackham, "Introduction," *Cicero: De Finibus Bonorum et Malorum*, trans. H. Rackham, LCL (Cambridge: Harvard, 1914), xi.

[67]Cic. *Fin.* 3.22.75.

[68]Ibid., 3.17.56-57.

[69]Ibid., 3.7.26-8.30.

those of the Cynics, were congenial to the conventional value placed upon power, money, honor, status, and rank. To the upper class Stoics, the values of the status quo were self-evident: "A man of good breeding and liberal education would desire to have the good opinion of his parents and relatives, and of good men in general."[70] "What man of honourable family and good breeding and education is not shocked by moral baseness?"[71] A wise man will be "law-abiding, conscious of his duty to the state,"[72] and will "desire to engage in politics and government".[73]

It is easy to see why so much of Stoic ethics was absorbed into the generally literate culture. Thus, many who were far removed from orthodox Stoicism read and appreciated Stoic writings. Such people did not object to the study of philosophy, "provided it be followed in dilettante fashion; but they do not think it ought to engage so large an amount of one's interest and attention."[74] Patrons or students of philosophers

> were in a position to pick the philosophy that suited them. They often mixed elements of several brands—Stoic the favorite, but also Epicurean, Peripatetic, Pythagorean, Academic, or Cynic—in a manner that showed their ignorance of the strict connections that ought to exist among all parts of a chosen system. It is, however, not too relativistic to doubt whether people generally choose any view because of its logic. It must instead form a harmony with economic interest, political bias, and social custom. We would not, for instance, expect from an aristocracy a delicate regard for the lower classes. Despite the most explicit teaching of Stoicism, later to be admitted to a changed situation, the Roman nobles of the first century did not look on all the world's population as their brothers—far from it. Nor was it they that would succor the slave. "Slavish" was the most common term of contempt among them; in contrast, "liberal" studies were "those that were fit for a free man," and the best of them was the study that "makes men free"—wisdom, in the Stoic sense. It was not for every man, only for the educated. Opinions of the masses should be ignored.[75]

---

[70]Ibid., 3.17.57.
[71]Ibid., 3.11.38.
[72]Ibid., 3.19.64.
[73]Ibid., 3.20.68.
[74]Ibid., 1.1.1. See also above, pp. 82-86.
[75]MacMullen, *Enemies*, 49.

Through these dilettantes and other sources, upper class persons generally believed that the Stoic σοφός was "not only prudent and just and brave, but also an orator (ῥήτωρ), a poet, a general, a rich man, and a king,"[76] and in another more telling list, the Stoic σοφός is known to be "at once handsome, gracious, liberal, eminent, rich, eloquent, (δεινὸν εἰπεῖν), learned, philanthropic," as opposed to one who is "ugly, graceless, illiberal, dishonored, needy, a poor speaker (ἀσθενῆ περὶ λόγον; cf. 1 Cor. 2:3, 2 Cor. 10:10), unlearned (περί λόγον ἀμαθῆ), misanthropic."[77] The former is distinguished as possessing "superiority" (ὑπεροχή, cf. 1 Cor. 2:1).[78]

Plutarch makes clear that people who know this particular Stoic doctrine apart from the full system think it means that if a person has wealth, high office, or eloquence which qualify him for honor, power, or fame, such a person is to be considered wise.[79] Thus, we find Horace satirizing people, like Staberius, who thought riches could qualify him as wise:

> All his life long he thought poverty a monstrous evil, and shunned nothing more earnestly, so that, if haply he had died less rich by a single penny, so far would he have thought himself the worse man. For all things—worth, repute, honour, things divine and human—are slaves to the beauty of wealth, and he who has made his 'pile' will be famous, brave and just. 'And wise [*sapiens*] too?' Yes, wise, and a king and anything else he pleases. His riches, as though won by worth, would bring him, he hoped, great renown.[80]

This popularized version of the Stoic doctrine could be easily employed by flatterers (κόλακες) who wished to gain the favor of persons of wealth, power, or repute:

> Flatterers proclaim that kings and wealthy persons and rulers are not only prosperous and blessed, but that they also rank first in understanding (φρονήσις, cf. 1. Cor. 4:10), technical skill, and every form of virtue. Again, some people will not even listen to the Stoics, when they call the wise man (σοφός) at the same time rich, handsome,

---

[76]Plut. *De tranq. an.*, *Mor.* 472A.
[77]Plut. *De frat. amor.*, *Mor.* 485A.
[78]Ibid, 485D.
[79]Ibid., 486E.
[80]Hor. *Sat.* 2.3.100.

> well-born, and a king; but flatterers declare of the rich man that he is at the same time an orator (ῥήτωρ) and a poet.[81]

This popularization of Stoic doctrine is reflected in a text by Sextus Empiricus, the skeptic philosopher (c. A.D. 200). He refutes any defense of rhetoric which claims that it's detractors confuse the good rhetoric of highly cultured people with the bad rhetoric of the less cultured:

> Some assert that as there are two forms of rhetoric, the one refined and in use among the wise, the other in use among inferior people, the accusation is not made against the refined kind but against that of the baser class.
>
> τινὲς φάσιν ὅτι διττῆς οὔσης ῥητορικῆς, τῆς μὲν ἀστειας καὶ ἐν σοφοῖς τῆς δὲ ἐν μέσοις ἀνθρώποις, τὴν κατηγορίαν γεγονέναι ού τῆς ἀστείας ἀλλὰ τῆς τῶν μοχθηρῶν.[82]

Sextus's diction displays the difference between the philosophical meaning of σοφός and the normal cultural meaning. Prior to the above passage, he attacks rhetoric's claim that it is used among the wise (ἐν σοφοῖς), because the wise man (according to orthodox Stoic doctrine) is never, or at least rarely, found. Yet in the above passage, he also admits that others assert the existence of two forms of rhetoric. One, ἀστείας (refined, elegant, witty speech; town-bred, polite[83]) is used among the wise (ἐν σοφοῖς). The other is used by μέσοις ἀνθρωποις (those of middle rank or middle class who are therefore mediocre).[84] These mediocre, middle level people are situated between the εὔποροι (those who are wealthy, full of resources, ingenious inventive[85]) and the ἄποροι (the poor, those without means who are helpless, who cannot undertake liturgies; ἄπορος is often used with ταπεινός[86] [cf. 2 Cor. 7:6, 10:1, 11:7]). To Sextus' imaginary interlocutor, the σοφοί are the opposite of the

---

[81]Plut. *Quomodo Adulator ab Amico Internoscatur*, *Mor.* 58E.
[82]Sext. Emp. *Math.* 2.43.
[83]LSJ, 260.
[84]LSJ, 1107.
[85]LSJ, 727-728.
[86]LSJ, 215.

μέσοι; i.e., the wise who claim to employ rhetoric in an admirable way are the cultured upper class as opposed to those just below them on the social scale. This is underlined by the corresponding opposition of the refined (τῆς ἀστείας) and the inferior (τῆς τῶν μοχθηρῶν).

We see, then, that the "wise" speaker was one who employed language in a manner which suited him to an upper class station. Such a person would be educated, cultured, literate, and persuasive.

The Foolishness of the Cross

The connection of rhetoric with social class is highly significant for 1 Cor., for the rhetorical situation must connect wisdom not only to the exigence of division but also to social status (1:26-28; cf 11:18, 22). The relationship between rhetoric and division we will investigate further in Chapter 6, and explicit references to status in Chapter 7. Here we will limit ourselves to 1:17, in which Paul contrasts speech which confers high status with speech about the cross.

As we have seen, the rhetorical structure indicates to the audience that 1:17 opens the argument against the behavior of 1:12. Paul claims that he did not preach in a status conferring manner, suggesting that he is responding to those who have so perceived him. Thus, Paul is responding not to division itself, but to the values which lie behind them. Those "of Paul" have perceived him as possessing the status indicator of eloquence, while those "of Apollos" perceive Apollos superior in this regard.

To persuade the Corinthians to change their values and behavior, Paul appeals to the narrative of community origins. In this narrative, Paul founded the community by preaching to them about the crucified Christ. Thus, he can refer to this narrative with a simple phrase meaningful only to community members: "the cross of Christ." To the Corinthians, Paul's preaching may have been persuasive, and thus "wise," but he reminds them that he had used this speech to draw the Corinthians into a world in which the "champion" is crucified. This

> 'word of the cross' (λόγος τοῦ σταυροῦ) ran counter . . . to Roman political thinking. . . . For the men of the ancient world, Greeks, Romans, barbarians and Jews, the cross was not . . . just any kind of death. It was . . . a matter of subjecting the victim to the utmost indignity. . . . The cultured literary world wanted to have nothing to to with it. . . . By the public display of a naked victim at a prominent place, . . . crucifixion . . . represented his uttermost humiliation. . . . Crucifixion was practiced above all on dangerous criminals and members of the lowest classes . . . in other words, groups whose development had to be suppressed by all possible means to safeguard law and order in the state. Because large strata of the population welcomed the security and the world-wide peace which the empire brought with it, the crucified victim was defamed both socially and ethically in popular awareness. . . . To assert that God himself accepted death in the form of a crucified Jewish manual worker from Galilee . . . could only seem folly and madness to men of ancient times. . . . When Paul talks of the 'folly' of the message of the crucified Jesus, he is therefore not speaking in riddles or using an abstract cipher. He is expressing the harsh experience of his missionary preaching and the offense that it caused, in particular the experience of his preaching among non-Jews, with whom his apostolate was particular concerned.[87]

In Paul's narrative world, the normal cultural narratives of eloquence and status are radically reversed. What persuades is speech about what is ordinarily unfit for contemplation: not a life which is cultured, wise, and powerful, but one marked by the worst shame and the lowest possible status. Paul's rhetoric of the cross thus opposes the cultural values surrounding eloquence.

This explains how Paul can at once attack rhetoric and yet employ it in that very attack. Traditionally, as we have seen, his interpreters have concluded that he rejected rhetorical devices of all kinds. Yet today we must take account of the relative sophistication of Paul's rhetoric. We cannot solve this paradox in the simple ways proposed by Timothy Lim and Peter Marshall. Lim falls into a *reductio ad absurdum* when he argues that Paul didn't reject "human communication in general, but that specific, studied art of persuasive speech as was practiced by orators and rhetoricians of the Graeco-Roman world and by at least some of the Corinthian preachers [Who? Apollos?], . . . which emphasizes the form rather than the

---

[87]Martin Hengel, *Crucifixion: in the Ancient World and the Folly of the Message of the Cross* (Philadelphia: Fortress, 1977), 5, 22-34, 38, 87, 89.

content."[88] Similarly, Marshall argues that Paul employed his rhetorical ability in the "grand style" when speaking, but turned it off when writing.[89] This makes little sense for two reasons. First, Paul's rhetoric is at least as artful in the very sections in which he "rejects" rhetoric as elsewhere.[90] Second, variations in style according to situation were standard rhetorical techniques and would only enhance Paul's rhetorical effectiveness.

Paul is not rejecting a "fancy" rhetoric in favor of a "plainer" one. Rather, as Lim inconsistently asserts, he is "willing to employ human eloquence."[91] Paul rejects not rhetoric, but the cultural values wedded to it:

> The value-system upon which Greek education had been built up is deliberately overthrown. Paul . . . reacted powerfully against the perversion of human relations which he saw inculcated by the ideals of higher education. It was a perversion because it enshrined the beautiful and the strong in a position of social power. In his own case he deliberately tore down the structure of privilege with which his followers wished to surround him.[92]

In addition to his rejection of the social role of rhetor and his reference to the narrative of the cross, Paul, as we shall see, employs a rhetoric of status reversal in other ways. But for now, we will restrict ourselves to further investigation into the meaning of σοφία λόγου and related phrases.

Roman Wisdom and Social Status

Another dimension of "wisdom" can be found in the Roman understanding of the term. This understanding would have have had great influence in a town which, though Greek, had been rebuilt by the Romans beginning in 44 B.C.E. They repopulated it with freed-

---

[88]Lim, 146, 149.
[89]Marshall, 388-393.
[90]For examples, see below, pp. 183-205.
[91]Lim, 149.
[92]Judge, "Reaction," 14.

men[93] and veterans[94] and others of neither the lowest nor highest status. Appian describes the Romans sent by Julius Caesar as τῶν ἀπόρων who asked for land.[95] Ἄπορος could mean "poor," but it also means "unmanageable," from its basic meaning of "having no way to get in or out."[96] Thus, "the reference could be to those who felt themselves locked into a certain social level through lack of opportunity."[97] Such persons fit well in Paul's rhetorical situation. As we shall see in Chapter 8 when we examine the dinners to which Paul refers in 11:17-34, these are the persons trapped in the middle, Sextus' μέσοι who are not wise and refined, but relatively inferior[98] (Judge's "socially pretentious persons").

Murphy-O'Connor comments that the majority of the freedmen

> were small shopkeepers, artisans, teachers, and secretaries. . . . Other freedmen must have been men of initiative and vision who, through the training gained in the service of their former masters, were aware of the ways to acquire capital and to deploy it wisely. Some would surely have acted as the agents of investors in Rome who recognized the tremendous economic potential of the site of Corinth.
>
> For both groups of freedmen the move to a new colony would have meant a step up the social ladder. . . . In addition, their children would have been full and free citizens in a land of golden opportunity.
>
> The first colonists would also have numbered slaves and, of course, freemen willing to gamble on the advantages of being in on the ground-floor of an enterprise which promised great rewards. Once the new colony grew it would have attracted far-sighted entrepreneurs. . . . Such infusions of new capital in a prime commercial situation inevitably generated more wealth, and within 50 years of its foundation many of the citizens had become men of very considerable means,[99]

such as Lucius Castricius Regulus, honored in an inscription as president of the Isthmian games, who between 7 B.C.E. and 3 A.D.

---

[93]Strabo 8.6.23c.

[94]Plut. *Vit. Caes.* 47.8.

[95]Appian *Pun.* 136, quoted in Wiseman, 497.

[96]LSJ, 215.

[97]Jerome Murphy-O'Connor, *St. Paul's Corinth: Texts and Archaeology*, Good News Studies, ed. Robert J. Karris, vol. 6 (Wilmington, DE: Michael Glazier, 1983), 113.

[98]See above, p. 168.

[99]Murphy-O'Connor, 66-7.

paid to renovate all the buildings and give a banquet for all the inhabitants.[100] "The prosperity of many of its citizens and of the city generally increased rapidly throughout the reign of Augustus," as indicated by the number of benefactors and the amount of building activity.[101] "The names of [Corinth's] ambitious citizens, their rivalries, and election promises are known to us from inscriptions recording their donations."[102]

Concerning such changes in economic status, MacMullen notes that "urban conditions favored mobility far more than did rural. For someone in manufacture and commerce on any scale at all, the wheel of chance spun much faster than for the man whose capital resided in land—hence, more rapid changes in status." MacMullen judges that the emergence of great fortunes were rare. Yet he grants

> a rather cautious acknowledgment that people who started with some minor skill or minor sum of money could indeed rise to relative affluence—could and did, in verifiable instances that aroused less surprise at their success than contempt of their origins. . . .
>
> Among those few, freedmen stood out. . . . Trimalchio is typical. He gave himself body and soul to his master, suppressed all pride. A fortune fell to him exactly as he hoped, and he somersaulted into a grand house and fame. The manners he assumed with his master he found perfectly natural among his guests: falseness and servility. . . . In Pompeii, freedmen and their descendants in the same proportion belonged to the governing aristocracy. . . . Nouveaux riches of this sort with their sudden successes deeply shocked the master class.[103]

This upper class shock led them to employ various means to reinforce the freedman's lower status in everything but money. As we shall see in Chapter 8, one significant place for this was the seating and portions at dinners.

The residents of Corinth, no matter how high they rose in riches and status in their own town, constantly lived in the shadow of Rome. Roman trade, government, and cultural institutions were ever present. From the time it was refounded as a Roman colony, the inscriptions

---

[100]Ibid., 14-15.

[101]J. Wiseman, "Corinth and Rome I: 228 B.C. - A.D. 267," *ANRW* 2.7.1, 503.

[102]Welborn, "Discord," 111.

[103]MacMullen, *Roman Social Relations*, 98-104.

are nearly all in Latin until the reign of Hadrian (117-138 C.E.).[104] While this indicates that Latin was the official language, it does not mean that Latin was more commonly spoken. Paul writes in Greek, and this corroborates what we might suspect from elsewhere. The old Greek city continued to be inhabited after the Romans plundered it in 146 B.C.E.,[105] most commerce in the area was done in Greek, and the inscriptions finally reverted to Greek. Thus, the Latin inscriptions probably mean that those who were honored or honoring others did so in the language which would underline their higher status as persons of Roman citizenship, descent or pretensions. This was apparently even true before the city was refounded in 44 B.C.E., when the residents who remained after the destruction were also apparently a mix of Greek and Latin backgrounds. Those who could afford it erected a Latin inscription honoring Hirrus, *legatus pro praetore* for the orator Marcus Antonius, grandfather of Mark Antony, celebrating the transportation of a Roman fleet across the isthmus in 102 B.C.E.[106] "Even if in many instances contact was sought with the older Greek tradition—the resumption of the Isthmian games, for example—the construction of an amphitheater nevertheless demonstrates how strong was the Roman, non-Greek influence."[107] Even the games showed Roman influence.[108]

This evidence of Roman influence makes it easy to imagine why the Corinthians would be hungry for status in Roman terms. No matter how high they rose, they always received less honor. Money and houses they might have, but good ancestry took many generations to purchase. Even if they had good ancestry, they were still mere provincials, residents of neither Athens nor Rome. But since their city was the gateway between Athens and the Peloponese as well as the major trade route between Rome and Athens, the Corinthians must have been very conscious of their status in the shadow of the two capitals. This would have been particularly true vis-a-vis Rome.

---

[104]John Harvey Kent, *Corinth VIII/3. The Inscriptions 1926-1950.* Princeton: American School of Classical Studies at Athens, 1966, 19.

[105]Wiseman, 491-496.

[106]Ibid., 495-7.

[107]Theissen, 158.

[108]Murphy-O'Connor, 15.

To live in the shadow of Rome would have been rather daunting to one who was conscious of status. "Citizens of the capital felt themselves vastly superior to men of any other origin." They displayed "an almost incredible snobbery."[109] The pride of the Roman upper classes was mirrored in the relative pride of citizens of other cities.

> They had [a] word, *asteios*, literally "urban" but by extension "fine," "refined," "good" in general, recalling but going beyond "urbane. . . . That quality triumphed in contrast with everything nonurban. i.e., rustic. But if everything about any city was good, then the bigger the city the better.[110]

We have already encountered this term in the report by Sextus Empiricus that rhetoric is often approved when it is refined (ἀστεῖος) and used by the wise (σοφοί), but criticized when used by less refined people, the μέσοι ἀνθρώποι, those who are not of the first rank, but neither are they poor.

Just as the Corinthians' money could not buy ancestry, even if they could move to Rome where it took vast sums to live in cultured style, it would not qualify them as Romans.

> Tacitus lists "among so many sorrows that saddened the city" in the year 33 the marriage of a woman of the royal family to someone "whose grandfather many remembered as a gentleman outside the senate, from Tivoli"—the horror of the mésalliance lying no more in equestrian rank than in the stain of small-town birth a bare two generations ago. . . . Cicero complained, "You see how all of us are looked down on who come from country towns." Cicero nevertheless goes on to say, "You might think [one] was speaking of a person from Tralles or Ephesus." Scorn of those provincial cities was after all quite understandable.[111]

However, even if money alone could not buy the "old boy" connections of the most acceptable *gymnasia*, it could buy teachers to lend a pretense of culture or even to actually educate oneself or one's children. It could also buy books (like Tramalchio's two libraries of

---

[109]MacMullen, *Roman Social Relations*, 58; cf. J.P.V.D Balsdon, *Romans and Aliens* (Chapel Hill: University of North Carolina, 1979), 24-25.

[110]MacMullen, *Roman Social Relations*, 58.

[111]Ibid., 58, citing Tac., *Ann.* 6.27 and Cic. *Phil.* 3.15.

Greek and Latin works). The status of being considered relatively "wiser" than other provincials was within reach.

The Roman Wise Man

The Romans, as we saw above in our discussion of popularized stoic ideas, were particularly drawn to the kind of wisdom which qualified a man as a competent public figure. This value is strongly and repeatedly reflected in their rhetorical tradition. Quintilian explicitly mentions the contrast between the claim of philosophers to be wise men, and his own view: the orator "should be a wise man [*sapiens*] in the Roman sense, that is, one who reveals himself as a true statesman, not in the discussions of the study, but in the actual practice and experience of life."[112] To the Romans, the Greeks had "too much talk, *loquacitas*, and too little common sense."[113] In practice speeches, we find such a public wise man contrasted with the "fool" [*stultus*], the same terminology employed by the Stoics and Cynics: "The wise man [*sapiens*] will die with manliness and honor on behalf of the republic, as opposed to the foolish man [*stultus*] who flees such peril to live in disgrace."[114]

In such contrasts, we see the typical connection of an honored description, *sapiens*, with social class. Thus, Quintilian allows that a *sapiens* may tell a lie, if for a good cause, but such behavior is reprehensible in slaves.[115] Again, a wise man is typically contrasted with the uneducated masses.[116]

Like their Greek counterparts' use of σοφία,[117] the Latin rhetoricians tend to leave the term *sapiens* for the philosophers,[118] preferring to use *prudentia* for rhetorical wisdom. Thus, although Cicero could refer to eloquence as "wisdom delivering copious

---

[112]Quint. 12.2.7, cf. 11.1.35.

[113]Balsdon, 32.

[114]Quint. 4.44.57.

[115]Ibid., 12.1.39.

[116]Ibid., 12.10.52.

[117]See above, pp. 157-58.

[118]Quint. 12.2.8.

utterance (*copiose loquens sapientia*),"[119] he generally upholds the wise character of rhetoric by calling it *prudens. Prudentia* tends to emphasize the more practical kinds of wisdom;[120] but the meanings of the words largely overlap, as when a statesman is first described as possessing *sapientia* and then *prudentia*,[121] or when the wisdom of the philosophers is called *prudentia.*[122] *Ad Herennium* explicitly shows that *prudentia* includes the meaning of σοφία by drawing upon a standard philosophical list of virtues, translating σοφία, δικαιοσύνη, ἀνδρεία, and σωφροσύνη as *prudentia, iustitia, fortitudo*, and *modestia*. Caplan comments that *Herennium's* definition of *prudentia* shows that it partakes of the nature of both σοφία and φρόνησις (cf. 1 Cor 4:10).[123]

When we add to our picture of Paul's world the pervasive Roman emphasis on practical wisdom, we can more easily imagine a rhetorical situation in which "wise speech" could have import far beyond "mere form." How one spoke was closely related to issues of social status that included education, power, wealth, birth, social relations, and tensions between urban/rural and Roman/Greek identity. "The wise of this age," of whom Paul writes in 1 Cor. 1:20, are "those who are trained in the artful literary and rhetorical devices, [i.e.], . . . the learned or politically dominant class."[124] Thus, when Paul received the report from Chloe's people that he and Apollos, as persuasive speakers, had become foci of divisive rivalries over status, he would easily (as he wrote in 11:18 in ironic understatement about other status related rivalries), "partly believe it."

---

[119]Cic. *Part. Or.* 23.79; cf. idem, *De Or.* 1.8.31.

[120]e.g., the wisdom of the Roman law compared to the lack of Greek wisdom: Cic. *De Or.* 1.44.197.

[121]Ibid., 1.2.8.

[122]Ibid., 3.31.122.

[123] Rhet. *Her.* 3.2.3: *Prudentia* is defined as "intelligence capable, by a certain judicious method, of distinguishing good and bad; likewise the knowledge of an art is called *prudentia*; and again, a well-furnished memory, or experience in diverse matters, is termed *prudentia*."

[124]F.C. Grant, 76-77.

CHAPTER V

RHETORIC AND STATUS

Explicit References Linking Rhetoric and Status

1 Corinthians

By reading the phrase σοφία λόγου in 1:17 in the light of the Greco-Roman culture of Corinth, we have moved a long way toward constructing key constituents of Paul's rhetorical situation: the ubiquitous presence of rhetoric itself and its relationship to rivalries over social status. Later verses which repeat the key words of 1:17 encourage the reader's confidence in this construction.

Expolitio

In 2:1, 2:4, and 2:13, Paul repeats his disavowal of wise speech. But each time, his phrasing is slightly different. In 2:1, Paul writes that when he came to the Corinthians "proclaiming the mystery [or testimony] of God (καττα γγέλλων τὸ μυστήριον [μαρτύριον] τοῦ θεοῦ)," he did so "οὐ καθ' ὑπεροχὴν λόγου ἢ σοφίας (not in superiority of word or wisdom)." Again in 2:4, his "speech (λόγος)" and "proclamation (κήρυγμά)" were "οὐκ ἐν πειθοῖς σοφίας λόγοις (not in persuasive wise words)." In 2:13, the apostles speak not in words taught by human wisdom (οὐκ ἐν διδακτοῖς ἀνθρωπίνης σοφίας λόγοις).

These repetitions serve a purely rhetorical function. That is, Paul is not saying anything new, but "amplifying" his theme of 1:17, using (ἐπ)ἐξεργασία or expolitio (refining or embellishing), which is

> dwelling on the same topic and yet seeming to say something ever new. It is accomplished in two ways: by merely repeating the same idea, or by descanting upon it. We shall not repeat the same thing precisely—for that, to be sure, would weary the hearer and not refine the idea—but with changes. . . . Our changes will be verbal when, having expressed the idea once, we repeat it once again or oftener in other, equivalent terms.[1]

Before hearing these amplifications, the audience has already been prepared for them by a number of devices. In 1:18-25, Paul has signaled that he is beginning a new topic (in support of the point he made in 1:17) by changing from the first person singular voice to the first person plural voice of 1:18-25. He then signals the end of this topic in 1:25 with a *conclusio*, "a brief argument, deducing the necessary consequences of what has been said or done before."[2] The second topic of 1:26-30 follows a similar pattern. He signals its beginning with another change in voice, now to imperative, second, and third-person. Again, in 1:29-30, Paul alerts the reader of the end of the second topic with another *conclusio*.

Then in 2:1, Paul alerts the reader that he is returning to his point of 1:17 by returning to the first- person singular, emphasizing this by placing ἐγώ in the emphatic position, "picking up, as it were, where he left off in 1:17."[3] Thus, we should not be thrown off by the phrase μυστήριον τοῦ θεοῦ. Whatever the meaning of μυστήριον later in 2:7, here it can be most naturally taken to refer to what he proclaimed when he first came and preached to the Corinthians. In any case, the correct reading may be μαρτύριον, "testimony."[4] In either case, Paul clarifies in the next verse (2:2) the subject of this testimony or mystery: Christ crucified. Then (2:3) he

---

[1] Rhet. Her. 4.42.55; cf. Quint. 8.3.88, 8.4.26-27; Theon, 1.172-174, 199-201, 2.115-123, 3.139-199; Robbins, *Jesus the Teacher*, 29, 64; Bonner, *Education in Ancient Rome*, 259; Kennedy, *NT Interpretation*, 29.

[2] *Rhet. Her.* 4.30.41; cf. Quint. 7.5.13.

[3] Humphries, 69.

[4] Conzelmann, 53, n. 6; cf. Barrett, *First Corinthians*, 62-63.

emphasizes his weak appearance as a rhetor, the opposite of the strength and boldness expected of a cultured orator. Rounding out the picture of anti-rhetorician, Paul then asserts (2:4) that just as his bodily presence was weak, so too was his speech. The rhetoric surrounding the third *expolitio* in 2:13 we shall examine below (pp. 200-205.)

The Superior Wise Speaker

In 2:1, the first *expolitio* of 1:17, which also forms the proposition of the argument of 2:1-5, Paul denies that his preaching was notable in its speech or wisdom (λόγου ἢ σοφίας). To this denial, he adds one important word: ὑπεροχή, which means "*projection*" or "*prominence*," but is used metaphorically to mean "*pre-eminence*" or "*superiority*." In reference to language, it can also mean an excess of words ("*periphrasis*" or "*prolixity*," "a circuitous mode of speech" which can be "one of the virtues of oratory"[5]) as opposed to *ellipsis*,[6] in which an omission of words "causes a blemish."[7] Since Paul is speaking about rhetoric, the latter meaning fits the context nicely, and the reader with an ear trained in rhetorical theory and/or practice would doubtlessly catch it. This is especially true since the previous verse (1:31) has such a strong *ellipsis* which "imitates ordinary speech."[8]

However, the shape of Paul's argument forces this narrow stylistic meaning to a secondary reference. Paul is not speaking primarily of style; rather, he has just finished (in 1:17-30) moving the attention of his audience from speech to cultural notions of status. Thus, 2:1 might be translated, "*I have not come as a superior person in speech or (human) wisdom.*"[9] Or, taking the κατά with the accusative as "a circumlocution for the possessive or subjective

[5]Quint. 7.6.59-61.
[6]LSJ, 1867.
[7]Quint. 8.6.21.
[8]BDF, §481.
[9]BAGD, 841.

genitive," it might be translated as "When I came, I did not preach with the speech or wisdom of superiority [or excess]."[10]

Thus, with the addition of the word ὑπερόχη, the explicit reference expands to include not only rhetoric, but the superior social status of those who master it. But this was already implicit in 1:17, since, as we have seen, σοφία λόγου would normally be taken as status-related, especially in the context of rivalries and the opposition to the cross. The nature of this opposition is brought out in 1:18-25, as Paul develops the paradoxical topic of the saving power of the "foolish" and "powerless" (low-status) λόγος τοῦ σταυροῦ versus the boasted power (high status) of σοφία λόγου.

In a passage we have used to illustrate the popularized Stoic meaning of "wise," Plutarch describes the social superiority of one who is richer or more learned or more famous. This person is on terms of hospitality with commanders and men of wealth, and can boast of his ancestors' great successes. Such a person possesses the "superiority and influence (ὑπερόχην καὶ δύναμιν, cf. 1 Cor. 1:26) so coveted" by others. This superiority "in repute and honor (ἐν δόξῃ καὶ τιμῇ)" provokes jealousy (ζηλοτυπία, cf. ζηλόω, ζῆλος in 1 Cor. 3:3, 13:4; 2 Cor. 12:20) in men of ambitious character.[11]

We also find Diodorus Siculus using ὑπεροχή in a context of competition for social status, including eloquence. He describes Tiberius Gracchus as the offspring of a distinguished family on both sides, who surpassed others in his generation "in sagacity, in skill as a speaker (λόγου δεινότητι) and, in short, in every acquirement (πάσῃ παιδείᾳ)." This was demonstrated by his ability to hold his own in debate, despite the greater prestige (ὑπεροχή) of his opponents.[12]

Similarly, Eunapius describes Sosipatra, as one who "by her surpassing wisdom (ὑπεροχὴν σοφίας)" made her own sophist husband Eustathius seem inferior and insignificant. Her fame traveled so far that Eunapius thought it fitting to include even a woman in his catalogue ἀνδρῶν σοφῶν. She deserved this honor on the basis of her

---

[10]BDF, §224.

[11]Plut. *De frat. amor.*, *Mor.* 485A-486D.

[12]Diod. Sic. 34/35.5.5.

wealthy family, her beauty, decorum, charm, and supernatural abilities. Once she achieved her stature as σοφός,

> ever on her lips were the works of the poets, philosophers, and orators; and those works that others comprehend but incompletely and dimly, and then only by hard work and painful drudgery, she could expound with careless ease, serenely and painlessly, and with her light swift touch would make their meaning clear.

Establishing a chair of philosophy in her own home (by the fourth century, sophists and philosophers had become almost indistinguishable in Eunapius's eyes), her students "positively adored and revered the woman's inspired teaching," while others were "overcome by her beauty and eloquence (τῶν λόγων)."[13]

In another passage, Eunapius, like Paul in 2:1-4, opposes ὑπεροχὴν λόγου to ἀποδείξις: "Maximus is one of the older and more learned students (ἐκπεπαιδευμένων) who, because of his lofty genius and superabundant eloquence (λόγων ὑπεροχὴν) scorned all logical proof (ἀποδείξις)." That is, Maximus felt no need to demonstrate the truth of his claims because he was so eloquent, while Paul conversely claims to need no eloquence because the truth of his gospel is demonstrated by God. Further, like the behavior Paul criticizes in Corinth, Maximus boasted "how greatly I surpass the common herd (οἱ πολλοὶ)".[14]

We should also note that Eunapius added praise of his heroes' spiritual wisdom in the practice of the mysteries. Thus, in the late fourth century C.E., we find the easy mixture of eloquence and mystery religions which had only begun to appear in the first century. Some argue that we should read this kind of spiritual eloquence into the Corinthian situation. Certainly, any adequate reading must somehow relate spiritual issues and eloquence in the rhetorical situation, since Paul and his Corinthians are concerned with both. Further, the later texts illustrate how in the fourth century "wise speech" could be that of one who was educated, cultured, of high status, *and* wise in the ways of the mysteries. As Horsley points out, we see the same type of connection between eloquence and spiritual

---

[13]Eunap. *VS* 466-469.

[14]Ibid., 475.

wisdom in Hellenistic Judaism as represented in Philo and the Wisdom of Solomon.[15] But to Philo, in good Stoic fashion, the religiously wise and eloquent person need only be metaphorically rich, well-born, and powerful. Philo despised the naked ambitions of sophistry as much as did most other philosophers.

Thus, even if Paul's disclaimers of superiority in wisdom or rhetoric refer obliquely to mystical rather than worldly status, the common usage of the first century as well as Paul's own context indicate a primary reference to social status. The "superiority" he renounces is that of the social status gained through eloquence.

An emphasis on status within a religious community might seem to demand a mystical context. However, our intuitive category of "religion" does not seem to work so well in Paul's world.

> It is hard to see how anyone could seriously have related the phenomenon of Christianity to the practice of religion in its first-century sense. From the social point of view, the talkative, passionate and sometimes quarrelsome circles that met to read Paul's letters over their evening meal in private houses, or the pre-dawn conclaves of ethical rigorists that alarmed Pliny, were a disconcerting novelty. Without temple, cult statue or ritual, they lacked the time-honoured and reassuring routine of sacrifice that would have been necessary to link them with religion. Instead of mislocating them under such an unhistorical rubric, then, we must first work out how they would have struck other people, as well as how they would have explained themselves to others.[16]

In the same vein, Meeks points out that "Christian associations" differed from ancient religious cults because the latter "had little to do with ethics. . . . Such instruction belonged rather to the schools of philosophy and rhetoric, and to the public discourse of philosophers and orators."[17]

By claiming not to have appeared as a superior rhetor, Paul eschews the Hellenistic rôle of the ideal public figure. We find this ideal typically expressed by Aeschines (4th c. B.C.E.) in language echoed in the Corinthian correspondence: "He ought to be free-born

---

[15]Horsley, "Wisdom," 224-239.

[16]Judge, "Social Identity," 212.

[17]Wayne A. Meeks, *The Moral World of the First Christians*, Library of Early Christianity, ed. Wayne A. Meeks, 6 (Philadelphia: Westminster, 1986), 114.

. . . have as a legacy from his ancestors some service which they have done to the democracy, . . . [and] be an able speaker (δυνατὸν εἰπεῖν; [cf. 1 Cor. 2:2: 2 Cor. 10:10]), for it is well that . . . his training in rhetoric and his eloquence persuade the hearers (παιδείαν τὴν τοῦ ῥήτορος καὶ τὸν λόγον πείθειν τοὺς ἀκούοντας)."[18]

Paul continues his *expolitio* in 2:2, now amplifying corollaries of his denial of status: the cross of Christ and his own weakness. Just as in the verse he is amplifying (1:17), he follows his denial of status as a rhetor with his reference to the narrative of community foundations in his proclamation of the cross. When he spoke among the Corinthians, he "decided (κρίνω) to hold before his mind's eye (εἶδον)" nothing but the crucified Christ. In other words, when he aimed to persuade through his speech, he *could* have kept in view the normal cultural benefit of enhancing his own and his hosts' status; but he chose not to. Instead, he chose to employ a kind of rhetoric that offended such expectations. He was weak and in much fear and trembling (2:3), instead of being bold and confident as Quintilian urges:

> Of all these qualities the highest is that loftiness of soul which fear cannot dismay nor uproar terrify nor the authority of the audience fetter further than the respect which is their due. For although the vices which are its opposites, such as arrogance, temerity, impudence and presumption, are all positively obnoxious, still without constancy, confidence and courage, art, study and proficiency will be of no avail. You might as well put weapons in the hands of the unwarlike and the coward. . . . Trachalus appeared to stand out above all his contemporaries, when he was speaking. Such was the effect produced by his lofty stature, the fire of his eye, the dignity of his brow, the excellence of his gesture, coupled with a voice which . . . surpassed the voice of all tragedians that I have ever heard.[19]

Hartman comments that

> Paul may have cut a miserable figure as a preacher as measured by the standards of rhetoric, but here he turns that into a reflexion on how the contents of the message of the cross harmonized with the conditions of the message—and of the messenger. Paul consciously

[18]Aeschin. *In Ctes.* 169-70.

[19]Quint. 12.5.1-5.

> puts his weakness and his anxiety into contrast with the confidence with which he and his addressees know that a good speaker ought to appear, and through this "anti-rhetor" God performed great things.[20]

Despite his weaknesses as a rhetor, the Corinthians still found him persuasive. For this reason, we must be careful not to take his protestations too seriously. Professional rhetors often affected weakness in an ironic method "by which one urbanely displayed one's own skill by affecting the lack of it."[21] Despite Quintilian's insistence on boldness, strength, and confidence, he also recognizes that

> We shall derive some silent support from representing that we are weak, unprepared, and no match for the powerful talents arrayed against us, a frequent trick in the *exordia* [introductions] of Messala. For men have a natural prejudice in favor of those who are struggling against difficulties. . . . Hence arose the tendency of ancient orators to pretend to conceal their eloquence, a practice exceedingly unlike the ostentation of our own times.[22]

A good example of such use of irony is found in Dio Chrysostom. Dio was highly sophisticated in his rhetorical skills but, after his "conversion," far more serious about his philosophy. He modestly refers to his "inexperience in simply everything, but especially in speaking (τοὺς λόγους), recognizing that I am only a layman (ἰδιώτης, cf. 2 Cor. 11:6)."[23] Similar to Paul's refusal to enter into rhetorical competitions, Dio writes, "My purpose . . . was . . . [not] to range myself beside those who habitually sing such strains, whether orators or poets. For they are clever persons, mighty sophists, wonder-workers; but I am quite ordinary and prosaic in my utterance, though not ordinary in my theme."[24]

Whether relatively weak or strong as a rhetor, Paul persuaded the Corinthians to receive his gospel. But he insists yet a third time (2:4) that this persuasion was not due to his personal eloquence.

---

[20]Lars Hartman, "Some Remarks on 1 Cor. 2:1-5," SEÅ 39 (1974), 118.
[21]Judge, "Paul's Boasting," 37.
[22]Quint. 4.1.8-10.
[23]Dio Chrys. *Or.* 42.3.
[24]Idem, *Or.* 32.39.

Persuasive Wisdom

In Paul's *expolitio* of 1:17 and 2:1 found in 2:4, he again denies that his word or his proclamation are connected to wisdom. But now he adds yet another word, "πειθοῖς." Πείθω, to persuade, was the central aim of rhetoric. Thus, "οὐκ ἐν πειθοῖς σοφίας λόγοις (not in persuasive wise speech)" is the clearest reference to rhetorical speech. But this phrase has textual problems, primarily because the normal adjectival form is πιθανός. These problems may be resolved if we accept the alternative reading οὐκ ἐν πειθοῖ σοφίας, "not in persuasiveness of wisdom."[25] In any case, no matter how we reconstruct the text, critics agree that Paul's use of the πείθω word

---

[25]Conzelmann agrees with the reading of NA^{26} because of the strength of the manuscript tradition (א* B D pc vg^{st} sy^{p}). The majority of MSS (א² A C Ψ M vg^{cl}; Did) add ἀνθρωπίνης before σοφίας, but this is widely regarded as almost certainly an addition, thus strengthening the reading of the other texts.

However, the reading of NA^{26} has serious problems. Πειθός is an otherwise unattested adjectival form, see BAGD 639. Πιθανός is the normal and widely attested adjective for πείθω. Those who follow the majority MSS solve this problem by noting that such a form could have arisen from the verb on the analogy of φειδός from φείδομαι. This assumption is strengthened by noting that the church fathers did not object to it. However, φειδός is a rare form; otherwise verbal adjectives almost always occur in -τος. Thus the adjective πειθοῖς is a textual corruption of the noun πειθοῖ: see BDF, §§47.4, 112; cf. Ludwig Radermacher, *Neutestamentliche Grammatik: das Griechisch des neuen Testaments im Zusammenhang mit der Volkssprache*, 2nd ed., HNT 1 (Tübingen: J. C. B. Mohr, 1925), 63. Furthermore, the occurrences of πιθανός are so numerous that it seems unlikely that we have simply lost the alternative form, and that Paul ignored the common word to coin his own.

Given these difficulties, Zuntz has cogently argued that the correct reading is ἐν πειθοῖ σοφίας, "in persuasiveness of wisdom." The noun form πειθοῖ is attested by several witnesses (according to Leitzmann : d g Or Ambr; Zuntz adds f vg^{AD} Ambst Sedul), though more often with λόγοις or λόγων. Zuntz argues that λόγοις was a gloss "invited by one of the most frequent scribal errors, namely, the doubling of the initial sigma of σοφίας." P^{46} (followed by F G) provides strong evidence that λόγοις was added by later scribes to make sense of its puzzling ἐν πειθοῖς σοφίας. See G. Zuntz, *The Text of the Epistles: A Disquisition upon the Corpus Paulinum* (London: Oxford University Press, 1953), 23-25; D. Hans Lietzmann, *An die Korinther I-II*, 5th ed., HNT 9 (Tübingen: J. C. B. Mohr, 1969), 11; Weiss, 49; Fee (88), accepts this position because "this reading is unquestionably the *lectio difficilior* and more easily explains how the others came about than vice versa."

proposed above, we accept a reading which includes a form of λόγος, it joins "persuasion" with both key words we have been examining, "wisdom" and "word." Thus, any reader who has been left wondering just what wisdom is at issue in the letter is now firmly guided by the implied author: the "wisdom" or "wise speech" is nothing other than rhetoric.

Also significant in this verse (2:4) is Paul's contrast of πειθώ and απόδειξις (the alternative reading to NA[26] is also to be preferred because it puts these words in parallel grammatical construction). Aristotle generally distinguishes απόδειξις (demonstration) from διαλεκτικός (dialectic). The former employs syllogistic reasoning proceeding from our knowledge (γνῶσις) of necessary premises to produce scientific knowledge (ἐπιστημονικός or ἐπιστήμη),[26] while the latter employs inductive or syllogistic arguments (λόγοι) based on generally accepted opinions (ἔνδοξος or δόξα which are held by the σοφοί) to produce "proof" (πίστις) or knowledge (γνῶσις). Rhetoric (ρητορική or τέχνας τῶν λόγων) is a kind of dialectic, that which relies on persuasion (πιθανός).[27]

We should note the number of linguistic parallels with Paul's language here: απόδειξις, γνῶσις, πίστις, λόγος, ἔνδοξος (in the sense of honor, i.e., who or what is held in high opinion: 3:10), σοφός, and πειθώ are all key words in 1 Cor. Thus, in an Aristotelian sense, 2:4-5 would read: "Though my speech and my proclamation persuaded you so that you have πίστις, this is not because I used rhetorical methods to sway you to γνῶσις based on the opinions of those who are usually honored as wise. Rather, your faith is grounded on something far more sure than clever arguments based on opinion. Your faith is as secure as a scientific proof arising from our knowledge of the necessary truths of God's spirit and power."

I am not implying that the Aristotelian texts suggest a world in which Paul and the Corinthians were having philosophical discussions about types of reasoning. However, Aristotle's language and categories were widely influential, especially in the debate between philosophy and rhetoric outlined above in Chapter Two. Paul could

---

[26]Arist. *An. Post.* 1.2.16-25 (71b).

[27]Arist. *Top.* 1.1 (100a.18-100b.23), 1.4 (101b.11- 16), 1.8 (103b.1-7), 1.11 (104b.1-3); idem, *Rh.* 1.1.1-3 (1354a), 1.1.11 (1355a).

easily be confronting the Corinthians' attitudes toward rhetoric by appealing to such widespread and popular philosophical commonplaces as its criticism of rhetoric's reliance on δόξα and πίστις, as opposed to philosophy's ἀποδείξις and ἐπιστήμη.

Furthermore, not just the philosophers but also the rhetoricians liked the word ἀποδείξις. Even Aristotle recognized a kind of rhetorical ἀποδείξις. Thus, rhetorical "proof (πίστις) is a sort of demonstration (ἀποδειξίς τις), since we are most strongly convinced (πιστεύομεν) when we suppose anything to have been demonstrated (δεδεῖχθαι)." He is referring not just to any rhetoric, not to the rhetoric of *pathos* or *ethos*, but to the rhetoric of *logos*: "rhetorical demonstration (ἀπόδειξις ρητορική) is an enthymeme, which generally speaking is the strongest of rhetorical proofs (τῶν πίστεων)," for "the enthymeme is a kind of rhetorical syllogism."[28]

Aristotle's understanding of enthymemes as rhetorical ἀπόδειξις became part of standard rhetorical teaching, as we see in Quintilian:

> I now turn to arguments, the name under which we comprise the ἐνθυμήματα, ἐπιχειρήματα, and ἀπόδειξις of the Greeks, terms which, in spite of their difference, have much the same meaning. . . . Some call the enthymeme a rhetorical syllogism. . . . An ἀπόδειξις is a clear proof; hence the use of the term γραμματικαὶ ἀπόδειξεις, "linear demonstrations" by the geometricians. . . . All authorities . . . define both [the *apodeixis* and the *epicheireme*] in the same way, in so far as they call both a method of proving what is not certain by means of what is certain. . . . To all these forms of argument the Greeks give the name of πίστεις, a term which, though the literal translation is *fides* "a warrant of credibility," is best translated by *probatio*, "proof."[29]

In these passages by Aristotle and Quintilian we see in microcosm the struggle between philosophy and rhetoric. The philosopher wishes to define rhetoric as an inferior even if necessary form of reasoning, while the rhetorician wishes to define syllogistic reasoning as a part of rhetoric. In this latter sense, Quintilian approves of the study of geometry among the other subjects: "Even the orator will sometimes, though rarely, prove his point by formal logic. . . . The

[28]Arist. *Rh.* 1.1.11 (1355a).
[29]Quint. 5.10.1-8.

most absolute form of proof is that which is generally known as γραμματικαὶ ἀπόδειξεις."[30] We have already encountered this sense in Eunapius' description of Maximus, in phrases like Paul's, yet taking the opposite side. Maximus scorns the use of "logical proof" (ἀπόδειξις) because he boasts of "superabundant eloquence" (λόγων ὑπεροχήν).

Thus, even if the situation constructed by the historically informed reader does not intersect the world of the philosophical traditions, it should intersect with the ubiquitous world of rhetoric.[31] Limiting the context to rhetorical discussions, we would read 2:4-5 as: "Though my speech and my proclamation persuaded you so that you have πίστις, your πίστις is not a γνῶσις gained through rhetoric which swayed you on the basis of the opinions of those who are honored as possessing superior, wise eloquence. Rather, your faith is grounded on something far more sure than clever arguments based on opinion. Your faith is based on the most absolute form of proof—the sure proof of God's spirit and power."[32]

Wise Speech Humanly Taught

A third *expolitio* on the theme of σοφία λόγου appears in 2:13 in the midst of Paul's topic of an alternative to cultural wisdom. Paul again adds a new phrase to the familiar words, emphasizing that the wisdom he renounces comes through education. Education, as we have seen, generally means rhetorical education. Thus, when Paul asserts that "we speak not in words taught by human wisdom (λαλοῦμεν οὐκ ἐν διδακτοῖς ἀνθρωπίνης σοφίας λόγοις)," the most natural teacher would be the rhetorical schools, as in Aristonymous Gnomologous, "πολλοὶ τοὺς υἱοὺς ῥήτορας διδάσκουσιν."[33] Taking into account Paul's previous uses of σοφία and λόγος, the Hellenistic reader would find the meaning unmistakable.

---

[30]Ibid., 1.10.37-38.

[31]Cf. Bünker, 49.

[32]Cf. Judge, "Reaction," 11-12: Paul pinpoints "persuasiveness as the excess he wishes to avoid. This is because his test of truth is that it comes from God and is demonstrated in positive human relations." Cf. Hartman, 116.

[33]Aristonymous Gnomologous, *Apud Stobaeum*, 3.4.105, in LSJ, 421.

The thought here parallels that of 2:4, where Paul contrasts ordinary human understanding through persuasion with understanding through the spirit of God. The parallel thought is emphasized with parallel structure, some of which reaches back to 1:17:

1:17:	οὐκ ἐν σοφίᾳ λόγου
2:4:	οὐκ ἐν . . . σοφίας λόγοις ἀλλ' ἐν . . . πνεύματος
2:13:	οὐκ ἐν . . . σοφίας λόγοις ἀλλ' ἐν . . . πνεύματος

These parallels alert the reader that 2:13 is another *expolitio* of 1:17, further indicating that Paul is not changing subjects in 2:6-16. In that section, he uses words which he had not used before, suggesting that they reflect peculiar Corinthian usage. These words definitely echo uses in mystery religions. However, they also echo far wider uses.

For example, the verb γινώσκειν is used only once before (1:21) but appears five times in this passage. While such knowledge could concern religious mysteries, it might just as well be "merely a matter of greater insight into things spiritual, the product of education and culture."[34] This certainly seems to be the sense of γνῶσις in 8:1.[35]

Similarly the τέλειος can be one who has completed the initiation ceremonies into the mysteries, but in the philosophical tradition it can refer to the true wise man. In even more general usage, a τέλειος can be the perfect citizen. A similar expression, οἱ ἐν τέλει is "found throughout Greek literature as a designation for 'the influential,' 'those in office.'"[36] Thus, its use in the mysteries to express a certain religious status merely reflects the general status related meaning of "accomplished," applied to such competitors in eloquence as historians and sophists.[37] This is the sense Isocrates uses to describe a τέλειος ῥήτωρ, meaning an exceptionally polished rhetor as opposed to an ἰδιώτης.[38] Philo also writes of a τέλειος ῥήτωρ to refer to the philosophical ideal of a rhetor (as opposed to

---

[34]Welborn, "Discord," 105; cf. Theissen, 134.

[35]Marshall, 204, 215.

[36]Welborn, "Discord," 106.

[37]LSJ, 1769.

[38]Isoc. *Antidosis* 199-200.

the sophist) who possesses the perfect synthesis of wisdom and eloquence.[39]

Thus, when Paul reverses his rhetoric in 2:6, now claiming that he does speak wisdom among "accomplished, high-status persons," (τέλειοι), he draws in his audience. "Ah, yes," Paul's implied audience should be saying to themselves, "You mean us, the ones who can boast of our wisdom." But they can sit easy for only half a sentence, for then comes "but not (δὲ οὐ)" the wisdom of the rulers of this world. Like the term τέλειοι,

> the same ambiguity attaches to the term Paul uses to characterize those from whom God has hidden his wisdom: οἱ ἄρχοντες (2:6, 8). We need not deny that the word has mythical connotations in this context, amid talk of μυστήριον and σοφία ἀποκεκρυμμένη (2:7), to recognize that Paul refers to political powers.[40]

Nor is it difficult to understand the connection of rulers to rhetoric. Rhetoric had three main public purposes: the law court (judicial rhetoric); display and praise (epideictic rhetoric) and politics (deliberative rhetoric). Rulers depended heavily on their own or their cohorts' power to persuade. In Paul's rhetoric, their reliance upon and confidence in such power blinded them to the apparently weak wisdom of God, and so exercised their supposed power over Christ's supposed weakness by crucifying him. This same reliance upon cultural wisdom has led the Corinthians to think of themselves as ruling like kings (4:8).

In Paul's anti-rhetoric, the high status of the τέλειοι is reversed. Now, the πνευματικοί (2:13, 15; 3:1) whose wisdom is not cultural strength, but divine weakness, take their place. Thus, Paul spoke not in words taught in human schools, but in λόγοις διδακτοῖς πνεύματος. In Plutarch we find a similar comment on the contrast between speaking, which is taught by people, and silence, which is taught by revelation: "In speaking we have men as teachers (λέγειν ἀνθρώπους διδασκάλους ἔχομεν), but in keeping silent we have gods, and we receive from them this lesson of silence at initiations into the

---

[39]Philo *Deter.* 132-3.

[40]Welborn, "Discord," 106.

Mysteries."[41] Of course, Paul refers not to divine silence but to divine words, as he read in LXX Isaiah 54:13: πάντας τούς υἱούς σου διδακτοὺς θεοῦ.[42] Here and elsewhere, Paul's rhetorical world is shaped by the rhetoric of the LXX. For "Paul ... is writing the Greek of a man who has the Septuagint in his blood."[43] In Paul's world, incarnated in a grammar of the cross drawn from the LXX, one seeks to be wise in a far different sense than in the world of Greco-Roman culture.

The Larger World of Paul

As Petersen points out, the narrative world of 1 Cor. is "embedded in the larger world of Paul known from all of his letters."[44] Particularly important here is 2 Cor., since it either continues the same narrative or revises it. There, we again find rhetoric playing a major rôle in the rhetorical situation. But even in other texts where rhetoric is not a major part of the situation, it still appears as a fixture of Paul's world.

We have already noted in Paul's letter to the Thessalonians his opposition to the typical rhetorical tactic of employing flattering speech (ἐν λόγῳ κολακείας: 1 Thess. 2:4-5; cf. Gal. 1:10). Such flattery is a pretext for advantage or greed (προφάσις πλεονεξίας [1 Thess. 2:5]), and thus "seeks glory from men" (ζητοῦντες ἐξ ἀνθρώπων δόξαν, 1 Thess. 2:6). This had long been a widespread criticism of rhetoric. For example, Petronius complained that rhetors "think first about what is calculated to please their audience."[45] Even rhetors might agree with this assessment, since one of the primary goals of rhetoric was to delight (the others were to move and to instruct). This contrasts with Paul's claim to have renounced such

---

[41]Plut. *De garr.*, *Mor.* 505f.

[42]Cf. Aristonymous Gnomologous, above; also Prov. 1:23, where personified σοφία proclaims διδάξω δὲ ὑμᾶς τὸν ἐμὸν λόγον.

[43]Arthur Darby Nock, "The Vocabulary of the New Testament," in *Essays on Religion and the Ancient World*, Vol. 1, ed. Zeph Stewart (Oxford: Clarendon, 1973), 347.

[44]Peterson, *Rediscovering Paul*, 17.

[45]Petron. *Sat.* 3.

tactics. He does not try to please people (ἀρέσκω). As in the Corinthian situation, such contrasting behavior is linked to the hardship Paul endures in working rather than taking money from the Thessalonians (1 Thess. 2:9). This ethical limitation of rhetorical persuasion within right conduct supports Paul's claim that his λόγος is θεοῦ, not ἀνθρώπων (1 Thess. 2:13).

These parallels are remarkable because the rhetorical situations in 1 Cor. and 1 Thess. are so different. Thus, we should interpret the parallels as responding to stable aspects of varying situations; in other words general, not special cultural conditions. Such conditions of the culture at large included perceptions of public speakers in the ancient world, perceptions which were usually tied to the status indicators of education, money, power, and birth.

We can hear these same parallels in 2 Cor., especially in chapters 10-12, but also, even if less explicitly, in the earlier chapters (probably a separate letter addressing a different stage in the developing rhetorical situation). In 1:12, Paul reminds his readers of his renunciation of the wrong kind of wisdom, which he now calls σοφία σαρκική.[46] Paul calls his renunciation a "boast" (καύκησις), now using positively the same word he has used in 1 Cor. to criticize the Corinthians' behavior (though also to describe the proper kind of boast: in God). This irony he develops by contrasting his "boast" and the boasts of those who seek status. In contrast to such worldly people who attempt to impress the audience with their sophistication, Paul emphasizes his sufferings and weaknesses (1:8) and the ordinariness and simplicity of his rhetoric (1:13).

In 1:17, Paul again raises the contrast between his behavior and that of the worldly person, who says "yes" and "no" at once. Such vacillation was a part of rhetorical training, since such education taught students how to argue any side of a question. This lack of

---

[46]We need not read any esoteric meanings into σαρκικός. Rather, "Paul employs the adjective to contrast what is worldly, material, and human with what is spiritual and divine (10:4; Rom 15:27; 1 Cor 3:3; 9:11). The wisdom described here is therefore the same as that about which Paul had previously written to the Corinthians: 'the wisdom of (this) world' (1 Cor 1:20; 3:19); 'of this age' (1 Cor 2:6); 'human' wisdom (1 Cor 2:5, 13). Here, where the *sophia sarkike* is contrasted with the *grace of God*, Paul must be thinking of wisdom which, however perspicacious, is still only human and finite." Victor Paul Furnish, *II Corinthians*, The Anchor Bible 32A (Garden City, NY: Doubleday, 1984), 128.

commitment to a particular point of view was often admitted by rhetoricians as a necessary weakness of rhetorical art, and was criticized by philosophers who called for a rhetoric committed to truth alone.

Again in 2:17, we find typical criticisms of sophists: they sell their rhetoric with concern for their own profit, thus earning the critical label of "merchant" (καπηλεύοντες τὸν λόγον). Even merchants of wares were suspected of dishonesty, so one who sold his speech was doubly suspect.[47] "The word [καπηλεύω] is used in the polemic of philosophers against inauthentic sophists or philosophers who sell their teaching for money."[48] The strength of this insult might be gauged by the inclusion of 11 citations of κάπηλος in MacMullen's "Lexicon of Snobbery," intended to illustrate "the brutality and feeling of disgust shown by the upper classes to the masses."[49] This upper class rhetoric is reflected in Paul's diction, since he puts together οἱ πολλοί with καπηλεύω. Thus, we again find money and status at issue: Paul employs familiar invective to undermine the supposed higher status of his professional, eloquent opponents. And again, Paul contrasts the behavior of other speakers with his own commission: θεοῦ ἐν Χριστῷ ἐλαλομεν.

In 4:5, Paul again employs a *topos* common to the criticism of sophists and rhetors, particularly in the imperial period: "we do not proclaim ourselves." Rhetors and sophists had always liked to perform showpieces.[50] *Epideictic* rhetoric was sometimes defined as existing primarily to call attention to the speaker rather than to the

---

[47]"The ancient stereotype of the merchant was of a person concerned only for profit and quite willing to adulterate the product or give short measure for the sake of it. . . . The huckstering of both wares and ideas at the time of the Isthmian Games (sponsored by Corinth) is described by Dio Chrysostom (VIII, 9)." Furnish, 178. Cf. Windisch, "καπηλεύω," *TDNT*, Vol. 3, 604: In the LXX, κάπηλος in Is. 1:22 and Sir. 26:29 express the "characteristic sense. . . . Every merchant stands under the suspicion of being a deceiver, a sinner; the word has an evil ring about it."

[48]Furnish, 603, cf. 178. Also cf. Ronald F. Hock, *The Social Context of Paul's Ministry* (Philadelphia: Fortress, 1980), 53; Furnish, 178; Marshall 320-21, 346. Windisch lists references in Plato, Lucian, Philostratus, and Aelius Aristides.

[49]MacMullen, *Roman Social Relations*, 138-141.

[50]See below, Chapter Six, pp. 254-58.

speech or the audience;[51] thus it is not surprising that *encomia* became the primary form of speaking in the Second Sophistic.[52] With the end of the Republic, opportunities for meaningful civic oratory nearly disappeared and declamation became the major public speaking event. Since such a declamation aimed to accomplish little more than the enhancement of the speaker's glory, rhetoric was increasingly criticized as an empty exercise in which the only subject proclaimed was the speaker himself.

We hear this contrast of Paul's rhetoric with typical cultural practices within the context of the vocabulary of 4:2, in which Paul describes unacceptable preaching as that which adulterates (δολόω) the word of God. The same word in noun form (δόλος, cunning deceit) Paul uses in 1 Thess. 2:3-4 to characterize rhetoric that aims to please people rather than God. Here, the verb δολόω is paired with πανουργία (craftiness), which "in the NT, as in the anti-sophistic polemic of the Greco-Roman world, is usually pejorative: 'craftiness,' 'cunning,' etc.[53] The same pair of words is combined by Lucian with καπηλεύω (to huckster, see above on 2:17) to describe "philosophers [who] sell their wines—most of them [*hoi polloi*] adulterating and cheating and giving false measure."[54]

In 5:11-12, like 1 Cor. 2:4, we encounter the word most associated with rhetoric, πείθω (to persuade). In this context, we hear the familiar contrast with those who boast in appearances (τοὺς ἐν προσώπῳ καυχωμένους). And in further parallel with 1 Cor., Paul's behavior is likened to the crucified Christ (5:14). But in 5:11, Paul seems to claim for himself what he rejects in 1 Cor. 2:4 and Gal. 1:10: "Knowing the fear of the Lord, we persuade people." This contrast has puzzled commentators,[55] who generally tend to assume that Paul has been accused of employing worldly and deceptive

---

[51] Arist. *Rh.* 1.3.1-3 (1358a-1358b): In epideictic rhetoric, the hearer is a "mere spectator" who judges "the ability of the speaker."

[52] Kennedy, *Classical Rhetoric*, 103.

[53] Furnish, 218; cf. Betz, *Der Apostel*, 104-5.

[54] Lucian *Hermot.* 59, cited by Furnish, 178.

[55] e.g., Barrett, *Second Corinthians*, 163-64; Furnish, *II Corinthians*, 306, 322.

rhetoric,[56] but then cannot explain why he does not simply repeat his denial of rhetorical techniques.

Paul's positive use of πείθω is reinforced by a metaphor in which the apostles act as ambassadors (πρεσβεύομεν, 5:20), since such rôles were normally taken by professional orators. To some extent, this metaphor of ambassadors serves the same purpose as that of οἰκονόμος ("steward") in 1 Cor. 4:1-2 and 9:17. In both, Paul takes on a relatively lower status position (he is not free to speak for himself), while enhancing the authority of his speech (he speaks with the authority of God).[57] On the other hand, πρεσβεύω is a higher status term than οἰκονόμος, and allows a certain irony, since it could also mean "to rank before, take precedence, rule over."[58] But Paul's power is only derived, "as if God were issuing his demands through us (ὡς τοῦ θεοῦ παρακαλοῦντος δι᾽ ἡμῶν)." This metaphor of derived strength is followed by yet another contrasting image of the powerlessness of Christ: "God made him sin." In this way, Paul can claim that when he πείθει (persuades), his speech, as any other πειθώ (persuasion), results in πίστις (belief); yet at the same time, he never abandons the renunciation, which he introduced in 1 Cor. 1:17, of the worldly relationship of rhetoric with power and status. Thus, Paul's view of rhetoric has not shifted; his more positive use of the word πείθω must be related to an altered rhetorical situation (see below). For now, we need only note that once again, rhetoric and status remain key ingredients in the developing rhetorical situations in Corinth.

In chapters 10-12, the references to rhetoric continue. In 10:4b-5, Paul again boasts, now in a strong military metaphor, of the power of his own rhetoric: "We destroy arguments and every proud obstacle to the knowledge of God, and take every thought captive to obey Christ." Once again, this rhetorical power is contrasted to that which is κατὰ σάρκα (10:3).

Paul goes on to discuss the rhetoric of his letters versus that of his oral preaching. He admits that others say that he writes strong

---

[56]However, "not every rhetorical denial is an accusation turned around!" Betz, *Galatians*, 56, n. 115.

[57]See below, pp. 316-18.

[58]LSJ, 1462.

letters, but when present, that he is physically weak with poor speech (10:10). These apparently contradictory claims often puzzle modern exegetes. For example, Schmithals argues that Paul's letters couldn't be that different from his speech. Following this logic, we must once again look not to Paul's direct references to rhetoric, but to some esoteric understanding of weakness as lacking spiritual power.[59] But such arguments miss the importance of the last of the five basic parts of rhetoric: When present, any lack of physical attractiveness, or any deficiency in delivery would be cause for severe criticism and loss of status. For example, Quintilian advises the aging orator to retire before being ridiculed for possessing knowledge, but not vigor:

> The orator depends not merely on his knowledge, which increases with the years, but on his voice, lungs, and powers of endurance. And if these be broken or impaired by age or health, he must beware that he does not fall short in something of his high reputation as a master of oratory. . . . Domitius Afer . . . when far advanced in years . . . pleaded amid the unworthy laughter of some, and the silent blushes of others, giving occasion to the malicious saying that he had rather "faint than finish."[60]

Paul's physical bearing when preaching to the Corinthians (1 Cor. 2:3: "weakness and fear and trembling"), or just his admission of it, could have provoked similar ridicule.

But in letters, these weaknesses are not apparent. Judge correctly points out that Paul's letters were read aloud in the congregation.

> His contemporaries actually found his letters, read by others, more rhetorically effective than anything he was able to put forward in person. . . . Is it possible that his readers, being professionally trained, really could put his work across in a way Paul himself, ἰδιώτης τῷ λόγῳ, could not?[61]

Paul admits that he is weak in appearance and delivery and that he is an ἰδιώτης τῷ λόγῳ, but is also, like Quintilian's aging orator,

---

[59]Schmithals, 176, Käsemann, "Die Legitimität des Apostels", and Betz, *Der Apostel*, 58, argue that the opponents of Paul disputed *both* his rhetorical eloquence *and* the possession of pneumatic eloquence. While this is possible, it is not necessary to understand Paul's rhetoric.

[60]Quint. 12.11.2-3.

[61]Judge, "Paul's Boasting," 37.

not without knowledge (11:6). Ἰδιώτης τῷ λόγῳ[62] is usually translated "unskilled" in speaking. In this sense, ἰδιώτης is the opposite of δεινός (clever, skillful; often paired with σοφός, see above).[63] But if we restrict the semantic range to this meaning, we miss many nuances of ἰδιώτης.

An ἰδιώτης may be one who is quite well trained in rhetoric, but does not practice it professionally.[64] We must remember that virtually all educated people were rhetorically trained, but only a small percentage spoke in the courts or declaimed in public. Thus, even Isocrates is among the ἰδιῶται, i.e., those whose profession is less public than a statesman or orator. Isocrates was certainly skilled and "professional" in our sense of the term; but he was an ἰδιώτης because he wrote but did not deliver speeches, claiming he was not gifted at the latter.[65] In this sense, the vast majority of Isocrates's students left school to enter private life (as ἰδιῶται). Only two or three a year enter public life, those who are "wiser in speech" (σοφωτέροι ἐν τοῖς λόγοις) and who are champions (ἀγωνιστάς) in the contests of oratory. Yet "those who have preferred to live in private have become more gracious in their social intercourse, keener judges of discourses (τῶν λόγων κριτάς, cf. 1 Cor 4:3) and more prudent counselors than most."[66] To Isocrates, at least, an ἰδιώτης is not necessarily an unwise or unskilled speaker, but one who may be well trained to compete in contests of verbal wisdom in writing or in more private settings, such as dinners (see below). Just such private settings, rather than the public ones of the professional orator, seem to have provided opportunities for Paul's speech.[67]

This is also brought out by Sextus Empiricus who uses ἰδιώτης to refer to the "private person" who hires an orator to speak for him.

---

[62]Betz, *Apostel*, 66; and Judge, "Paul's Boasting," amply illustrate how this "admission" could have been no more than irony for rhetorical effect.

[63]LSJ, 374.

[64]Kennedy, *NT Interpretation*, 95.

[65]Isoc. *Against the Sophists* 14.

[66]Idem, *Antidosis* 200-204 (including Norlin's notes).

[67]Stanley Kent Stowers, "Social Status, Public Speaking and Private Teaching: The Circumstances of Paul's Preaching Activity," *NovT* 26, 1984; cf. Judge, "Early Christians," 125-137.

We should also note Sextus' other descriptions of the ἰδιώτης.[68] Such a "common" or "plain" (ἀφέλεια: artless, simple; in rhetoric: simple, affecting simplicity or artlessness of style[69]) person's speech is itself "ordinary" (τόν ἰδιωτικὸν τύπον), and characterized by "weakness" (ἀσθένεια, cf. I. Cor. 1:27, 4:10; II. Cor. 10:10, 11:21, etc.), as opposed to that of the rhetor, whose speech is characterized by "airs of superiority" (ὑπεροχαῖς, cf. 1 Cor 2:1) and trickery (πανουργία, cf. 1 Cor. 3:19, II. Cor 4:2, 11:3, 12:16). But it is the very artlessness and weakness which, Sextus argues, actually makes the speech of the ἰδιώτης more persuasive than that of the trained orator, whose trickery and airs of superiority are despised by ordinary people.[70] Thus, ἰδιώτης λόγος means "everyday speech."[71] Similarly, as we saw above, Dio Chrysostom could claim to be more persuasive because he was an ἰδιώτης.[72]

A similar contrast appears in Plutarch. He reports that Aristarchus jeered at the crowd of sophists (πλῆθος τῶν σοφιστῶν) by saying "that in the old days there were barely seven Sophists [the Seven Wise Men], but that in his own day an equally large number of non-sophists (ἰδιώτας) could not easily be found."[73] This passage is particularly interesting, since here we find Plutarch referring to the Seven Wise Men of his *symposion* as the archetypes for the sophistry which became debased by too many claimants to the title. In his mockery of this competition, all claim to be sophists rather than ἰδιῶται. But Paul, by calling himself ἰδιώτης, resists this pretentious, competitive tendency.

But even this admission does not disqualify him from the claim of articulating an intelligible and weighty message. Plutarch explicitly uses the term in this sense in relation to the conviviality of the dinner party. The ἰδιῶται could refer to "men without erudition" as opposed to "learned men" (πεπαιδευμένων); but such ἰδιῶται may still be relatively articulate and knowledgeable: "If some few men

---

[68]Sext. Emp. *Math.* 2.83.

[69]LSJ, 287.

[70]Sext. Emp. *Math.* 2.76-83.

[71]LSJ, 819, citing Dion. Hal. *Dem.* 2 and Longinus 31.2.

[72]Dio. Chrys. *Or.* 42.3 (quoted above, p. 194).

[73]Plut. *De frat. amor.*, *Mor.* 478C.

without erudition are present, included in a large company of learned men . . . they will take no wholly inarticulate part in talk and ideas."[74] Again, Paul could be saying, "I may not be a wise and witty conversationalist, but I still have something important to say."

'Ἰδιώτης can also refer explicitly to social status. As we have already seen in Isocrates, from it's basic meaning, a "private person," derives its common use to mean "one in a private station, as opposed to one holding public office, or taking part in public affairs." Thus, it could mean one who did not have the status of a ῥήτωρ, an ἄρχων (cf. 1 Cor. 2:6-8) or a βασιλεύς (cf. 1 Cor. 4:8). Going further, it can mean "an average man" as opposed to a person of distinction, or a "common man" or "plebeian."[75] For example, Plutarch ridicules the flatterer for confusing a "private citizen" (ἰδιώτης) or the "poor" with a "ruler" or the "rich."[76]

Thus, we see that Paul's admission of his status as ἰδιώτης τῷ λόγῳ fits the whole context of competition over social status related to rhetoric. The continuation of this issue into 2 Cor. adds coherence to the argument that rhetoric and status are part of Paul's exigence in 1 Cor. This argument is enhanced by a general observation about 2 Cor. which parallels what we have noted about 1 Cor. 1-4:

> One is struck in particular by the fact that there is no direct information about the 'doctrinal' stance of the opponents, not even in 11:4. Whatever doctrinal basis the actions and attitudes of Paul's rivals may have had, the actions and attitudes themselves are what Paul attacks, so the personal dimensions of the conflict are much more apparent than the doctrinal aspects of it. One of the merits of Theissen's analysis of the situation at Corinth is his recognition that *social* as well as *theological* differences separated Paul from his opponents, and that one of the key points at issue was the apostle's decision to remain financially independent of his congregation.[77]

Not only Theissen, but Hock and Marshall point to the issue of financial support as continuing through the two letters, an issue

---

[74]Plut. *Queast. conv.*, 1.1 (*Mor.* 613E).

[75]LSJ, 819.

[76]Plut. *Quomodo adululator ab amico internoscatur*, *Mor.* 58F; cf. idem, *Conv. sept. sap.*, *Mor.* 157C.

[77]Furnish, *II Corinthians*, 53.

always important to the tenuous social status of teachers. Hock argues that Paul's perceived status as a sophist was diminished in the eyes of those with upper class pretensions because he worked as an artisan, which was perceived by upper class persons as servile activity.[78] In other words, "expecting to be paid for one's eloquence is seen by the Corinthians as a mark of professional eminence; in contrast Paul is depicted as an amateur (an ἰδιώτης) or worse.[79] Marshall accepts this, but argues that more central to Paul's exigence, at least in 2 Cor., was the dishonor and loss of status Paul's hosts and patrons suffered when he refused their gifts. This loss of honor and status also threatened to produce a loss of power, since the exchange of gifts functioned to build alliances. For these reasons, the Corinthians, following the lead of their higher status leaders, rejected Paul in favor of apostles who would play the cultural game of enhancing the status of the patrons by playing the rôle of sophists who allowed their hosts to outdo their teaching with gifts of money.[80]

But we also see different exigences addressed in 1 Cor. 1-4 and 2 Cor. In 1 Cor., we have no hint of outsiders, while throughout 2 Cor. we encounter ample evidence that they have arrived.[81] Furthermore, in 1 Cor., Paul resists any characterization of him as a wise orator, pointing instead to his weaknesses as a speaker (a

---

[78]Hock, 60-64.

[79]Meeks, *First Urban Christians*, 72.

[80]Marshall, 243, 276, 326-340, 359, 397.

[81]"It has too often been assumed that the troubles with which Paul deals in these chapters were a simple continuation of those that appear in the first epistle; in particular that the trouble-makers of the second epistle are the same persons as those described in I Cor. 1:12 as the Christ-group. . . . Important, . . . however, is the simple but too often neglected observation that whereas I Cor. 1.12 deals with native inhabitants of the Corinthian church, 2 Cor. 10-13 is directed against strangers who intrude themselves into the church from without." Barrett, *Essays*, 14; cf. Furnish, 52.

common rhetorical device in certain situations to strengthen persuasive appeal). In 1 Cor., he addresses an audience who perceives him as a Hellenistic σοφός suitable for divisive allegiance. But in 2 Cor., the tables have been turned on Paul. No longer is the problem an over-valuation of his rhetorical skills by some; now the Corinthians have rejected Paul as an inferior rhetor compared to the "super-apostles." To preserve his authority, Paul must defend himself as a credible rhetor, yet still within his theological constraint of the cross, which opposes cultural sources of power and status.

Implicit References Linking Rhetoric and Status in I Corinthians

Wise Man or Fool?

After introducing his themes of wisdom, speech, and cross in 1 Cor. 1:17, Paul expands these in 1:18 by contrasting wise speech with the foolish speech of the cross. Listening with an ear for common usage, we must ask whose speech is considered foolish.

The "fool" is the standard antonym for the "wise." Thus, the fool was the loser in the competition for the honor of being considered wise. Since, as we have seen, this competition generally included verbal skills, the foolish speaker in contrast to the wise speaker is a familiar figure in Greco-Roman literature. The foolish speaker is one who does not use speech in accordance with cultural expectations.

One of the most common fools in Greco-Roman literature is the chatterer, who, according to Horace, lacks *communis sensus* (here, *savoir faire*, sense of propriety)[82] so that he is avoided by persons of culture. Thus, Plutarch writes in his essay *De Garrulitate* that the chatterer (ἀδολέσκος) is he who is not σοφός because he will not receive σοφοὺς λόγους.[83] Rather, his speech is like the foolish talk (μωρολογία, cf. 1 Cor. 1:18) of a drunken man.[84] He is unlike those "who can pack much sense into a short speech [who] are more

[82]Hor. *Sat.* 1.3.66-77.

[83]Plut. *De garr.*, *Mor.* 502C.

[84]Ibid., 504B.

cf. 1 Cor. 1:26) and royal (βασιλικός, cf. 1 Cor. 4:8) education (παιδεία)."[86] The chatterer lacks the great virtues of

> hearing and being heard; neither of these can happen to talkative persons, but even in that which they desire especially they fail miserably. . . . They desire listeners and cannot get them, but every one runs away headlong. If men are sitting in a public lounge or strolling about in a portico, and see a talker coming up, they quickly give each other the counter-sign to break camp. . . . When a chatterbox comes into a dinner-party [συμποσία] or social gathering, every one grows silent, not wishing to furnish him a hold. . . . And so it is a talker's lot . . . to find . . . as table companions . . . only conscripts.[87]

The chatterer's great sin is his inability "to secure listeners who either pay attention or believe what they say. . . . The speech (λόγος) of babblers is ineffectual and fruitless."[88] Their attitude was inconceivable to a rhetorically cultured Greek, for they "appear to regard speech as the least valuable of all things. They do not, therefore, meet with belief (πίστις) which is the object of all speech. For this is the proper end and aim of speech, to engender belief in the hearer; but chatterers are disbelieved even if they are telling the truth."[89] In contrast to such fools, Plutarch praises the persuasiveness (πειθώ, cf. 1 Cor. 2:4) and charm (χάρις) of the orator Lysias.[90]

Such a fool who fails to use language in a socially acceptable manner suffers a loss of prestige: "Speech (λόγος), which is the most pleasant and human of social ties, is made inhuman and unsocial by those who use it badly and wantonly, because they offend those whom they think they please, are ridiculed for their attempts at gaining admiration, and are disliked because of the very means they employ to gain affection."[91]

Not just the chatterer, but any loser in the competition was in danger of being called a fool. For example, Plutarch reports that

---

[86]Ibid., 506C.
[87]Ibid., 502E-503A.
[88]Ibid., 503B.
[89]Ibid., 503D.
[90]Ibid., 504C.
[91]Ibid., 504E.

Dionysius the Elder, ruler of Syracuse from 405-367 B.C.E., entered a contest in speech. Rather than losing as a fool, he won as a king:

> Dionysius the Elder, when the speakers who were to address the people were drawing by lot the letters of the alphabet to determine their order of speaking, drew the letter M; and in answer to the man who said, 'You speak foolishly (μωρολογεῖς), Dionysius,' he replied, "No! Monarch I am to be," and after he had addressed the people he was at once chosen general by the Syracusans.[92]

This same story of Dionysius is related by Diodorus Siculus in a way that further illustrates the status relations of rhetoric. In Diodorus's account, Dionysius attacks the oligarchical power of the current rulers, using democratic rhetoric: "Consequently he advised them to choose as generals not the most influential citizens (δυνατωτάτους, cf. 1 Cor. 1:26) but rather . . . the more humble (ταπεινοτέρους, cf. 2 Cor. 7:6, 10:1, 11:7)" who will not plunder the country "since they fear their own weakness (ἀσθένειαν, cf. 1 Cor. 1:25-27, 2:3, 4:10, 8:7-12, 9:22, 12:22; 2 Cor. 11:21-30, 12:5-10, 13:4-9)." Thus stirring up the crowed "by suiting every word of his harangue to the people to the predilection of his hearers," the people chose Dionysius as their general. He built up his power by appealing to the people's envy of the most influential citizens (δυνατωτάτοις) who they stigmatized as superior (ὑπεροχή, cf. 1 Cor. 2:1).[93] As we can see from this diction, and as we shall see further in the next chapter, Paul employs such democratic rhetoric of weakness as a counter to the more normal upper-class oligarchic rhetoric of status. Here, we can see that Dionysius may sound like a fool when judged by such oligarchic standards, but he demonstrates his lack of foolishness through the power of his rhetoric. He is no fool because his "weak" appeal to the people becomes strength.

---

[92]Plut. *Regum et imperatorum apophtegmata*, *Mor.* 175C-D.

[93]Diod. Sic. 13.91.4-93.3.

Thus, when we hear Paul's rhetoric with the ears of a Hellenist, we discern that when he asserts that his word is foolish, he is contrasting his own low status position to the high status position of the wise. He speaks as one who has no influence, one who knows not how to use language properly, who cannot claim the honorific title of σοφός, one who has no friends, who is indeed powerless in a society where power depends on such friendship. But from such rhetoric of weakness, paradoxically, flows power.

Wisdom: Human and Divine

"Foolish speech" is introduced by Paul to set up a paradox about his "word of the cross." This λόγος is speech about a person of the lowest status: a crucified criminal. Such speech must be considered weak and foolish, for it celebrates the opposite of all upper class values enshrined in the canons of rhetoric. But Paul's rhetoric forces the context away from upper class values to the community's narrative of origins and self-identity: "to us who are being saved. . . . We preach Christ crucified . . . to those who are called" (1:18, 24). When seen in this context, what the culture calls foolish the community ought to call powerful and wise.

This paradox leads him to general theological reflection in 1:19 in his citation of Isaiah 29:14. Here, and again in other citations in 1:26-31 and 3:19-20, Paul argues that Scripture addresses the situation he encounters in Corinth. Although we should not be too quick to assume that Paul interprets these citations in the light of their original contexts, the passages to which he points all prescribe humility for those who exalt themselves on account of their wisdom.

In addition to these negative connotations of wisdom, Paul uses σοφία positively in 1:24, 30; 2:6-7; 3:10; 6:5, and 12:8, against the negative connotations elsewhere. The reader can best make sense of this apparent contradictory usage by assuming that Paul finds some distinction between good wisdom and bad. Since both the rhetorical situation and the contexts of the three citations include seeking status on the basis of wisdom, we would do well to look for the distinction not in particular wisdom theologies, but in the ethical issues of seeking to achieve status in human eyes.

potter. (29:16)[94] For this reason, the poor and those without hope shall be exalted (29:19), while the arrogant man (ὑπερήφανος) perishes.

In 1:26, Paul recalls the language of LXX Jer. 9:22, and cites 9:23 in 1:31. By setting the σοφός in the list with the strong and the rich, the Jeremiah passage critiques those who boast in their intellectual, political, and economic power. Jer. 9:23/1 Cor. 1:31 emphasize that the issue is not boasting itself, but boasting in one's self instead of in God: i.e., the issue is who is exalted.[95]

In 3:19, Paul cites Job 5:12-13, lines from a speech of Eliphaz. Again, the wise man (σοφός) is overthrown by God because he is crafty (πανούργως, πολυπλόκος). These wise men are the counselors to the mighty, whom Eliphaz prays might perish in war, while the weak (ἀδύνατος, cf. 1 Cor. 1:26) escape from the hand of the politically powerful (δυνάστης). But in Job, like Isaiah, wisdom can be positive. Thus, God is σοφός διανοίᾳ (9:4), and his σοφία is δύναμις (11:6, 12:12); righteous people may also have wisdom (12:2) and be called σοφός (15:2, 18) because God gives his wisdom to them (15:8).

The other citation in 3:20, of LXX Ps. 93:11, strongly guides the reader who knows the Psalm to distinguish positive from negative wisdom. Paul changes the word ἀνθρώπων to σοφῶν, even though ἀνθρώποι appear as a synonym in the next verse. This emphasizes Paul's close association of the two words when σοφία carries the negative connotation (2:5: σοφία ἀνθρώπων). In the Psalm (v. 8), the fools (μωροί) are those who do not know God's wisdom (συνήσις, φρονήσις) These fools are the unrighteous powerful, those who kill widows and orphans (v. 6). Those with such foolish ways of thinking are bidden to be instructed by the Lord (παιδεύω, διδάσκω, vv. 10, 12, cf. 1 Cor. 2:13), for he teaches knowledge (γνῶσις, cf. 1 Cor 1:5). Thus, Paul alters the wording so that it fits his context, but at the same time is faithful to the sense of the Psalm in distinguishing the foolishness of human wisdom versus the human need of divine

---

[94]Cf. the citation of Is. 64:4 in 2:9, where the issue is again sin, not doctrine, and where again in close context comes the image of the potter and the clay (64:8).

[95]Gail R. O'Day, "Jeremiah 9:22-23 and 1 Corinthians 1:26-31: A Study in Intertextuality," *JBL* 109 (1990) 259-267.

wisdom. Furthermore, this human wisdom is once again characterized by rebellious misuse of power.

Paul's Septuagintal rhetoric draws the reader into a world in which wisdom can be either good or bad. Good wisdom teaches humility before God; this is the same humility commended in further citations: in 2:9 of Isaiah 64:4 and in 2:16 of Isaiah 40:13. Bad wisdom is a human stance which arrogantly uses knowledge and power for one's own exaltation.

The Wise Man, the Scribe, and the Debater

The contrast in 1:18 between those who are perishing (ἀπολλυμένοι) and those who are being saved (σωζομένοι) not only moves the discourse from cultural to community identity, it also locates that identity within the larger narrative of God's salvific activity. This narrative of universal salvific activity continues in 1:19, which appeals to the long-standing theological dynamic of human versus divine wisdom.

Having universalized the discussion in this manner, Paul employs an *expolitio* of 1:19 in 1:20, repeating the sense of the citation in phrases redolent with more language from Isaiah,[96] but now expanding the term σοφός with the list σοφός, γραμματεύς, and συζητητής. Taken in this universalized sense, σοφός becomes a generic term for a person, whether Greek or Jew, who claims to be humanly wise. This is borne out by the following terms which refer to scholars of both the Jewish and Hellenistic worlds.

---

[96]LXX Is. 19.11-12: "The princes of Tanis shall be fools (μωροὶ), as for the king's wise (σοφοὶ) counselors, their counsel shall be turned into folly (μωρανθήσεται). . . . Where are now your wise men (σοφοί)?" 33:6, 18 reaches back to 1 Cor. 1:18: "Our salvation (σωτηρία) is our treasure: there are wisdom (σοφία) and knowledge (ἐπιστήμη). . . . Where are the scribes (γραμματικοί [Aquila: γραμματεῖς])? Where are the counselors? Where is the one who counts the people?"

The Debater

The third term, συζητητής, while unusual, is easily understood as a "disputant," i.e., one who jointly inquires into a matter.[97] Such a dispute (ζητῆμα) may be a philosophical investigation or an official or judicial inquiry,[98] i.e., a rhetorical exercise by a philosopher or rhetor. Thus, "debater" is a good translation for the disputant familiar in Corinth, from law courts to lecture halls to dining rooms.

Just as the Corinthians would have tended to view Paul as a σοφός, so too does he fit the mold of a συζητητής. A ζητῆμα, notes Quintilian, is the "main question" of a case is "on which two or more plausible opinions may be advanced."[99] Debate (*altercatio*) on this and lesser questions Quintilian describes in the following passage which I quote at some length, because of the striking similarities to the type of rhetoric Paul employs in his correspondence:

> The art of debate turns on invention alone, does not admit of arrangement, has little need for the embellishments of style, and makes no large demand on memory or delivery. . . . Debate consists of attack and defense . . . This brief and discontinuous form of oratory. . . . consists of questions and replies. . . . Even mediocre speakers have not without some reason acquired the reputation of being good advocates simply by their excellence in debate. Some on the other hand think they have done their duty to their clients by an ostentatious and fatiguing display of elaborate declamation and straightway march out of court attended by an applauding crowd and leave the desperate battle of debate to uneducated performers who often are of but humble origin. . . .
>
> For debate the chief requisites are a quick and nimble understanding and a shrewd and ready judgment. For there is no time to think. . . . The skilled debater must be able to control his tendency to anger. . . . The statements of our opponents have not merely to be refuted: they are often best treated with contempt, made light of or held up to ridicule, methods which afford unique opportunity for the display of wit. . . . The debater's task is not one that suits a meek temper or excessive modesty. . . . Those who have given a careful study to the arguments that are likely to be pro-

[97]LSJ, 1670.

[98]LSJ, 756; cf. Kennedy, *Rhetoric in the Roman World*, 15.

[99]Quint. 3.11.1-4.

> duced by their opponents or the replies which may be made by themselves are almost always ready for the fray.[100]

Such debates characterized not only an important court-room activity, but that form of declamation known as the *controversiae*: "It is most profitable to agree with a fellow student on some subject, real or fictitious, and to take different sides, debating it as would be done in the courts."[101] Even on the secondary level, as Theon's *Progymnasmata* show (esp. Ch. 10), students learned the tools for this kind of debate. In the exercises and declamations, wit and wisdom were even easier to display, since one's opponent was only imaginary. Thus, the συζητητής, in the context of Paul's rhetoric about rhetoric, most naturally refers to the rhetorician skilled at declamation and extemporaneous courtroom displays. Increasingly, such persons were called sophists, and were sought by all status seekers as prizes.

Grammateus

The second term, γραμματεύς, is more puzzling. Given the emphasis on Hellenistic wisdom both in the rhetorical situation and in Paul's universalizing rhetoric, it is understandable why Barrett and the NIV understand γραμματεύς as a generic term for a Hellenistic "scholar."[102] However, as Fee correctly points out,[103] "it is simply not found among Greeks for their scholars or teachers." Rather, as Schmithals asserts, γραμματεύς in this context "is terminologically unambiguous: γραμματεύς is, as a translation from סופר, a technical term for the Jewish teacher of the law."

However, Schmithals is not justified in concluding "that Paul in his argumentation against the wisdom of the world also sets himself

---

100Ibid., 6.4.

101Ibid.

102LSJ, 359, referring to Aesch. *Fr.* 358, but noted as *si vera lectio.* Indeed, it is difficult to read the passage in this way; the sense seems rather to be "an able writer." The passage is also quoted by Plutarch, *Quest. conv.*, *Mor.* 625D.

103Fee, 70. Among Greeks and Hellenists, it is a very frequent term for clerk or secretary, including titles of town officials with considerable status. However, this translation would not fit into the list: "Where is the wise man, where is the secretary, where is the debater of this age?"

against Jewish theology."[104] This conclusion seems obvious to Schmithals, since he assumes that we must be looking for theological "contents" disembodied from social contexts. Schmithals's logic forces him to interpret Paul as meaning that all wisdom, Jewish and Greek, is opposed to God. But we have already pointed out that Paul, like the Scripture he cites as authoritative, finds only certain kinds of wisdom objectionable. Certainly the man who wrote that "the law is holy, and the commandment is holy and just and good (ὁ νόμος ἅγιος καὶ ἡ ἐντολὴ ἁγία καὶ δικαία καὶ ἀγαθή)" (Rom. 7:12) and that he himself was was "as to the law a Pharisee, . . . as to righteousness under the law blameless (κατὰ νόμον Φαρισαῖς . . . κατὰ δικαιοσύνην τὴν ἐν νόμῳ γενόμενος ἄμεμπτος)" (Phil. 3:5-6) was not opposed to the wisdom of the law, even as interpreted by scribes.[105]

Even without recourse to other letters, we find no basis in 1 Cor. for seeing Jewish theology under attack. Particularly important is 1:22, where Paul identifies the wisdom at issue as that sought by Greeks, not Jews.

> It is this clear statement of Paul's that makes it so difficult to root the use of wisdom in this passage in the Jewish wisdom tradition as many do. The fact that Paul identifies it as a Greek characteristic and then uses all his rhetorical energy *against* "the wisdom of this world," which the *Greeks* seek, seems to demand a Hellenistic derivation of the Corinthian position; unless, of course, it is to be found, as Horsley argues, in Hellenistic Judaism, which Paul perceived to be more Greek than Jewish. But that, too, seems doubtful.[106]

It is doubtful, Fee argues, because "if Paul is attacking a form of Hellenized Judaism, it is most perceptible as Hellenism, not Judaism."[107] Fee finds many other indications that 1 Cor. addresses a predominantly Gentile audience, including the mention of the Corinthians' former idolatry (6:10-11; 8:7; 12:2) and their practice of

---

[104]Schmithals, 27.

[105]The literature on Paul and the law is extensive, but see especially E.P. Sanders, *Paul and Palestinian Judaism* (Philadelphia: Fortress, 1977).

[106]Fee, 74, n. 32.

[107]Ibid., 14, n. 36; cf. Munck, 148-149.

attending pagan temple feasts (8:1-10:22).[108] "Nothing in the letter *cannot* be explained in the light of its Greco-Roman origins; whereas several items are extremely difficult to explain on the hypothesis of Hellenistic Jewish origins."[109] "Thus, the picture that emerges is one of a predominantly Gentile community. . . . Although they were the Christian church in Corinth, an inordinate amount of Corinth was yet in them, emerging in a number of attitudes and behaviors that required radical surgery without killing the patient."[110] That is, the exigence was not Hellenistic-Jewish doctrine, but "attitudes and behaviors" of Hellenistic culture.

Such Hellenistic "attitudes and behaviors" were not absent from Judaism in Paul's day. In certain respects, Jews reflected general Hellenistic tendencies. Since Paul's rhetoric appears to address such tendencies rather than specific doctrines, we might enrich our understanding of the rhetorical situation by looking for attitudes rather than doctrines. The rhetorical force of the γραμματεύς, then, might be to amplify the same social tendencies of status seeking which Paul perceives as related to the divisions in Corinth.

---

[108]Fee, 4.

[109]Ibid., 14.

[110]Ibid, 4. Ironically, the only text which offends a reading of 1 Cor. as addressed to Gentile tendencies is 1:22-23; for why would Paul mention the Jewish tendency to seek signs and to find the cross a cause of stumbling if peculiarly Jewish error is not an issue? The answer may be that, as Conzelmann points out, Paul *theologically* equates the Jews' seeking signs with the Greeks seeking wisdom, since both exalt human judgement over divine activity. This may be understood as a universalizing rhetorical and theological move to include the Jews in the audience, much like Rom. 2:17-3:19. But since, unlike in Romans, Paul gives no further attention to peculiarly Jewish concerns (except for the collection for Jerusalem in 16:1-3), the reader is not helped by including any such concerns in the exigence. In fact, Jews reappear only in strongly universalizing passages (a universalizing tendency which is also the theological intent of Romans and Galatians): 1 Cor 9:20, 12:13. Rather than focus on peculiar Jewish errors, Paul theologically and rhetorically includes Jews in the exigence spawned by Hellenism.

Scribes and Social Status

"Scribe" named a variety of Jewish rôles, including many which overlapped those of Greek and Roman clerks. But this type of Jewish clerk fits no better into Paul's list than their gentile counterparts. On the other hand, a scribe could also be a Jewish scholar,[111] which fits quite well into the list: "Where is the wise man, where is the Jewish scholar, where is the Greek debater of this age?"[112]

1) Ben Sira

The social rôle of the Jewish scribe in the Hellenistic period is most fully described by Ben Sira. Here, particularly in Sirach's grandson's Greek translation known in Paul's world, we find the scribes' social rôle overlapping that of other Hellenistic scholars. We also find scholarship characterized as "wisdom":

> The wisdom of the scribe (σοφία γραμματέως) comes with the
> wealth and time for leisurely scholarly pursuits (σχολή).
> whoever is free from toil can become wise.
> How can one become wise who guides the plow . . . ?
> So with every engraver and designer . . .
> So with the smith sitting by the anvil . . .
> So with the potter sitting at his wheel . . .
>
> They are not sought out for the council of the people,
> nor are they prominent in the assembly.
> They do not sit on the judge's bench,
> nor can they understand law and justice.
> They cannot expound the instruction of wisdom,
> nor are they found among the rulers.

---

[111]Encyclopedia Judaica (Jerusalem: Keter, 1972) 15:81-82. Talmudic literature uses סו פר for Torah scholars and copyists. But in earlier literature, scribes appear alongside other notables (I Macc. 7:12-13,; Test. Patr. Levi 8:17; Jos. Ant. 12:142; Luke 11:42-52), and are the equivalent of sages and elders, or even office-holders in the Temple and courts.

[112]Judge ("Reaction," 11) argues that "In 1 Cor 1:20 Paul challenges the three main types of tertiary scholar of his world: the rationalistic philosopher ('the wise'), the Jewish legal expert ('the scribe') and the rhetorician ('the debator')." Cf. Hartman, 119.

How different the person who devotes himself to the fear of God
and to the study of the Law of the Most High!

He is in attendance on the great,
and has entrance to the ruler.
He travels among the peoples of foreign lands.

Many will praise his understanding;
his fame endures to the end of the age (τοῦ αἰῶνος, cf. 1 Cor. 1:20)
Unfading will be his memory,
through all generations his name will live.
Nations (ἔθνη) will speak of his wisdom,
and the assembly (ἐκκλησία) will declare his praises.
While he lives he is one out of a thousand,
and when he dies he leaves a good name.[113]

Ben Sira connects wisdom to status in typically Hellenistic ways: the wise enjoy wealth, freedom from manual labor, influence, and honor. This is emphasized by the description of the wise person as cultured (πεπαιδευμένος, 21:23, 31:19) and eloquent:

A wise person by his speech (ὁ σοφός ἐν λόγοις) endears himself,
But the blandishments of fools (μορῶν) are poured out in vain.

A wise person by his speech (ὁ σοφός ἐν λόγοις) advances himself.
a prudent person pleases the great (ἄνθρωπος φρόνιμος ἀρέσει μεγιστᾶσιν).

(20:13, 27)

Like philosophers, sophists and rhetors, Ben Sira apparently ran a school (οἶκος παιδείας, 51:23) where he taught wisdom. He promises his students that along with other benefits, this wisdom will bring wealth (51:25-28). "Here the 'zeal for education' in Jewish wisdom and the Hellenistic world come together."[114]

---

[113]LXX *Sir.* 38:24-29, 32-34; 39:4, 9-11. This and other translations are adapted from Patrick W. Skehan and Alexander A. Di Lella, *The Wisdom of Ben Sira*, The Anchor Bible 39, ed. William Foxwell Albright and David Noel Freedman (New York: Doubleday, 1987).

[114]Hengel, *Judaism and Hellenism*, 132.

With such zeal inevitably comes the kind of competition which leads to division: "Presumably there were various wisdom schools in the Jerusalem of Ben Sira with different trends, sometimes conflicting with each other. The characterization of different kinds of teachers [37:19-26] might be a reference to this."[115] While Ben Sira himself is a Hellenistic σοφός, his main opponents are those Jews who also consider themselves wise, but on the basis of their Hellenistic sophistication rather than fidelity to the law:

> The whole of wisdom (σοφία) is fear of the Lord;
> complete wisdom (σοφία) is the fulfillment of the Law.
>
> There is a cleverness (πανουργία) that is detestable, . . .
>
> Better those with little understanding who fear God,
> than those of abounding in intelligence (φρονήσις) who violate the Law.
>
> The wise man (ἀνὴρ σοφός) will not hate the law. . . .
> (19:20, 23-24; 32:2)

This tie of wisdom to study and keeping of the law "provided the possibility of repudiating an alien autonomous wisdom which refused any association with the law. Accordingly, he warns against *false 'striving for wisdom.'* "[116]

Despite Ben Sira's opposition to unadulterated Hellenistic wisdom, his rhetorical situation demanded accommodation, "for even a fundamentally conservative scribe like Ben Sira would have to adapt himself to the learned arguments of his time, if only to be heard and understood by his pupils and his opponents in the youth of the aristocracy." Thus, we find some influence of popular Stoicism "in his apologetic and polemic statements."[117] Sirach also displays echoes of Greek gnomic poetry and comedy.
In view of the international character of the wisdom tradition in the Hellenistic period, we cannot exclude the possibility of the transmigration of sayings from gnomic Greek thought, tragedy and comedy, by word of mouth. Finally, the influence of Greek conventions can

---

[115]Ibid., 132.
[116]Ibid., 141.
[117]Ibid., 148.

be seen in Sirach's extensive account of dining customs [31:-32:13] and in his positive attitude toward the doctor [38:1-15], which ran counter to an orthodox rigorism.[118]

Such strong parallels with those considered wise in Hellenistic culture means that Ben Sira's views were "probably influenced by Greek social and educational ideals."[119] This is particularly noteworthy, since Ben Sira wrote the original Hebrew text in Jerusalem in the 2nd century B.C.E., and generally resists Hellenistic ideas in favor of Jewish wisdom. After two hundred more years of Hellenization of the Jews (even taking into account further reaction against it), and in Greece rather than Jerusalem, Paul's inclusion of γραμματεύς with other σοφόι could only make even more sense.

The parallels of Ben Sira's social norms to typically Hellenistic ones is all the more striking because it contrasts with his scriptural allusions which oppose such attitudes. One should be humble before God, and accept his teachings rather than arrogantly pursue human speculative knowledge (3:17-24). The poor, oppressed, and widows must be helped, and even treated with deference (4:1-10, 35:16-22). Ben Sira advises not to seek a place of honor, nor flaunt one's wisdom; rather, one should humble oneself, accepting laborious manual labor, and esteem oneself as no better than others (7:4-17). He recognizes that wealth perverts the heart (8:2), that the rich generally abuse the poor unjustly (13:1-24) and that a poor person or slave can be wise (10:23-11:4; however, even here, Ben Sira maintains that the rich and powerful, even if not wise, deserve honor). Arrogance (ὑπερηπανία, cf. Rom. 1:30) is hateful to God, and an absurd attitude before one's Maker (10:7-18, cf. 1. Cor. 4:7) who brings down the arrogant and enthrones the humble. True wisdom is contrasted with shrewdness (πανουργία, 19:20-27; cf. 1 Cor. 3:19; 2 Cor. 4:2, 11:3); the former is the fear of the Lord (φόβος κυρίου, cf. 2 Cor. 5:11: εἰδότες οὖν φόβον τοῦ κυρίου ἀνθρώπους πείθομεν), the latter is unrighteousness (ἄδικος, cf. 1 Cor. 6:1, 11) and deceit (δόλος, cf. 2 Cor. 4:2, 11:13, 12:16).

---

[118]Ibid., 150.

[119]Anthony J. Saldarini, *Pharisees, Scribes and Sadducees in Palestinian Society: A sociological Approach* (Wilmington, DE: Michael Glazier), 257.

In other words, Ben Sira's views of wisdom are at times not far from Paul's. He even criticizes the way status is related to speech:

> The rich speaks and all are silent,
> his speech (λόγος) they extol to the clouds.
> The poor speaks and they say, "Who is that?"
> If he stumbles they knock him down.
> (13:23)

Ben Sira thus maintains a certain tension between the upper class Hellenistic social values he takes for granted and doctrines drawn from Jewish wisdom and prophetic traditions. The extent to which his social world is upper class he further reveals in his advice on slaves:

> Fodder and whip and loads for an ass;
> food, correction, and work for a household slave (οἰκετῃ).
> Make a slave work and he will look for his rest;
> let his hands be idle and he will seek to be free.
> Yoke and harness are a cure for stubbornness;
> and for a mischievous slave, tortures and torments.
> (33:25-27)

2) The Letter of Aristeas

Ben Sira attempted to bridge the worlds of his scriptures and his Hellenistic social environment. The extent to which he was Hellenized is debated, but no one doubts the Hellenization of Aristeas displayed in his letter to Philocrates.
Aristeas' views . . . reflect the unique social, intellectual, and spiritual climate of the Egyptian Jews in the [late] second century BCE, when their numbers and prestige had made them a considerable element in the population and before anti-Semitism had raised its head. Aristeas shows us that the Egyptian Jews embraced the dominant culture enthusiastically, and assimilated their own to it to the extent of adopting its social usages, literary forms, and philosophical beliefs insofar as they were not in direct opposition to central religious tenants of their own. The High Priest himself is praised as a *kalokagathos* (3), which may fairly be rendered "a Greek gentleman,"

and the translators are distinguished for their *paideia* (121), which means Greek culture.[120]
The high priests are also described with the word λογιωτάτης, "most learned or eloquent"[121] (5) and as possessing ὑπεροχή, "eminence"[122] (cf. 1 Cor. 2:1).

Aristeas thus reinforces the impression of the social ideal of the Jewish leaders gained from Ben Sira as cultured and eloquent Hellenists. This is especially true of the scribes who translate the scriptures from Hebrew to Greek. Though the word γραμματεύς is never used for these scholars, they are described as "elders who possess skill (ἐμπειρία) in the law",[123] and who transport and transcribe the texts—all scribal activities.[124] Further, as Saldarini points out, translating the Bible is also "a scribal act and many attributes assigned to the translators are those assigned to high ranking or well born scribes in other texts." Saldarini goes on to emphasize the ideal social rôle of the scribe as parallel to other Hellenistic wise men:

> The translators are described as "best" or "excellent" (*aristoi*), a characteristic of aristocrats in Greece. They have distinguished parentage and "education" or "scholarship" (*paideia*) and they know both the literature of the Jews and of the Greeks. They have some specifically Greek accomplishments, including a talent for talking about the law (the ability to speak well was an essential Greek virtue for the educated person). . . . They are not uncouth, nor conceited in dealing with others and they can listen and comment appropriately. In addition, they are also qualified for embassies. . . . The description of this group also fits the wisdom ideal of the scribe attached to the highest levels of the ruler's court and has much in common with the scribe as depicted in Ben Sira. The translators and the scribe are wise men who know the whole tradition, can function in international situations, and have the talent to be leaders, judges, and scholars.[125]

---

[120]Hadas, 63-64.
[121]*Aristeas* 5.
[122]Ibid., 175.
[123]Ibid., 39.
[124]Ibid., 46.
[125]Saldarini, 260, referring to *Aristeas* 120-127.

3) New Testament

Putting together the evidence from Ben Sira and Aristeas, we are left in little doubt that Jewish scribes were frequently viewed as Hellenistic σοφοί. As in most cases, we have less evidence from the first century C.E. (unless Aristeas is dated then[126]).

Most important here are the Gospels, which frequently mention Palestinian scribes in the early Church's Hellenistically shaped narratives. In the gospels, the scribes are presented as scripture scholars (Mark 9:11, 14; 12:28-35, Matt. 2:4, 7:29, 17:10, 23:2-3) who debate (συζητέω, Mark 9:14-16, 12:28; cf. 1 Cor. 1:20). Further, they seek a sign (σημεῖον, cf. 1 Cor. 1:22), and are rebuked for this as a rejection of κήρυγμα and σοφία (i.e., the LXX good wisdom), and are offered instead the death of Jesus (Matt. 12:38-42; cf. Mark 8:11, 1 Cor. 1:22). The scribes of past ages are classed with prophets and wise men (σοφοί [again, the good kind], Matt. 23.24), but the first century scribes are criticized for seeking honor. In particular parallel to the competition among Hellenistic wise men, they like to take the seats of honor (πρωτοκαθεδρίαι, πρωτοκλισίαι, Mark 12:39, Luke 20:46, Matt. 23:6) in the synagogue and at dinners (δείπνοις, cf. 1 Cor. 11:20-21). These honors, reflecting and reinforcing their status, are joined with political influence. They have close relations with the chief priests and elders (or οἱ πρῶτοι τοῦ λαοῦ, Luke 19:47) in Jerusalem (Mark 8:31 11:27, 14:43, 14:53, 15:1; Matt 2:4, 16:21, 26:57, 27:41; Luke 9:22, 20:1, 22:66; Acts 4:5) with whom they join to uphold the status quo.

On the basis of such evidence, Judge argues that the early Church put Jesus in a category with the scribes, calling both *rabbi.* But Jesus, like Paul, also contrasted with cultural expectations of teachers, and these also focused on the cross:

> What was the social status of a rabbi? The title is a form of address usually reserved for the scribes. . . . They form a professional élite, entered by merit and above all by training. . . . The chief priests and elders, who sat in the Sanhedrin and administered the government under Roman supervision, were drawn from an

---

126R. J. H. Shutt, "Letter of Aristeas," in *The Old Testament Pseudepigrapha*, ed. James H. Charlesworth (New York: Doubleday), 1985, 8.

> exclusive landed aristocracy. Scribes were frequently associated with them. . . . Jesus' bitter attacks on their social pretensions and arrogance (Matt. xxiii) are excellent evidence for the social distinction their professional abilities earned them. It must not be allowed to distract attention from the fact that Jesus is also one of them. . . . Jesus was not, however, the sort of person who might have expected to acquire this status in the normal course of events. He came from an unlikely family, and lacked the normal education. . . . But it is not a carpenter who thus commands the attention of all sections of the community: it is a proved master in the law of Israel. . . . Incredible and unpalatable though it was, the expertise was self-authenticating, and Jesus in due course began to enjoy the social esteem the status carried. The Pharisees recognized a rival, but also a peer. . . . The cup of passion . . . was the cup of rejection by the nation and of incomprehension by the disciples; it was the cup of renunciation of all temporal hope of triumph.[127]

We should also not ignore Paul's own use of γραμματεύς in 1 Cor. 1:20, the verse under discussion. "Paul seems to be referring to well known terms for educated intellectual leaders in the Greco-Roman world, of which scribe is one."[128]

4) Rabbinic Literature

"The figure of the scribe in rabbinic literature is consistent with scribes in other literature."[129] That is, scribes are not a cohesive group, but are characterized by a variety of social rôles including copyists, persons who write letters and documents, and teachers and interpreters of scripture who possess a significant degree of authority. We have focused on this last group, since they appear to have been perceived as among the Hellenistic σοφοί.

Many scholars have noted a variety of ways that the scribal tradition of the rabbinic literature reflects Hellenistic culture. These are summarized by Hengel, who points to 1) the emergence of the authority of the individual teacher; 2) disputes over whether teachers should be paid; 3) the master-pupil relationship which "has its model less in the Old Testament than in Greece"; 4) "the dialectical form of

---

[127]Judge, "Early Christians," 9-11.
[128]Saldarini, 268.
[129]Ibid., 272.

instruction which could almost be termed 'Socratic' . . . [which] may have been influenced by the model of the Greek rhetorical schools"; and 5) the ideal of universal education through elementary schools, where "instead of Homer, the Hebrew Bible, and especially the Pentateuch, held pride of place in instruction."[130]

Jewish scribes, then, fit well into the Hellenistic world. They competed with others who boasted of the superiority of their wisdom. Their competition was inevitably shaped by the dominant Hellenistic culture. Even the most conservative Palestinian scribes apparently had their culture shaped in reaction to Hellenism and its rhetorical education. This does not mean that their ideas merged with those of gentile thinkers, though in warding off Hellenism they absorbed a great deal of philosophical influence, as is patent, for example, in the "Wisdom of Solomon."

Though we find considerable differences in ideas, we find greater parallels in social rôles. The scribes, like sophists and rhetors, ran schools, asserted their authority, sought to be perceived as wise, gained status if they were so perceived, and were thus able to enjoy the benefits of a cultured life. Thus, it should not surprise us that a Jewish scribe can be called either a σοφός or a συζητητής.[131] The titles would have been particularly fitting in the ears of a cosmopolitan resident of Corinth, who witnessed a steady stream of Hellenized wise men of various nationalities whose social rôles were all constrained by Hellenistic cultural expectations.

Once the reader is aware of the consistency of these cultural expectations, Paul's inclusion of the γραμματεύς in his list becomes less puzzling. We can read it not as a shift away from the themes of division, rhetoric, and status to a sudden rejection of Jewish theology, but part of the rhetoric which universalizes the Corinthian situation. Just as the Corinthians have followed normal cultural practice by

---

[130]Hengel, *Judaism and Hellenism*, 81-2. See also the excellent summary by Kinneavy, *Rhetorical Origins*, 57-91, and especially on scribes, 84-86.

[131]According to Wilckens (*Weisheit*, 27), ζήτειν was used to translate דרש and בקש among Jews as describing the profession of the teacher of Scripture, and συζητητής can be a direct translation of the rabbinical title דרשן. However, Wilckens wrongly concludes that such evidence of translation dictates interpretation of 1 Cor. This must be sought not from disincarnate lexical information, but within a meaningful response to the rhetorical situation, which focuses on generally Hellenistic, not peculiarly Jewish, culture.

viewing speakers in categories of social status, so has the entire Hellenized world, Jewish and Gentile. The reader is not bidden to reject Jewish wisdom, but to reject certain values of Hellenistic culture endemic in the competition over wisdom and status.

Conclusion

We have seen that Paul's reference to rhetoric in 1:17 is not isolated. Rather, rhetoric is repeatedly a factor to which Paul must respond in various situations, especially the developing situation in Corinth. In these Corinthian situations, rhetoric is a two-edged sword: it provides Paul with tools for persuasion; but it also carries implicit messages of status which offend the Cross as the basis of unity. In 1 Corinthians 1-4, Paul emphasizes through repetition that he is responding to a situation in which the Corinthians have perceived him and Apollos as high status rhetors suitable for divisive allegiances. Such divisions, we shall see next, were a normal part of Hellenistic culture.

CHAPTER VI

RHETORIC AND DIVISIONS

We should have little difficulty imagining a world in which rhetoric causes divisions, since rhetorical utterances by nature compete for allegiance. However, as we saw above, the divisions which alarm Paul are not a matter of such allegiance to competing ideas, but allegiance to various speakers. A modern reader may have difficulty imagining how the "mere" rhetoric of speakers rather than their "content" could cause such factionalism. Again, we may inform our reading by referring to social history.

Contests in Verbal Wisdom

In the Hellenistic milieu, speakers frequently competed for allegiance. This competition was a normal part of the culture; for "the Greeks made a contest out of everything. To do so was as characteristic of their nature as to pursue restraint and moderation." At Olympus, "crowds applauded the most frenzied straining to be immoderately fleet of foot, strong of hand, or sweet of voice."[1]

This competitive nature was always part of classical rhetoric, in which speakers contested not just *what* word but *whose* word would prevail. Competition over who has a λόγος τοῦ σοφοῦ was not limited to claims to philosophical truth. Rather, such competition was

[1]MacMullen, *Enemies*, 66, 185.

part of rhetoric even before it was conceptualized, as evidenced by the tradition of agonistic speech practiced to determine the wiser speaker.[2] When Gorgias visited Athens in 427 B.C.E. to demonstrate and teach how to prevail rhetorically, he worked within traditions already established by the agonistic poets satirized in Aristophanes' *Frogs*:

> O Muses, the daughters divine
> of Zeus, the immaculate Nine,
> Who gaze from your mansions serene
> on intellects subtle and keen,
> When down to the tournament lists,
> in bright-polished wit (γνωμοτύπων) they descend,
> With wrestling and turnings and twists
> in the battle of words to contend (ἀντιλογοῦντες).
> O come and behold what the two
> antagonist poets can do,
> Whose mouths (δεινοτάτοιν στομάτοιν) are the swiftest to teach
> grand language and filings of speech:
> For now of their wits (σοφίας) is the sternest
> encounter (ἀγὼν) commencing in earnest.[3]

Such contests of speech (ἀγῶνα λόγων) and wisdom were the business of all speakers throughout antiquity. Not just poets, but sophists[4] and rhetors tried to be champions. Thus, Diodorus Siculus can describe employing ρητορικοὺς λόγους as entering ἐν τοῖς λόγοις ἀγῶνας.[5] As Isocrates points out in the passage noted above, those students trained in rhetoric who are "wiser in speech" (σοφώτεροι ἐν τοῖς λόγοις) are honored as champions (ἀγωνισταί) in contests of speech.[6]

These traditions of competition in wise speech continued into Paul's day. Plutarch portrays Homer and Hesiod as such contestants

---

[2]PW, s.v. "Logos," which quotes a fragment from Eur. *Antiop*. fr. 189: ἐκ παντὸς ἄν τις πράγματος δισσῶν λόγων ἀγῶνα θεῖτ' ἄν, εἰ λέγειν εἶν σοφός.

[3]Ar. *Ran*. 875-884.

[4]e.g., Pl. *Prt*. 335A: Protagoras asserts, "I have undertaken in my time many contests of speech (ἀγῶνα λόγων ἀφικόμην)" which led to being considered "superior" (βελτίων).

[5]Diod. Sic. 20.2.1.

[6]Isoc. *Against the Sophists* 14.

(ἀγωνισταί). Already the most esteemed poets among the wise (τῶν σοφῶν οἱ δοκιμώτατοι ποιηταί), the judgment (κρίσις) between the two was difficult because they shared such equal repute (δόξα). For this reason, the poets resorted to riddles, like those of the competitions at symposia (see Chapter 8), to decide who should be honored as the wisest.[7]

Such competition in σοφοί λόγοι sometimes became quite divisive. Just as bitter divisions arose between sophists and philosophers, so one philosopher and another or one rhetor and another were often strenuous competitors. The group following a particular teacher could be so strong that they could be described as a *secta*, a "sect" or "party." This is the word Seneca the Elder uses to describe the followers of Apollodorus versus Theodorus, rival rhetoricians in Rome in the first century B.C.E.[8]

The importance of this particular division is emphasized by Quintilian. He criticizes rhetoricians who *ought* to claim allegiance to one of these teachers, but who fail to do so: "One of these gentlemen . . . when asked whether he was a follower of Theodorus or Apollodorus replied, 'Oh! as for me, I am all for the Thracians [i.e., I am far more interested in gladiatorial contests]. . . . He could hardly have found a neater way to avoid confessing his ignorance."[9]

As I mentioned above, under the Empire the practical public value of rhetoric declined as opportunities for free political speech were curtailed. In this situation, declamation increasingly became the major opportunity for oratorical displays, and teachers of rhetoric were the main declaimers. In the courtroom or assembly, the contests were partly over pleasing performance, but primarily over results. In classrooms, the competition might be over theory. But in declamations, as in increasingly popular epideictic oratory, the contest was not between rival goals or theories, but between rival performers.

This drive for adulation, we learn from Seneca the Elder,[10] often overcame the more basic goals of rhetoric. Declaimers were

---

[7]Plut. *Conv. sept. sap.*, *Mor.* 153F-154A.

[8]Sen. *Controv.* 10.pr.15.

[9]Quint. 2.11.1-2.

[10]c. 55 B.C.E. to 40 C.E.; his works were written toward the end of his life, making him a close contemporary of Paul.

easily criticized as concerned "to win approval for yourself rather than for the case."[11] They attracted large crowds, and bitterly competed to win admiration and avoid ridicule.[12] Boys thronged to the schools[13] and idolized their teachers,[14] and they along with the crowds at the declamations[15] greeted successful sallies with frequent applause.[16] The more successful would declaim before the powerful, even emperors.[17] People would flock to the newest orator, just as they would to the newest actor or gladiator.[18] According to Quintilian's disapproving comments, when fellow students declaimed, others would "stand up or leap from their seats in the expression of their applause" so that

> every effusion is greeted with a storm of ready made applause. . . . In the schools today we see boys stooping forward ready to spring to their feet: at the close of each period they not merely rise, but rush forward with shouts of unseemly enthusiasm. . . . The result is vanity and empty self-sufficiency. . . . [They become] intoxicated by the wild enthusiasm of their fellow pupils.[19]

Such behavior was not limited to the schools or declamation halls. The political realities of the Empire created an atmosphere in which crowds were ready to back one speaker or another:

> Romans no longer had a voice of any significance in affairs of state, and cities Italian or provincial were run by rich oligarchies. The withering of democratic institutions could by no means cure people of the habit of holding opinions essential to the government to discover and, if possible, to conciliate. Emperors, their legates and procurators, and municipal magistrates still had to reach their fellow citizens, and for the purpose no place came so pat as the

---

[11]Sen. *Controv.* 9.pr.1.

[12]Ibid., 7.pr.8-9.

[13]Ibid., 3.pr.15.

[14]Ibid., 2.pr.1.

[15]Ibid., 4.pr.2.

[16]Ibid., 9.pr.2. Cf. Bonner, *Roman Declamation* (Liverpool: University Press, 1949), 41-2; M.L. Clarke, *Higher Education in the Ancient World* (Albuquerque: University of New Mexico, 1971), 43; Quint. 8.5.13-14, 10.5.18.

[17]Sen. *Controv.* 2.4.12.

[18]Ibid., 4.pr.1.

[19]Quint. 2.2.9-12.

> theater. . . . Emperors, consuls, prefects, great noblemen and women, religious sects and leaders, popes and pretenders, the level of taxation or of the grains supply, all were attacked or applauded by the most ungovernable elements of the population in an atmosphere created by the obscenity of pantomime and the brutality of gladiation.[20]

These competitive and divisive tendencies contributed to the rise of the Second Sophistic. In that movement of the second century C.E., we find the earlier tendencies grown to grotesque exaggeration. Thus, the professors now became great sophists who inspired "cultural contests" between rival groups or cities. They had

> pupils, or rather disciples, who spread the fame of the master. . . . A polemical literature came into being in the form of tracts by warring sophists, denouncing each other with wit and erudition. . . . Empty titles and imagined superiority meant much to the local citizenry. . . . Sophists were cause for boasting, as were building, canals, or coinage. . . . At Rome, observed Philostratus, consulars and sons of consulars applauded one sophist and then the other, starting a "rivalry such as kindles the keenest envy and malice even in the hearts of wise men."[21]

These contests between groups and cities for the boast of the greater champion of eloquence are probably more typical after the 1st century C.E. But the values lying behind them were firmly in place, including the status accorded the more *asteios* or *urbanitas*. Throughout the centuries, rhetoric often divided Greco-Roman people who competed for status in the "thirst for honor, the contest for applause."[22]

Apparently, Paul was perceived as among such persuasive speakers.[23] He had preached among the Corinthians (1:17; 2:1, 4;

---

[20]MacMullen, *Enemies*, 171-72. Note Quintilian's parallel of cheering for rhetoricians and gladiators, Quint. 2.11.2 (quoted above, p. 254).

[21]Bowersock, 39, 89-90l; cf. Clarke, *Rhetoric at Rome*, 130.

[22]MacMullen, *Roman Social Relations*, 62.

[23]Munck (138) similarly argues: "The Corinthians regarded the Christian message as wisdom like that of the Greeks, the Christian leaders as teachers of wisdom, themselves as wise, and all this as something to boast about." But Munck anachronistically projects the social role of 2nd century sophists from Philostratus' account of the Second Sophistic into the first century. Moreover, he exaggerates the role of philosophy for the sophists. As I have argued, virtually

3:1; 15:1), and as a result of his preaching a community had formed around him. Similarly, in Luke's narrative world, Paul "argued (διελέγετο)" in the Corinthian synagogue, and "persuaded (ἔπειθέν)" Jews and Greeks. Silas and Timothy found him "occupied with preaching (συνείχετο τῳ λόγῳ)" and "testifying (διαμαρτυρόμενος)." Turning away from the Jews because of their opposition, he turned to the Gentiles who "when they heard believed" (ἀκούοντες ἐπίστευον). The Jews accuse Paul, telling Gallio that he persuades (ἀναπείθει) contrary to the law, but to Gallio, this is only a matter περὶ λόγου. Paul remained for eighteen months, speaking (λαλέω) and teaching (διδάσκω).

Thus, we can understand why Paul has concluded that the Corinthians implicitly, if not explicitly, had regarded him as a persuasive rhetor, i.e., as σοφός. Apparently, those "of Paul" still considered him adequate in this rôle. But others soon preferred Apollos as the σοφός of a rival group.

The Role of Apollos

Paul refers to Apollos several times. His name, like that of Paul, Cephas, and Christ, forms one of the four slogans of 1:12. But Paul and Apollos garner far more attention than the other two (3:4-9, 3:22, 4:6; cf. 16:12). Those "of Apollos" and those "of Paul" are singled out as the target of Paul's rhetoric (4:6). For these reasons, the slogans "I am of Paul" and "I am of Apollos" dominate the exigence. The other two slogans may be read as no more than hyperbole.

Those of Christ

The slogan "I am of Christ" has presented interpreters with particular difficulties; it has been variously explained as a gloss, as Paul's own slogan in response to those of the Corinthians, as rhetorical hyperbole, as the slogan of gnostic opponents, or as yet one more slogan adopted by those who would use Christ as a champion

---

any content, even cookery, could serve to establish eloquence and wisdom.

to set themselves above the other groups.[24] The last explanation, that a fourth group reacted to the others by saying "You may claim human teachers as your wise man, but Christ is ours!" makes good sense of Paul's rhetoric, since his next phrase (μεμέρισται ὁ Χριστός) could be taken as a criticism of such a claim.[25] But it could also be read as a rhetorical flourish. The grammar would be the same; whether it would have been read by the Corinthians as ironic or as referring to an actual slogan is lost to us. But in either case, since not history but interpretation is our goal, the rhetoric has the same force: these kinds of divisions cannot be justified even if Christ is the champion.

Those of Cephas

The rôle of Cephas is very vague; we have no other indication that he ever visited Corinth. But he does appear again in 3:22, 9:5, and 15:5, so the Corinthians are at least familiar with him as an important figure. Some take 9:5 as indicating that Peter did visit Corinth, since Paul expects the Corinthians to know that he traveled with his wife.

Whatever the historical rôle of Cephas, Paul's rhetoric does not prompt the reader to imagine Peter as a cause of *theological* division. As Fee points out,

> All the evidence of 1 Corinthians seems to speak against it. Whatever some meant when they said, 'I follow Cephas,' it had not brought about the theological divisions in the church envisioned by F. C. Baur, and frequently repeated thereafter. [e.g, Manson, Barrett, and Vielhauer.] Despite the opinions of many, not a

---

[24]For a summary, see Hurd, 101-106.

[25]Fee (58-59) cautiously points out that "the grammar of the passage seems to demand that there were in fact Corinthians saying such a thing. But beyond that all is speculation, including the suggestion that this was a party with a definable theology." Most likely, those who used such a slogan constituted no distinct group, but persons who attempt to rise above rest who boast in men. Yet in doing so, they fall into their own spiritual elitism. Conzelmann (33) rightly rejects the possibility that ἐγὼ δὲ Χριστοῦ is Paul's own declaration, for it allows no link between 1:12 and 1:13.

> single item in 1 Corinthians explicitly suggests a Judaizing faction in the church. . . . More likely there is a personal allegiance factor here, involving some who had been converted and baptized under his ministry.[26]

On the other hand, Cephas may never have visited Corinth. If 9:5 is read as indicating that he had visited, the same must then also be true of "the other apostles and the brothers of the Lord" mentioned there. Rather, Cephas and the other apostles may simply be known through tradition (15:5-7). So, again, it is possible to read the slogan ἐγὼ δὲ Κηφᾶ as rhetorical hyperbole.

Those of Apollos

Apollos has a much clearer rôle. In 3:4-9 and 4:6, Paul emphasizes that whatever the status of the other slogans, the ones connected to Paul and Apollos are central to the exigence. This major rôle for Apollos has tempted many exegetes to argue that he introduced a theology which caused divisions. As we have already seen, Paul's rhetoric points away from theological division.[27] Rather than assuming theological issues, if we follow the path from Paul's rhetoric to the rhetorical situation that provoked it, we might arrive at a very different conclusion.

Apollos worked in Corinth after Paul "laid the foundation (3:10), "watering" what Paul had "planted." Thus, in the letter's implied narrative, he too gathered a following through preaching and teaching. Luke (Acts 18:25ff) portrays Apollos as a Jew, born in Alexandria, an ἀνήρ λόγιος who, like Paul, "spoke and taught" (ἐλάλει καὶ ἐδίδασκεν). Some time after Paul had left Corinth, Apollos went there to help "those who already believed," i.e., had already been persuaded (πεπιστευκόσιν) by Paul.

Apollos's Alexandrian origin has given rise to an enormous amount of speculation about his possessing a Philo-like theology. We have already seen that even if this were true, it was not relevant to the exigence. And we have very little basis on which to speculate.

---

[26]Fee, 57-58.

[27]See above, pp. 140-47.

The Alexandrian origin he shared with Philo means very little, since the city of perhaps a million residents had a large and varied Jewish population with many kinds of scholars.

On the other hand, in the world of Acts, like that of 1 Cor., Apollos appears as a persuasive speaker. Luke describes Apollos as an ἀνηρ λόγιος, which can mean one who is "learned," "cultured," or "skilled in words," i.e., "eloquent"[28] It is the same phrase reported by Plutarch as Augustus's praise of Cicero.[29] In Attic Greek, the meaning tends to be "learned," while in Koine, it tends to be "cultured" or "eloquent."[30] This is just what we would expect from rhetoric's rise to academic and cultural prominence in the Hellenistic period, since the ordinary understanding of "learned" came to mean one who was rhetorically educated. Given the context of preaching, Luke certainly seems to be referring to rhetorical ability.

Although any speculation about Alexandrian origins is risky, we are on much firmer ground when we assume that any educated Alexandrian was well trained in rhetoric. Indeed, even Philo studied, used, and honored it, and was himself sent as a spokesman to represent the Jews before the emperor. He was thoroughly acquainted with rhetorical theory in all its details, as well as the debates between philosophy and rhetoric.[31] "Philo displays a consistent evaluation of eloquence. He criticizes its abuse and distortion but highly values its proper use."[32] Moreover, his discourse was "profoundly rhetorical," employing "precise rhetorical treatment. He knew to adapt inclusively the weapons of his rhetoric to the public he was trying to pedagogically influence, convince, or inspire." He was determined to employ "the weapons of true eloquence" to insure both the interpretive and apologetic success of his discourse. In fact,

---

[28]BAGD, 1056.

[29]Plut. *Cic.* 49.5.

[30]MM, 378; F. F. Bruce, "Apollos in the New Testament," *Ekklesiastikos Pharos* 57 (1975), 356.

[31]J. Leopold, "Philo's Knowledge of Rhetorical Theory," *Two Treatises of Philo of Alexandria*, eds. D. Winston and J. Dillon, Brown Judaic Studies, 25 (Chico, CA: Scholars Press, 1983), 129.

[32]Horsley, "Wisdom of Words," 226.

> The rhetorical code of persuasion . . . is at the base of his hermeneutic. . . . There is apparently no model or structure, hallowed in the canones [*sic*] of rhetoric, from which he has not profited or has not strategically adapted to his ambitious literary project. The adoption and strategic adaptation of the conventions of Hellenistic rhetoric is so evident in his treatises that the most simple and direct exegesis of a text is performed with remarkable frequency, in conformity with its structural codes. . . . In the majority of cases, his ideas are exhaustively dissected and the outline of his thought architectronically trimmed and invigorated as far as the structures of argumentation consecrated in the canones [*sic*] of the orators permit.[33]

"In short, [Philo's] methods were thoroughly rhetorical."[34] At the same time, we should remember that Philo did not differ from other educated Jews in this regard. Like all educated Hellenists, Jews, whether Palestinian or Diaspora, were thoroughly acquainted with rhetorical teaching and employed it in their own systems of thought and practice.[35] Thus, Luke's comment that Apollos was not only "ἀνὴρ λόγιος," but also "δυνατὸς ἐν ταῖς γραφαῖς" does not set him apart as a pneumatic whose eloquence was a sign of special spiritual status. Rather, it could have described any Jew of that

---

[33]Manuel Alexandre Jr., "Rhetorical Argumentation as an Exegetical Technique in Philo of Alexandria," *Hellenica et Judaica*, eds. A. Caquot, M. Hadas-Lebel, and J. Riaud (Paris: Peeters, Leuven, 1986), 21-25.

[34]T. Conley, "Philo's Use of *Topoi*," *Two Treatises of Philo of Alexandria: A Commentary on De Gigantibus and Quod Deus Sit Immutabilis*, eds. David Winston and John Dillon, Brown Judaic Studies, 25, eds. Jacob Neusner, Wendell S. Dietrich, Ernest S. Frerichs, B. Twiss Sumner, and Alan Zuckerman (Chico, CA: Scholars Press, 1983), 174.

[35]David Daube, "Rabbinic Methods of Interpretation and Hellenistic Rhetoric," *Hebrew Union College Annual*, Vol. 22 (Philadelphia: Jewish Publication Society, 1949), 257, points to the recognized parallels between Philonic and Palestinian hermeneutical principles, both of which are also paralleled in Hellenistic rhetorical teaching. Daube concludes that "it is far more likely that [Philo] learned them from his general studies at Alexandria" than that he was influenced by Palestinian Rabbinism. "Cicero did not sit at the feet of Hillel, nor Hillel at the feet of Cicero; and there was no need for Philo to go to Palestinian sources for this kind of teaching. . . . The true explanation lies in the common Hellenistic background." Daube's thesis (p. 240) is that "Hellenistic rhetoric is at the bottom both of the fundamental ideas and presuppositions from which the Rabbis proceeded and of the major details of application. . . . In its beginnings, the Rabbinic system of hermeneutics is a product of the Hellenistic civilization then dominating the entire Mediterranean world."

period who excelled in the widespread practice of adapting rhetorical teaching to scriptural exegesis.

Philo was among the rhetors not only as exegete. His eloquence was recognized by his fellow Jews when they appointed him an ambassador to Gaius Caligula in 38-39 C.E.[36] In this rôle, he was much like the spokesman of the Jerusalem high priest Ananaias, who came to Felix with a certain rhetor Tertullos ("ῥήτορος Τερτύλλου τινός," Acts 24:1). It is even closer to the metaphor Paul applies to himself in 2 Cor. 5:20, when he is attempting to bolster his authority as an ambassadorial rhetor.[37]

Of course, Philo was not primarily a rhetor, but a philosophical theologian who employed rhetoric, and as such was one of those rare intellectuals who had a command of both. His rhetorical knowledge and practice once again testify to the ubiquity of rhetoric. In fact, Apollos's Alexandrian origins place him in one of rhetoric's very centers. Even if we picture him as Philonic, we find a rhetor, and in this both he and Philo would have been counted as wise. And such wisdom could certainly divide a community's allegiance.

Alexandrian Rhetoric

If Apollos was an attractive rhetor, the nature of Alexandrian rhetoric becomes relevant. This has been studied in depth by Robert W. Smith.[38] Judging by Smith's study, Philo represents an important but small part of the actual rhetoric of the large, highly cosmopolitan city.

All "except for the native Egyptians, who with rare exception remained on the fringes of society" became culturally Greek. "The large number of rhetorical papyri found in Egypt prove the significant rôle the spoken word in theory and practice had in Greco-Roman education." In the Library and Museum, sophists, rhetoricians,

---

[36]Joseph. *Ant.* 18.257f; Philo *Leg.*

[37]See p. 211.

[38]Robert W. Smith, *The Art of Rhetoric in Alexandria: Its Theory and Practice in the Ancient World* (The Hague: Martinus Nijhoff, 1974).

philosophers, literary critics, and philologists taught side by side, rather than competing as in Athens, Rome, and Tarsus.[39]

However, this sophisticated tertiary education, while highly influential within the Library and Museum, seems to have had limited influence on the general rhetoric of the city. Rather than following prominent Alexandrian sophists or rhetors, schools on the primary and secondary levels seemed "to have copied rather closely the procedures in Rome and Antioch." In fact, the evidence indicates that only a few rhetors or orations received special honor. Nor did the city produce prominent rhetorical handbooks. The one exception helps prove the point: Aelius Theon's *Progymnasmata*, aimed at secondary education, lamented the common lack of study of philosophy by students of rhetoric, and of theory before practice.[40]

In place of the scholarly rhetoric of the Library and Museum, Smith argues that Alexandrian rhetoric was generally demagogic. He speculates that Augustus's denial of an assembly helped push rhetoric into the street, where it was shaped by the riotous nature of the city.

> Audiences in any era largely determine the kind of speech an orator can give on specific occasions, and ancient authorities repeatedly struck the note of the riotous, jealous, and superficial character of Alexandria's population. Egyptians, Jews, and Greeks required little provocation for melees [arising from ethnic rivalries] which in their wake frequently left many dead.[41]

Ethnic rivalries were a particular problem for Jews. Though they often surpassed their counterparts in other parts of the Empire in education, Greek culture, independence, reputation, and wealth, they largely lived in isolated communities. For this reason, Jews often "saw the Greeks as intolerant bigots unable to come to terms with other nationalities or races who did not conform to Greek culture and religion."[42] When Jews enjoyed financial success, it was often as merchants, smiths, and industrialists; as we have seen, this kind of status-inconsistent group seems to have been a major part of Paul's

---

[39]Ibid, 19.
[40]Ibid., 133-35.
[41]Ibid., 20.
[42]Ibid., 21.

Corinth. A style of rhetoric shaped among Alexandrian Jews could easily succeed in the similar social dynamic of Corinth.

The tensions between the three ethnic communities (Jewish, Greek, and Egyptian) caused numerous riots, especially from 30 B.C.E. to 170 C.E.[43] We have no primary evidence of "whose oratory precipitated the recorded cries, but since the inflammatory spoken word always arouses and is the instrument by which harbingers of ill-will marshall forces in hours of crises, we can be certain that politico-religious demagogues played a significant rôle. . . . The tongue of the orator wielded its power."[44] In the major riot of 38 A.D., just before Apollos appears in Paul's world, Jews were flogged, dragged through streets, compelled to eat pork, and killed. Flaccus encouraged Greeks in this behavior, labeling Jews as foreigners and aliens. This behavior was hardly temporary; in the riots of 115-117 A.D., the Jewish population was nearly annihilated.

Thus, we should not imagine the typical Alexandrian Jewish orator to be as cool as the philosopher-rhetor Philo. Rather,

> angry men, bred in a restive city and fearless in their character, emerge in numerous deliberative and legal documents of Greco-Roman Alexandria. The excitement of their rhetoric came not from their cultivated artistic ability but from the boldness and vehemence with which they presented their evidence, arguments, and theses. Only men foredoomed to death or at least convinced that the truth lay on their side could have dared such presentations.[45]

Smith speculates that Apollos "must have had some considerable practice in his hometown prior to journeying to Ephesus, and perhaps had studied rhetoric there." Some of the Corinthians, according to 1 Cor. 1:12, claimed to belong to the Apollos camp, suggesting "his persuasive ability."[46]

Even in the official rhetoric of Alexandria, we find the same characteristics. The ambassadors and gymnasiarchs of the first and second centuries C.E. were

---

[43]Ibid., 28.

[44]Ibid., 28-29.

[45]Ibid., 72.

[46]Ibid., 75.

> sufficiently sympathetic with the city's causes to speak and even to die for them, much as Christians and Jews died under persecution for their faith. The altercation between emperor and accused reached fever-pitch at times as each openly charged the other with partisanship, incompetence, or insolence. . . . Unlike rhetoricians and students in schools, . . . these spokesmen were much bolder in their challenge of Roman authority.[47]

In the rhetoric of the 3rd century C.E., including that of the reconstituted assembly, Smith finds the same characteristics:

> While the papyrological accounts always break off before we learn all we should desire of either the substance or the rhetorical theory, they do reveal that speakers sometimes heatedly debated municipal issues in the senate, fearlessly attacked the puerile and unrestrained conduct of the people, and ingratiated or insulted the emperor to his face. . . . Alexandria seems to have been only modestly influenced if at all by the extant theories of rhetoric.[48]

Like embassies and senate debates, the rhetoric of the law courts also played more to the people than to cultured expectations. "At times, the situation got out of hand and the people became so intoxicated with merriment that Dion said (Orat. XXXII, 68) that if one passed a courtroom he could not determine whether a trial or a drinking party was in progress."[49] Such a style of rhetoric, highly suitable to drinking parties, might have brought Apollos great success in Corinth, where, as we shall argue in chapter 8, the drinking parties were an important setting for competition among the wise.

"As elsewhere in the Empire, resident and itinerant sophists also orated for the public, though not as freely and extensively as in Antioch and Rome. Philo tells us that in his day Alexandria's lecture halls and theaters were crowded almost daily with auditors of discourses on virtue and other topics."[50] The florid, Asianist style had been introduced to Ptolemaic Alexandria by traveling sophists who visited the Delta by at least the third century B.C.E., bringing the latest fads which Alexandrians could hardly resist.[51] This

---

[47]Ibid., 51.
[48]Ibid., 58-59.
[49]Ibid., 62.
[50]Smith cites Philo *Judaeus* 1.5.
[51]R.W. Smith, 130-31.

Asianist style, "which enjoyed a heady vogue precisely in that age and in those areas through which Paul moved," was, "as Norden has contended, the rhetoric [Paul] fought and by which he himself was found wanting."[52]

Smith points out that the Alexandrian Christians benefited from this rhetorical tradition which escaped the cultural limitations of more classical practice. According to Harnack, "'the church [in Alexandria] understood how to present Christianity in forms which were suited to the varied grades of human culture, and this feature undoubtedly proved an extraordinary aid to the propaganda of the religion,' though later the large numbers of uneducated members would prove embarrassing to the church's existence and spiritual growth."[53]

Apollos's experience in Alexandria, then, probably prepared him to preach in a way which could bring great success among οἱ πολλοί, or at least those with less than the highest cultural backgrounds. Once again, we see how rhetoric was closely related to issues of status.

Toward a Meaningful Narrative

An understanding of Alexandrian rhetoric allows the reader to construct a narrative which can make sense of how Apollos's rhetoric could be related to the exigence. The reader can imagine that Paul viewed Apollos as a typically Alexandrian rhetor: energetic, enthusiastic, playing to the tastes of the masses. This was especially likely if Apollos had experienced or even fled because of the anti-Jewish riots of 38 A.D. By this experience, he could have been further formed into a typical Alexandrian orator as described above by Smith: a man "foredoomed to death or at least convinced that the truth lay on [his] side." It is certainly striking that Luke describes him as "boiling in spirit" (Acts 18:25: ζέων τῳ πνεύματι, which we certainly need not take as a sign of enthusiasm foreign to Paul, since Paul recommends just such behavior in Romans 12:11). With such passion, only he and

[52]Judge, "Paul's Boasting," 41.

[53]R.W. Smith, 80, citing Harnack, *The Mission and Expansion of Christianity*, Vol. II, 175 & Vol. I, 219ff.

Paul are described in Acts as "speaking boldly" (παρρησιάζομαι). Such rhetoric could easily have appealed to those Corinthians who were not the most sophisticated.

By the same token, that same rhetoric might have offended the more sophisticated listeners. Not only was it roughly hewn, its Greek, and worse, Asianist tradition set it far apart from the proper Latin which never took root in Alexandria. In this Greek city of Corinth which tried to be Roman, the reader can easily imagine that the higher status Corinthians yearned to impress Roman visitors with the propriety of their speech, and were embarrassed by anything that sounded less cultured. They might have heard Apollos's rhetoric as characterized not just by Asianism, but by demagoguery.[54]

The Greco-Roman texts amply illustrate the cultured disdain for the kinds of rhetoric which appealed to less sophisticated tastes. For example, Quintilian is forced to admit that the rhetoric which "slaves and barbarians sometimes achieve" is usually considered

> the more vigourous. . . . The uninstructed sometimes appear to have a richer flow of language, because they say everything that can be said, while the learned exercise discrimination and self-restraint. . . . [The uninstructed] seek only for such themes as may beguile the ears of the public even at the cost of appealing to the most perverted tastes. . . . Well, let the world credit them with as much genius as it pleases, as long as it is admitted that such praise is an insult to any man of real eloquence. . . . These creatures have another weapon in their armoury: they seek to obtain the reputation of speaking with greater vigour than the trained orator by means of their delivery. For they shout on all and every occasion and bellow their every utterance "with uplifted hand," to use their own phrase, dashing this way and that, panting and gesticulating wildly and wagging their heads with all the frenzy of a lunatic. Smite your hands together, stamp the ground, slap your thigh, your breast, your forehead, and you will go straight to the

---

[54]On the upper class disdain and popular approval of demagoguery, see Dale Martin, *Slavery as Salvation: The Metaphor of Slavery in Pauline Christianity* (New Haven: Yale, 1990), 86-116, and my Chapter Seven, pp. 318-22. Martin argues that Paul employs this two-edge sword in 1 Cor. 9:19-22 to challenge the upper-class socio-rhetorical world while appealing to those of lower class. Could Paul be simultaneously attempting to regain the confidence of the less sophisticated followers of Apollos while continuing to challenge the higher-class values of those "of Paul"?

> heart of the dingier [lower class][55] members of your audience.[56]

Such boisterous rhetoric could easily contrast with that of Paul, who, according to Luke, was born a Roman citizen of Tarsus, "no insignificant city" (Acts 21:39), a major center of Hellenistic education. Luke's Paul was further educated in Jerusalem (Acts 22:3), and well travelled throughout the Hellenistic world. As research increasingly shows, and despite his overt protestations, Paul's rhetoric displays a well-developed understanding of the rhetorical conventions taught in the schools.

Thus, Paul's rhetoric might have been more appealing to more sophisticated tastes, Apollos to the less cultured. This does not mean that the Pauline and Apollos groups were divided by lines of class or income, but by level of education and culture. The two are not necessarily equated in any social group; this is especially true in a mercantile economy like Corinth's, where significant income and power could be achieved by those of lower levels of status and education. If Apollos's group were all poor, they would have had no patron to feed and house their teacher, nor to provide meeting places and other needs of the group. Further, even if we are persuaded by Theissen's equating of the "strong" with upper class and the "weak" with lower class,[57] we read no hint that these divisions of chapters 8-12 parallel those of chapters 1-4. In other words, both those of Paul and those of Apollos had "strong" and "weak" members, i.e., patrons and clients.

However, the divisions of chapters 8-12 along class lines and the divisions of chapters 1-4 between patronal groups according to favored teachers are both grounded in competition for status. The fiercest competition for status often occurs among those at a similar level of society, and can be fueled by one group's perception of the other's status inconsistency. As we shall see, upper class Greco-Roman writers could be highly critical of the rhetoric of those whose

---

[55]"*pullatus* = wearing dark clothes, *i.e.* the common people, as opposed to the upper classes wearing the white or purple-bordered toga." Butler, in Quintilian, Vol. 1, 286, n. 2.

[56]Quint. 2.11.7-12.12.

[57]Theissen, 121-143.

income, but not their birth or παιδεία, surpassed their own. In other words, the leaders of the Apollos group could have been *nouveau riche* (νεόπλουτος) patrons with tastes that ran more to Alexandrian street rhetoric. Though rich, they were not considered wise or well-born, but vainglorious upstarts.[58] If they were also still ἰδιῶται who had not yet acquired public office or political friendships, neither were they as powerful as upper class oligarchs. Paul's assertions of 1:26 would have particularly stung them. But they also would have stung his own patrons, who by their divisive behavior demonstrated their own relative insecurity about status.

Paul as Σοφός

Paul points to his relative weaknesses as an orator in part to disclaim any responsibility for the behavior of the "ἐγὼ εἰμι Παύλου" group. As we have seen, these admissions of weakness come back to haunt him when the "superlative apostles" of 2 Cor. use them against him. In 2 Cor., he defends himself by pointing to his relative strengths as an orator which he claims to have used for the sake of his mission. These claims are credible, since to persuade his audience of the truth of the gospel, he had to speak in a way persuasive to those whose ears and values were Hellenistic and therefore rhetorical.

Thus, Paul was constrained by his situation to operate within the recognized social rôle of σοφός, and at the same time to resist it. This was a particularly strong constraint for Paul, since, as he reveals, his relationships were with the higher status and therefore better educated Corinthians. First, he claims to have baptized only Crispus, Gaius, and the household of Stephanus (1:14-16). According to Theissen's analysis, these are among the most certainly higher status members of the church.[59] Crispus was a ruler of the synagogue and head of a household; his conversion was apparently influential in bringing others into the church (Acts 18:8). Gaius housed Tertius (and Paul?) and hosted the entire church (Romans 16:23). Thus he

---

[58]LSJ, 1169.

[59]Theissen, 69-119.

was a major patron of the church, possessing a house large enough to hold λαὸς πολύς (Acts 18:10). He also seems to be closely related to the "city-treasurer" Erastus, another presumably high status Corinthian. Stephanus, like Chloe (1 Cor. 1:11), heads a household; he also patronizes the church, is in a leadership position, and travels with Fortunatus and Achaicus to see Paul in order to continue his long relationship with Paul as the head of the first household in Achaia to be converted through Paul's ministry (16:15-19). Judge asserts that "it seems a likely guess" that Stephanus, Fortunatus, Achaicus, and Cloe were leaders of the Pauline faction.

Others of means also patronized Paul. According to Luke, Titius Justus, a "God-fearer" who lived next to the synagogue housed him (Acts 18:7). Phoebe of Cenchraea Paul calls προστάτις (Rom. 16:1-2) of himself and many others, the technical term for patron.[60] Further, she is a διάκονος τῆς ἐκκλησίας, probably meaning that she patronized the Corinthian church, just as the household of Stephanus devoted themselves to διακονίαν τοῖς ἁγίοις as fellow laborers with Paul and so place the rest of the church in a position of submission to them as clients (1 Cor. 16:15-18, cf. 1 Thess. 5:12-13). Paul gives Phoebe first place in his list of important persons, and goes on at length to recommend her to the church in Rome for friendship and hospitality, an upper class custom.[61] "She is travelling to Rome, and Paul places his followers there under obligation to attend to her interests, which nicely illustrates the way in which he supported the system of patronage in return for the security it afforded him."[62]

Patronage by such persons allowed Paul to pursue his primary goal of preaching. Socially, Paul would have been perceived as among the sophists, those "visiting professional preachers" who relied "upon the hospitality of their admirers, all expert talkers and persuaders. . . . St. Paul provided himself with a secure social position, consciously or unconsciously, by adopting the conventions of the sophistic profession."[63] As we have seen above on Paul's

---

[60]BAGD 718; LSJ, 1526-27; Judge, "Early Christians," 129; Marshall, 142.

[61]On friendship and recommendation, see Marshall, 1-34, 91-124, 133-151 passim.

[62]Judge, "Early Christians," 129.

[63]Judge, "Early Christians," 125-26.

status as ἰδιώτης, Stowers cogently argues that Paul was constrained to preach in synagogues and homes. Thus,

> it is no accident that patrons, households and house churches are so prominent in the letters of Paul the missionary. . . . An invitation to teach in someone's house would provide Paul with . . . a sponsor, an audience and credentials as a certain type of speaker corresponding to a specific genre of speaking event. Above all, speakers needed some type of social status or a recognized role. . . . When Paul says 'I baptized the household of Stephanus,' it is probably correct to assume that the preaching which led up to these baptisms occurred not in a marketplace or a gymnasium, but in someone's house.[64]

These were not the only higher status Christians with whom Paul had long and close relations. Judge lists

> as many as forty persons in the class of people who either actually did sponsor Paul's activities or are referred to in a way that implies that they probably did, or would have done had occasion arisen. They all belong together as persons of substance, members of a cultivated social elite, and in particular as sympathizers with Jewish thought, since it was usually through the synagogue connection that they met St. Paul.[65]

Of particular importance are Aquila and Prisca. Theissen judges them to have significant financial resources because they managed to remove themselves from Rome (Acts 18:2), were still able to employ and house Paul (Acts 18:3), house a church (Rom. 16:5, 1 Cor. 16:19), and travel long distances and remain for long periods (Acts 18:18-26). Their patronage appears lavish and widespread, since the entire gentile church owes them thanks (Rom. 16:5).

Prisca and Aquila also patronized Apollos. But Apollos's relationship with them (Acts 18:26-27) appears somewhat different from Paul's. Paul apparently kept the ledger of exchanges even, avoiding a client's obligations (thus, his patrons are his fellow workers). He earned their patronage with his teaching, while perhaps insulting them by not accepting monetary gifts.[66] But Apollos was

---

[64]Stowers, "Public Speaking and Private Teaching," 68.
[65]Judge, "Early Christians," 130.
[66]Marshall, 232 passim.

more on the receiving end: he received teaching as well as other help, including the money Paul refused (see below).[67] Further, Paul could boast that, at least in this particular case, he did not need a letter of recommendation (2 Cor. 3:1) from a patron, but Apollos needed one because of his less secure status with the church (Acts 18:27).

The *nouveau riche*, who wished to gain status through money, would be particularly frustrated by Paul's refusal of their gifts, and delighted if Apollos would accept them. In fact, Paul is aware that all the other apostles, except Barnabas but including Cephas and presumably Apollos, accepted gifts (1 Cor. 9:5-6). Paul does not criticize them, because he considers it an apostle's right to do so, and he accepts gifts from other churches.[68] But in Corinth, he refused all monetary gifts in his desire to be a "champion" apostle (9:24-27; note the irony here). He adapted his behavior to the particular situation (9:20-23), perhaps suspicious from the first that the ambitious Corinthians would treat him as a resident sophist.[69] That decision led some to criticize him, perhaps especially those who boasted of their "friendship" with (i.e., patronage of) Apollos: "Didn't Apollos speak with words that moved us far more than Paul's, and didn't he adorn our house with his professional presence rather than dishonor it with the dirty hands of an artisan?" Those who criticize Paul he describes in a slightly, and perhaps significantly differently list than 1:26: they too are wise and powerful, but instead of well born, they are "held in repute" (ἔδοξοι, 1 Cor. 4:10).

If the leaders of the Pauline group are imagined to be higher status than the leaders of the Apollos group, this helps the reader make sense of several other factors in the Corinthian letters. First, it explains why Paul tends to identify with the "strong," yet takes the position of the "weak" (1 Cor 8, 10:23-30). Theissen persuasively argues that the "strong" are the higher status Corinthians. While the Apollos group also has "strong" members, the strongest are the leaders of Paul's group. Many of the "strong" had been God-fearers, who would be more likely to accept Paul's sophisticated theological arguments such as "an idol has no real existence" (8:4). Paul cannot

---

[67]προσλαμβάνω, see LSJ, 1518-19; BAGD, 717.
[68]Marshall, 220-22 passim.
[69]Hock, 61.

disagree with his own teaching, but he does object to the use to which the "strong" are putting it: to exalt themselves at the expense of the "weak." As in ch. 1, he criticizes most those who claim to be closest to him.

Presuming a higher status for Paul's patrons also explains why he seems to identify with their values, but then turns them upside down. For example, he counts working with his hands as a hardship which contributes to his low status (1 Cor 4:10-13). Only upper class persons, those who never worked, considered manual labor to be shameful. Those who had were still earning their money through successful trades were proud of their accomplishments.[70] Though employing upper class values, he simultaneously contrasts his position to that of the "wise, strong, and honored" (4:10), language which recalls the wise, powerful, and well-born of 1:26. These aspects of Paul's rhetoric make most sense as addressed to his higher status patrons.

Paul's manual labor created a problem of status inconsistency for those Corinthians who expected their resident sophists or philosophers to accept good salaries. This status problem made him even more dependent on his patrons' status if he were to initiate his new type of speaking to found a new type of community. He needed patrons who could supply more than money; in their toleration of his transgressions of normal patron-client relationships, they must be willing to "risk their necks" for him (Rom. 16:4). "The importance of private residences for his teaching activity was crucial. Paul needed a platform, a legitimate context."[71] Paul was "promoting a new kind of community education for adults. This involved him in a confrontation with his own churches because they wanted him to adopt the status in life that was appropriate to a tertiary teacher."[72]

Apollos, on the other hand, entered a situation in which the context had already been legitimized by Paul's success. Apparently having no scruples against receiving gifts, he needed only a host who could provide such material necessities. But he did not need from his patrons the conferral of status as Paul did; for this he could rely on

---

[70]MacMullen, *Roman Social Relations*, 120.

[71]Stowers, "Public Speaking and Private Teaching," 71.

[72]Judge, "Reaction," 12.

the recommendations of others, such as Paul, Aquila, and Prisca. In other words, he needed only the one thing the *nouveau riche* could supply: money. In exchange, he could confer upon them, as the hosts of an eloquent teacher who appeared professional in his acceptance of gifts, the status they lacked as "wise." These wealthy church members who lacked other status indicators could not afford the status inconsistency of Paul, with his manual labor and refusal of gifts. Thus, it makes sense for the reader to imagine that these νεοπλούτοι would want to claim Apollos as their own wise man to compete with leaders of the more cultured group.

This scenario also relieves the reader of wondering why Apollos is not mentioned in 2 Cor., especially since Paul expected him to return (1 Cor. 16:12). In 2 Cor. 10-12, at least some Corinthians are being attracted to Jewish "superlative apostles" who "class and compare themselves" with Paul, criticizing the weakness and foolishness of his rhetoric while boasting of the wisdom of their own (2 Cor. 10:10-11:22). If Apollos appealed to the higher status Christians as a philosopher-rhetor like Philo, we might expect him to be claimed by those who wanted such superlative rhetoric. We would at least expect to hear some reference to the earlier problems with rhetoric if Paul in both cases was being criticized for using less cultured rhetoric than other preachers, first Apollos and now the superlative apostles. But if the situations were not the same, the lack of reference to Apollos and to the earlier problems makes more sense. That is, in 1 Cor. Paul is resisting being characterized as the high status, eloquent leader of the "wise." In 2 Cor., he is resisting a problem from the other front: now better rhetors than he have attracted his higher status followers, so he is criticized for being a lower status fool.

Though this scenario helps make sense of Paul's rhetoric better than parallels of Apollos with Philo, the reader is not constrained to accept it. Instead, the reader may leave Apollos's rôle rather vague. On the other hand, the reader may choose to narrate a world like the one above to meaningfully locate Apollos in the intersecting stories of Paul's Corinth and social history. With this or a similarly satisfying narrative, the reader is better able to interpret the text as a meaningful response to an implied exigence.

Conclusion

Whatever narrative the reader constructs, the evidence examined thus far suggests certain constraints. We have already seen that Paul is addressing an exigence of division based on the Corinthians' perceptions of his and Apollos's status as wise rhetors. In this chapter, we have seen that just as rhetoric and its relationship to status are a normal part of a Hellenist's world, so too are competitive divisions among the supporters of different rhetors. Thus, our narrative will be constrained to include groups who are attempting to enhance their status by supporting either Paul or Apollos as the superior wise man. Precisely how these general dynamics worked themselves out in Corinth is open to various possible narratives. However, Luke's descriptions of Apollos, especially his Alexandrian origins, have led us to abundant material to further enrich and constrain our narrative so that it makes better sense of these chapters, of later ones, and of parts of 2 Cor. (especially chapters 10-12). In any case, the reader can now be quite confident that two Hellenistic speakers who essentially agreed with one another could easily become sources of division without ever intending to. To this situation Paul responds.

CHAPTER VII

SOCIAL STATUS AS AN EXPLICIT ISSUE

Paul's rhetoric appears to respond to an exigence of division based upon competition for social status, in which each of the groups of 1:12 claims, or is reacting to others' claims, to have a wiser teacher, i.e., one's whose cultured eloquence indicates and confers status. Having raised this exigence in 1:12-17, Paul in 1:18 then contrasts the σοφία λόγου valued by the Corinthians with the foolishness of ὁ λόγος τοῦ σταυροῦ. We have already seen that foolish speech indicates low status. To this opposition between the wisdom of *paideia* and the foolishness of *kerygma*, Paul adds another opposition between strength and weakness. As we shall see, these terms are, like wisdom and foolishness, standard status-related vocabulary. Once introduced, Paul plays upon this opposition of foolishness and weakness versus wisdom and strength (1:23-25).

Wise, Powerful, and Well-Born

That social status is a constraint in the situation Paul addresses becomes even more certain once he begins a new *topos* in 1:26-30. These verses have been greatly studied as providing information for the social description of the Corinthian community. But the relationship between their social implications and the rhetoric of the whole section and its implied situation has not received sufficient attention.

For example, Conzelmann recognizes the references as sociological ("the group comprises the educated, the influential, the people of distinguished family"), but sees this only as an example arbitrarily drawn from the Corinthian situation to assert theology, i.e., Paul's christological adaptation of Jewish theology concerning the overthrow of the lofty and exaltation of the lowly.[1] Barrett sees only a slightly greater connection to situation in that the Corinthians tend to glory in men (3:21).[2] Fee, on the one hand, recognizes something more than examples to support theology: the Corinthians' low social status contradicts their values expressed in their boasts and divisions. On the other hand, Fee wrongly divides sociology and theology:

> But sociology is not Paul's concern; his is theological, and he is capitalizing on the less-than-pretentious social standing of the majority . . . to make his point. . . . God has forever aligned himself with the disenfranchised. . . . Every middle-class or upper-class domestication of the gospel is therefore a betrayal of that gospel.[3]

In a few words, Fee loses the insights of his previous comments, now interpreting Paul's language as an exposition of theology relevant to all times and places. Our modern liberalism might be comfortable castigating those at the top of the heap. But Paul points out that the Corinthians are struggling for status because they *lack* it, at least relative to those with the bluest blood, the best education, and the most power and money. If anything, we might characterize it as an ambitious person's domestication of the gospel.[4]

---

[1]Conzelmann, 49-51.

[2]Barrett, *First Corinthians*, 59.

[3]Fee, 78-82.

[4]I am reading 1:26 with virtually all translators: an assertion that not many were wise, powerful, or well-born. However, W. Wuellner offers a different reading, taking the ὅτι as interrogative. Thus, 1:26 would be a question expecting a positive response: "Were not many of you . . . ?" (Wilhelm Wuellner, "The Sociological Implications of 1 Corinthians 1:26-28 Reconsidered," in *Studia Evangelica*, Vol. 6, ed. Elizabeth A. Livingstone [Berlin: Akademie-Verlag, 1973], 666-672). However, even Wuellner judges the Corinthians to be *petite bourgeoisie* with some upper class and poor. Wuellner's grammatical arguments, as far as I am aware, convinced no one until O'Day's "Jeremiah 9:22-23 and 1 Corinthians 1:26-1:31," 259-267. O'Day argues further that 1:27-1:28 does not refer to the sociological standing of the majority of Corinthians, but to the cross of Christ.

But Paul's rhetoric cannot be directly translated to a theology for all times and places; rather, it confronts the Corinthians' values and actions within a specific language world. As Dale Martin correctly asserts,

> We cannot be content to outline Paul's language purely in theological terms; we must also examine how that theological language relates to social structures, conflicts between groups of people, and struggles for power. The conflict at Corinth was not a debate about abstract theological concepts. It was a struggle between different groups of people with different ways of viewing the world, indeed, different ways of actually structuring the world. Paul entered that struggle, a struggle for the right to define reality.[5]

Attempting to tie together the sociological descriptions of 1:26 with Paul's rhetorical response, J. Bohatec argued that the community in Corinth suffered at the hands of those who were educated, powerful, rich, and socially elite because the community consisted primarily of uneducated, poor, powerless people with no social standing.[6] The ancient world, Bohatec correctly asserts, was clearly divided between a small upper class who held money and power and the rest of the people whom the upper classes held in contempt (though he wrongly equates the lower class with slaves[7]). This, Bohatec argues, is the situation Paul confronts in 1:26-29, opposing the arrogance of the rich and powerful, in terms similar to Philonic parallels drawn from the Hebrew Scriptures. From parallels to 1:26

However, she does not explain why the singular of 1:17-25 becomes plural in 1:26-28. Yet I must agree that 1:26-28 *includes* the cross and 'weak' apostles, as well as lower class Christians, as theological counterparts to status κατὰ σάρκα. In any case, even if we accepted 1:26 as an interrogative expecting a positive response, this affects the rhetorical situation very little. Paul is still attacking boasting in status, including rhetoric, with the anti-rhetoric of the cross.

[5]Martin, 146.

[6]J. Bohatec, "Inhalt und Reihenfolge der 'Schlagworte der Erlösungsreligion in 1 Kor 1.26-31," *Theology* 24 (1948), 252-71. Bohatec's article is also unusual in attending to the meaning the reader can draw from Paul's impressive rhetoric, insisting that one should go beyond Weiss in appreciating more than the stylistics of rhetoric. For a contrasting low view of rhetoric, see Barrett (*First Corinthians*, 58), who finds meaning *in spite* of rhetoric: "rhetorical though the words are, they are not meaningless."

[7]see below, pp. 316-17.

in Jeremiah 9:23-24 and various Hellenistic sources, Bohatec demonstrates that sociological realities are the issue addressed by the verse.

According to Bohatec, the sociological aspects of the situation are not isolated examples drawn for theological illustration, but appear as central issues variously addressed by Paul. We see this especially in his admonitions to avoid lawsuits in 6:1-11, since the powerful could and generally did triumph over the weak in court. Bohatec might well have pointed to the following illustration from Petronius:

> Of what avail are laws to be where money rules alone, and the poor suitor can never succeed? The very men who mock at the times by carrying the Cynic's wallet have sometimes been known to betray the truth for a price. So a lawsuit is nothing more than a public auction, and the knightly juror who sits listening to the case approves, with the record of his vote, something bought.[8]

The function of this rhetoric in 6:1-10 has been thoroughly examined by Alan Mitchell.[9] Though he shows no awareness of Bohatec's article, Mitchell also finds a connection between these verses and social status. He argues that Paul is attempting to define the boundaries of the community by differentiating their methods of settling disputes from those of the world. This aspect of his argument is not very convincing, since he also argues that Paul is suggesting a standard Roman method: private arbitration. Mitchell's emphasis upon group boundaries is drawn from his adviser, Wayne Meeks, but he employs this concept less vigorously than his teacher. Paul is indeed aiming to define and strengthen community boundaries, but by appeal to *values* reflected in legal actions, not the form of the action itself. This value centered rhetoric explains why Paul can eclectically employ rhetorical themes drawn from the culture—he reassembles these themes into a new *gestalt*.

Mitchell points out that private arbitration was often preferred by poorer litigants, because of "the obstacles to getting a fair trial. . . . The evidence points to the fact that going to court was costly and

---

[8]Petron. *Sat.* 14.

[9]Alan Mitchell, *1 Corinthians 6:1-11: Group Boundaries and the Courts of Corinth* (Ph.D. diss., Yale, 1986).

inconvenient, and that the wealthier members of society seemed to be favored by the Romans courts."[10] Mitchell goes on to argue that if the wealthy members are suing each other, this eliminates the issue of status. But this is too simplistic a notion of competition for status. As we have already seen and will see further below, the competition was often keenest among those nearer the top who were ambitious to climb higher, or at least not suffer any loss of prestige. For this reason, an argument like Bohatec's makes more sense: Paul is beseeching the Corinthians to recognize that just as their wisdom comes from Christ, not from men, their justification comes from Christ, not the courts. So too does their dignity in sanctification, and their freedom (redemption). Thus, Paul's argument is a paradoxical confrontation with the social values of ancient culture.

Wilckens found Bohatec's argument about the social references of 1:26 thoroughly persuasive, even though Bohatec's thesis of confrontation with culture did not match his thesis of confrontation with the Corinthians' theology. Since Wilckens' thesis runs counter to the rhetorical force of Paul's language, he argues for a polyvocal meaning for 1:26: not only are the Corinthians socially unesteemed, they are, like all human efforts, nothings. This then allows Wilckens to shift the focus of his interpretation from sociological reference and confrontation with culture to rarified theological debate.[11]

The tension in Wilckens' interpretation between surface sociological reference and hidden theological reference is dissolved in the readings offered by Pearson, Horsley and Davis. They perceive no tension because they simply abandon any sociological reading. Striving to harmonize 1:26 with their speculative reconstruction of a Corinthian theology, these critics ignore the rhetorical force in favor of linguistic parallels to Hellenistic sources. Pointing to passages from Philo, they assert that Paul refers not to the sociological position of the Corinthians when God called them, but to their boast of spiritual status as metaphorically well-born, honored, and royal on the basis of their wisdom.[12]

---

[10]Ibid, 97, 211.

[11]Wilckens, *Weisheit*, 41-43.

[12]Pearson, *Pneumatikos-Pseukikos*, 40. Horsley, "Pneumatikos vs. Psychikos: Distinctions of Spiritual Status among the Corinthians," *HTR* 69 (1976), 282-288; idem, "Gnosis in Corinth: 1 Cor 8:1-6," *NTS* 27 (1980),43-45; idem, "Wisdom of

One problem with these parallels, as Fee points out, is that "none of their examples brings this set [wise, powerful, well-born], nor anything quite like it, together." In contrast, "Munck has mustered a considerable amount of evidence to show that part of the "boast" of the sophists was precisely that they belonged to the 'wise, powerful, and well born.'"[13] However, Fee is too impressed by Munck's parallels, for Munck relies exclusively on evidence of the Second Sophistic in Philostratus' *Vitae Sophistarum* and *Eunapius' Vitae Philosophorum et Sophistarum.*[14] The social position of sophists in the second to the fourth centuries appears to be more consistent and higher than that of rhetors in the 1st. Yet, the later sophists were heirs of the long and close relationship between rhetoric and status. "The social and political influence of the rhetors of the late republic and early empire can be discerned clearly by anyone who cares to look; in the second century it simply cannot be missed, so conspicuous are the intellectual and (in many cases) lineal descendants of those earlier men of culture."[15]

Despite the difficulties of Pearson's and Horsley's Philonic parallels, they are impressive. Thus, the Corinthians might well have been using these terms in this sense, and we might well hear echoes of such usage in other passages, such as 4:8. But in 1:26, Paul asserts that few Corinthians could claim to be wise, powerful, or well-born κατὰ σάρκα, not κατὰ πνεύματος. Proto-gnostics would have responded, "Of course we aren't powerful or well born according to the flesh. We have become so according to the spirit. That's just our point." What rhetorical force 1:26 has in the rhetorical situation of proto-gnosticism I cannot imagine, nor do the proponents of this argument seem to ask this question. Parallels are not enough.

They are not enough for another reason which has been frequently pointed out by critics of this approach: the parallels seem to be common features of Hellenism beyond Judaism.[16] As I have

---

Words," 232-33; Davis, 74-78.

[13]Fee, 80-81.

[14]Munck, 162, n. 2.

[15]Bowersock, 43.

[16]e.g., R. Grant, "The Wisdom of the Corinthians," in *The Joy of Study: Papers on New Testament and Related Subjects Presented to Honor Frederick Clifton Grant*, ed. Sherman E. Johnson (New York: MacMillan, 1951), 51-52.

pointed out above, Stoics asserted that only the wise man was truly rich, honored, powerful, and royal, and Philo seems to be picking up standard Stoic teaching. Popular Stoicism frequently emphasized the enjoyment of both metaphorical and actual money, power, and status on the basis of a conflation of philosophical and cultural wisdom. While the presence of Philonic language is sheer speculation, popular Stoicism was so widespread that we can be confident its language was part of the communis sensus of Paul's audience.

Moreover, such language makes sense of the force of Paul's rhetoric in 1:26. The Corinthians are competing for status; Paul points out the absurdity of any such struggles for status in the light of their own situation when God called them. They were not chosen because they had any status; quite the opposite, God has chosen to use things and people without worldly status. If God not only overlooks status, but positively turns it upside-down, then the Corinthians' boastful, divisive behavior is absurd in the context of their own narrative of community origins. Interpreting the rhetoric in this way allows the reader to continue to construct a situation which fulfills the imaginative requirement of cohesion. Paul is not digressing from the exigence of division into a discourse on mystical claims, but tying that exigence closer to the whole situation which included constraints of status perceptions.

In contrast to the parallelism employed in history of religions approaches, E.A. Judge launched a new era in NT criticism by promoting the study of social contexts. Adopting an implicitly rhetorical approach, Judge asserts

> that ideas are never satisfactorily explained merely by discovering their philosophical connections. They must be pinned down in relation to the particular circumstances in which they were expressed.... The New Testament is not an orderly statement of dogma, but a heterogeneous collection of writings addressed to various occasions ... There will normally be a particular construction to be placed on them in relation to the particular situation. ... Thus the present study concentrates not on the writers, but on the readers.[17]

[17]Judge, *Social Pattern*, 8-9.

Judge points out that social situations affect their participants in far deeper ways than simply providing terminologies. Rather, early Christian communities in their "thinking and behavior naturally reflect the social institutions" of the Hellenistic Roman republic. "That many of the readers practiced the Jewish religion does not make their situation irrelevant to their thinking. They still lived under the Hellenistic social institutions and largely shared in the common tradition of civilization." Ideas in the New Testament can to some extent be understood as "a reaction to the situation."[18]

Among Judge's observations, he revises earlier scholars' assessments of the social position of Christians. His conclusions have now become the basis of a wide consensus. First, the Christians did not include any members of the upper classes: "Christians rarely met members of the Roman aristocracy; very few people did. What we want to discover are the affiliations of Christians within their own communities. . . . Their membership seems to have been drawn from a surprising variety of stations."[19] Though not the richest members of the empire, the Corinthian community had sufficient resources to contribute to the collection for the Jerusalem church (1 Cor. 16:1-3; 2 Cor. 9:1-5).

Paul seems to be a fairly distinguished member of society, with impeccable Jewish credentials and good relations with those in power (Rom. 11:1, 2 Cor. 11:22, Gal. 1:13-14, Phil. 3:4-6). Judge fills out this picture primarily from a somewhat indiscriminate use of Acts. But he can also point out that, as in Acts, the Paul of the letters moved freely among the best circles not only of Palestinian but of Hellenistic society (Rom. 16:23). Furthermore, he displayed a cultured sensitivity to humiliations:

> 'We are made as the filth of the world, and are the off-scouring of all things unto this day' (1 Cor. iv. 13) is certainly not the complaint of a person to whom social affronts were normal. On the contrary, they are felt as indignities he ought not to have been subjected to. Under the same heading come his occasional periods of manual labour. . . . Normally he expected to be supported at

---

[18]Ibid., 14-17.
[19]Ibid., 54.

the charges of the groups who enjoyed his religious leadership (1 Cor. 9:4; 2 Cor. 11:8, 12:13).[20]

This touchiness Paul displays principally in his relationship with the Corinthians. Judge interprets this as evidence that the Corinthians have "forced him into an embarrassing position by their own airs." These "Corinthian social pretensions" can be seen in their "snobbery and divisions": e.g., they split into factions to support rival leaders (1 Cor. 1:12), sued each other in the public courts (1 Cor. 6:7), poisoned the common meal with selfishness (1 Cor. 11:21), and were generally riddled with

> debates, envyings, wraths, strifes, backbitings, whisperings, swellings, tumults (2 Cor. 12:20). But this was natural in a group that had enjoyed the attentions not only of the mercurial Paul but of the impressive Alexandrian theologian, Apollos (Acts 18:24-28) and others, and was entertained by a number of generous patrons (Rom. 16:1, 2, 23; 1 Cor. 1:16, 16:15; Acts 18:8). The ... exclamation 'not many wise . . . , not many mighty, not many noble, are called' (1 Cor. 1:26) plainly admits this situation. Taking the words at their face value, they merely imply that the group did not contain many intellectuals, politicians, or persons of gentle birth. But this would suggest that the group did at least draw upon this minority to some extent. However, it is hardly intended as a factual statement. Properly evaluated as a piece of impassioned rhetoric, it leaves no doubt that in their own opinion, and presumably also in that of their contemporaries, they were anything but a collection of unintelligent nonentities. Paul in fact states this later. 'Now ye are full, now ye are rich, ye have reigned as kings without us. . . . We are fools . . ., but ye are wise . . .; we are weak, but ye are strong; ye are honourable, but we are despised' (1 Cor. 4:8, 10). His aim is to disabuse them of such ideas, and to clear his gospel of any suggestions of depending on human qualifications for success. The stress on his own humiliation is meant to drive the point home by contrast with their behavior.
>
> The Corinthians . . . were dominated by a socially pretentious section of the population . . . . Beyond that they seem to have drawn on a broad constituency, probably representing the household dependents of the leading members. The interests brought together in this way probably marked the Christians off from the other unofficial associations, which were generally socially and economically as homogeneous as possible. Certainly the phenome-

[20]Ibid., 58.

> non led to constant differences among the Christians themselves.[21]

Using his implicitly rhetorical approach of listening with ears imaginatively attuned to the culture of the original audience, Judge constructs the outlines of a meaningful reading of 1 Cor. 1:26. This reading is becoming increasingly persuasive as a supplement or even alternative to those which attempt to trace parallels, backgrounds, or trajectories of the key words of 1:26 in narrowly religious contexts. While the latter have succeeded in finding these parallels, the direction of such research has moved from gnosticism to Hellenistic Judaism, and verges on general Hellenism. Meanwhile the rôle of such general Hellenistic status issues in the Corinthian situation continues to grow.

A major impetus for this direction of research has been the work of Gerd Theissen. In a series of important articles, Theissen argues for a larger rôle for sociological factors. He focuses on the Corinthian community, partly because Paul's Corinthian correspondence provide us with such a wealth of information, but also because this information suggests the importance of sociological factors in those situations.

1 Cor. 1:26-29 are key verses in Theissen's argument. He follows Bohatec and Judge in concluding that "although it is true that by means of these designations social relationships are seen in a theological light, the sociological implications of the concepts cannot be denied."[22] Theissen adds to Bohatec's numerous Hellenic and Hellenistic parallels, not only to the three terms in 1:26, but also to those in the following verses (τὰ ἀσθενη, "the weak"; τὰ ἰσχυρά, "the strong"; τὰ ἐξουθενημένα, "the despised"; τὰ μὴ ὄντα, "nothings"). These parallels amply illustrate that all these terms normally refer to high or low social status. Among these parallels, Theissen and Bohatec both point to the following passage in Philo which contains numerous similarities to the Corinthian correspondence in terminology, oppositions, the connection of wisdom to other aspects of

[21]Ibid., 59-60.

[22]Theissen, 71.

worldly status, and the easy mixture of sociological and theological comment:

> [Concerning] "the affairs of men" (τὰ ἀνθρώπων πράγματα). . . . Are not private citizens (ἐξ ἰδιωτῶν) continually becoming officials (ἄρχοντες) and officials private citizens, rich men (ἐκ πλουσίων) becoming poor men (πένητες) and poor men men of ample means, nobodies becoming celebrated (ἔνδοξοι), obscure people (ἄδοξοι) becoming distinguished, weak men (ἐξ ἀσθενῶν) strong (ἰσχυροι), insignificant men (ἀδυνάτων) powerful (δυνατοὶ), foolish men (ἐξ ἀφραινόντων) men of understanding (συνετοὶ), witless men (ἐκ παραπαιότων) sound reasoners (εὐλογιστότατοι). Such is the road on which human affairs go up and down, a road liable to shifting and unstable happenings,[23]

in contrast to the stable, high position of God.[24]

In addition to the same or similar terms found in 1 Cor. 1:26-29, Philo refers to the "human" of 2:5, the "rulers" of 2:8, the "rich" of 4:8, and the "private person" of 2 Cor. 11:6. Concerning this last term, Philo's use again illustrates how an ἰδιώτης could mean nothing more than one without governmental authority. Such a person, in Philo's opposition, is clearly lower in status than a ruler; but at the same time his status does not preclude other indicators of high status, including eloquence.

Theissen focuses on the parallel idiomatic uses of τὰ μὴ ὄντα in opposition to ἐυγενεῖς and concludes that

> the last of the three categories mentioned (wise, powerful, of noble birth) is of unmistakable sociological significance. Because this particular term in the series goes beyond the catchwords of the preceding context, it can be assumed that in the new paragraph (1:26ff), Paul has a social fact in mind and probably intends the first two categories to be understood sociologically as well. The "powerful" would be influential people; the "wise," those who belong to the educated classes (that is, "wise according to worldly standards") for whom wisdom is also a sign of social status. . . . In my opinion there can be no doubt about the sociological implications of the language of 1 Cor. 1:26-29.[25]

---

[23]Philo *De somniis* 155-6.

[24]Ibid., 157-158.

[25]Theissen, 71-72.

Theissen's careful analysis has received further nuancing in an article by Sänger, who attempts to sharpen our sense of the reference of δυνατοί.[26] Like Bohatec and Theissen, he considers the meaning of σοφοί beyond dispute: those who possess the σοφία τοῦ κόσμου of 1:18-3:23. "The σοφοί are members of the educated/cultured (*gebildeter*) circle, those who belong to the social elite." This is indicated by the parallel of σοφός with δυνατός/ἰσχυρός and σοφοί/δυνατοί with εὐγενεῖς. The latter term refers to "people of esteemed families, of high birth, to whom a suitable conduct—we can even say a suitable character—should correspond." These are the same as "those who are honored" (ἔνδοξοι) of 4:10. Similarly, the lowborn often are likened to the bad or evil. So, in Hellenistic diction, we hear an unmistakable sociological reference in three sets of parallels and corresponding antonyms:

σοφοί	=	φρόνιμοι vs. μωροί
δυνατοί	=	ἰσχυροί vs. ἀσθενεῖς
εὐγενεῖς	=	ἔνδοξοι vs. ἄτιμοι

Sänger correctly points out that εὐγενής is not an equivalent term for wealthy. Rather, as his numerous textual parallels illustrate, it is used exclusively to refer to honor or high prestige, not to wealth alone. Wealth did not guarantee high prestige or credentials of high origin or character. As MacMullen observes, in the competition for status, "affluence obviously constituted one important factor," but, among the upper classes, it was not enough. One thing a moneyed person might lack was *paideia*:

> They laughed at ill-educated slips and slurs of speech; . . . Those who went on to advanced training in rhetoric and a career of eloquence were hailed by crowds of supporters and laudatory decrees, by claques and plaques. Here then is a second factor: great learning, great power as a speaker, style and taste in one's address.[27]

---

[26]D. Sanger, "Die *dunatoi* in 1 Kor 1:26," *ZNW*, 285-91.

[27]MacMullen, *Roman Social Relations*, 107.

On the other hand, to those lower on the social scale, money did accord status:

> When we turn from what was expected of a Roman senator to a decurion of Tymandus (some of whose peers could barely read or write), we confront quite another scale of values. The army veteran, even more explicitly, points the difference. It was not his years in camp that brought him honor, it was not likely to be his lineage, and hardly his cultivation. His neighbors valued him because, as one says, "He's *got* it"—meaning money alone. His mustering-out bonus and his savings allowed an ex-private to assume the leadership of a village, an officer to enter the council of some large provincial center. . . . When we get right down to it, wealth seems to earn respect by itself, to the degree it is accumulated.[28]

Turning his attention to the δυνατοί, Sänger again agrees with Theissen, Bohatec, and Judge that they are people of influence. But Sänger presses this reference further by examining just how people came to be influential and powerful, and concludes that δύνατος can be used as a technical term for political power derived from economic muscle. With this we might compare MacMullen's observation with supporting citations that οἱ δυνατοί (*potentes*) was "the common term for magnates," the landlords whose economic, political and legal power dominated the life of the poor.[29] Similarly, Welborn notes that "the δυνατοί are the πλούσιοι throughout Greek literature."[30] Thus, we find Artemidorus speaking of three economic categories: very *powerful* men and women, those of moderate means, and the poor (τοῖς μὲν μέγα δυναμένοις ἀνδράσι καὶ γυναιξὶν . . ., τοῖς δε μετρίοις . . ., τοῖς δὲ πένησιν).[31] Yet the words were not strictly equivalent, as is evident from Plutarch's list of praises similar to Paul's: "eloquent, rich, or powerful (λόγιος ἢ πλούσιον ἢ δυνατὸν)."[32]

Thus, the terms "weakness" and "strength" (whether δυνατός or ἰσχυρός) were status-related.

---

[28]Ibid., 108, 117.

[29]Ibid., 163, n. 52; cf. LSJ, 453.

[30]Welborn, "Discord," 97.

[31]Artemidori Daldiani *Onirocriticon* 2.34.

[32]Plut. *De se ipsum citra invidiam laudando*, 12 (*Mor.* 543A).

> Usage of the terms both in a wide cross-section of Hellenistic writers and in Paul himself indicates . . . that the terms carry strong social connotations. 'Weakness' is the state of those without power or status, and 'strength' is the state of those who do have status. 'Weakness' connotes humiliation in the eyes of others, rather than inadequacy in one's own.[33]

So, in 1:26, Paul connects economic and political power with good birth. Though a person might have only good birth or power, more often than not a person had neither or both. Inheritance could confer riches and office, and the connections of good birth often enabled people to amass even greater fortunes and power. Conversely, money was a prerequisite for entry into the upper class. As MacMullen notes,

> To pay for the enormously expensive role in the community that would, over the span of some generations, ennoble one's line; to pay the fees and voluntary subscriptions to the gymnasium through which one's culture and accent might satisfy polite circles; to maintain one's household in proper fashion—all required a handsome income. It was taken for granted by the aristocracy. Without it, social ambitions could never be treated seriously. By itself, however, it did not constitute respectability.[34]

Thus, Sänger, like Theissen and Judge, argues that Paul is referring to the presence of at least a few cultured, rich, and/or well-born people in the Corinthian congregation. However, this conclusion must be carefully nuanced. As pointed out above, the richest and most powerful members of society were probably not even in the congregation. Moreover, Paul's assertion that "not many of you were wise according to flesh, not many powerful, not many well-born," suggests that even the highest status Corinthians are only of middling status. They are the μέσοι, the μέτριοι, the νεόπλουτοι we have encountered in various sources. Challenged by Paul's assertions, the audience must cope with their relative *lack* of status rather than their

---

[33]Christopher Forbes, 19. See also idem, "'Strength' and 'Weakness' as Terminology of Status in St. Paul: The Historical and Literary Roots of a Metaphor, with Specific Reference to 1 and 2 Corinthians" (unpublished B.A. Honors thesis, Macquarie University, 1978; unavailable to me).

[34]MacMullen, *Roman Social Relations*, 108.

relative *boast* of status. Like magic, the glass that was half full becomes half empty.

The Corinthians are competing because they are, in typical Greco-Roman fashion, both proud of whatever status they have, and envious of those with higher status.

> Even those of lower rank would boast of what they could, identifying themselves, for example, by the initials *s.* for *servus* or *serva,* "slave," or *l.* for *libertus* or *liberta*, "freedman" or "freedwoman." . . . It is important to recognize that they did tend to classify themselves and one another. Even slaves within a household ranked themselves; those with more desirable jobs had higher prestige than menials and had the fact recorded on their tombstones: "nurse," "pedagogue," "valet."[35]

For this reason, Paul's rhetoric can be effective. On the one hand, the Corinthians are boasting of the high status they enjoy by association with a wise teacher. On the other hand, by the rules of the same status game, they lack the indicators of the highest status. As we shall see further, Paul's rhetoric suggests the presence of people with money who suffer status dissonance from their lack of other status indicators.

In any case, the meaning of the language is clear. In Roman society, we find

> three standards of prestige: time, money, place. The further back . . . , the more . . . , the closer to Rome . . . —these were the lines of thought drawn defensively around one's position to keep others out. A fourth we may call vaguely, culture. One might fail by the test of the first three and yet sneer at one's patron, as Lucian did at his employers or as the dinner guests sneered at Trimalchio.[36]

The "wise, powerful, and well-born" are none other than the elite of ancient times.

From this we can conclude several things. Paul is addressing a situation in which competition for status over the prestige of eloquence is related to the widespread cultural competition for status.

---

[35]Meeks, *Moral World*, 32-34.

[36]MacMullen, *Roman Social Relations*, 122.

This competition is based on several status indicators summed up by MacMullen as time, money, place, and culture, i.e., good birth, wealth and power, *urbanitas*, and *paideia*. These same indicators Paul sums up as "wise, powerful, and well-born." Elsewhere he adds "rulers" (2:6-8), "rich" and "kings" (4:8), and "honored" (4:10). Thus, the exigence Paul perceives is deeper than division itself. The divisions are alarming because they are tied to worldly competition for status, a competition whose values diametrically oppose those of the cross of Christ.

Status and Boasting

Paul explicitly refers to such boasting of status in the context of his list of status indicators. He connects the two ideas theologically in 1:29, 31: "God chose what is low and despised in the world, even things that are not, to bring to nothing things that are, so that no human being might boast in the presence of God. . . . As it is written, 'Let him who boasts, boast of the Lord.'"

Paul's rhetoric reveals that he is addressing an audience in which he perceives boasts of worldly status to be a problem. As we pointed out above, he strengthens this rhetoric with the explicit scriptural citation in 1:31 of Jeremiah 9:22-23 which continues the implicit citation of those same verses in 1:26. The Jeremiah text admonishes the wise man, the mighty man, and the rich man to cease boasting of their wisdom, might, and riches in the face of God's activity:

> Μὴ καυχάσθο ὁ σοφὸς ἐν τῄ σοφίᾳ αὐτοῦ,
> καὶ μὴ καυχάσθω ὁ ἰσχυρὸς ἐν τῃ ἰσχύι αὐτοῦ,
> καὶ μὴ καυχάσθω ὁ πλούσιος ἐν τῳ πλούτῳ αὐτοῦ,
> ἀλλ ἤ ἐν τούτῳ καυχάσθω ὁ καυχώμενος,
> συνίειν καὶ γινώσκιν ὅτι ἐγώ εἰμι κύριος
> ποιῶν ἔλεος καὶ κρίμα καὶ δικαιοσύνην επὶ τῆς γῆς.

As O'Day remarks, Paul

> read the Corinthian situation through the lens of Jeremiah (or *mutatis mutandis*, Jeremiah through the lens of the Corinthian situation) because of the exigency of the situation. . . . Jeremiah's critique of wisdom, power, and wealth as false sources of identity

that violate the covenant are reimaged by Paul as a critique of wisdom, power, and wealth that impede God's saving acts in Jesus Christ.[37]

In the rhetorical situation, then, boasting is connected to status, including the status of being perceived as wise. But it is also connected to the divisions of 1:12 and the σοφία λόγου of 1:18-25. In 3:4, he has returned to the exigence and slogans of 1:12. Then in 3:5, he introduces his alternative to the evaluation of himself and Apollos as champions of division: they are not wise rhetors with high status, but servants (διάκονοι) who were persuasive (δι' ὧν ἐπιστεύσατε). As servants, the gospel is not theirs to possess; rather each has what God has given him (ἑκάστῳ ὡς ὁ κύριος ἔδωκεν). In fact, they are nothing (οὐ τι, 3:7, cf. 1:28). Only God is exalted. His servants may have different work assigned, but they are not to be set one over the other because of this difference; rather they are united in their work (3:8a). Changing his metaphor from servants to field workers, Paul insists that unlike sophists who are patronized for their status enhancing presence, the apostles deserve no more wages from God than what they earn through their labor (3:9b-15). To this issue of wages we shall return below.

Following Paul's rhetoric of the apostles' rôles as servants or workers, Paul in 3:18-19 returns to the theme of the foolishness of worldly wisdom. Then, in 3:21-22a he again makes clear that such wisdom centers on boasting in men (καυχάομαι ἐν ἀνθρώποις), which in the context of 3:4 and 3:22 should be read as referring to their divisive boasting in apostles: "So let no one boast of men. For all things are yours, whether Paul or Apollos or Cephas."

After the climax of 3:21b-23, Paul employs another *expolitio*. In 4:1, he repeats and amplifies the point of 3:5, where he had opposed the Corinthian perceptions of the apostles with his questions, "What then is Apollos? What then is Paul?" The answer, as we have seen, is that they are to be seen not in terms of status and boasting, but as servants. In 4:1-2, Paul puts the same point in the form of a statement: "*Thus* a man should regard us," as servants. Now he uses the terms ὑπερέτης and οἰκονόμος. Paralleling the thought of 3:5, that they are not wise men to be honored because they are persua-

[37]O'Day, 266-67.

sive, but "servants through whom you were persuaded (διάκονοι δι' ὧν ἐπιστευσατε, 3:5)," here they are to be regarded as slaves (ὑπηρέται) who are trustworthy and believable house stewards (πίστοι οἰκονόμοι, 4:1-2).

In 4:6, Paul describes his own rhetoric: he has "transferred as in a figure of speech" (μετασχηματίζω)[38] the rhetoric of status to himself and Apollos. But the rhetoric is reversed: he and Apollos are not to be spoken of as sources of status enhancing wisdom, but as mere servants.

> Paul is intent on awakening his audience's attention to the fact that things are not what they seem to be. In fact, in using the term *metaschematizein* ("to transfer as in a figure") . . . Paul expressly states the parenetic purpose behind his remarks. . . . At least the Christian patrons [wish] to resemble those of other groups around sophists and professional rhetoricians. If, then, it was these same highly placed Christians who were guilty of lionizing one teacher over another (1:10; 3:4), of vaunting their own knowledge (3:1; 6:12; 8:13), of making distinctions in the community rooted in pride (4:7; 5:2), or of slighting the poor at the assemblies (11:17-34), then Paul would have to proceed with caution. . . . Paul offers his own example . . . as a help for the community to see things for what they are and not take them as they seem to the world.[39]

Paul as Servant

The function of servant language in Paul's rhetoric later in the letter, in 9:15-23, has been thoroughly investigated by Dale Martin. Martin argues that chapter 9 is a digression, framed by the *inclusio* of chapter 8 and 10 which both address the issue of the weak, the strong, and meat sacrificed to idols. Accepting Theissen's arguments that the categories of "weak" and "strong" are status related, Martin argues that Paul writes a fictitious defense in chapter 9 against imaginary interlocutors to portray himself to the strong as an example to be imitated.[40]

---

[38]LSJ, 1117; BAGD, 51; Conzelmann, 85-86; F.H. Colson, "μετεσχηματισα I Cor. iv 6," *JTS* 17, 379-384.

[39]Benjamin Fiore, "'Covert Allusion' in 1 Corinthians 1-4," *CBQ* 47 (1985), 89-101.

[40]Martin, 77-80.

Martin argues that in 9:17 Paul portrays "himself as Christ's slave *oikonomos*," using

> status-specific language precisely because his goal is to change the behavior of a particular group in Corinth, those who are themselves taking their own high positions too seriously. Throughout chapter 9, Paul constructs his arguments in terms that were loaded for the higher-status Christians at Corinth, because it is that group he is addressing. They were unwilling to change their lifestyles in order to please less important Christians. They did not want to give up their perquisites, such as their philosophical freedoms and their social activities, which included eating meat; they wanted to remain leaders of the church at Corinth but from a secure position of social superiority. Paul's choice of imagery emphasizes that he, their first leader, is a high-status person who has taken on low status. He challenges the other leading Christians to do the same. . . . His rhetoric overturns the clear categories of his contemporary readers, who assume that leaders are free, exercise authority, and do not work, whereas lower-status persons do work. Paul's language forces his readers who share upper-class views to think of leadership in confusing ways that stress the ambiguity—not the "givenness"—of normal status indicators.[41]

The same rhetorical purpose and situation Martin finds in chapter 4, where

> Paul addresses certain persons at Corinth who are "filled," "rich," and who "reign like kings" (4:8). In contrast to these people, Paul says that he and his co-workers are of low status: they are foolish instead of wise, weak instead of strong, dishonored instead of famous. Paul juxtaposes these different pairs of terms in an obvious play on status positions. It is no accident that the next sentence mentions very real indicators of Paul's low status: hunger, thirst, nakedness, abuse, homelessness, and manual labor. . . . Paul contrasts the apostles' weakness with the strength of "certain" people at Corinth. His assertion of his authority and his call to imitation are directed at those "certain ones" who judge their own positions by normal criteria of social status. . . . Paul targets the ones on top, the wise, rich, strong, and free.[42]

These high status Christians "think of Christians leadership as modeled on the benevolent, free, high status *sophos*," which Paul

---

[41]Ibid., 79-80, 82.

[42]Ibid., 122-23.

opposes with his metaphor of being an οἰκονόμος of Christ in 9:16-18.[43]

Paul as Οἰκονόμος

While the status of slaves always appeared low in the view of the upper class, Martin points out that those lower on the Roman social scale might hear such language as ambiguous. This was particularly true of οἰκονόμοι, "those slaves who worked as stewards of households or businesses; they were sometimes plantation managers or financial bursars."[44] Although οἰκονόμος did not necessarily designate a slave, in the context of Paul's self-description as διάκονοι and ὑπηρέται in 1 Cor. 3:5 and 4:1-2 it should be read as referring to slave stewards.

Just as Paul wrote that οἰκονόμοι should be πιστοί, so does Artemidorus *Oneirocritica*, a dream handbook which is

> a valuable source of attitudes of the lower strata of Greco-Roman society. As it is a practical handbook on the interpretation of dreams, its concerns remain close to the everyday concerns of ordinary people: health, financial state, business transactions, social relations. Furthermore, because it relates dreams of all persons—not just those of kings and the elite—it offers at least indirect access to desires and attitudes of the lower classes, including slaves of various levels. . . .
>
> Artemidorus splits the slave population into two basic groups: common slaves and those 'in a position of trust' [n.: *pepisteumenoi*]. The *oikonomos* word group is sometimes used to refer to someone in the second category, but the terminology is flexible. Such people may be designated as slaves "held in trust" (*en pistei*), or as those honored by their masters or having many possessions.[45]

Thus, οἰκονόμοι enjoyed certain status indicators higher than many free persons, including the derived authority and power of the owner, status by relationship with the owner, and perhaps considerable financial means.

---

[43]Ibid., 135.

[44]Ibid., 15.

[45]Ibid., 20-21, citing Artemidorus, 1.35, 1.74, 2.9, 2.30, 2.47, 2.49, 4.15, 4.61.

Though Martin does not comment on the slave terms of 1 Cor. 4:1-2, several parallels with 9:16-18 are apparent. First, we find not only the general parallel of Paul's self-designation as a slave, but also the close parallel between 4:1, where Paul speaks of himself as an οἰκονόμος of the mysteries of God who has been found faithful (πιστός), and 9:17, where Paul has been entrusted with a stewardship of the gospel (οἰκονομίαν πεπίστευμαι). Furthermore, words used by Artemidorus in close association with the οἰκονόμος are found in 4:1-2: not only the πίστις word group, but also his list of "different kinds of slaves in what seems an order of ascending status:" after "servers (*therapontes*)" comes Paul's two terms of 4:1-2: "underlings or helpers (*hyperetai*)" and "stewards (*oikonomoi*)."[46] In both chapters 4 and 9, then, Paul rhetorically claims to be an οικονόμος to confront those who would boast of their status. In both chapters, these claims aim to remove the basis for the boasts of the "strong" while simultaneously enhancing Paul's authority on alternative grounds.

Paul as Demagogue

We might also note a connection between Paul's designations of himself as an οἰκονόμος in 1 Cor. and as an ἰδιώτης in 2 Cor. 11:6. As we saw above, ἰδιώτης is often used to designate a status position of one who does not have the honor of public office. In an extended passage about the qualifications for having dreams with public significance, Artemidorus uses the term in this way. He opposes the ἰδιώτης to a king (βασιλεύς), a master (δεσπότης), a magistrate (ἄρχων), a general (στρατηγός), or one of the nobility (μεγιστάν). In contrast to such persons, private citizens are those to whom only small matters have been entrusted (ἰδιῶται μικρὰ πεπιστευμένοι).[47] Since Artemidorus tends to use the term πεπιστευμένοι as an equivalent for οἰκονόμος, his diction reveals a close relationship between the status implications of the ἰδιώτης and the οἰκονόμος.

---

[46]Martin, 34.

[47]Artemidorus, 1.2.

These congruences are even more striking when we notice that Artemidorus allows one exception to the relatively lower state of the ἰδιώτης:

> It has never happened that a dream which has a meaning for the entire state has been seen by a single private citizen; it has been seen, rather, by many and in the same way—some of whom announce it publicly while others do so individually and in private. And so it comes about that the seer is not a private man (ἰδιώτης), but the people (δῆμος), which is in no way inferior (ἥττων) to a general or a ruler.[48]

This exception is striking because it relates directly to the second metaphor of slavery outlined by Martin: the demagogue's slavery to the people, to which, Martin argues, Paul appeals in 1 Cor. 9:19-22. Like the metaphor of the οἰκονόμος, Paul's demagogic rhetoric serves to enhance his authority at the same time that he transgresses the normal hierarchy of status. In other words, Paul, though on the one hand an ἰδιώτης or δημότης[49] with no public authority according to ordinary upper class stan- dards, gains that authority by direct appeal to the people.[50] According to Artemidorus, the people as a whole, though individually only ἰδιῶται, can rise to the same status as a king, ruler, or other member of the wise, powerful, and well-born. Thus, Artemidorus puts the demagogue in the same category as a ῥήτωρ or a rich man who has been appointed to some office, as opposed to a poor man or one who is rich yet has not held office (i.e., an ἰδιώτης).[51] This relationship between the ἰδιώτης, rhetoric, and demagoguery is brought out by Plutarch, who comments that an ἰδιώτης of δημοτικός dress and appearance can "attain power and rule the multitude" only if "he possesses persuasion and attractive speech."[52]

From below, demagogic power is a marvelous leap-frogging of status barriers, but from above, it is mere slavishness to the people.

---

[48]Artemidorus, 1.2. Translation adapted from *Interpretation of Dreams*, trans. Robert J. White (Park Ridge, NJ: Noyes Press, 1975), 18.

[49]The two words can be used synonymously. LSJ, 387.

[50]For this function of demagogic rhetoric, see Martin, 86-135.

[51]Artemidorus 1.17.

[52]Plut. *Praecepta Gerendae Reipublicae*, *Mor.* 801E.

In this vein, Plutarch criticizes the "self-praise of a demagogue, of a would-be sophist, or of one who courts plaudits and cheers."[53] As we shall see below, such self-praise, though widely practiced, risked back-firing if perceived as an attempt to claim a status to which one was not entitled by cultured standards. Apparently, the "superlative apostles" in 2 Cor. attempted to employ such invective against Paul, accusing him of "commending himself" (ἑαυτοὺς συνιστάνειν 2 Cor. 3:1, cf. 4:2), "boasting a little too much in our authority (περισσότερόν τι καυχήσωμαι περὶ τῆς ἐξουσίας ἡμῶν, 10:8)." Such boasting could be criticized because it "immoderately" (εἰς τὰ ἄμετρα, 10:13, 15) claimed authority beyond normal upper class standards of status. Though the "superlative apostles" also boast of themselves, theirs is within upper class norms of eloquence (10:10, 11:6), leisure (10:15, 11:23), birth (11:22), and power (11:20-21); in short, they boast in their worldly position (5:12) viewed humanly (5:16). Paul is merely an ἰδιώτης (11:6), a person with no power or status. Yet his success with the people (10:14-16) commends him (3:2). Thus, Paul's demagogic rhetoric informs us in yet one more way how he could be "an ἰδιώτης, yet not without knowledge," i.e., not in the category of a professional orator or public official, yet with equivalent authority as slave to the people of God, "abasing himself" (ταπεινῶν) as an οἰκονόμος without pay, so the people might be "exalted" (ὑψαω, 2 Cor. 11:5-7).

Paul's use of demagogic rhetoric to overthrow the oligarchic world of the higher status Corinthians has also been noted by Welborn. As I argued in chapter 3, Welborn unnecessarily limits the entire situation to the politics of oligarchy versus democracy. Nevertheless, these aspects of power are still present within the more general references to status. Welborn points out that Paul's terms in 1:26

> are the very terms employed by Greek writers from the time of Solon to designate the major class divisions. . . . The supporters of oligarchic government are referred to as the "wise" (σοφόι or φρόνιμοι), the "powerful" (δυνατοί), the "nobly-born" (εὐγενεῖς, γενναῖοι, or γνώριμοι) all substitutes for "the rich"; while "the poor," the supporters of democracy, are styled in

---

[53]Plut. *De se ipsum citra invidiam laudando* 16 (*Mor.* 545C).

> antithesis the "vulgar" (μωροί or βάναυσοι), the "weak" (ἀσθενεῖς), the "lowly-born" (ἀγενεῖς or δημοτικοί). . . . It is obvious whose view of society is reflected in these terms. The absolute dichotomy they express corresponds to the wide gulf between the rich and the poor in the ancient economy. Paul uses the established terminology ironically: God has inaudibly inverted the accepted values, an acoustic phenomenon for which only the elect have ears.[54]

Given the different status associations of these terms depending upon the relative status position of the audience, Paul's rhetoric in 4:1-2 and 9:16-18 not only challenged, within upper class diction, the normal upper class assumptions about status, but identified Paul with those lower on the social scale. At the same time it served to reassert Paul's authority as a representative of Christ. Just as Paul writes about "transferring" status language "as in a figure of speech" to himself and Apollos (4:6), Martin notes that Paul "redefines the arena for status by taking it out of normal discourse and placing it within the symbolic universe of the household of Christ."[55]

The Ethos of the Faithful Οἰκονόμος

We also find striking parallels between chapters 3-4 and chapter 9 concerning both money and Paul's defense against those who would interrogate him. In both 9:3 and 4:3, Paul refers to those who ἀνακρίνει him, which can mean to interrogate him as in a court.[56] "Paul's language in 4:1-5 leaves little doubt that his opponents sought to 'examine' his credentials in quasi-judicial proceedings."[57]

In the context of 4:3, the accusers are those who would question whether he is a speaker worthy of confidence (πιστός). To establish or destroy such credibility was one of the strongest and most basic techniques of rhetoric. Following Aristotle, such appeal to persuasiveness or the lack of it based on character was usually called ἦθος, which renders a speaker worthy of confidence (πιστός) so that the

---

[54]Welborn, "Discord," 96-97.
[55]Martin, 66.
[56]LSJ, 109.
[57]Welborn, "Discord," 107.

audience is ready to believe him (πιστεύω).[58] Some, Paul says, might accuse him of falling short in this regard. (4:3).

Since some are claiming allegiance to another apostle, they would inevitably compare the *ethos* of their own rhetor to that of Paul, finding their own teacher worthy of greater praise (ἔπαινος, 4:5). "Evidently, the leaders of the opposing factions were also men of substance, for the terms that Paul uses to characterize those who would examine his apostolic credentials in 1 Cor. 4:10—'wise' (φρόνιμοι), 'strong' (ἰσχυροί), and 'held in repute' (ἔνδοξοι)—are, like the epithets in 1:26, euphemisms for 'the rich.'"[59] Paul attempts to counter this interrogation of his *ethos* as in a court (ἀνακρίνω) or by a human tribunal (ἀνθρωπίνη ἡμέρας, 4:3).[60] In place of the rhetoric of status employed by the Corinthians, he "transfers" (4:6) to the apostles the discourse of the faithful οἰκονόμος. In this alternative discursive world, the apostles are at once low status but with the high authority of their master. Paul also transfers this discourse from the human to the divine sphere: only God will interrogate and judge him (4:4-5). Again, human cultural values involving rhetoric are contrasted with the ways of God.

In chapter 9, Paul is also defending himself against those who would interrogate him (ἀνακρίνουσίν, 9:3). Once again, the issue is his authority, i.e., whether his character makes his speech a credible directive for action. Here, Paul addresses the implications of his refusal of financial support. Rather than receive the wages (μισθός) of a free worker, Paul receives the reward (μισθός) of being a faithful οἰκονόμος of God (9:17-18). Only in his rôle as οἰκονόμος does, ironically, he have any boast (καύχημα). This boast would be emptied (κενόω) if he instead worked as a higher status free person, just as the cross would be emptied (κενόω) if he allowed others to boast of him as a high status speaker of σοφία λόγου (1:17).

We find the same idea of faithful stewardship in 4:2 as an *expolitio* of 3:5, where Paul moves from the metaphor of servanthood to that of hired field workers who receive the fitting wage for their

---

[58]Arist. *Rh.* 1.2.3-4; cf. Quint. 6.2.18-19.

[59]Welborn, "Discord," 98.

[60]LSJ, 770; cf. BAGD, 347: "a day appointed by a human court." On character assassination through interrogation, see Quint. 5.7.26, 30; *Rhet. Her.* 2.6.9. See also on comparison, pp. 341-44.

labor. He is the one who plants (φυτεύω) and receives his wages (μισθός) for his labor. This is nearly the same imagery he uses in 9:1 in defense of his right as a worker to claim the fruit of the vine he has planted (φυτεύω), a right he has refused to exercise. In both places he also combines the metaphors of wages for field workers and for temple workers. All these parallels only strengthen a reading which sees the same status-related issues being addressed in similar ways in both places.

All this status-related language Paul has transferred to himself and Apollos so that the Corinthians may not be puffed up (φυσιόω, 4:6, a variant of φυσάω, "to blow, or puff," which can be used metaphorically to mean "to puff up, or make vain" or "to swell with pride"[61]). Paul admonishes them not to "be inflated with pride each on behalf of the one [leader] against the other (εἷς ὑπὲρ τοῦ ἑνος φυσιοῦσθε κατὰ τοῦ ἑτέρου,[62] . . . boasting (καυχάομαι)" as if whatever they possess were not a gift. This rhetoric of status, boasting, and divisiveness he follows with two contrasting status descriptions: the first of the Corinthians, being rich (πλουτέω) and reigning as kings (βασιλεύω); versus a second of the apostles, as criminals sentenced to die (επιθανάτιος) like gladiators (θέατρον). Then (v. 10) comes a familiar series of contrasts (μοροὶ/φρόνιμοι; ἀσθενεῖς/ἰσχυροί) whose function as status descriptions is made certain by the final pair: you are ἔνδοξοι, we are ἄτιμοι. The final term is then expanded by a *peristasis* catalogue which culminates in the lowest possible status for the apostles as the dirt one cleans off and discards. The section ends by returning to those who are puffed up, but now Paul makes clear that he refers to actually, not just potentially, arrogant persons (4:18-19). Paul's rhetoric in this section, then, continues to tie together competitive boasting in social status as related to the divisions of 1:12.

---

[61]LSJ, 1963; cf. Welborn, "Conciliatory," 332.

[62]The translation is from C.F.D. Moule, *An Idiom-Book of New Testament Greek*, 2nd ed. (Cambridge: University Press, 1959), 64: "ὑπέρ with the genitive means *on behalf of, with a view to, concerning*." Cf. Marshall, 204: the Corinthians are "puffed up each on behalf of one person—Paul, Apollos, Cephas—against another. Though it is better to see the reference in the ἵνα clause to Paul and Apollos rather than to the Corinthians themselves being puffed up against each other, the latter rendering is also possible."

The Rhetoric of Praise

The boasts of status Paul confronts were a normal part of Greco-Roman culture. As we saw in Chapter 6, these boasts often focused on competitions among favored rhetors. The status gained by association with a wiser rhetor gave one greater grounds for boasting of one's own status in comparison with another's. Thus, comparison of teachers and boasting of one's own status were closely related.

The norms for any praise, including comparison and self-praise, were set out by the rhetoricians in discussions of the rhetoric of *ethos*. Among the standard topics for this rhetoric are things frequently found in the Corinthian correspondence. These are classified by the rhetoricians as, first (in Theon's typical list), "external qualities," including "good breeding (εὐγένεια ἀγαθόν), . . . education (παιδεία), friendship (φιλία), reputation (δόξα), public office (ἀρχή), wealth (πλοῦτος), an easy death." The second category includes the "bodily qualities (τοῦ σώματος)," among which "are health, strength (ἰσχύς), beauty, quick wit." The third category covers virtues evident in deeds, the first of which is always practical wisdom (φρόνιμος).[63]

Such lists had long been established in both Greek and Roman philosophical and rhetorical traditions[64], and Aristotle expounds on them at great length in his *Rhetoric*.[65] The Greek equivalents Caplan gives to the list in *Ad Herennium* are similar to those in Theon and include: εὐγένεια, πλοῦτος, δυνάμεις, εὐδοξία, and τιμή, all key words in 1 Cor. (substituting ἔνδοξος for εὐδοξία). Wisdom appears as *prudentia*.[66] Cicero likewise refers to the external attributes for praise as "public office, money, connections by marriage, high birth, friends, country, power, and all other things that are understood to belong to this class." and the first virtue as

---

[63]Theon *Prog*. 9.15-24.

[64]For citations, see Caplan's note *a* in *Rhet. Her.* at 1.6.10 (p. 174).

[65]Ar. *Rh*. 1.5.3-18 (1360b-1362a), 1.9.1-13 (1366a-b).

[66]*Rhet. Her.* 3.6.10. This list closely parallels that of Aristotles' components of happiness (εὐδαιμονία, Arist. *Rh*. 1.5.4).

prudentia.[67] Quintilian restricts his list to "wealth, power, and influence" as key subjects for praise.[68]

Paul parodies the Corinthians' praise of himself and Apollos as well as their self-praise. In 1 Cor. 4:9-13, he portrays his "external attributes" as the opposite of "rich, wise, strong, and honored." His bodily attributes are likewise the opposite of strength of body: he is ill-fed, ill-clothed (4:11) and "with you in weakness (ἀσθενεια) and in much fear and trembling" (2:3). His actions are likewise contemptible for an upper class person: he works as a tradesman, which makes him servile (4:12). Worse, his actions display weakness rather than strength: when he is reviled, he blesses; when persecuted, he bears it; when slandered, he conciliates (1 Cor. 4:12-13).

Paul parodies praise as part of his reverse rhetoric, since praise functioned to reinforce the status hierarchies and their attendant values. As Theon notes, "it is customary to flatter (κολακεύω) the living" since praise of noble actions overcomes "the jealousy of the mob (οἱ πολλοί), for 'with the living, jealousy,' according to Thucydides, 'arises because of rivalry.'"[69] Even self-praise, wrote Plutarch, when used within proper bounds of modesty and truthfulness, shows that the speaker refuses to be humbled, and so humbles (μὴ ταπεινοῦσθαι ταπεινούσης) and overpowers envy (φθόνος). "For men no longer think fit even to pass judgement on such as these, but exult and rejoice and catch the inspiration of the swelling speech, when it is well-founded and true."[70] In such self-praise we see how "the love of status, philotimia . . . [when] understood to its depths, goes further to explain the Greco-Roman achievement" than any other word.[71]

However, when praising oneself, one had to be careful to avoid being perceived as unjustifiably boastful. Upper class people were quick to criticize anyone equal to or beneath them who attempted to claim a status to which they were not entitled. Just as φιλοτιμία had a positive sense when the status was recognized, it could also be used

---

[67]Cic. *Inv. Rhet.* 2.59.177.

[68]Quint. 3.7.14.

[69]Theon *Prog.* 9.26-28.

[70]Plut. *De se ipsum citra invidiam laudando*, *Mor.* 540D.

[71]MacMullen, *Roman Social Relations*, 125; 168, n. 14; 201, n. 99.

in a negative sense to mean an ambitious display, or ostentation when the status sought was not recognized by others. Especially significant for the exigence of 1 Cor. 1-4, in the plural it can refer to the very jealousies, rivalries, and party feelings which Theon claimed it could overcome.[72]

Thus, self-praise was a dangerous tool, Plutarch tells us, in his essay, "On Inoffensive Self-Praise," because it could easily appear "to aim to gratify ambition (φιλοτιμίας) and an unseasonable appetite for fame." This only serves to underline the speaker's lack of status, for

> when those who hunger for praise cannot find others to praise them, they give the appearance of seeking sustenance and succour for their vainglorious appetite from themselves. . . . When they . . . try to rival the honor that belongs to others and set against it their own accomplishments and acts in the hope of dimming the glory of another, their conduct is not only frivolous, but envious and spiteful as well.

Such persons will possess the qualities of being "puffed up, vainglorious, or proud (ἀλαζονεία καὶ κενότητα καὶ φιλοτιμία)."[73] Flatterers can easily "puff up" (φυσῶσιν) such an ambitious ἀλαζών. Such self-praise is often characteristic of "soldiers and the newly rich (νεοπλούτους) with their flaunting and ostentatious talk." But it is also characteristic of "sophists, philosophers and commanders who are full of their own importance and hold forth on the theme."[74]

The negative evaluation of ambition which seeks to "cheat" the status system is evident in Quintilian's criticism of "the ostentatious poor person [*pauper ambitiousus*]" who does not have the necessary rooms and furniture for proper hospitality, so that his furniture "is sure to show signs of wear through being used for such a variety of different purposes."[75] This kind of criticism is greatly embellished in *Ad Herennium* in a humorous narrative describing "a man who is not actually rich, but parades as a moneyed man," one who "thinks it admirable that he is called rich." He is criticized for displaying

---

[72]LCL, 1941.

[73]Plut. *De se ipsum citra invidiam laudando*, 3-4 (*Mor.* 540A-D).

[74]Ibid, 22 (547E).

[75]Quint. 2.4.29.

"empty boasting [*gloria*: thirst for glory, ambition, pride, boasting, bragging] and showing-off [*ostentatio*]." In short, he is a "boastful man" [*gloriosus*].

This "boastful man" was familiar to the rhetorical tradition, especially in its frequent reliance upon Theophrastus' *Characters*.[76] Theophrastus describes the "ἀλάζων (pretentious or snobbish person)" who lays claim to advantages he does not possess. The details about the behavior of such a character are strikingly similar to those in Ad Herennium. The ἀλάζων uses deceit to make his small number of possessions appear to be quite large. Yet, like Quintilian's "*pauper*," who possesses enough furniture and housing to make a pretense of the life-style of the rich, the ἀλάζων is far from impoverished. He has a servant, some money in the bank, and, though he does not own a home, rents one that suits his pretensions.[77]

The same character appears again in Epictetus: "The braggart (ἀλάζων)" is "a tasteless and worthless person." who shows himself off to οἱ πολλοί as a "rich man and an official (πλουτοῦντα καὶ ἄρξοντα)" Epictetus warns his students against such social climbing:

> Observe the means by which you must achieve your pretense: You will have to borrow some paltry slaves; and possess a few pieces of silver plate, and exhibit these same pieces conspicuously and frequently, if you can, and try not to let people know that they are the same; and possess contemptible bright clothes, and all other kinds of finery, and show yourself off as the one who is honored by the most distinguished persons; and try to dine with them, or at least make people think that you dine with them; and resort to base arts in the treatment of your person, so as to appear more shapely and of gentler birth than you actually are.[78]

Similar to the character of ἀλάζονεία is that of μικροφιλοτιμία (petty pride), which Theophrastus defines as "a vulgar [ἀνελεύθερος: servile] appetite for distinction [τιμή]; . . . The μικροφιλότιμος [is] of a kind that when he is invited out to dine must needs find place to dine next to the host." Like the ἀλάζων, he makes an ostentatious display of his possessions. But unlike the ἀλάζων, the

---

[76]*OCD*, 1058.

[77]Theoph. *Char.* 23.

[78]Epict. 4.6.3-4.

μικροφιλότιμος is actually upper class, for he is a knight and a magistrate. Yet, though he is rich, he is not of the highest status, for he seeks to sit next to the generals (στρατηγοί) in the theater. He invites philosophers, sophists, and others to use his private wrestling place "for their displays which he himself attends, coming in late so that the company may say one to another, 'That is the owner of the wrestling-place.'"

Such arguments were so common they are listed among the *topoi* by the rhetoricians. According to *Herennium*, "We shall be using the topics of Temperance [*modestia*] if we censure the inordinate desire for office [*honoris*, i.e., honor, esteem, position, glory, fame], money, or the like."[79]

Employing such *topoi*, Philo criticizes boastfulness (ἀλαζονεία) in a passage which, by its parallels with the Corinthian correspondence, especially 1 Cor. 4:6-13, illustrates the sense of Paul's diction. Boastfulness, writes Philo, is particularly displayed by those who enjoy riches (πλοῦτοι) and honors (δόξοι) and high offices (ἡγεμονίαι). Filled (κόρος) with their privileges, they fall into "insolence" (ὕβρις). They "at once" (εὐθὺς) become "elated" (διαιρόμενοι) and "puffed up" (φυσώμενοι). Having become rich, they make others poor; having received great glory and honor (δόξα καὶ τιμή), they bring ingloriousness and dishonor (ἀδοξία καὶ ἀτιμία) to others. They prefer jealousy and envy (φθόνος καὶ βασκανία) to thankfulness. Such persons regard themselves as richer (πλουσιώτατος), worthy of greater honor or rank (ἐντιμότατος), of greater beauty, honor, or nobility (κάλλιστος), stronger (ἰσχυρότατος), wiser (φρονιμώτατος), more temperate (σωφρονέστατος), more just (δικαιότατος), more eloquent (λογιώτατος), more knowledgeable (ἐπιστημονικώτατος); while everyone else they regard as poor, disesteemed, unhonored, foolish, unjust, ignorant, offscourings (καθάρματα), nothings (τὸ μηδέν). The only cure for them is to remember that God says that he "gives you strength to make power" (σοι δίδωσιν ἰσξὺν ποιῆσαι δύναμιν). One who understands that his strength is a divine gift will take account of his own weakness (ἀσθένεια) and will overthrow his arrogant pride (ὑπέραυχος φρόνημα) in thankfulness.[80]

---

[79]*Rhet. Her.* 3.3.5.

[80]Philo *De Virtutibus* 51, 161-174.

Beside illustrating Paul's diction, Philo also shows the thin line between boastfulness and hurtful arrogance (ὕβρις). Theon points to the latter as the most obvious example of a *topos*: "The charge of being an insolent person [ὑβριστός] is universal and undisputed, and so is called a commonplace [τόπος]. By starting out from such a charge, as from a familiar place, we readily have an abundant supply of arguments."[81]

Thus, with ears attuned to a Greco-Roman audience, Paul's rhetoric would be taken as accusing the Corinthians of boastful, status-seeking behavior. This "rhetoric of status" has been noted by Peter Marshall in an important and sweeping extension of the work of Judge and Theissen. Marshall emphasizes the strongest type of such rhetoric, the accusation of ὕβρις: a prideful, arrogant or insolent attitude of superiority, usually resulting in insulting behavior which brings shame and feelings of outrage to the victim. *Hybris* was

> traditionally and closely associated with the term κόρος, 'fulness', 'satiety' or 'having too much', and the verb κορέννυμι (passive or middle), 'to be sated or glutted with a thing', 'having one's fill of a thing'. They are virtually equivalent in meaning being used interchangeably in many instances. Both notions are frequently joined with *ploutos* and *hybris* is said to either produce *koros* or *ploutos*, or to be produced by them. Overindulgence or wealth caused a person to become a *hybristes* or he may be said to indulge further because he is *hybristes*. Wealth is implicit in behaviour of the *hybris* kind.[82]

The "fullness" was often associated with eating and drinking too much, which was generally possible only for the rich. Thus, the *hybristes* had plenty of everything, and this was related to his attitude of superiority. This attitude often led to insulting actions which brought shame upon others and pleasure to the *hybristes*. "The rich treat people just as they like because they think that they are the most important people in existence, and that if anyone objects they will be able to buy off trouble, by compensation or by bribery of officials."[83] *Hybris* frequently results in political or social discord

---

[81]Theon *Prog.* 6.13-16.

[82]Marshall, 183-184.

[83]N.R.E. Fisher, "Hybris and Dishonour," *Greece and Rome* 23 (1976), 182 (quoted by Marshall, 186).

and factions, especially between the powerful and the masses. In sum, *hybris*

> is primarily a social concept which indicates the breach of one's assigned status and thus results in dishonour and shame. It is most commonly caused by undue pride in strength and wealth, both of which are given by the gods. The hybrist is regarded as a fool (*aphron*), a man who is not aware of his own limitations; a boaster (*alazon*) who pretends to possess praiseworthy qualities which he does not have or only possesses in limited measure; a vain man who gives himself to *hybris* due to his wealth and false conception of his superiority over both his equals and inferiors.[84]

The *hybrist* as wealthy person is described by MacMullen:

> Secure in interlaced wealth, acquaintance, and kinship, gentlemen earned yet another nickname: "the Haughty." They earned it by conspicuous consumption expressive of their vast resources and, by implication, an insult to the poor. They earned it by their progress through the streets, sweeping *hoi polloi* to the walls. . . . "'I am superior to you,'" Epictetus imagines one of them saying, "'for my father has consular rank.' . . . A boast of influence was equally common. . . . "[85]

Paul employs this rhetoric to criticize those who are boasting on the typical grounds of culture, power, and birth (1:26, 29; 3:18). Like the hybrist, they have become puffed up in a competitive fashion (4:6). In an even more telling application of ὕβρις *topoi*, Paul accuses the Corinthians of being sated (κεκορεσμένοι), enriched (ἐπλουτήσατε), and reigning as kings (ἐβασιλεύσατε). The last reference, if alone, could be taken to echo only the boast of popular Stoicism that the wise man is a king. But when combined with the first, it has the unmistakable ring of accusations of *hybris*.

With this accusation, Paul has heightened his rhetoric from criticism of boasting to accusation of crime, for ὑβρις often included actual violent crime. In this case, the more powerful the offender, the greater the potential to harm those less powerful. Thus, the worst offender was the tyrant. "The *koros* and *hybris* of a king far

---

[84]Marshall, 194.

[85]MacMullen, *Roman Social Relations*, 110.

exceed that of a wealthy man. As an absolute ruler, the Hellenistic king was above the law and independent of his subjects."[86]

The rhetoric of the ὕβρις of the ruler also included the phrase πάντα ἔξιστιν, which "not only described the total freedom of the king to do as he pleased, but represented a popular catchcry of a person of rank and amounted to an assertion of independence from his fellow man and to those who would impinge upon his freedom." This catchcry, and other examples of "the traditional terminology of freedom" in 1 Cor. 6, 8, and 10, were used "by the wealthy and powerful in Greek literature as a means of justifying hybristic behaviour." This parallel and many others are used by Marshall to argue

> that reference to *hybris* rather than gnosis provides a satisfactory explanation of the attitudes and conduct of the Corinthians. . . . The term represents a familiar and contemporary tradition of long standing in Greek life and thought, something which cannot yet be claimed with any confidence about the primitive gnostic/pneumatic movement. By comparison, it offers a recognizable and more comprehensive context in which to explain the complex of nuances (e.g., status, excess, measurement, moderation, superiority, shame, freedom, knowledge) which appears in the passages.[87]

Marshall concludes that the "arrogant" whom Paul criticizes must be this sort of haughty rich person, and to some extent this fits the situation. Yet Paul never uses the term ὕβρις, and the type of behavior displayed by Theophastus's ἀλάζων generally fits Paul's rhetoric better. Marshall refers to Theophrastus's ἀλάζων, but he fails to point out that this character, from the point of view of the upper class, is *not* rich. The distinctive quality of the ἀλάζων is his boasting in an attempt to gain a status he does *not* possess. Similarly, the μικροφιλότιμος has a vulgar or servile appetite for esteem beyond his station. Thus, while Marshall correctly argues that those Paul criticizes in 1 Cor. 1-4 must be *relatively* rich and powerful, they are also likely to be those who are not of the highest status, but seek it at the expense of each other and those beneath them.

---

[86]Marshall, *Enmity*, 188, 209.

[87]Marshall, 189, 215, 218, 404.

On the other hand, the presence of ὕβρις *topoi* cannot be ignored. The difference between the ὑβριστής and the ἀλάζων seems to be mainly a matter of point of view. Complaints about ὕβρις behavior comes from equals or inferiors who suffer from insulting haughtiness or violence. Criticisms of the ἀλάζων come from above, from those who resent the tasteless pretensions of those trying to push their way up. As Philo shows, an ἀλάζων could become a ὑβριστής once he had the power.

The mixture of the two themes in Paul would thus best be read as responding to the competitions of relatively higher status persons who are trying to push higher. Whether they are haughty or boastful would depend upon the relative position of the person criticizing the behavior. But to Paul, like Philo, any such behavior is the same violation of scriptural calls for humility before God.

In Paul's rhetorical world, *hybristic* behavior was also confronted by the cross. As we noted in Chapter 4, a crucified champion was perceived as foolishness. *Hybristic* behavior was enjoyable because it brought shame on others, emphasizing one's own honor by comparison. Those whose humiliation was public suffered the worst shame. A crucified person was the diametric opposite of a *hybrist*.

Self-Praise as Comparison in 2 Corinthians

Whatever the status level of the Corinthians, they later tolerated hybristic behavior from the "superlative apostles" who boast of their own persons (2 Cor. 5:12) and accomplishments (11:17), including their eloquence (10:5-6), authority (11:12), strength (10:10, 21), and descent of family and race (11:22). The Corinthians, Paul writes, bear it when one or another of these fools (ἀφρονων) arrogantly displays his strength, seeking honor he does not deserve: he "makes slaves of you, or preys upon you, or takes advantage of you, or puts on airs, or strikes you in the face." (11:20)

These superlative apostles were using comparison to recommend themselves (2 Cor. 10:12, 18). This was a standard feature of Hellenistic culture, as numerous examples cited by Forbes demonstrate. Forbes concludes that

> self-advertisement was a prime characteristic of popular teachers. The convention of comparison was practiced as part of this self-advertisement. . . . It is clear that a major part of Paul's critique of his opponents is directed toward their (to him) extravagant self-praise, formulated in frequently invidious comparison. Consistent conventions relating to self-praise can be shown to exist from at least 100 B.C., through Paul's time, and beyond. The conventions of third-person encomium were simply adapted into first-person speech. However, it was widely conceded that self-praise was an odious business, and one that no decent person would indulge in, except in certain fairly clearly defined circumstances. . . . I believe it is fair to say that the educated Hellenistic world in which Paul moved knew of conventions of self-praise, but believed that they required great delicacy if they were not to be misused, as they led all too easily to ἀλοζονεία and ὑπεροψία, which were closely related to ὕβρις. Like self-comparison, self-praise was a dangerous, though occasionally useful tool.[88]

The standard themes for comparison were the same as those for praise. According to Theon, comparison is a rhetorical technique to enable the audience to determine the superiority (ὑπεροχή, cf. 1 Cor. 2:1) of one person over another.

> When we compare (συγκρίνωμεν) characters (πρόσωπα, cf. 2 Cor. 5:12), we will first set side by side [their external qualities:] their noble birth (εὐγένεια) [according to nation and race], their education (παιδεία), their children, their public offices (ἀρχαί), their reputation (δόξα); their bodily health, as well as whatever else I said earlier, in the chapter 'On Encomia,' about bodily good qualities and external good qualities." After these items, we will compare their actions.[89]

When the super-apostles compare themselves with Paul to demonstrate their own superiority, they point to their "external" attributes, those τοῦ σώματος, and their deeds. By doing so, they compare and boast ἐν προσώπῳ rather than ἐν καρδίᾳ (5:12), i.e., as Theon advises, according to the person as he appears in his worldly accomplishments. This Paul also describes as "proclaiming themselves" (κηρύσσειν ἑαυτοὺς, 4:5); as looking according not to what is unseen (which is a superiority beyond all superiority, καθ'

---

[88]Christopher Forbes, 7-10.

[89]Theon *Prog.* 10.13-18.

ὑπερβολὴν εἰς ὑπερβολὴν,[90] 4:17-18), but to what is seen; as perceiving a person according to the flesh (εἰδέναι τινά κατὰ σάρκα, 5:16) and as boasting according to the flesh (πολλοὶ καυχῶνται κατὰ σάρκα, 11:18). He also apparently turns against his opponents their accusation of boasting immoderately (εἰς τὰ ἄμετρα καυχῆσθαι, 10:13, 15).

In comparing themselves to Paul, the superlative apostles have admitted that he is eloquent in his letters (2 Cor. 10:10), but his eloquence is no match for theirs, for he is not a professional orator (11:6), nor any kind of σοφός (11:16-19). Furthermore, he cannot boast of his descent (11:22). Turning to things τοῦ σώματος, he again compares unfavorably to their strength (ἰσχύς): ἡ παρουσία τοῦ σώματος ἀσθενὴς (10:10).[91] This they have amplified by pointing out that that his physical weakness contributes to the weakness of his eloquence, for his λόγος ἐξουθενημένος. For deeds displaying their virtues, they can boast like a general of their victorious actions in the service of their patron Christ (11:23-33) and the visions he granted them in return (12:1-7).

Paul attempts to turn the comparison ἐν προσώπῳ to his favor. In birth, he matches at least their claims of Jewish origin (11:22). But in virtually all other respects, he attempts to turn their boasts against them so they might be perceived as going beyond the limits of acceptable boasting into ἀλάζωνεια or even ὕβις ("boasting immoderately [ἄμετρος]," 10:13). He parodies their boasting, casting them in the rôle of the foolish (ἄφρων) ἀλάζων or ὑβριστής.

In 1 Cor., as we saw above, Paul had also confronted boastful attitudes with another strategy: "reverse rhetoric." By 2 Cor., his authority has been questioned partly because the superlative apostles can point to the superiority of their persons. Paul answers these comparisons with even more of this "reverse" rhetoric, again hitting the standard themes of "external attributes," things τοῦ σώματος, and deeds (2 Cor. 4:7-9, 6:4-10, 11:23b-33, 12:7-10). As Marshall asserts,

---

[90]The cognate ὑπερβολία, is a synonym of ὕβρις and κόρος, LSJ 1861.

[91]The phrase τοῦ σώματος clearly places "weakness" here as part of the bodily attributes, but, as pointed out above, in general the term has a wide status-related reference.

> "super-apostles" have made invidious comparisons between themselves and [Paul]. . . . The rival apostles resorted to the traditional exercise of comparison, and such popular topics of encomium as their social position, power and deeds, to cast Paul in an unfavourable light as a man who lacked culture.

Whether Marshall is also correct to assert that "the majority of the Corinthians were persuaded by it" we cannot say. But those to whom Paul's rhetoric is addressed, the higher status leaders, were persuaded, "and their susceptibility suggests that they shared a common system of values with the rival apostles."[92]

Once we see that this value system was a constant throughout the changing rhetorical situations Paul faced in Corinth, we can better appreciate the rôle that issues of status, boasting, and rhetoric play in the particular situation addressed in 1 Cor. Marshall attempts to do this by projecting the problems of 2 Cor. back into the situation of 1 Cor. Pointing to the issue of Paul's refusal of money in both letters, he argues that Paul has offended normal friendship relations by refusing the rich Corinthians' gift in return for his teaching. This, he suggests, might have caused the divisions of 1 Cor. 1:12: those who are not "of Paul" responded to his insult by changing their allegiance to another "friend."[93] Those "of Paul" remain loyal despite the insult. However, even to the extent that Marshall's arguments about money are otherwise convincing, his particular point about the divisions of 1:12 encounters the same problem as so many others: Paul strongly disapproves of those who are "of Paul." Thus, the behavior of those "of Paul" is no less "*hybristic*" than the behavior those "of Apollos." The problem in 1 Cor. 1-4 is not primarily money, or insults, but divisions based on ambitious, boastful, status-seeking attitudes and behavior which led to rivalries and party spirit.

Conclusion

We had already seen in previous chapters that Paul is confronting a situation in which the Corinthians have perceived him and

---

[92]Marshall, 200, 384.

[93]Ibid., 264.

Apollos as cultured rhetors, and have formed into groups championing one or the other. In this chapter, we have seen that Paul focuses on the issues of status and boasting, further persuading us that the divisions are based on such issues, and that it is such values that so alarm Paul. His response draws on Septuagintal rhetoric as an alternative to Hellenistic rhetoric about status. But the latter he also employs in a way that undermines normal status hierarchies, while simultaneously re-establishing his authority as servant. This anti-rhetoric takes the form of rhetoric normally used by ambitious people who want to enhance their status through boasting, comparison, and competitive divisions. Paul will not allow himself, the Gospel, Christ, or the Corinthians to submit to such cultural categories. Instead, he offers a paradoxical vision of strength through weakness.

Before we narrate this situation more fully, our imaginations might be further enriched by looking at another place that rhetoric and status probably interacted in Corinth—at their dinners

CHAPTER VIII

ELOQUENCE AT DINNER

Our search for clues to aid our imaginations in constructing a rhetorical situation have produced several important ones:

1) Paul is responding to an exigence of division in the community in the name of at least two teachers, himself and Apollos.
2) This division is not tied to significant differences among the teachers' doctrine or character, nor to their rôles as baptizers.
3) The division is related to rhetoric, i.e., cultural wisdom. In Hellenistic culture, perceptions of one's rhetorical, cultural wisdom are an important determinate of status. Thus, the divisions were rivalries for the status of having the wisest teacher.
4) The Corinthian rivalries are part of their normal Hellenistic boasts of status in terms of education or culture, political power, and genteel birth. They also compare their favored apostles in these terms. By 2 Cor., they clearly favor apostles who compare themselves with Paul in similar terms.
5) Paul focuses on this status-seeking behavior as the problem behind the divisions, both through explicit references and rhetorical methods aimed at undermining its underpinnings in the Corinthians' socio-linguistic world.

Before employing our imaginations to knit these factors together into a coherent situation, we can find further clues in the direction set by Theissen's research. Particularly important here is the information Theissen gleans from 1 Cor. 11 on the conflict at the Lord's Supper. In that chapter, Paul "is silent about . . . theological motives. . . . Only the social causes of the conflict emerge more clearly. Therefore it may be suggestive to put forward the thesis that this conflict has a social background."[1]

The Symposion

The social setting to which Theissen appeals is that of the evening meal, the δεῖπνον (*cena*), which was nearly always combined with the συμπόσιον (*convivium*), the drinking party. The social norms of the meal were well established, reaching back into classical Greece through Imperial Rome. While some variation occurs, these mainly adapt the standard customs to suit particular functions.[2]

Theissen offers little argument for his treatment of the Corinthian δεῖπνον within these norms of the Greco-Roman συμπόσιον. But others have vindicated the appropriateness of this setting. Aune points to five aspects of overlapping perceptions:

1) The *symposion* always had religious significance. It generally began with offerings of food to a divinity and concluded with libations and the singing of hymns; sacrificial meat was frequently preferred for the δεῖπνον. With such typical meals Paul explicitly compares the κυριακὸν δεῖπνον (1 Cor. 11:20; 10:14-22). "The force of this analogy is dependent on the actual similarities between the Lord's Supper and other religious meals. It seems clear that the Corinthian Christians understood the Lord's Supper in terms of the same conceptual framework that they brought to bear on other sacral meals within their experience."

---

[1]Theissen, 146.

[2]Dennis Edwin Smith, *Social Obligation in the Context of Communal Meals: A Study of the Christian Meal in 1 Corinthians in Comparison with Graeco-Roman Communal Meals*, Th.D. Thesis, Harvard, 1980; David E. Aune, "*Septum Sapientium Convivium*, 71; "Symposia," *DKP*, 449; "Convivium," *DKP*, 1301.

2) The Christians assembled to eat (συνερχόμενοι εἰς φαγεῖν, 11:33). "Paul is clearly offended by the structure and decorum which marked the sacral meals of the Corinthian community; one suspects that the root of the conflict lies in Paul's perception of the synthesis of Greek versus Judaeo-Christian socio-religious traditions and customs." 3) "What offends Paul most is the inequality and disorder of the proceedings." These were common problems of *symposia* as evidenced by the frequent attempts of those like Plutarch to mitigate such practices. "The 'disorder' at Corinth seems fairly representative of the real nature of such occasions."

4) Paul's comment that some are drunk "appears to be a note of realism," typical of Graeco-Roman *symposia.*

5) The structure of the assemblies seems to have been influenced by the *symposia* patterns. "The δεῖπνον is clearly set at the beginning, and . . . concludes (μετὰ τὸ δεῖπνον, 1 Cor. 11:25) with a ceremony involving wine."[3]

Symposia could be private or public. Christian assemblies would fall somewhere between the two, since they were held in private homes, but their gatherings most closely parallel ancient associations (which also sometimes met in homes). Theissen points out that the dinners of the congregation in Corinth differed from those of other ancient associations

> in regard to their social composition. These associations of the ancient world were, to a great extent, socially homogeneous. Religious associations give evidence of expressing class-specific forms of sociability to an even greater degree than do professional groups of persons bound together by common occupation, where members of different social strata, such as more and less wealthy merchants, could meet. By contrast, the Hellenistic congregations of early Christianity, as we find them in Corinth and Rome, display a marked internal stratification. In Corinth only a few are "wise," "powerful," and "of noble birth" (1 Cor. 1:26), but they seem to dominate and stand in contrast with the majority of members who come from the lower strata.[4]

Theissen deduces several ways in which the "differing expectations, interests, and self-understandings that are class-specific" have

[3]Aune, "*Septum*," 75-78; cf. D.E. Smith, *Social Obligation.*

[4]Theissen, 146.

contributed to divisions (σχίσματα, 11:18) at the Lord's supper. First, those with a higher social status can provide food for the whole group, while the poorer ones must depend on the others' generosity. These wealthier people own their own houses (οἰκίας ἔχετε, 11:22; e.g., Gaius, who is "host to me and to the whole church," Rom 16:23), as opposed to those who have nothing (τοὺς μὴ ἔχοντας). Each of the richer members eats his or her own meal (τὸ ἴδιον δεῖπνον, 11:21), getting drunk while the poorer members go hungry.

These poorer members went hungry because the richer ones treat the food they brought as private (τὸ ἴδιον δεῖπνον), not to be shared with the whole congregation. "It is not inconceivable that there was a larger portion of food for those whose contribution made the meal possible in the first place. Various associations or clubs in antiquity observed such distinctions in allotment and officially recognized . . . 'larger shares in feasts for officials and staff members.'"[5] Such differences merely ritualized everyday conditions, as a guest at Trimalchio's feast summed it up: "I swear I cannot get hold of a mouthful of bread today. . . . The little people come off badly; for the jaws of the upper classes are always keeping carnival."[6] Frequent shortages "proved the existence of class tensions" and were the commonest cause of riots in almost every province and period of the empire.[7]

Not only would the upper class expect larger portions as more honored members, they also might have expected better food.[8] "For some Corinthians it would not be at all strange to think that common meals, involving people of varied social status, should include food of varying quality. Such practice is well attested for the period."[9]

This difference in food was not so much intended to save money, but to reinforce distinctions in status, as Juvenal makes clear:

> You may perhaps suppose that Virro grudges the expense; not a bit of it! His object is to give you pain. For what comedy, what

---

[5]Theissen, 154, quoting PW, s.v. "Collegium;" cf. D.E. Smith, *Social Obligation*, 123.

[6]Petronius, 44.

[7]MacMullen, *Enemies*, 180.

[8]Pliny *Ep.* 2.6; Mar. *Epigr.* 1.20, 3.49, 3.60, 4.85, 6.11, 10.49.

[9]Theissen, 156; cf. D.E. Smith, *Social Convention*, 37.

> mime, is so amusing as a disappointed belly? His one object, let me tell you, is to compel you to pour out your wrath in tears, and to keep gnashing your molars against each other. . . . In treating you thus, the great man shows his wisdom.[10]

Such hybris intended to display one's "wisdom," notes MacMullen, was a common feature of the dinner setting:

> Nothing rewarded such efforts [at status climbing] more richly than the power they afforded to insult someone else in a lower station. Invite him to dinner and he came, sure to be shown a place at table that demeaned him, a serving of food that left him hungry, cheap wine, and the insolence of the servants—servants in this respect taught by their master.[11]

In addition to bigger and better portions of food, Theissen suggests that the rich possibly separated themselves physically "and at their own table." He points to J. Weiss' comment: "That members sat in groups, some together at separate tables, would have been unavoidable."[12] These insights are on target, but they are surprisingly uninformed by archaeology. This is corrected by Murphy-O'Connor, who points to the evidence that the typical dining room could hold nine couches for reclining[13] (i.e., not sitting at tables; many rooms had as few as seven couches).[14] Vase paintings show two or even three sharing a couch, thus allowing a capacity of 18 or even 27, though archaeological remains generally show couches only large enough for one occupant.[15] Plutarch also implies that couches are shared, and that some wealthy people "build showy dining-rooms that hold thirty couches or more".[16]

But such showy displays are criticized as interfering with the real purpose of the gathering: conversation. For this reason, smaller

---

[10]Juvenal, *Satires*, V.156-170.

[11]MacMullen, *Roman Social Relations*, 111.

[12]Theissen, 151, quoting J. Weiss, *Korintherbrief*, 293.

[13]Murphy-O'Connor, 155-159.

[14]Athen. *Deip.* 2.47, also testifies that "besides the triclinia dining-rooms with three couches, there were in ancient times rooms with four, seven, nine, and even higher numbers.

[15]D.E. Smith, *Social Obligation*, 9.

[16]Plut. *Quest. Conv.* 5.6 (*Mor.* 679A-680B).

gatherings were generally preferred.[17] This explains why a number of small dining rooms rather than one large one was the rule in public buildings, such as the Asklepieion at Corinth (3 rooms with seven couches each).[18] In any case, "the whole church" (1 Cor. 14:23) could not be accommodated in the dining room (especially if room was left for the "shadows," the normal and expected uninvited guests brought by upper class friends). Thus,

> it became imperative for the host to divide his guests into two categories; the first-class believers were invited into the triclinium while the rest stayed outside. . . . the host must have been a wealthy member of the community and so he invited into the triclinium his closest friends among the believers, who would have been of the same social class. The rest could take their places in the atrium, where conditions were greatly inferior. Those in the triclinium would have *reclined* . . . whereas those in the atrium were forced to *sit*. The space available made such discrimination unavoidable, but this would not diminish the resentment of those provided with second-class facilities.[19]

Plutarch remarks on the insult of this kind of division: "If space gives out because it has been spent on too great a crowd, then the host himself is guilty of a kind of insult to his guests."[20] The likelihood of separate quarters is even more likely if the houses were equipped with a feature found in the dining rooms at the Sanctuary of Demeter and Kore at Corinth (late 6th c. to ca. 146 B.C.E.): a smaller room adjacent to the dining room with a stuccoed bench along three walls. This room was "evidently used as a sitting or waiting room."[21] This sitting room might have been reserved for

---

[17]Ibid., 5.5 (*Mor.* 679B). Cf. Ath. *Deip.* 1.1: The 24 guests at this *symposium* "was more like a muster-roll than a list of guests at a banquet (συμποτικός)."

[18]D.E. Smith, *Social Obligation*, 227-230, from Carl Roebuck, *Corinth XIV: The Asklepieion and Lerna* (Princeton: The American School of Classical Studies at Athens, 1951).

[19]Murphy-O'Connor, 158-159. It is not clear why Murphy-O'Connor refers to the dining room as a Roman *triclinium*, which had three couches along three walls, each holding at least three diners. The archaeological evidence suggests that Corinth would have had the typical Greek pattern of seven or nine smaller Greek couches arranged along all four walls. See D.E. Smith, *Social Obligation*, 113.

[20]Plut. *Quaest. Conv.* 5.5 (*Mor.* 678F).

[21]Wiseman, 472; cf. D.E. Smith, *Social Obligation*, 235-39.

those who arrive late for whom no room remains in the dining-room, or for those whose rank did not qualify them to recline,[22] since reclining had been a symbol of aristocratic life from classical Greece through the late imperial period.[23]

In addition to differences in food, location, and posture, Smith points out another division suggested by 1 Cor.: differences in the time one had to eat. "If it was the wealthy who were the real offenders in eating a private meal, then that would also explain why they could begin earlier than the others. The wealthy would have leisure time in the evening, whereas the working classes would arrive late to the meeting."[24] This scenario is suggested by 1 Cor. 11:34, where Paul exhorts the wealthier Corinthians to "wait for one another" (ἀλλήλους ἐκδέχεσθε), meaning that προλαμβάνει in 11:21 also "necessarily has a temporal connotation; some began to eat before others."[25]

The leisurely arrival of the wealthy might have had further status-related causes, as Juvenal complains:

> When the rich man has a call of social duty, the mob makes way for him as he is borne swiftly over their heads in a huge Liburnian car. . . . He will arrive before us; hurry as we may, we are blocked

---

[22]Dennis E. Smith, "Dining and Dining Rooms in the Corinth of 1 Corinthians," unpublished paper presented at SBL, 1989.

[23]D.E. Smith, *Social Obligation*, 33-35.

[24]Ibid., 189. Earlier (pp. 6-7, 25-26), Smith outlines the typical afternoon schedule for a member of the upper class: exercise, bathing, perfuming, and attiring oneself for dinner. In the summer, the Romans preceded this regimen with a siesta. cf. Murphy O'Connor, 160: "Since the host's friends were of the leisured class they could arrive early and feast on larger portions of superior food while awaiting the arrival of lower class believers who were not as free to dispose of their time. The condition of those reclining in the triclinium could hardly be disguised from those who had to sit in the atrium."

[25]Murphy O'Connor, 161. Theissen's objection to a temporal reading hinges on his insistence that the words of institution in 11:23-25 mean that the bread was consecrated *before* the meal. Thus, the entire congregation would be present from the beginning. However, while the cup is certainly blessed after the meal, the tradition Paul relates mentions no time for the blessing and breaking of the bread. In fact, Mark and Matthew's version of the words of institution suggest by the present participle ἐσθιόντων that the blessing and breaking of the bread took place during the meal.

> by a surging crowd. . . . My legs are beplastered with mud; huge feet trample on me from every side.[26]

Yet another way that the higher status person could keep the lower status one waiting is illustrated by Lucian: just as the rich person reserves the biggest and best for himself, so also he reserves special service from the servants. In this way, "one is hungry and another is drunk" (1 Cor. 11:21). Thus, Lucian bids Saturn concerning the celebration of the Saturnalia,

> Tell them to invite the poor to dinner, taking in four or five at a time, not as they do nowadays, though, but in a more democratic fashion, all having an equal share, not one man stuffing himself (ἐμφορεῖσθαι) with dainties with the servant standing waiting for him to eat himself to exhaustion, then when this servant comes to us he passes on while we are still getting ready to put out our hand, only letting us glimpse the platter or the remnants of the cake. And tell him not to give a whole half of the pig when it's brought in, and the head as well, to his master, bringing the others bones covered over. And tell the wine-servers not to wait for each of us to ask seven times for a drink but on one request to pour it out and hand it to us at once, filling a great cup as they do for their master. And let the wine be one and the same for all the guests—where is it laid down that he should get drunk on wine with a fine bouquet while I must burst my belly on new stuff?[27]

Yet one more possible source of temporal differences along class lines should be added: the rôle of household slaves. Normally they would serve the meal to the master of the house and his guests, and take their own meal separately. But what would happen in households in which both slaves and master were members of the same Christian *ekklesia*? Would not the slaves tend to resent that they must wait to share the communal meal while others go ahead with their meals and get drunk? One reason that reclining indicated status was that it required servants.[28] There were certainly slaves in the Corinthian church (1 Cor. 7:21); further, since entire households were

---

[26]Juv. *Sat*. 3.239-248. Out of context, this passage suggests the mixing of social classes at the same social function. But Juvenal's portrayal of himself as poor reflects not true poverty, but merely the gap between his own moderate means and those of the fabulously wealthy; see below.

[27]Lucian *Sat*. 21-22.

[28]D.E. Smith, *Social Obligation*, 35.

converted, they probably included at least some household slaves. In 1:16 and 16:15, Paul notes that he baptized the household of Stephanus (τὸν Στεφανᾶ οἶκον) which collectively "is devoted to the service of the saints." Similarly, according to Acts 18:8, "Crispus believed in the Lord, together with all his household" (σὺν ὅλῳ τῷ οἴκῳ).

> The *oikos* (or *oikia*; Latin *domus* or *familia*) mentioned when the New Testament reports the conversion of someone 'with all his house' is . . . defined by . . . the relationship of dependence and subordination. The head of a substantial household was thus responsible for—and expected a degree of obedience from—not only his immediate family but also his slaves, former slaves who were now clients, hired laborers, and sometimes business associates or tenants. The floor plans of some of the houses that have been excavated in Pompeii or on Delos can be read as a kind of physical diagram of some of these relationships: . . . centrally located, a dining room in which the *paterfamilias* might enjoy the company of his equals and friends from other households, or entertain his *clientela*, or do both at once (with each assigned his fitting place.)[29]

The "fitting place" for the household slaves would of course be waiting on the master and his friends, while the rest found their "fitting places" either in the dining room or seated outside. But within the dining room, too, there was a competition for seating and room for resentment. The "first place" was normally reserved for the host or most honored guest; other places were reckoned as "high" or "low" according to their proximity to the first place. "Such distinctions and honors were considered essential to the makeup of cultured society, and the formal meal normally functioned within society to buttress its view of status."[30] The norm was to give to "family, wealth (γένεσις, πλοῦτος, cf. 1 Cor. 1:26), or official position (ἄρχων, cf. 1 Cor. 2:8)" or any other "prestige (ἔνδοξος, cf. 1 Cor. 4:10)"[31]

> the position that suits it, one which does honor to the outstanding man, leaves the next best at ease, and exercises the judgement

[29]Meeks, *First Urban Christians*, 30.
[30]D.E. Smith, *Social Obligation*, 55.
[31]Plut. *Quaest. Conv.* 1.2 (*Mor.* 618A).

> (διάκρισις, cf. 1 Cor. 4:7, 11:29, 31) and sense of propriety of the host. For the man of quality does not have his honor and his station in the world, yet fail to receive recognition in the place he occupies at dinner; nor will a host drink to one of his guests before another, yet overlook their distinctions in placing them at table.[32]

Thus, when Paul asks "Who distinguished you? (τίς σε διάκρινει;)," he may be responding to Corinthian claims to be regularly distinguished in this way. Paul picks up the same language to emphasize that it is the *whole* body, the crucified body, not the exaltation of the individual, which is to be distinguished (11:29).

The honor of choice seating was particularly important for those who were ambitious to claim status, such as Theophrastus' μικροφιλοτίμιος, who, as we saw above, "when he is invited out to dine must needs find place to dine next to the host."[33] Plutarch portrays such a person in his description of a foreigner who arrived at Timon's dinner "like a grandee (εὐπάρυφος) out of a comedy, rather absurd with his extravagant clothes and train of servants; and when he had run his eyes round the guests who had settled in their places, he refused to enter, but . . . said that he saw no place left worthy of him."[34]

Distinctions of honor according to seating naturally occasioned further insults.[35] One reason was the difficulty of deciding relative worth, since status was determined by a number of indicators; thus, "the decision is not easy, differing as the guests do in age, in influence (δυνάμις), in intimacy, and and in kinship. . . . If we humble some of them and exalt others, we shall rekindle their hostility and set it aflame again through ambitious rivalry [φιλοτιμία]."[36]

All the above factors of quality and portion of food, leisurely versus late dining, and seating position worked together to reflect and reinforce status hierarchies. This is well illustrated by Lucian in his "*symposion* laws" (νόμοι συμπότικοι) for the *Saturnalia*, which satirize the normal practice in which the rich enjoy private feasts

---

[32]Ibid., 1.2 (*Mor.* 616B).

[33]Theoph. *Char.* 23.

[34]Plut. *Quaest. Conv.* 1.2 (*Mor.* 615D).

[35]Ibid., 1.2, 1.3; idem, *Conv. sept. sap.*, *Mor.* 148F-149A; cf. D.E. Smith, *Social Obligation*, 36.

[36]Plut. *Quaest. conv.* 1.2 (*Mor.* 616D-E).

(καθ' αὑτοὺς οἱ πλούσιοι ἑορτάζουσι).[37] Instead, the festival allows an occasion for slaves to enjoy the prerogatives of the upper class:

> Each man shall take the couch where he happens to be. Rank, family, or wealth shall have little influence on privilege. All shall drink the same wine, and neither stomach trouble nor headache shall give the rich man an excuse for being the only one to drink the better quality. All shall have their meat on equal terms. The waiters shall not show favor to anyone, but shall neither be too slow nor be dismissed until the guests choose what they are take home. Neither are large portions to be placed before one and tiny ones before another, nor a ham for one and a pig's jaw for another—all must be treated equally. . . . Each guest shall stay and go as he likes. When a rich man gives a banquet to his servants, his friends shall aid him in waiting on them.[38]

One's place in this hierarchy at meals depended on a number of status factors. A prerequisite, and perhaps even sufficient factor for the honor of place was the possession of a relatively large home and enough money for food and slaves to host the meal. Thus, in the language of 1:26, the host was among the relatively δυνατοί. He or she was probably also among the relatively εὐγενεῖς, not only because money and birth often went together, but because the relationships of friendship and clientelia represented at a meal built up over time, usually over generations. The rest of the places were then assigned according to these same criteria, as well as some others, such as age. As we shall see, one of these other criteria, the third on Paul's list in 1:26, was apparently of great importance to the Corinthians: the ability to speak wisely. Thus, the competition for status at the Corinthian's dinners is a good place to look for clues to our exigence of division caused by boasting in wise speech and speakers.

---

[37]Lucian *Sat.* 11.

[38]Lucian *Sat.* 17-18.

Collegia

In arguing for the frequency with which portions differed according to status, Theissen compares the Christian *ekklesia* to Graeco-Roman clubs. He does not argue in detail for the aptness of this comparison, but others have done so in a convincing manner. Although we have no evidence that Christian groupings were ever given legal status as associations,

> there need be no doubt that . . . they were not distinguished in the public's mind from the general run of unofficial associations. Like many others they could be labelled conveniently from the god whose patronage they claimed. 'Christ-ites' is certainly not the sort of name they would have chosen for themselves. . . . This distaste of the Christians for the name that was gratuitously bestowed upon them, however, certainly does not mean that they were unwilling to be thought of as forming an association of the usual kind. On the contrary it would hardly have occurred to them to raise the question in the first place. It was taken for granted. . . . The term *ecclesia* (*sc.* meeting) itself, and the names for the various officials may have developed special connotations within the Christian community, but to non-Christians, and to Christians themselves in the early stages, they need have suggested nothing out of the ordinary.[39]

Christian *ekklesia* were classified with *collegia* partly because they were at times perceived as a group which threatened the Roman order. In all periods, *collegia* threatened to become political. "In the Ciceronian age the *collegia* became involved in political action; many were suppressed in 64 B.C. and again by Caesar, after a temporary revival by Clodius."[40] Under Augustus, every *collegium* had to be officially sanctioned, except for burial clubs. (Through this loophole, clubs ostensibly organized only for burial purposes actually enjoyed social activities, especially dinners.) "Reviewing the whole collection of stories in which societies figured as villains, we can see why earlier emperors feared the promiscuous multiplication of *factiones*," while

---

[39]Judge, *Social Pattern*, 44-45; cf. D.E. Smith, *Social Obligation*, 138-139.
[40]*OCD*, s.v. "Clubs, Roman."

under later emperors, "these groups of workers came handiest to the ambition of a demagogue."[41]

For these reasons, Trajan advises Pliny not to organize a *collegium* of firemen, because such societies frequently become factional troublemakers. "Whatever title we give to them, and whatever our object in giving it, men who are banded together for a common end will all the same become a political association (*hetaeriae*) before long."[42] Pliny had already recognized the dangers; he had proposed limiting the number of members, taking care to limit membership to bona-fide firemen, and otherwise preventing them from diverting their privileges to any other purpose.[43]

As we can see in Pliny's correspondence with Trajan, the line between *collegia*, *factiones*, and *hetaeriai* was not sharp. *Hetaeriai* was sometimes used for associations of a wholly private character, such as guilds and clubs, but generally it designated political factions.[44] Pliny uses the word to refer to Christians, reporting that Christians had ceased to gather for their communal meals when Trajan's edict was announced banning *hetaeriai*.[45] This indicates that both writer and implied recipient of Pliny's letter understand the Christian assembly to be included within the edict. Their association is a *collegium* which has passed over into an *hetaeriae*. As Judge comments, this is "an important point which shows that the Christians were distinguished from the other unofficial associations neither by the authorities nor by themselves, and also that the ban was not intended to apply to the strictly religious gatherings of any association, but merely to its social occasions."[46]

In other words, Trajan's edict aimed at the threat these *collegia* or *hetaeriai* posed to the socio-political unifying function of public rituals and meals. For this same reason Augustus had limited unofficial clubs to monthly meetings, at which they could do nothing other than deposit their contributions to burial funds. When the

---

[41]MacMullen, *Enemies*, 178.

[42]Pliny *Ep.* 10.34.

[43]Ibid, 10.33.

[44]*OCD*, s.v. "Hetairiai."

[45]Pliny *Ep.* 10.96.

[46]Judge, *Social Pattern*, 48-49.

Christians submitted to Trajan's edict by ceasing their communal meals, most still did not return to a normal social life with its meals in the temples. In their case, the edict's purpose had failed. Those who did worship in the temples were tolerated, but Pliny began to execute those who would not. His reason for persecuting Christians, beyond following established practice, was that their worship was drawing people "of all ranks" from the temples, the festivals, and the sacrifices. In other words, he saw the social order of the state, ritualized in worship at established temples, threatened by the Christian resistance to these rituals. Thus, Pliny followed the normal tolerance of religious beliefs except for those for whom the Christian *collegium* had become a political *hetaeriae*.

This political threat was not present in Paul's Corinth, since the Christian group was new and small. But the conflict between their gatherings and the civic ones which normally included dinners with worship and sacrifices was already deeply troubling the young community (1 Cor. 8:7, 10; 10:21). In sociological terms, they were in the process of defining their group identity and boundaries, a process which Paul hopes to influence with his letter. In this process, the place of meat sacrificed to idols was debated, and so was the place of other typical practices of the meals of *collegia* including the assigning of places, portions, and quality of food according to status. Thus, it is not surprising that Lucian called Christian groups θίασοι, one of the typical designations of the regularly scheduled meetings of clubs or associations, including religious ones.[47] Those, like Christians and Jews, with peculiar religious rites, "needed and got from each other special comfort through their comradely congregations."[48]

Since the Corinthians saw themselves as a *collegium*, it is easy to imagine how behavior Paul criticizes could to them have seemed completely normal.

> Terms like *convivae* . . . declared that the fellows shared . . . their meals together. . . . Friends liked to get together to eat, drink, and be merry. Moralists grumbled that they ate too much; . . .

---

[47] Aune, "*Septum*," 72-75, referring to Lucian *Peregr.* 2 and Ath. *Deip.* 5.185.

[48] MacMullen, *Roman Social Relations*, 83.

> worse, they drank too much. . . . If piety counted for much, conviviality counted for more. In a setting as rich and well-furnished as they could afford, . . . like dined with like, drawn together by the sharing of neighborhood, social class, occupation, or simple congeniality. . . . Even the young met with the young and the old with the old. . . . It is as if no principle of either inclusion or exclusion could meet all demands—as if every conceivable private sympathy required expression. Where two neighbors at a corner pub today will raise their glasses and at most exchange a friendly "Cheers!" the two in antiquity seem to have said, "Be it resolved, to call ourselves the society of. . . ."[49]

Perhaps, "Be it resolved, to call ourselves the society of Paul" or "of Apollos."[50]

Status within Collegia

Though members of a *collegia* were expected to contribute something to their meals (as opposed to family *symposia* in which the host provided all the fare), most clubs depended on the support of a wealthy patron who donated gifts of food and money. "In return for the beneficence of the patron, a guild would honor him with titles and dedications. These honors added to the status of the patron which therefore was the return for his investment."[51]

In addition to the honors due the patron, honors were also accorded to officers of the club. For example, in the statutes of the college of Diana and Antinous, a Roman burial society founded in 136 C.E., the *quinquennalis*

> shall receive a double share in all distributions. It was voted further that the secretary and the messenger shall . . . receive a share and a half in every distribution. It was voted further that any member who has administered the office of *quinquennalis* honestly

---

[49]Ibid., 77-82.

[50]M. Mitchell (116) objects to Welborn's assertion that the slogans of 1:12 are political because extant ancient political slogans never appear in the genitive. But the titles of collegia did take this form. E.g., the association "of Zeus (τοῦ Διος);" see Colin Roberts, T. C. Skeat, and A. D. Nock, "The Gild of Zeus Hypsistos," *HTR* 29 (1936), 40-41; cited in D.E. Smith, *Social Obligation*, 261. So too did rival sects devoted to rhetoricians: Quint. 2.11.1-2.

[51]D.E. Smith, *Social Obligation*, 121-122.

> shall [thereafter] receive a share and a half of everything as a mark of honor. . . . It was voted further that any member who moves from one place to another so as to cause a disturbance shall be fined.[52]

Smith comments concerning this passage that the function of the *quinquennalis* was

> parallel to that of a host or symposiarch at a formal banquet. As such, he would sit in the position of honor and would preside over the order of the meal. . . . The rule against taking another's place so as to cause a disturbance suggests that a value was placed on one's assigned position at the meeting. This of course, makes sense in the context of a banquet meeting, where each position at table had a value assigned to it. To take another's position would therefore be a personal insult and a seditious act toward the community.[53]

Rivalries over status could easily lead to disorder, so clubs typically attempted to enact rules to prevent this. For example according to the rules of the Egyptian "Gild of Zeus Hypsistos" preserved in a papyrus dated ca. 69 to 58 B.C.E., "It shall not be permissible for any one . . . to make factions (σχίσματα), or to leave the brotherhood of the president for another, or for men to enter into one another's pedigrees (γ[ε]νεαλογ[ήσειν])."[54] "The most obvious explanation for the cause of a genealogical dispute would be the situation at table whereby one's status was indicated by his position. Such a situation inevitably caused jealousies, and an ensuing argument over relative degrees of status would evidently degenerate into a comparison of family backgrounds."[55] Thus, in this brief passage we have parallels to the status-related tensions within dinners addressed in 1 Cor. 11., as well as to the divisions of 1 Cor. 1-4: one leader is favored over another ("to leave the brotherhood of the president for another") in a situation of jealousies

---

[52] *Statutes of the College of Diana and Antinous*, trans. Naphtali Lewis and Meyer Reinhold, *Roman Civilization* (New York: Harper, 1966), 2.18-25, cited in D.E. Smith, *Social Obligation*, pp. 258-259.

[53] D.E. Smith, *Social Obligation*, 127.

[54] Colin Roberts, T. C. Skeat, and A. D. Nock, "The Gild of Zeus Hypsistos," *HTR* 29 (1936), 40-41; cited in D.E. Smith, *Social Obligation*, 261-62.

[55] D.E. Smith, *Social Obligation*, 148.

"over relative degrees of status [which] would evidently degenerate into a comparison of family backgrounds."

As Welborn comments, this "illustrates what must have been one of the most important functions of such associations under the empire: they provided scope for the exercise of the . . . deeds appropriate to a public career," deeds for which the opportunities in that period were curtailed. "In the church, Greek converts may have hoped to experience some of the δύναμις and ἐλευθερία of which they heard the apostle speak."[56]

In any period, lower class persons might harbor such hopes of glory as 'big fish in a small pond.'

> Humble artisans . . . enjoyed a certain standing in the community solely through their incorporation. . . . No one found their honorific decrees . . . in the least ridiculous. . . . The arrogation of fancy titles raised no laugh. . . . It followed that their internal organization should ape the high-sounding terminology of larger, municipal bodies, the nomenclature of officialdom, and honors like *proedria* and the award of gold crowns in their meetings. At least the larger craft associations constituted in every detail miniature cities.
>
> [They focused] their energies on the pursuit of honor rather than economic advantage. . . . They cared a lot more about prestige, which the members as individuals could not ordinarily hope to gain, but which, within a subdivision of their city, competing with their peers, they could deal out according to a more modest scale of attainments. Associations thus resembled the whole social context they found themselves in and imitated it as best they could. Like everyone else, they sought status.[57]

Symposia and Schismata

With imaginations enriched by these references to the customs of the *symposion*, we can more easily construct a situation to which Paul's rhetoric meaningfully responds in 1 Cor. 11:17-34. In typical fashion for ancient *symposia*, σχίσματα have arisen. Paul is not surprised by this (μέρος τι πιστεύω), since divisions are inevitable (δεῖ γὰρ καὶ αἱρεσεις) if those who are esteemed (οἱ δόκιμοι) are

---

[56]Welborn, "Discord," 111.

[57]MacMullen, *Roman Social Relations*, 75-77.

to be conspicuous (φανεροὶ). These divisions are the result of jealousies and rivalries over such honors as place, portion, or quality of food and wine. The winners proudly go ahead with their own meals, and in the typical manner of *symposia*, they get drunk, which frequently fueled any divisive behavior. Meanwhile, the less esteemed (ἃ δοκοῦμεν ἀτιμότερα εἶναι, 12:23) go hungry. Thus, those who are honored by providing houses and food are dishonoring (καταισχύνω) those who have not.

This last reference to bringing shame or dishonor upon those who "have not" is somewhat puzzling if we imagine them to be poor, since honor and shame was normally much more a concern for the upper class. But οἱ μὴ ἔχοντες need not refer to the poor, since in literature about meals a common *topos* had developed in which the "poor" who suffered at the hands of the rich were not actually poor, but upper class persons who were not as rich as their hosts. For example, Plutarch's brother Timon spoke against "the rich lording it over the poor," but all attending the banquet to which he refers were upper class.[58] Similarly, Juvenal complains of the lot of the *pauperis* who suffers at the hands of the *nouveau riche*. But by *pauperis*, he means an upper class person who is down on his luck:

> Is a man to sign his name before me, and recline on a couch above mine, who has been wafted to Rome by the wind which brings us our damsons and our figs? . . . Of all the woes of luckless poverty none is harder to endure than this, that it exposes men to ridicule. 'Out you go, for very shame,' says the marshal; 'out of the Knights' stalls, all of you whose means do not satisfy the law.' Here let the sons of panders, born in any brothel, take their seats.[59]

Such former *equites* hardly qualify as poor. They still can afford slaves, but have lost enough money so they do not own houses: "You must pay a big rent for wretched lodging, a big sum to fill the bellies of your slaves, and buy a frugal dinner for yourself." They would like to advance back up the social ladder through marriage, inheritance, or appointment, but this is itself expensive, since "we all live in a state of pretentious (*ambitiosus*) poverty."[60] Martial is similar to Juvenal

---

[58]Plut. *Quaest. conv.* 1.2 (*Mor.* 616F).
[59]Juv. 3.81, 152-56.
[60]Ibid., 165-83.

in his self-descriptions of poverty, writing that his life was relatively simple and his city dwelling inadequate, and that he continually had to find ways to get himself invited to the dinners of the rich. Yet he maintained both a country villa and an apartment in Rome.

Thus, Smith is quite right to point out that in 1 Cor. 11, "the levels of social class cannot be assumed to be widely divergent. Indeed, since Paul's instructions do not address a problem of poverty, such as by providing for a distribution to the poor, it would appear that the distinctions are not very great."[61] The lack of provision for a distribution is especially striking since Paul emphasizes the collection for the church in Jerusalem to which each Corinthian is to contribute regularly (1 Cor. 16:2) from what he or she has (ἐκ τοῦ ἔχειν, 2 Cor. 8:11-12). This should not be a burden for the Corinthians, for they have abundance (περίσσευμα) compared to the need (ὑστερημά) of the church in Jerusalem, whom Paul apparently considered the poor (τοί πτώχοι) whose needs he was eager to remember (Gal 2:10; cf. Acts 11:29-30). The Church in Corinth undoubtedly included persons of various social positions, mostly not of the highest positions (1 Cor 1:26) and including slaves (1 Cor 12:13), but we can make best sense of the text if we imagine the problems to have arisen not among the highest or lowest levels of society, but among those with social pretensions who were most concerned with gaining a greater share of honor and most sensitive to insults which brought shame.

Sophia at Dinner

Just as the honor of receiving or being relatively near the first seat at a dinner was a microcosm of the *proedria* of large public events, so was the competition at each dinner a microcosm of the larger struggle to be recognized as σοφός. In fact, as we saw above, the main purpose of collegia and dinners was often considered to be the enjoyment of convivial conversation: "It is worse to take away the pleasure of conversation at table than to run out of wine.

---

[61]D.E. Smith, *Social Obligation*, 191-92.

Theophrastus in jest calls barbershops 'wineless drinking parties' just because of the chatter of those who come to sit there."[62]

For this reason among others, the competition to be recognized as eloquent was far wider than the contests of orators of who we have ample testimony.[63] These could intersect with honors gained at dinners. For example, Plutarch writes that when, during the Isthmyan games, Sospis

> entertained in his home his closest friends, all men of learning (φιλολόγοι), I was present too. At the clearing away of the first course, someone came in to present Herodes the professor of rhetoric (ῥήτωρ), as a special honour, with palm-frond and a plaited wreath sent by a pupil who had won a contest with an encomiastic oration.[64]

But it was not just orators who sought such honor. For those with upper class values, eloquence was an important indicator of status.

> To Juvenal, for instance, nothing is more ridiculous than the farmer who tries to pass as a product of the schools of urban elegance and cultivation. . . . Since the surviving sources are of course mostly the work of men who valued literature, it is not surprising to find in them many contemptuous references to yokel accents and lack of education. Country folk had no books, their choice of words was out of date and uncouth, they dropped their aitches; in contrast *urbanitas*, meaning city fashions but above all those of the capital itself.
>
> That value blended with loyalty to one's whole culture. A pure Latin was the pride of the ruling race. . . . One blushed to be detected in an un-Roman slip. . . . Claudius only exaggerated a very common prejudice when he withdrew the grant of citizenship from a man who could not speak good Latin. *Urbanitas* opposed not only *rusticitas* but *peregrinitas* [foreign manners or ways] as well.
>
> Similarly the Greeks. . . . We can easily see what distressed the highly educated: the gulf that opened gradually between the prose and poetry of the classical period and what was being written or spoken even in good circles of Roman Athens or Alexandria. But,

---

[62]Plut. *Quaest. conv.* 5.5 (*Mor.* 679A).

[63]See Chapter VI.

[64]Ibid., 8.4.1 (723A).

> as inscriptions prove, away from the city each mile marked a further deviation from correctness.[65]

Thus, ambitious people were always competing to be perceived as *asteios*, *urbanitas*, or *sophos*, and one of the primary settings for this competition was the dinner or *symposion*. This is strongly reflected in *symposia* literature, prolifically produced after the model provided by Plato's and Xenophon's *Symposia*. These works emphasized that the entertainment portion of the *symposion*, which was often taken up with music or acting, should be dedicated to philosophical dialogue. Through the influence of this popular literary genre, the ideal *symposion* included the enjoyment of cultured conversation, including popular philosophy or sophism. For this reason, Plutarch wrote that

> the Romans are fond of quoting a witty and sociable person who said, after a solitary meal, "I have eaten, but not dined today," implying that a "dinner" always requires friendly sociability for seasoning. . . . The most truly godlike seasoning at the dining-table is the presence of a friend or companion or intimate acquaintance—not because of his eating and drinking with us, but because he participates in the give-and-take of conversation.[66]

Because of this rôle of conversation at dinner, problems could easily arise in the Christian *ekklesia*, since members were expected to dine with persons not of their own choosing. As Plutarch writes, "to have the company of others forced upon one" is particularly unpleasant

> at dinner. . . . A dinner party is a sharing of earnest and jest, of words and deeds; so the diners must not be left to chance, but must be such as are friends and intimates of one another who will enjoy being together. . . . You could not get good and agreeable company at dinner by throwing together men who are different in their associations and sympathies.[67]

---

[65]MacMullen, *Roman Social Relations*, 30-31.

[66]Plut. *Queast. conv.* 7.praef. (*Mor.* 697C-D).

[67]Ibid., 7.6 (708D).

When conversation is not convivial, there can arise "waves of strife (ἔρις, cf. 1 Cor. 1:11, 3:3, 12:20) or rivalry (φιλονεικία, cf. 1 Cor. 11:16)," "reviling (λοιδορία, cf. 1 Cor 4:12)," or discussion that deviates "into an unpleasant squabble or a contest in sophistry" with "political and legal controversies" and "gales of eloquence."[68] Thus, the problems Paul confronted in 1 Cor. 1-4 and 11 might have been predicted by Plutarch, who would have advised against mixing people with a wide spectrum of educational backgrounds.

We have already looked at one important example of the *symposion* literature of Paul's time in Plutarch's *Convivium septum sapientum* ("Dinner of the Seven Wise Men"). There we discovered that σοφία was repeatedly used to mean cultured cleverness. The σοφός, who enjoys that title because of worldly status outside the dinner, aims to enhance his honor by competing in riddles and other witty conversations of sophistic quality. For this reason, the seating arrangements were important. As we saw above, dining rooms were limited in size to enhance conversation, and one's place was a matter of honor not only because of the traditional honor assigned each seat, but because a lower place might put one next to a less wise conversation partner. Thus, here just as in his *Quaestiones conviviales*, Plutarch emphasizes that one must not trust in luck regarding one's dining companions; otherwise one will end up sitting next to an unsuitable companion. Rather, the places, as usual, must be carefully arranged according to honor.[69]

A major reason for care in seating was to avoid dining companions who could not conduct cultured conversation, i.e., fools.[70] This would have been especially important if the gathering were in one of the large dining rooms built by ostentatious rich people, since

> too many guests . . . prevent general conversation (λόγων κοινωνία); they allow only a few to enjoy each other's society, for the guests separate into groups of two or three in order to meet and converse, completely unconscious of those whose place on the couches is remote and not looking their way because they are separated from them by practically the length of a race course. . . . So it is a mistake for the wealthy to act in the manner of youthful

---

[68]Plut. *Quaest. conv.* 7.8-9.

[69]Plut. *Conv. sep. sap.*, *Mor.* 148A, F; 149A.

[70]Plut. *De Gar.* 503A; quoted above, p. 223.

> insolence (νεανιεύομαι, i.e., with ὕβις), building dining rooms that hold thirty or more. . . . However, we must forgive this display, for they consider wealth, unless it has witnesses and . . . spectators, no wealth but something blind indeed and cut off from the world.[71]

Even if the host were not ostentatious, seating arrangements were important for conversation with one's neighbors. This is why Lamprias claims that one secret of a good *symposion* was careful seating arrangements; his formula is to "supply what suits him to the man who lacks it and invite him who is eager to learn to recline below a learned man, . . . the young who like to listen below the old who like to talk, etc."[72]

Even more than enjoying neighbors with whom one could share conversation suitable to one's social station, one of the main benefits of better seats was greater opportunity to display one's wit. This was easiest for those with the best seats, since the opportunity for conversation was normally apportioned "on the basis of wealth or rank."[73] Customarily, not just "the continuous toasts and the serving of food" but also "the conversation and discourse as well shall be in strict conformity with the order of the guests's seating."[74] Any host who fails to follow these customs "is committing a theft" for he "turns an individual's prerogative (i.e., according to the worth of each individual: ἴδιον τὸ κατ' ἀξίαν ἑκαστου, cf. 1 Cor. 11:21) into common property. . . . He offends each one of them by depriving him of his accustomed honor."[75]

We find many of these typical features of *symposia* in *Sirach*. As we have already seen, Ben Sira in many ways represents the social norm of the *sophos*. In this role, he offers his advice to those who would attend a *symposion*. First, he advises one given the honor of

---

[71]Plut. *Quaest. Conv.* 5.5 (*Mor.* 679B).
[72]Ibid., 1.2 (618E).
[73]Plut. *Conv. sep. sap.*, *Mor.* 154D.
[74]Plut. *Quaest. conv.* 1.2 (*Mor.* 616E).
[75]Ibid., 1.2 (617C).

being the symposiarch[76] to resist the temptation to act boastfully. Rather, one can win praise through better manners:

> If you are chosen to preside at dinner, be not puffed up (ἐπαιρω,
> to swell up, cf. 2 Cor. 10:5, 11:20),
> but with the guests be one of them.
> Take care of them first before you sit down—
> see to their needs, then take your place,
> To share in their joy
> and win praise for your hospitality.

He then goes on to mention the competition in speech:

> You who are older, it is your right to talk,
> but temper your wisdom, not to interrupt the singing.[77]
> Where listening is in order, do not pour out discourse,
> and flaunt not your wisdom (σοφίζω) at the wrong time.[78]

Another important example of *symposion* literature roughly of Paul's time to which we have already frequently referred (because of its wealth of references to *symposia* customs) is Plutarch's *Quaestiones conviviales.* The form itself emphasizes the conversational nature of the evening meal. This is a time when "talk abounds (ἐν λόγοις πλεονάζοντα)"[79] among the cultured (πεπαιδευμένων) on almost any subject. The presence of a few men without erudition (ἰδιῶται) will not spoil the sharing of popular philosophi-cal talk and ideas. If the party is dominated by ἰδιῶται, however, the conversation will range even more widely than does Plutarch's popular philosophy.

Some *symposia* texts were satires. For example, Persius mocks the kind of competition that went on in the Roman *convivium* of Paul's time. A pretentious person will aim to have others flatter him for his knowledge, aiming to have

---

[76]i.e., to preside (ἡγούμενος) "is a reference to the custom of selecting a banquet master, called in Gr literature *symposiarchus* or *architriklinos* (this word is used to describe the official of the wedding feast at Cana in John 2:8-10). . . . It was a great honor for a person to be chosen banquet master." Skehan and Di Lella, 391.

[77]A *symposion* often had various entertainments besides conversation.

[78]*Sirach*, 32:1-4.

[79]Plut. *Quaes. Conv.* 1.1 (613C).

> a finger pointed at one, and to hear people say, 'That is the man.' . . . See, now, the sons of Romulus, having well dined, are asking over their cups, 'What has divine poesy to say?' Whereupon some fellow with a purple mantle round his shoulders lisps out with a snuffle some insipid trash. . . . The great men signify their approval. . . . The lesser guests chime in with their assent. . . . But I decline to admit that the final and supreme test of excellence is to be found in your 'Bravo!' (*euge*) and your 'Beautiful!' (*belle*) . . . You know how to present a shivering client with a threadbare cloak, and then you say, 'I love the truth; tell me the truth about myself!' How can the man do that? Would you like *me* to tell you the truth? You are just a fool.[80]

Lucian also satirized this kind of competition in his *Συμποσίον*. His meal, which celebrates a wedding, brings together as guests of a rich man who is interested in culture (παιδεία) a number of learned people (οἱ σοφοί; σοφοί ἄνδρες, τοί σοφωτάτοι)[81] who were "clever in words (περιττός ἐν τοῖς λόγοις),"[82] both philosophers and literary men (οἱ ἀπὸ πιλοσοφηίας καὶ λόγων), including a grammarian and a rhetorician.[83] The whole company is arranged "according to the esteem in which each was held (ὡς ἕκαστος ἀξίας εἶχε)." But this immediately caused a protest from the Stoic, who insisted that because he is an old man he should have precedence (πρότερος) over the Epicurian despite the latter's membership in the leading family in the city (γένος τοῦ πρώτου ἐν τῄ πόλει).[84] With the passing of the cup came the usual conversations (ὁμιλίαι).[85] As at most symposia, the group became drunk, and "the room was full of uproar. Dionysodorus the rhetorician was making speeches, pleading first on one side and then on the other, and was getting applauded by the servants who stood behind him. Histiaeus the grammarian, who had the place next him, was reciting verse."[86] The competition for applause became fierce, until the quarreling (ἔρις,[87]

---

[80]Pers. 1.26-56.
[81]Lucian *Symp.* 10, 35, 48.
[82]Ibid., 34.
[83]Ibid., 6.
[84]Ibid., 9.
[85]Ibid., 15.
[86]Ibid., 17.
[87]Ibid., 1, 35.

cf. 1 Cor. 1:11, 3:3, 2 Cor 12:20) spread to all the σοφοί, which the unlettered folk (ἰδιῶται) found quite amusing.

The behavior of Lucian's σοφοί typifies the general competition for applause and the resultant ἔριδες. In particular, Lucian's Cynic Alcidamas can help us appreciate Paul's reaction to the "superlative apostles." Alcidamas "burst in uninvited," which most of the other guests took to be "an impudent thing (ἀναίσχυντος)," and so said witty things under their breath, including that he was "being foolish (ἀφραίνω, cf. 2 Cor. 11). . . . But nobody dared (τολμάω, cf. 2 Cor. 10:2, 12; 11:21) to speak out, for they all feared he who was really 'good at the war-cry,' and the noisiest of the Cynic barkers, for which reason he was considered a superior person (ἀμείνων) and was a great terror to everybody."[88] He boasts that he is "invincible in courage, unfettered in intellect (ἐλευθερος τὴν γνώμην) and strong in body (τὸ σῶμα καρτερός, cf. 2 Cor. 10:9)."[89] Finally, he started a fight, "for he was jealous because the other fellow [a clown] was making a hit and holding the attention of the room."[90] Who "made a hit" or "held the attention" of the *ekklesia* appears to be a recurrent issue in Corinth as well.

If upper class persons expected to compete in cultured conversation, it is not surprising that they resented those with lower status who attempted to use conversation to gain recognition as wise. This is particularly apparent in Petronius' *Satyricon*, in which the *nouveau riche* freedman Trimalchio hosts a feast attended by other freedmen, some also rich. Petronius portrays Trimalchio like Theophrastus' μικροφιλοτιμίας and satirizes the feast as an uncouth *symposion* of typical form:

> Tramalchio had the first place kept for himself in the new style. . . . The course had now been removed, and the cheerful company (*convivium*) proceeded to turn their attention to the wine, and to general conversation. Tramalchio lay back on his couch and said, . . . "One must not forget one's culture (*philologia*) even at dinner."[91]

---

[88]Ibid., 12.
[89]Ibid., 16.
[90]Ibid., 19.
[91]Petron. *Sat.* 31, 39.

Tramalchio proceeds to display his sophistication, first in a speech about astrology. The guests "applauded his elegance (*urbanitas*)," finally crying out "*Sophos!*"[92] He verbally fences with the rhetorician Agamemnon, pointing out what he might have summarized as "even if I am not a professional orator, I am not without knowledge," 2 Cor. 11:7): "I do not practice in court myself, but I learned literature for domestic purposes. And do not imagine that I despise learning. I have got two libraries, one Greek and one Latin." Agamemnon responds by telling of the *controversia* (a kind of declamation) he delivered that day: "'A poor man and a rich man were once at enmity.'" Tramalchio's reply, "'But what is a poor man?'" again receives the praise from Agamemnon, "'Very clever [*urbanus*],'" and all of Tramalchio's sallies were given "the most extravagant admiration."[93]

Tramalchio thus enjoys his guests' approbations as wise, while others fear being considered foolish, such as the narrator, the freedman Encolpius who is studying rhetoric: "I cursed my dullness (*stupor*) and asked no more questions, for fear of showing that I had never dined among decent people (*honestus*, i.e., honored, well-born)."[94] Similarly, Niceros is "afraid your clever friends (*scholasticus*, i.e., a student of rhetoric) will laugh at me."[95] But Tramalchio assures his guests that Niceros "never talks nonsense: he is very dependable, and not at all a chatterbox"[96] (i.e., the fool we have met in Plutarch).

Other guests are more ready to fight for the esteem of possessing wise eloquence. One, a farmer, complains to the rhetorician Agamemnon, "You look as if you were saying, 'What is the bore (*molestus*, a nuisance) chattering for (*arguto*, to say foolishly)? . . . You are not of our cloth, and so you make fun of the way we poor

---

[92]Ibid., 39.

[93]Ibid., 48.

[94]Ibid., 41. As Balsdon (24) comments, "People were respectable or common, *honesti* or *vulgares*, generally a matter of birth. . . . Society at large was destined to crystallise into two broad classes, the *honestiores* (outside Rome, largely the town-councilor, *decuriones*) and the *humiliores*."

[95]Ibid., 61.

[96]Ibid., 63.

men talk. We know you are mad with much learning."[97] Later, one of Trimalchio's fellow freedmen challenges the boy Giton, Encolpius' fellow student of rhetoric, to a battle of wits in the typical *symposion* fashion of a riddle: "I will show you that your father wasted the fees, even though you are a scholar in rhetoric. . . . Solve this riddle. . . ."[98]

The same disdain Petronius shows for ambitious *nouveau riche* appears in Juvenal's satire of upper class Roman women. Roman women were allowed at *symposia* (as Greek women increasingly were) but their place would not normally have been to participate in the verbal competition. Thus, Juvenal complains that "the most intolerable of all is the woman who as soon as she has sat down to dinner" asserts her literary opinions.

The grammarians make way before her; the rhetoricians give in; the whole crowd is silenced: no lawyer, no auctioneer will get a word in, no nor any other woman; so torrential is her speech. . . . She lays down definitions, and discourses on morals, like a philosopher; thirsting to be deemed both wise *(docta)* and eloquent (*fecunda*), she ought to tuck up her tunic knee high [like a man].[99]

To compete for esteem as wise and eloquent was expected of upper class men, but these same men resented it if someone else, a woman or a freedman, entered the same competition.

Symposia and Teachers

In the symposia literature we have surveyed, the presence of eloquent, educated, cultured teachers is portrayed as the ideal, and the competition to achieve this ideal became so banal it was commonly satirized. In this competition, teachers who qualified as especially σοφός sometimes enjoyed particular attention for the honor their presence could provide. Thus, patrons of teachers would invite them to dinner, e.g. Lucian's rich man we met above, who is interested in culture (παιδεία) and so invited a number of learned

---

[97]Ibid, 46.
[98]Ibid, 58.
[99]Juv. 6.434-446.

people (οἱ σοφοί; σοφοί ἄνδρες, τοί σοφωτάτοι) who were "clever in words (περιττός ἐν τοῖς λόγοις)," both philosophers and literary men (οἱ ἀπὸ φιλοσοφηίας καὶ λόγων), including a grammarian and a rhetorician. Athenaeus tells us of one Larensis who "took pride (φιλοτιμίας) in gathering about him many men of culture (παιδεία) and entertained them with conversation as well as things proper to a banquet, now proposing topics worthy of inquiry, now disclosing solutions of his own."[100]

Teachers could enhance the status not only of the host but of all those who conversed with him. Thus, Plutarch points out that if a guest is jealous on account of his lower seat, that jealousy can be mitigated by assigning that person a place next to a teacher/professor (καθηγτής).[101] The extent of the honor given such a teacher was mocked by Lucian in his *Symposion*: when Ion the Platonic philosopher, who is the teacher of the groom, arrives "they all arose in his honor and received him like a supernatural being; in short it was a regular divine visitation, the advent of Ion the marvelous."[102]

The honor given wise guests is extensively portrayed in *Aristeas*. We have already seen in this letter and in *Sirach* that Hellenistic Jewish scribes entered the general cultural competition for being considered wise and eloquent, and above we saw in *Sirach* that any cultured Jew could enter into the competition at a *symposion*. *Aristeas* describes a series of *symposia* over seven days in which the Jewish scribes are portrayed as wiser than the Egyptian philosophers. The king, wishing to show his esteem for the scribes, invites them to dinner (δεῖπνον/συμπόσιον). He has the couches carefully arranged so that half of them would recline on each side of him in order of seniority, "leaving nothing undone to show the men honor (τίμη)." The king invites each in turn to speak on some subject, after which each is greeted with applause or other approval. The ninth speech is on *symposia*, and mirrors the general ideals: "One ought to invite lovers of learning. . . . Such men . . . have cultivated (παιδεύω) their minds." As one would expect of such men, Aristeas was very

[100]Ath. *Deip.* 1.2:

[101]Plut. *Quaest. conv.* 1.2 (*Mor.* 617D).

[102]Lucian *Symp.* 7.

impressed with the "power of their discourse (τὴν τοῦ λόγου δύναμιν, cf. 1 Cor. 1:18, 2:4-5, 4:19-20).[103]

Lucian and other satirists enjoy poking fun at such learned guests at rich men's dinners, in part because the type of genteel *symposion* idealized by Plutarch and Aristeas contrasts with the actual pseudo-sophisticated drunken competition of wits that seems to have been more the norm. Though Ion and others are presented as philosophers, their rôle at dinners was not philosophical but rhetorical. According to Plutarch, philosophers are not even invited by many, for they fear the guests will be bored by their serious discourse. The only kind of philosopher who is a fit guest is one who can learn to "consider the character of the guests." If his drinking companions are unwilling to listen to philosophy, he "will change his role, fall in with their mood," and choose "topics of discussion that are particularly suitable for a drinking-party . . . to entertain and instruct his companions." Because of the mixed audience and convivial nature of the *symposion*, even people of good taste (οἱ χαρίεντες) who wish to discuss philosophy will rely on persuasion (πιθανός), not demonstration (ἀποδείξις).[104]

Such genteel urbane distaste for philosophical conversation was especially acute among the Romans, to whom Greeks were "the world's greatest chatterboxes. Not only did they talk too much, but at the wrong time. The learned Greek . . . was often gauche, *ineptus*, a bore. . . . They talked shop, their own shop, in a manner offensive to polite conversation."[105] Perhaps Paul did not cater to such genteel tastes, since he claims to have taken the opposite approach, relying not upon adaptable persuasion, but upon the persuasion of the "shop-talk" of the gospel (1 Cor. 2:4). He was willing to adapt his ways to the weak, but he pointedly leaves out any mention of willingness to adapt himself to the strong (1 Cor. 9:22). According to Luke (Acts 20:7), Paul at a δεῖπνον in Troas prolonged his speech (λόγος) until midnight, so that one young man, sitting in the window (presumably because of a lack of space in the typically small dining room) "sank into a deep sleep as Paul talked (διαλέγομαι) still

[103]*Aristeas*, 180-299.

[104]Plut. *Quaest. conv.*, 1.1 (*Mor.* 612E-615B).

[105]Balsdon, 32, citing Strabo 3, 4, 19, 166.

longer." No wonder some of the Corinthians changed their preference to Apollos as the featured speaker of the Christian *symposion*. Perhaps they were like Trimalchio, who wished to have inscribed on his sepulcher that despite his religious, civic, and economic accomplishments, "He never listened to a philosopher."[106]

Sophists at Dinner

Though philosophers were often considered poor guests if they did not speak in a rhetorical manner, those who fashioned themselves as sophists were frequently invited to *symposia*. In fact, a sophist who was clever enough at flattering speech could keep himself fed through invitations to one dinner after another. This type of person Athenaeus calls a "dinner-chasing sophist."[107] Since a "dinner-chaser" is a synonym for parasite,[108] the dividing line between sophists and parasites was not always clear, since both in their own ways sought to please their audience.

Such sophists were among those who helped transform the title "parasite" from meaning "dining companion" to "sponger." Parasites were frequently criticized as flatterers, those who are always looking to please their hosts for their own ends. In Lucian's description, a successful parasitical sophist could profit quite well by such subservience. His work "On Salaried Posts in Great Houses" warns against taking such posts, for it puts one "on trial in the friendship of our wealthy men—if the name of friendship may be applied to that sort of slavery on their part."[109] In other words, when a teacher accepts a rich person's salary, he sacrifices ἐλευθερία in the bonds of a patron-client relationship. Some, though, say

> that men were thrice happy when, besides having the noblest of the Romans for their friends, eating expensive dinners (δεῖπνα) without paying any scot, living in a handsome establishment, and travelling in all comfort and luxury, behind a span of white horses,

---

[106]Petr. *Sat.* 72.
[107]Ath. *Deip.* 1.4.
[108]Ibid., 6.242.
[109]Lucian *Merc. Cond.* 1.

> perhaps, with their noses in the air, they could also get no inconsiderable amount of pay for the friendship which they enjoyed and the kindly treatment which they received.[110]

Such clients, or "friends," of rich Romans, here and elsewhere in the Imperial period, are preferred because they are Greeks, though the attitudes of Romans towards the more ancient culture remained fickle. These philohellenic Romans think the Greek teachers "confer a tremendous benefit by turning wretched phrases."[111] They included not only philosophers, but "grammarians, rhetoricians, musicians, and in a word all who think fit to enter families and serve for hire as educators (παιδείας)." All these teachers were treated by their paymasters as a single class. Along with these come "the rest of the mob (ὁ ἄλλος πλῆθος), such as athletic instructors (γυμναστής) and parasites (κόλαξ, i.e., a flatterer), ignorant (ἰδιώτης, cf. 2 Cor. 11:6), petty-minded, naturally abject (ταπεινός, cf. 2 Cor. 10:1) fellows" who also take such positions, but are suited to it by their low station and lack of a trade (ἄτεχνος). "They enter households in the first instance to encounter this insolence (ὕβρις), and it is their trade to bear and tolerate it." But educated men (πεπαιδευμένοι) should be indignant (ἀγανακτέω) and try to regain their freedom (ἐλευθερία),[112] or they will end up being compared with "flatterers and loafers and buffoons" themselves.[113]

The categories and terminology here are so closely parallel to the Corinthian situation they hardly need comment. Paul, as ἰδιώτης and ταπεινός (at least by 2 Cor.) places himself among the "the mob" of low status teachers. But he also escapes slavery and *hybris* by having a trade. The superlative apostles place themselves among the higher class of teachers who "turn a phrase" and receive pay.

The rich man wants such sophists around him to enhance his own status. Though he claims to desire the "wisdom (σοφία) of Homer or the eloquence (δεινότητος) of Demosthenes or the sublimity of Plato," he really wants to impress others. Since "everybody knows you for a grammarian or a rhetorician or a philosopher,

---

[110]Ibid, 3.
[111]Ibid, 17.
[112]Ibid., 4.
[113]Ibid., 24.

it seems to him the proper thing to have a man of that sort . . . It will make people think him . . . a person of taste in literary matters (παιδεία)."[114]

As in all patron-client relationships, the teacher does not just confer status, but gains it and other advantages. Among the things that entice men to become "slaves (δοῦλοι) instead of freemen" are the rich dinners.[115] They "put themselves into the power of the rich to treat as they will" partly because they seek "the mere name of associating with men of noble family (εὐπατρίδαι) and high social position. There are people who think that even this confers distinction and exalts them above the masses."[116]

Lucian relates the kind of pitfall such a person can encounter. One day your master

> calls you up and asks you a casual question. Then you sweat profusely, your head swims confusedly, you tremble (τρόμος, cf. 1 Cor. 2:3) inopportunely, and the company laughs at you for your embarrassment. . . . Good men call this modesty, forward men (τολμηροί, cf. 1 Cor. 6:1, 2 Cor. 10.12, 11:21) cowardice (δειλία), and unkind men lack of breeding (ἀπαιδευσίαν).[117]

In Corinth, Paul trembles, then tries to use this timid demeanor to his advantage by portraying himself as modest. Unkind Corinthians call his trembling a lack of breeding and some turn to a more suitable apostle. When the superlative apostles arrive, they directly attack his character as weak and cowardly (2 Cor. 10:1).

When the rich man displays his learning, he is "praised and felicitated." But the teacher must compete for recognition, so you end up

> jealous (φθονέω) of your rivals. . . . No doubt there are many who side against you and for others in your stead. . . . Then too imagine a man with a long beard and grey hair undergoing examination to see if he knows anything worth while, and some

---

[114]Ibid., 25.
[115]Ibid., 7.
[116]Ibid., 9.
[117]Ibid., 11.

> thinking that he does, others that he does not! Then a period intervenes, and your whole past life is pried into.[118]

Again, the parallels to Paul's Corinth are apparent. Some are siding with him, but some who side with other teachers are examining him, not just about what he knows, but about his *ethos*.

Lucian imagines that in the teacher's first dinner, he is given a place "a little above the rich man." When the *symposion* begins, the host "drinks your health, addressing you as 'the professor' (διδάσκαλος) or whatever it may be. You take the bowl, but because of inexperience you do not know that you should say something in reply, and you get a bad name for boorishness." Then, "subject after subject is discussed." But some of the host's old friends become "jealous of you, . . . some of whom you had previously offended when the places at table were assigned because you, who had only just come, were given precedence over men who for years had drained the dregs of servitude." The rivals may undertake a "campaign of slander (διαβολή)"[119]—an apt description of the activities of the "superlative apostles."

At later dinners, the teacher is no longer "held in the same esteem (ἔντιμος) and admiration by the company," he is given the poorest portions and quality of food and drink, and he ends up hungry and thirsty.[120] Finally, he is entirely rejected in favor of another.[121]

What Lucian describes in great detail, Juvenal portrays briefly in his biting portrayal of such guests in the homes of the rich (again, Greeks whose education impresses their Roman patrons):

> And now let me speak at once of the race which is most dear to our rich men. . . . I cannot abide, Quirites, a Rome of Greeks. . . . Quick of wit (*ingenium velox*) and of unbounded impudence (*audacia perdita*), they are as ready of speech (*sermo promptus*) as Isaeus, and more torrential. . . . He has brought with him any character you please; grammarian, orator, geometrician, painter, trainer, or rope dancer; augus, doctor or astrologer. . . . These

---

[118]Ibid., 11-12.
[119]Ibid., 16-18.
[120]Ibid., 26-28.
[121]Ibid., 40.

> people are experts in flattery, and will commend the talk of an illiterate or the beauty of a deformed friend. . . . He has always the best of it, being ready at any moment . . . to throw up his hands and applaud if his friend spit or hiccup nicely, or if his golden basin make a gurgle when turned upside down. . . . All my long years of servitude go for nothing. Nowhere is it so easy as at Rome to throw an old client overboard.[122]

Perhaps Corinth treated Paul in a similar way. Paul seems to be resisting the Corinthians' perceptions of him and Apollos as wise teachers who enhance the status of their hosts by making them appear wise. Perhaps it was not just his rôle as a preacher/orator that shaped their perceptions in this way. As Judge and Stowers insist, we must imagine the primary setting for Paul's speech in private homes; and in those homes the primary setting for speech was at the *deipnon/symposion*. Since we know that such dinners were a frequent, probably primary, perhaps even only gathering, we should imagine Paul constrained by cultural expectations of teachers at dinners, including the normal competition for status as wise.

Conclusion

In earlier chapters, we have seen that the rhetorical situation consists of an exigence of division constrained by status-related values including the value placed on rhetoric. While the issue of rhetoric does not explicitly reappear in the rest of the letter, the issues of status and division are prominent, especially in the dinners of chapter 11. When we examine Greco-Roman dining customs, we find not only the related issues of status and divisions, but also of rhetoric. Since evidence persuades us that the Corinthian dinners were perceived within Hellenistic cultural expectations, the presence of divisive competitions over eloquence at the Corinthian dinners becomes strongly implied in the narrative we construct. Such a narrative can tie the letter together into a response to a single, even if complex, rhetorical situation.

---

[122]Juv. 3.58-125; cf. Ath. *Deip*. 3.236-245.

CONCLUSION

As readers of Paul's letter, we intuitively and naïvely construct a narrative of the rhetorical situation to which he responds. As historians, we search for clues to further enrich and constrain our imaginations in order to revise our narrative both to satisfy our critical convictions and to provide more meaningful readings of the text. These clues have led to the following conclusions:

Paul is responding to an exigence of division among the Corinthians. These divisions are a result of the Corinthians' competitions for status. As other Hellenists, they compete to be recognized as wise (cultured), well-born, and rich or powerful. When Paul arrived among them, their relationship with him was shaped within the social norms for visiting sophists (i.e., eloquent teachers). They gladly provided the patronage Paul needed to establish a congregation. Paul needed such patronage to give him a legitimate platform to address the gentiles. Among Jews, he could speak in the synagogue, but among gentiles he, as an amateur rhetor, lacked a platform until invited to speak in the homes of his patrons. The Corinthians, in return, gained honor through hosting him, especially at their evening meals followed by cultured discussion.

The Corinthians were particularly ambitious because of their status inconsistency. While Corinth was a major urban center with lots of money, even its leading citizens were overshadowed by high status Romans, especially since the Corinthians tended to be nouveau riche. Thus, when Apollos arrived to carry on Paul's work, the two teachers quickly became occasions for competitive and divisive boasting. The different backgrounds of Paul and Apollos in, respectively, Asia Minor and Alexandria, gave them different rhetorical training and experience. While we might imagine Alexandrian rhetoric to be more sophisticated, the opposite appears to be true. Thus, Apollos, who, unlike Paul, apparently took money from his patrons, seems to have appealed to those with even greater status inconsistency.

We should, then, construct a narrative in which each of at least two competing groups of patrons and their clients boast that they have the wiser teacher. To exalt themselves over the other group, they employ normal comparitive rhetoric, not only finding their own teacher wiser than that of the other group, but themselves wiser or richer or of better birth. Comparison included not just praise and self-praise, but accusations against the competitor. Thus, Paul also has to defend himself against such charges and the resultant loss of authority, particularly against the charge that he was less than cultured in refusing gifts and working as a craftsman.

Just as others formed themselves into clubs to enjoy status not available in the general culture, so too did these Corinthians use their Christian association as the occasion to compete for status. Thus, at the dinners, the patrons of the teachers particularly gained honor and enjoyed it in the best seats, and the others competed for honored seats with the best food, drink, and service. The best seats also gave them the opportunity to compete further to be considered wise (cultured) conversationalists. Meanwhile, they also enjoyed the pleasure of being among the "wise," "strong," "well-born," "honored" ones rather than the "weak," "foolish," "nothings" who did not even rate a space in the dining room with its fine food and conversation.

All this Paul found alarming. The Corinthians had received his message about Christ, but they had not absorbed the ethical implications of their decision. In other words, Paul is attempting to define group boundaries differently than the Corinthians. They see themselves as yet one more Hellenistic group in which one could compete for and enjoy status in a smaller field than the entire city or even empire. Thus, their group is defined as a microcosm of the general culture differentiated only by its particular kind of wisdom, which is then typically seen as an occasion for boasting (this is also true of the spiritual gifts of chapters 12-14). Just as the community mirrors cultural norms of boasting, so too do they fail to differentiate themselves in the areas of sexual ethics, settlement of disputes, or religious participation outside the church.

Paul insists that modeling the church on such attitudes and behaviors of the outside world betrays the heart of the gospel. Christians should not exalt themselves over one another, since their hero is the lowest status person in the world. They should not champion one apostle over another, since the apostles are, like Christ, servants. They should not divide themselves from one another, because Christ suffered and died and rose again equally for all. The persuasiveness of Paul's message is not to be attributed to the status of rhetorical skill (even if he has it), but to the authority he derives from his master. This authority he not only speaks but acts in suffering, a humble attitude he enjoins the Corinthians to imitate.

Having concluded our search for historical clues, we are ready to write a new narrative. As an imaginative exercise, such a narrative treats the evidence more flexibly and intuitively than does formal historical critical work. Thus, it is a move toward what Paul Ricoeur calls a "second naïvete."[1] I have written the narrative in the voice of the Paul I find implied in the text. This is not an attempt to psychologize the historical Paul. It is simply an exercise in aid of interpretation, since "the task of hermeneutics is to bring back to discourse the written text."[2]

A Narrative of the Rhetorical Situation

I arrived at Corinth fully convinced that I was once again to preach the gospel of my crucified Lord. As was my usual practice, I went first to my fellow Jews. The Lord aided this task by sending me a devout, truth-seeking Jewish couple, Aquila and his wife Prisca, newly arrived at Corinth from Rome. They soon received my gospel and become my devoted helpers.

They invited me to stay in their home and to accept their money so I might preach without hindrance. I accepted their hospitality, but

---

[1]Loretta Dornisch, "Symbolic Systems and the Interpretation of Scripture: An Introduction to the Work of Paul Ricoeur," *Semeia* 4 (1975), 16.

[2]Paul Ricoeur, "Biblical Hermeneutics," *Semeia* 4 (1975), 67.

I refused their offers of monetary gifts. I explained to them that I had no qualms against receiving such gifts. Indeed, as I later wrote to the congregation, I am firmly convinced that a preacher of the gospel deserves his pay. Later, when Prisca and Aquila offered Apollos such help, I had no objection. But I would not receive such gifts from the Corinthians, even though I had received and continue to receive such gifts from other congregations. For I quickly perceived that Corinthians are a peculiar lot. Money plays a part in their lives in a way unmatched in the towns of my other congregations. I don't mean that these Corinthians were aristocrats. On the contrary, they were mostly ordinary folk, many of them freedmen or slaves. But the remarkably active business, banking, and trade of this city, famous throughout the world, allowed many of them to multiply their money. With these new "riches," they tried to simulate, even if sometimes rather crudely, the lives of Roman aristocrats. Even genuine aristocrats like to buy teachers to show them off to their friends, robbing the teachers of their freedom. To such slavery I would submit neither myself nor the gospel of Christ.

Instead, I worked at the craft I have kept active even through my years of proclaiming the gospel. I thank God that Aquila and Prisca bought a shop engaged in that very craft of tentmaking. With all the caravans passing through Corinth, with their bags of coins of merchants from Athens to Rome, they had more than enough work for me.

My hosts also introduced me to the elders of the synagogue. They allowed me to speak, but, as I had come to expect, most did not receive my teaching favorably. Some, though, were more receptive and are in the congregation to this day, including Crispus, the ruler of the synagogue whom I baptized along with his whole household.

So I turned to the gentiles. Though I had already spoken to several as the Lord gave me opportunities, I was determined to fulfill my commission to speak to as many as possible. For this reason, I left the home of my Jewish hosts and accepted the hospitality of gentiles so I would have greater opportunity to speak to their friends. My first host was the god-fearer Titius Justus whom I had met in the synagogue; later I accepted Gaius' hospitality because he had one of the largest homes in town (Gaius was also one of the few I baptized in those early days before I turned the task over to others.) Each of these hosts was uneasy with my refusal of gifts of money. They were embarrassed by my lowly trade, and by the shame they suffered by not being able to claim me as fully their "friend." But in those early days, my hosts were so won over by the power of my message that they forgave me these insults.

I stayed with this young congregation for many months, sometimes aided by Silas and Timothy. When the congregation seemed stable enough, I left them under the care of Stephanus and his household. I left for Ephesus, now accepting the generous assistance of my travelling companions, Prisca and Aquila (outside Corinth, I had no reason to refuse such provision).

While in Ephesus, we met an impressive Jew named Apollos, who had come from Alexandria. He was an enthusiastic preacher of Christ, speaking in that rousing way that only Alexandrians seem to master. I knew God had sent this man to further the gospel, but his message was as yet immature. While I was engaged in other congregations, Prisca and Aquila offered him their hospitality and support while they instructed him further in my gospel. They also told him of the young congregation in Corinth, and he was anxious to be of service there. So Prisca and Aquila wrote him a letter of recommendation to the patrons of the Corinthian congregation.

Once Apollos arrived, he excited the congregation. They were impressed with how persuasively he could argue from the Scriptures, even confounding those Jews who refused to receive God's Messiah. His manner of preaching and teaching contrasted very much with my own. I had first learned to speak in the same way as other boys in Tarsus, through many repetitions of the *gymnasmata* before the dour gaze of my teachers. If not for my years of listening and speaking in the synagogue, if not for the enthusiasm I found first in persecuting Christians and then in proclaiming Christ, if not for my ear trained through years of travel throughout the world, I would have been no vessel at all for God's message. As it is, I am but a poor earthen vessel, but God's message is so powerful he can use even me.

But Apollos is another matter. He tells me that he did not suffer long the boring lessons of his schooling. In Alexandria, he says, one need not be a professional orator to speak before the public. All manner of men spoke in that tumultuous city, and those who could sway a crowd of ordinary people prevailed in the contests in speech. The streets, Apollos said, were his school of rhetoric. With such a vessel, the gospel could go far.

Indeed it did. By now, the church included all sorts of people, not just the wealthy heads of houses and their households. I learned from the reports of Chloe's people that many of these folk preferred Apollos's fiery preaching over my own plainer style. But others, especially my original converts, were rather offended by his lack of dignity. Apollos accepted the hospitality of some of the former group, who were moneyed but less cultured than my hosts. These hosts began to boast that Apollos, their "friend" because he accepted their hospitality and monetary gifts, was more eloquent than I. This boastful and divisive behavior became particularly apparent at the Lord's *deipnon*, where Apollos's animated speech dominated the conversation. We learned that his own devotees had begun to fight among themselves for the honor of sitting nearest him, and once he left, for the honor of taking his seat or one near it. Their weaker members they exiled to another room. And those "of Paul" were behaving in just the same way.

From there, Chloe's people told me, things got really out of hand. I became even more convinced than ever that I had been right to refuse my hosts' offers of money. Even after all my teaching and that of Apollos, the Corinthians still could not discern the difference between the human, fleshly ways of this world which is passing away and the spiritual ways of Christ. They began to think of their dinners not as meetings of the whole church, but as an association devoted to the wisdom "of Apollos" or "of Paul." Treating our association as if it were any other, they called their worldly attitudes "wise" and therefore "spiritual." Just as a group gathered around a sophist boast in his wisdom, so were those "of Apollos" or those "of Paul" boasting. Those of Apollos compared me unfavorably to him, even attacking my character by pointing out my *faux pas* in refusing money, my long and monotonous manner of speech, my weakness of body and voice. Even more painful to me, those who proclaimed loyalty to me answered in kind, accusing Apollos of being crude and his followers of being ostentatious and uncultured.

Let it not be so! How could those for whom I labored, for whom Apollos labored, for whom Christ died, now turn their backs on this message of service and exalt themselves one over another, and in the name of their very teachers! They might as well empty the gloriously shameful cross of suffering and worship those with worldly success, the rulers of this age.

When I heard these reports, I again wrote to the Corinthians. Perhaps through my poor words, the transcendent power of Christ could change their immature and worldly hearts. Perhaps even those who disliked my manner of speaking could hear my words when they did not have to suffer my poor personal appearance and delivery. In any case, I had no choice; God had given me a commission.

I began my letter as my teachers had taught me. Faced with an audience I must rebuke, I employed the "subtle" type of introduction. I tried to win over my audience by first praising them, touching many of the topics I would later raise. Then I introduced the main point on which I wished to challenge them: their worldly behavior and attitudes of boasting and divisiveness. The situation made this letter particularly difficult: my own amateur rhetoric and that of Apollos provoked this crisis, yet I could only fight it with more rhetoric.

My strategy, then, was to disarm the worldly attraction of our rhetoric, and indeed to turn the Corinthians away from all such worldly attitudes which would exalt human achievements. Whether this important opening section of my letter will be effective, I do not know. Time will tell, but I fear that these Corinthians have brought so much of the world and its ways into the church that there is no undoing it.

Their worldly behavior I know not just from this report of Chloe's people. Other reports, including their own letter, have grieved me about their worldliness. I have written them before about such matters, including instructions to refuse membership to people who will not repent of the most obvious worldly sins, such as idolatry and drunkenness. But they not only fail to purify themselves in this way; they persist in such behavior themselves. They participate in idol-worship, and honor members who engage in the most shameless sexual sins.

But it is their typically worldly ways of climbing one over the other in their ceaseless desire for honor that most disturbs me, for it is this which most directly offends my gospel of the cross. If they suffer some loss of honor, they are even ready to leave the wisdom of the church and take their disputes before unrighteous gentiles. And they care more for the honor of eating fine meals with their pagan friends than with offending the consciences of the weaker members of the congregation.

Perhaps most disturbing of all is the way they bring these worldly attitudes into the meetings themselves. I already mentioned the shameless treatment of the weaker members by the stronger members, whether those who favored me or Apollos. In the early days, we did not have these problems in our dinners. Most of the first members were accustomed to dining with people like themselves, but even the slaves who came in as members of the converted households were welcomed. There was plenty of room in Gaius's large dining room if we shared the couches, and the novelty of being "one in Christ" gave us all a common subject of conversation. But, I have learned, as the church grew to include more of *hoi polloi*, the stronger members were no longer so hospitable. In fact, they began to treat the weaker members with ordinary worldly contempt. Their own honor in seating, conversation, food, and leisurely eating and drinking became more important to them than the sharing of the crucified body of Christ! Let it not be so!

Well, I have written my letter and sent it on its way. The problems aroused by my rhetoric I hope I have put right with yet more rhetoric. In fact, I added one last section before sending my final greetings, in which I recalled the best sermon I preached to the Corinthians. Perhaps if I can recall them to the heart of the message — the crucified and risen Lord — they will forget their worldly focus on the human qualities of the rhetoric itself.

But given all the words that have been spoken to these Corinthians, I am beginning to despair that they will ever repent of their worldly attitudes. Things could even get worse. All that needs to happen is for some so-called apostle to appeal to their worldly desires and they will embrace him enthusiastically and follow him down whatever Satanic path he leads.

But if not the Corinthians, perhaps others will one day read this letter and find it persuasive. Perhaps God will use this letter to help protect his Church from the corruption of the world. That corruption may take different forms, yet it is ever the same. How ironic that only through the tools of this world, such as its rhetoric, can God save his church from the world. After all, as I wrote to the Corinthians, we cannot escape the corruption of the world by removing ourselves from it. But we must deal with the world as if we had no dealings with it.

So I have treated my own rhetoric: as if I did not use rhetoric.

BIBLIOGRAPHY

Reference Works

Bauer, Walter. *A Greek-English Lexicon of the New Testament and Other Early Christian Literature.* 2nd ed. trans., adapted, and augmented by William F.Arndt, F. Wilbur Gingrich, and Frederick W. Danker. Chicago: University Press,1979.

Bennet, Charles E. *New Latin Grammar.* 3rd ed. Boston: Allyn and Bacon, 1918.

Blass, F., and A. Debrunner. *A Greek Grammar of the New Testament and Other Early Christian Literature.* 9th-10th ed. Translated and revised by Robert W. Funk. Chicago: University of Chicago Press, 1961.

Hammond, N. G. L., and H. H. Scullard, eds. *The Oxford Classical Dictionary.* 2nd ed. Oxford: Clarendon, 1970.

Institute for New Testament Textual Research and the Computer Center of Munster University. *Concordance to the Novum Testamentum Graece.* 3rd ed. Berlin: Walter de Gruyter, 1987.

Liddell, Henry George, and Robert Scott. *A Greek-English Lexicon.* 9th ed. Revised by Henry Stuart Jones with Roderick McKenzie. Oxford: Clarendon, 1968.

Morton, A. Q., S. Michaelson, and J. David Thompson. *A Critical Concordanceto I and II Corinthians.* The Computer Bible, eds. J. Arthur Baird and David Noel Freedman, no. 19. Wooster, Ohio: Biblical Research Associates, 1979.

Moule, C. F. D. *An Idiom-Book of New Testament Greek.* 2nd ed. Cambridge: University Press, 1959.

Oxford Latin Dictionary. Oxford: Clarendon, 1968-80.

Smyth, Herbert Weir. *Greek Grammar.* Revised by Gordon M. Massing. Cambridge:Harvard, 1956.

Ancient Texts

Aristeas to Philocrates. Jewish Apocryphal Literature, ed. Solomon Zeitlin, ed. and Translated by Moses Hadas. New York: Harper, 1951.

Aristophanes. Translated by Benjamin Bickley Rogers. LCL. Cambridge: Harvard, 1924.

Aristotle. *The "Art" of Rhetoric.* Translated by John Henry Freese. LCL. London:Heinemann, 1926.

________. *Topics.* Translated by E.S. Forster. LCL. Cambridge: Harvard, 1960.

Artemidori Daldiani. *Onirocriticon.* Leipzig: Teubner, 1963.

Athenaeus. *The Deipnosophists.* Translated by Charles Burton Gulick. LCL. London:Heinemann, 1928.

Butts, James R. "The Progymnasmata of Theon: A New Text with Translation and Commentary." Ph.D. diss., Claremont, 1986.

Cicero. *De Finibus Bonorum et Malorum.* Translated by H. Rackham. LCL. Cambridge:Harvard, 1914.

________. *De Oratore, De Fato, Paradox Stoicorum, De Partionie Oratoria.* Translated by E. W. Sutton. LCL. Cambridge: Harvard, 1942.

________. *De Inventione, De Optimo Genere Oratorum, Topica.* Translated by H. M.Hubbell. LCL. Cambridge: Harvard, 1949.

[Cicero] Ad C. Herennium: De Ratione Dicendi (Rhetorica ad Herennium). Translated by Harry Caplan. LCL. Cambridge: Harvard, 1954.

Dio Chrysostom. *Discourses.* Translated by J.W. Cohoon and H. Lamar Crosby. LCL. Cambridge: Harvard, 1932-1951.

Diodorus Siculus. *Bibliotheca historica.* Translated by C. H. Oldfather, Charles L. Sherman, Bradford Welles, Russel M. Geer, and Francis R. Walton. LCL. Cambridge:Harvard, 1933-1967.

Epictetus. *The Discourses as Reported by Arrian, The Manual, and Fragments.* Translated by W. A. Oldfather. LCL. Cambridge: Harvard, 1925-1928.

The Greek Anthology. Translated by W. R. Paton. LCL. Cambridge: Harvard, 1960.

Homer. *The Iliad.* Translated by A. T. Murray. LCL. London: Heinemann, 1924-25.

Horace. *Satires, Epistles and Ars Poetica.* Translated by H. Ruston Fairclough. LCL. Cambridge: Harvard, 1926.

Isocrates. Translated by George Norlin. LCL. Cambridge: Harvard, 1928-1929.

Josephus, Flavius. *Jewish Antiquities.* Translated by H. St. J. Thackery, RalphMarcus, Allen Wikgren, and Louis H. Feldman. LCL. Cambridge: Harvard, 1930-1965.

Juvenal. Translated by G. G. Ramsay "Satires." In *Juvenal and Persius*. LCL. London: Heinemann, 1928.

Lucian. Translated by A.M. Harmon, K. Kilburn, and M.D. MacLeod. LCL. Cambridge: Harvard, 1913-1967.

Martial. *Epigrams.* Translated by Walter C.A. Ker. LCL. Cambridge: Harvard, 1919-20.

Nestle, Erwin, Eberhard Nestle, Kurt Aland, Matthew Black, Carlo M. Martini, Bruce M. Metzer, and Allen Wikgren, eds. *Novum Testamentum Graece.* 26th ed.Stuttgart: Deutsche Bibelstiftung, 1979.

Persius. "Satires." Translated by G. G. Ramsey. In *Juvenal and Persius*. LCL. Cambridge: Harvard, 1928.

Petronius. "Satyricon." Translated by Michael Haeseltine. In *Petronius*. LCL. Cambridge: Harvard, 1969.

Philo. Translated by F.H. Colson, G.H. Whitaker, and J.W. Earp. LCL. Cambridge: Harvard, 1929-1962.

Philostratus and Eunapius. *The Lives of the Sophists.* Translated by Wilmer Cave Wright. LCL. Cambridge: Harvard, 1921.

Plato. *Phaedrus.* Translated by Harold North Fowler. LCL. Cambridge: Harvard, 1914.

________. *Protagoras.* Translated by W.R.M. Lamb. LCL. Cambridge: Harvard, 1924.

________. *Lysis, Sympsium, Gorgias.* trans W.R.M. Lamb. LCL. Cambridge: Harvard,1925.

Pliny. *Letters.* Translated by William Melmoth, revised by W.M.L. Hutchinson. LCL. Cambridge: Harvard, 1915.

Plutarch. *Moralia.* Translated by F.C. Babbitt et al. LCL. Cambridge: Harvard, 1927-1969.

Quintilian. *The Institutio Oratoria.* Translated by H. E. Butler. LCL. Cambridge, Harvard, 1920.

Rahlfs, Alfred, ed. *Septuaginta.* Stuttgart: Privilegierte württembergische Bibelanstalt, 1935.

The Elder Seneca. *Declamations.* Vol. 1-2 (*Controversiae* and *Suasoriae*). Translated by M. Winterbottom. LCL. Cambridge: Harvard, 1974.

Sextus Empiricus. Translated by R. G. Bury. Vol. 4: Against the Professors. LCL. Cambridge: Harvard, 1949.

Strabo, and Geography. *Geography.* Translated by Horace Leonard Jones. LCL. Cambridge: Harvard, 1917-1932.

Tacitus. *Dialogus, Agricola, Germania.* LCL. Cambridge: Harvard, 1939.

Theophrasus. *Characters.* Translated by J.M. Edmonds. LCL. Cambridge: Harvard, 1929.

White, Robert J. *Interpretation of Dreams.* (Artemidorus' *Oneirocritica*), Translated by Robert J. White. Park Ridge, NJ: Noyes Press, 1975.

Secondary and other Modern Works

Achtemeier, Paul J. "*Omne Verbum Sonat:* The New Testament and the Oral Environment of Late Western Antiquity." *Journal of Biblical Literature* 109 (1990): 3-27.

Alexandre, Manuel, Jr. "Rhetorical Argumentation as an Exegetical Technique in Philo of Alexandria." In *Hellenica et Judaica*, eds. A. Caquot, M. Hadas-Lebel, and J. Riaud, 13-27. Paris: Peeters, Leuven, 1986.

Apel, Karl-Otto. Tranlated by Linda Gail DeMichiel "Scientistics, Hermeneutics, Critique of Ideology: An Outline of a Theory of Science from an Epistemological-Anthropological Point of View." In *The Hermeneutics Reader*, ed. Kurt Mueller-Vollmer, 321-46. New York: Continuum, 1989.

Aune, David E. "Septum Sapientium Convivium." In *Plutarch's Ethical Writings and Early Christian Literature*, ed. Hans Dieter Betz, 51-105. Studia ad Corpus Hellenisticum, eds. H. D. Betz, G. Delling, and W. C. van Unnik, Vol. 4. Leiden: E. J. Brill, 1978.

________. *The New Testament in its Literary Environment.* Library of Early Christianity, ed. Wayne A. Weeks, no. 8. Philadelphia: Westminster, 1987.

Austin, John C. *How to Do Things with Words.* Oxford: Clarendon, 1962.

Baird, William. "Review: *Wisdom and Spirit: An Investigation of 1 Corintians 1:18-3:20 against the Background of Jewish Sapiential Traditions in the Greco-Roman Period* by James A. Davis." *Journal of Biblical Literature* 106 (1987): 149-51.

Balsdon, J. P. V. D. *Romans and Aliens.* Chapel Hill: University of North Carolina, 1979.

Barrett, C. K. *A Commentary on the First Epistle to the Corinthians.* 2nd ed. New York: Harper & Row, 1968.

________. *Essays on Paul.* Philadelphia: Westminster, 1982.

_______. "Apollos and the Twelve Disciples of Ephesus." In *The New Testament Age: Essays in Honor of Bo Reicke*, Vol. 1, ed. William C. Weinrich, 29-39. Macon, Ga.: Mercer, 1984.

Beker, J. Christian. *Paul the Apostle: The Triumph of God in Life and Thought.* Philadelphia: Fortress, 1984.

Bell, Richard H. "Introduction: Culture, Morality, and Religious Belief." In *The Grammar of the Heart: New Essays in Moral Philosophy & Theology*, ed. Richard H. Bell, xi-xxviii. San Francisco: Harper & Row, 1988.

Betz, Hans Dieter. *Der Apostel Paulus and die sokratische Tradition: Eine exegetische Untersuchung zu seiner "Apologie" 2 Korinther 10-13.* Tübingen: J.C.B. Mohr, 1972.

_______. *Galatians: A Commentary on Paul's Letter to the Churches in Galatia.* Philadelphia: Fortress, 1979.

_______. "The Problem of Rhetoric and Theology according to the Apostle Paul." In *L'Apôtre Paul: Personalité, Style et Conception du Ministère*, ed. A. Vanhoye, 16-48. Bibliotheca Ephemeridum Theologicarum Loveniensium. Leuven: University Press, 1986.

Bitzer, Lloyd F. "The Rhetorical Situation." *Philosophy & Rhetoric* 1 (1968): 1-14.

_______. "Functional Communication: A Situational Perspective." In *Rhetoric in Transition: Studies in the Nature and Uses of Rhetoric*, ed. Eugene E. White, 21-38. University Park: Pennsylvania State University, 1980.

Black, C. Clifton. "Rhetorical Criticism and Biblical Interpretation." *Expository Times* 100 (1989): 252-58.

Bohatec, J. "Inhalt und Reihenfolge der 'Schlagworte der Erlösungsreligion' in 1 Kor 1.26-31." *Theology* 24 (1948): 252-71.

Bonner, Stanley F. *Roman Declamation in the Late Republic and Early Empire.* Liverpool: University Press, 1949.

________. *Education in Ancient Rome: From the Elder Cato to the Younger Pliny.* Berkeley: University of California, 1977.

Booth, Alan D. "Elementary and Secondary Education in the Roman Empire." *Florigelium* 1 (1979): 1-14.

________. "The Schooling of Slaves in First-Century Rome." *Transactions of the American Philological Association* 109 (1979): 11-19.

Booth, Wayne C. *The Rhetoric of Fiction.* 2nd ed. Chicago: University of Chicago, 1983.

Bowersock, G. W. *Greek Sophists in the Roman Empire.* Oxford: Clarendon, 1969.

Bradley, David G. "The *Topos* as a Form in the Pauline Paraenesis." *Journal of Biblical Literature* 72 (1953): 238-46.

Bréhier, Émile. *The History of Philosophy: The Hellenistic and Roman Age.* Tranlated by Wade Baskin. Chicago: University of Chicago, 1965.

Brinsmead, Michael. *Galatians—Dialogical Response to Opponents.* Chico, CA: Scholars' Press, 1982.

Brinton, Alan. "Situation in the Theory of Rhetoric." *Philosophy & Rhetoric* 14 (1981): 234-48.

Bruce, F. F. "Apollos in the New Testament." *Ekklesiastikos Pharos* 57 (1975): 354-66.

Bultmann, Rudolf. *Der Stil der paulinischen Predigt un die kynisch-stoische Diatribe.* Göttengen: Vandenhoeck & Reprecht, 1910.

________. *History of the Synoptic Tradition.* Tranlated by John Marsh. New York: Harper & Row, 1963.

Bünker, Michael. *Briefformular und rhetorische Disposition im 1. Korintherbrief.* Göttinger Theologische Arbeiten, ed. Georg Strecker, no. 28. Göttingen: Vandenhoek & Ruprecht, 1983.

Burke, Kenneth. *A Rhetoric of Motives.* New York: Prentice-Hall, 1950.

________. "Rhetoric and Poetics." In *Language as Symbolic Action*, 296-307. Berkeley: University of California, 1966.

Caplan, Harry. "Introduction." In *[Cicero] Ad C. Herennium: De Ratione Decendi (Rhetorica Ad Herennium)*, vii-xl. LCL. Cambridge: Harvard, 1954.

Childs, Brevard S. *The New Testament as Canon: An Introduction.* Philadelphia: Fortress, 1984.

Clark, Donald Lemen. *Rhetoric in Greco-Roman Education.* New York: Columbia University, 1957.

Clarke, M. L. *Rhetoric at Rome: A Historical Survey.* London: Cohen & West, 1953.

________. *Higher Education in the Ancient World.* Albuquerque: University of New Mexico, 1971.

Colson, F. H. "μετεσχηματισα I Cor. iv 6." *The Journal of Theological Studies* 17 (1916): 379-84.

Conley, T. "Philo's Use of *Topoi.*" In *Two Treatises of Philo of Alexandria: A Commentary on De Gigantibus and Quod Deus Sit Immutabilis*, eds. David Winston and John Dillon, 171-78. Brown Judaic Studies, eds. Jacob Neusner, Wendell S. Dietrich, Ernest S. Frerichs, B. Twiss Sumner, and Alan Zuckerman, no. 25. Chico, CA: Scholars Press, 1983.

Consigny, Scott. "Rhetoric and Its Situations." *Philosophy & Rhetoric* 7 (1974): 175-85.

Conzelmann, Hans. *1 Corinthians.* Tranlated by James W. Leitch. Philadelphia: Fortress, 1975.

Culpepper, R. Alan. *Anatomy of the Fourth Gospel: A Study in Literary Design.* Philadelphia: Fortress, 1983.

Dahl, N. A. "Letter." In *The Interpreter's Dictionary of the Bible*, Vol. Supplementary, ed. G. A. Buttrick, 538-41. Nashville: Abington, 1962.

________. "Paul and the Church at Corinth According to 1 Cor. 1:10-4:21." (also available in *Christian History and Interpretation*, ed. W. Farmer and C.F.D. Moule [Cambridge: University Press, 1977], 313-335). In *Studies in Paul*, 40-61. Minneapolis: Augsburg, 1977.

Daube, David. "Rabbinic Methods of Interpretation and Hellenistic Rhetoric." In *Hebrew Union College Annual*, Vol. 22, 239-64. Philadelphia: Jewish Publication Society, 1949.

Davis, James A. *Wisdom and Spirit: An Investigation of 1 Cor. 1:18-3:20 against the Background of Jewish Sapiential Traditions in the Greco-Roman Period.* Lanham, MD: University Press, 1984.

Deissmann, Gustav Adolf. *Paul: A Study in Social and Religious History.* 2nd ed. Tranlated by W. Wilson. London: Hodder & Stoughton, 1926.

________. *Light from the Ancient East: The New Testament Illustrated by Recently Discovered Texts of the Graeco-Roman World.* 4th ed. Tranlated by L. Strachan. New York: George A. Doran, 1927.

Dibelius, Martin. *From Tradition to Gospel.* New York: Doubleday, 1966.

Dockhorn, Klaus. "Hans-Georg Gadamer's *Truth and Method.*" Translated and edited by Marvin Brown, *Philosophy & Rhetoric* 13 (1980): 160-80.

Dornisch, Loretta, "Symbolic Systems and the Interpretation of Scripture: An Introductin to the Work of Paul Ricoeur." *Semeia* 4 (1975), 1-21.

Doty, William G. *Letters in Primitive Christianity.* Philadelphia: Fortress, 1973.

Eagleton, Terry. *Literary Theory: An Introduction.* Minneapolis: University of Minnesota, 1983.

Ebeling, Gerhard. "Word of God and Hermeneutic." In *The New Hermeneutic*, eds. James M. Robinson and John B. Cobb Jr., 78-110. New Frontiers in Theology: Discussions among Continental and American Theologians, Vol. II. New York: Harper & Row, 1964.

Ellis, E. Earle. "Paul and His Opponents." In *Christianity, Judaism, and Other Greco-Roman Cults*, ed. J. Neusner. Leiden: Brill, 1975. (also in *Prophecy and Hermeneutic in Early Christianity*, 80-115. Grand Rapids: Eerdmans, 1978).

Fee, Gordon D. *The First Epistle to the Corinthians.* Grand Rapids: Eerdmans, 1987.

Fiore, Benjamin. "'Covert Allusion' in 1 Corinthians 1-4." *Catholic Biblical Quarterly* 47 (1985): 85-102.

Fiorenza, Elisabeth Schüssler. *The Book of Revelation: Justice and Judgement.* Philadelphia: Fortress, 1985.

________. "Rhetorical Situation and Historical Reconstruction in 1 Corinthians." *New Testament Studies* 33 (1987): 386-403.

Fish, Stanley E. *Is There a Text in This Class?* Cambridge: Harvard, 1980.

________. "Interpreting the Variorum." In *Reader-Response Criticism: From Formalism to Post-Structuralism*, ed. Jane P. Tompkins, 164-84. (also in Stanley Fish. *Is There a Text in This Class?* [Cambridge: Harvard, 1980]) Baltimore: Johns Hopkins, 1980.

________. "Literature in the Reader: Affective Stylistics." In *Reader-Response Criticism: From Formalism to Post-Structuralism*, ed. Jane P. Tompkins, 70-100. Baltimore: Johns Hopkins, 1980b.

________. *Doing What Comes Naturally: Change, Rhetoric, and the Practice of Theory in Literary and Legal Studies.* Durham, NC: Duke University, 1989.

Forbes, Christopher. "Comparison, Self-Praise, and Irony: Paul's Boasting and the Conventions of Hellenistic Rhetoric." *New Testament Studies* 32 (1986): 1-30.

Forbes, Clarence A. "The Education and Training of Slaves in Antiquity." *Transactions of the American Philological Association* 86 (1955): 321-60.

Froehlich, Karlfried. "Biblical Hermeneutics on the Move." In *A Guide to Contemporary Hermeneutics: Major Trends in Biblical Interpretation*, ed. Donald K. McKim, 175-91. Grand Rapids: Eerdmans, 1986.

Fuchs, Ernst. "The New Testament and the Hermeneutical Problem." In *The New Hermeneutic*, eds. James M. Robinson and John B. Cobb Jr., 110-45. New Frontiers in Theology: Discussions among Continental and American Theologians, no. Vol. II. New York: Harper & Row, 1964.

________. *Studies of the Historical Jesus.* Studies in Biblical Theology, eds. C. F. D. Moule and et al, Translated by Andrew Scobie. Naperville, IL: Allenson, 1964.

Funk, Robert Walter. "The Hermeneutical Problem and Historical Criticism." In *The New Hermeneutic*, eds. James M. Robinson and John B. Cobb, 164-97. New Frontiers in Theology: Discussions among Continental and American Theologians, no. Vol. II. New York: Harper & Row, 1964.

_______. *Language, Hermeneutic, and the Word of God.* New York: Harper & Row, 1966.

_______. "The Apostolic Parousia: Form and Significance." In *Christian History and Interpretation: Studies Presented to John Knox*, eds. W. R. Farmer, C. F. D. Moule, and R. R. Niebuhr, 249-68. Cambridge: Cambridge University, 1967.

Furnish, Victor Paul. *II Corinthians.* The Anchor Bible, eds. William Foxwell Albright and David Noel Freedman, no. 32A. Garden City, NY: Doubleday, 1984.

Gadamer, Hans-Georg. *Reason in the Age of Science.* Translated by Frederick G. Lawrence. Cambridge: MIT, 1981.

_______. *Truth and Method.* New York: Crossroad, 1984.

_______. "Rhetoric, Hermeneutics, and the Critique of Ideology." Translated by Jerry Dibble. In *The Hermeneutics Reader*, ed. Kurt Mueller-Vollmer, 274-92. New York: Continuum, 1989.

Gager, John. *Kingdom and Community: The Social World of Early Christianity.* Englewood Cliffs, NJ: Prentice-Hall, 1975.

Georgi, Dieter. *The Opponents of Paul in Second Corinthians.* Philadelphia: Fortress, 1986.

Gitay, Yegoshua. *Prophecy and Persuasion: A Study of Isaiah 40-48.* Forum Theologiae Linguisticae, ed. Erhardt Guttgemanns, no. 14. Bonn: Linguistica Biblica, 1981.

Grant, F. C. "Rhetoric and Oratory." In *The Interpreter's Dictionary of the Bible*, Vol. 4, ed. G. A. Buttrick, 75-78. Nashville: Abington, 1962.

Grant, Robert M. "The Wisdom of the Corinthians." In *The Joy of Study: Papers on New Testament and Related Subjects Presented to Honor Frederick Clifton Grant*, ed. Sherman E. Johnson, 51-55. New York: MacMillan, 1951.

________. "Hellenistic Elements in 1 Corinthians." In *Early Christian Origins: Studies in Honor of Harlod R. Willoughby*, ed. A. Wikgren, 60-66. Chicago: Quadrangle, 1961.

________. *Early Christianity and Society: Seven Studies.* New York: Harper & Row, 1977.

Grassi, Ernesto. *Rhetoric as Philosophy: The Humanist Tradition.* Translated by John Michael Krois and Azizeh Azodi. University Park: Pennsylvania State University, 1980.

Grosheide, Frederick Willem. *Commentary on the First Epistle to the Corinthians.* Grand Rapids: Eerdmans, 1953.

Habermas, Jurgen. "On Hermeneutics' Claim to Universality." In *The Hermeneutics Reader*, ed. Kurt Mueller-Vollmer, 294-319. New York: Continuum, 1989.

Halloran, Stephen M. "Language and the Absurd." *Philosophy & Rhetoric* 6 (1974): 97-108.

Hart, J. H. A. "Apollos." *The Journal of Theological Studies* 7 (1906): 16-28.

Hartman, Lars. "Some Remarks on 1 Cor. 2:1-5." *Svensk Exegetisk Årsbok* 39 (1974): 109-20.

Harvey, A. E. *Jesus and the Constraints of History.* Philadelphia: Westminster, 1982.

Heinrici, C. F. Georg. *Das erste Sendschreiben des Apostel Paulus an die Korinther.* Berlin: Wilhelm Hertz, 1880.

________. *Das zweite Sendschreiben des Apostel Paulus an die Korinthier.* 7th ed. Göttingen: Vandenhoeck & Ruprecht, 1890.

Hengel, Martin. *Judaism and Hellenism: Studies in Their Encounter in Palestine During the Hellenistic Period.* Translated by John Bowden. Philadelphia: Fortress, 1974.

________. *Crucifixion: In the Ancient World and the Folly of the Message of the Cross.* Translated by John Bowden. Philadelphia: Fortress, 1977.

________. *Acts and the History of Earliest Christianity.* Philadelphia: Fortress, 1979.

________. *Jews, Greeks, and Barbarians: Aspects of the Hellenization of Judaism in the Pre-Christian Period.* Translated by John Bowden. Philadelphia: Fortress, 1980.

Hering, Jean. *The First Epistle of Saint Paul to the Corinthians.* Translated by A. W. Heathcote and P.J. Allcock. London: Epworth, 1962.

Hock, Ronald F. *The Social Context of Paul's Ministry.* Philadelphia: Fortress, 1980.

Horner, Winifred Bryan, ed. *The Present State of Scholarship in Historical and Contemporary Rhetoric.* Columbia: University of Missouri, 1983.

Horsley, Richard A. "Pneumatikos vs. Psychikos: Distinctions of Spiritual Status among the Corinthians." *The Harvard Theological Review* 69 (1976): 269-88.

________. "Wisdom of Words and Words of Wisdom in Corinth." *Catholic Biblical Quarterly* 39 (1977): 224-39.

________. "The Background of the Confessional Formula in 1 Kor 8:6." *Zeitschrift für die neutestamentliche Wissenshaft und die Kunde des Urchristentums* 69 (1978a): 130-35.

________. "How Can Some of You Say, 'There is no Resurrection of the Dead'?: Spiritual Elitism in Corinth." *Novum Testamentum* 20 (1978b): 203-31.

________. "Spiritual Marriage with Sophia." *Vigiliae Christianae* 33 (1979): 30-54.

________. "Gnosis in Corinth: 1 Cor 8:1-6." *New Testament Studies* 27 (1980): 32-51.

Hubbell, H. M. "Introduction." In *Cicero: De Inventione, De Optimo Genere Oratorum, Topica*, vii-xiv. LCL. Cambridge: Harvard, 1949.

Humphries, Raymond Alexander. "Paul's Rhetoric of Argumentation in 1 Cor. 1-4." Ph.D. diss., Graduate Theological Union, 1980.

Hurd, John Coolidge. *The Origin of 1 Corinthians.* 2nd ed. Macon, GA: Mercer University, 1983.

Hurst, L. D. "Apollos, Hebrews, and Corinth: Bishop Montefiore's Theory Examined." *Scottish Journal of Theology* 38 (1985): 505-13.

Ijsselling, Samuel. *Rhetoric and Philosophy in Conflict: An Historical Survey.* Translated by Paul Dunphy. The Hague: Martinus Nijhoff, 1976.

Iser, Wolfgang. "The Reading Process: A Phenomenological Approach." In *Reader-Response Criticism: From Formalism to Post-Structuralism*, ed. Jane P. Tompkins, 50-69. Baltimore: Johns Hopkins, 1980.

Jaeger, Werner. *Early Christianity and Greek Paideia.* Cambridge, Mass.: Belknap Press, 1961.

Jamieson, Kathleen M. Hall. "Generic Constraints and the Rhetorical Situation." *Philosophy & Rhetoric* 6 (1973): 162-70.

Jeanrond, Werner G. *Text and Interpretation as Categories of Theological Thinking.* Translated by Thomas J. Wilson. New York: Crossroad, 1988.

Jordan, Mark D. "Ancient Philosophic Protreptic and the Problem of Persuasive Genres." *Rhetorica* 4 (1986): 309-33.

Judge, E. A. *The Social Pattern of Christian Groups in the First Century.* London: Tyndale, 1960.

________. "The Early Christians as a Scholastic Community." *Journal of Religious History* 1 (1960-61): 4-15, 125-37.

________. "The Conflict of Educational Aims in New Testament Thought." *Journal of Christian Education* 9 (1966): 32-45.

________. "Paul's Boasting in Relation to Contemporary Professional Practice." *Australian Biblical Review* 16 (1968): 37-50.

________. "St. Paul and Classical Society." *Jahrbüch Für Antike und Christentum* 15 (1972): 19-36.

________. "The Social Identity of the First Christians: A Question of Method in Religious History." *Journal of Religious History* 11 (1980): 201-17.

________. *Rank and Status in the World of the Caesars and St. Paul.* Christchurch, New Zealand: University of Canterbury, 1982.

________. "The Reaction against Classical Education in the New Testament." *Journal of Christian Education* 77 (1983): 7-14.

Kane, Francis I. "Peitho and the Polis." *Philosophy & Rhetoric* 19 (1986): 99-124.

Kasemann, Ernst. "Die Legitimität des Apostels." *Zeitschrift für die neutestamentliche Wissenshaft und die Kunde des Urchristentums* 41 (1942): 33-71.

Kaster, Robert A. "Notes on 'Primary' and 'Secondary' Schools in Late Antiquity." *Transactions of the American Philological Association* 113 (1983): 323-46.

Kennedy, George A. *The Art of Persuasion in Greece.* A History of Rhetoric, Vol. 1. Princeton: Princeton University, 1963.

________. *Quintilian.* New York: Twayne, 1969.

________. *The Art of Rhetoric in the Roman World: 300 B.C.-A.D. 300.* A History of Rhetoric, Vol. 2. Princeton: Princeton University, 1972.

________. *Classical Rhetoric and Its Christian and Secular Traditions from Ancient to Modern Times.* Chapel Hill: University of North Carolina, 1980.

________. *New Testament Interpretation through Rhetorical Criticism.* Chapel Hill: University of North Carolina, 1984.

Kent, John Harvey. *Corinth VIII/3: The Inscriptions 1926-1950.* Princeton: American School of Classical Studies at Athens, 1966.

Kingsbury, Jack Dean. *The Christology of Mark's Gospel.* Philadelphia: Fortress, 1983.

Kinneavy, James L. "Contemporary Rhetoric." In *The Present State of Scholarship in Historic and Contemporary Rhetoric*, ed. Winifred Bryan Horner, 167-213. Columbia: University of Missouri, 1983.

________. *Greek Rhetorical Origins of Christian Faith: An Inquiry.* Oxford: University Press, 1987.

Kirby, John T. "The Rhetorical Situations of Revelation 1-3." *New Testament Studies* 34 (1988): 197-207.

Der Kleine Pauly. S.v. "Convivium" and "Symposion.". Stuttgart: Alfred Druckenmüller, 1964-75.

Koester, Helmut. "Ulrich Wilckens: Weisheit und Torheit." Review, *Gnomon* 33 (1961): 590-95.

________. "*GNOMAI DIAPHOROI*: The Origin and Nature of Diversification in the History of Early Christianity." In *Trajectories through Early Christianity*, eds. James M. Robinson and Helmut Koester, 114-57. Philadelphia: Fortress, 1971.

________. *History, Culture, and Religion of the Hellenistic Age.* Philadelphia: Fortress, 1982.

Kovesi, Julius. *Moral Notions.* London: Routledge & Kegan Paul, 1967.

Kummel, Werner George. *Introduction to the New Testament.* Revised ed. Tranlated by Howard Clark Kee. Nashville: Abingdon, 1975.

Wissowa, G., ed. *Paulys Real-Encylopädie der classischen Altertumswissenshaft.* Neue Bearbeitung. S.v. "Logos" and "Sophia" by Leisegang and "Symposium" and "Symposium Literature" by Hug. Stuttgart: J.B. Metzler, 1893-1980a.

Lemcio, E. "The Intention of the Evangelist, Mark." *New Testament Studies* 32 (1986): 187-206.

Leopold, J. "Philo's Knowledge of Rhetorical Theory." In *Two Treatises of Philo of Alexandria*, eds. D. Winston and J. Dillon, 129-36. Brown Judaic Studies, no. 25. Chico, CA: Scholars Press, 1983.

Lieberman, Saul. *Greek in Jewish Palestine.* New York: Jewish Theological Seminary, 1942.

________. *Hellenism in Jewish Palestine.* New York: Jewish Theological Seminary in America, 1950.

Lietzmann, D. Hans. *An die Korinther I-II.* 5th ed. enlarged by Werner Georg Kümmel. Handbuch zum Neuen Testament no. 9. Tübingen: J. C. B. Mohr, 1969.

Lim, Timothy H. "Not in Persuasive Words of Wisdom, but in the Demonstration of the Spirit and Power." *Novum Testamentum* 29 (1987): 137-49.

Long, A. A. *Hellenistic Philosophy: Stoics, Epicureans, Skeptics.* London: Gerald Duckworth and Company, 1974.

Luedemann, Gerd. *Opposition to Paul in Jewish Christianity.* Tranlated by M. Eugene Boring. Minneapolis: Fortress, 1989.

MacDonald, Dennis Ronald. *There is no Male and Female: The Fate of a Dominical Saying in Paul and Gnosticism.* Harvard Dissertations in Religion, no. 20. Philadelphia: Fortress, 1987.

MacMullen, Ramsey. *Enemies of the Roman Order.* Cambridge: Harvard, 1966.

________. *Roman Social Relations: 50 B.C. to A.D. 284.* New Haven: Yale, 1974.

Malherbe, Abraham J. *Social Aspects of Early Christianity.* 2nd ed. Philadelphia: Fortress, 1983.

________. *Ancient Epistolary Theorists.* Society of Biblical Literature: Sources for Biblical Study, ed. Bernard Brandon Scott, no. 19. Atlanta: Scholars, 1988.

Marrou, H. I. *A History of Education in Antiquity.* Tranlated by George Lamb. New York: Sheed & Ward, 1956.

Marshall, Peter. *Enmity in Corinth: Social Conventions in Paul's Relations with the Corinthians.* Wissenschaftliche Untersuchungen zum Neuen Testament, eds. Martin Hengel and Otfried Hofius, no. 2. Rheihe 23. Tübingen: J.C.B. Mohr (Paul Siebeck), 1987.

Martin, Dale, *Slavery as Salvation: The Metaphor of Slavery in Pauline Christianity.* New Haven: Yale, 1990.

McCasland, S. V. "Education, New Testament." In *The Interpreter's Dictionary of the Bible*, Vol. 2, ed. G. A. Buttrick, 34-38. Nashville: Abingdon, 1962.

Meeks, Wayne A. *The First Urban Christians: The Social World of the Apostle Paul.* New Haven: Yale, 1983.

________. *The Moral World of the First Christians.* Library of Early Chistianity, ed. Wayne A. Meeks, no. 6. Philadelphia: Westminster, 1986.

Miller, Arthur B. "Rhetorical Exigence." *Philosophy & Rhetoric* 5 (1972): 111-18.

Mitchell, Margaret Mary. "Paul and the Rhetoric of Reconciliation: An Exegetical Investigation of the Language and Composition of 1 Corinthians." Ph. D. diss., University of Chicago Divinity School, 1989.

Mueller-Vollmer, Kurt. "Introduction: Language, Mind, and Artifact: An Outline of Hermeneutic Theory Since the Enlightenment." In *The Hermeneutics Reader*, ed. Kurt Mueller-Vollmer, 1-53. New York: Continuum, 1989.

Muilenburg, James. "Form Criticism and Beyond." *Journal of Biblical Literature* 88 (1969): 1-18.

Mullins, Terence Y. "Topos as a New Testament Form." *Journal of Biblical Literature* 99 (1980): 541-47.

Munck, Johannes. *Paul and the Salvation of Mankind.* London: SCM Press, 1959.

Murphy-O'Connor, Jerome. *St. Paul's Corinth: Texts and Archaeology.* Good News Studies, ed. Robert J. Karris, no. Vol. 6. Wilmington, DE: Michael Glazier, 1983.

Nock, Arthur Darby. In *Essays on Religion and the Ancient World*, Vol. I, ed. Zeph Stewart, 49-133. Oxford: Clarendon, 1973a. Also in *Essays on the Trinity and the Incarnation*, ed. A. E. J. Rawlinson (1928), 51-156 "Early Gentile Christianity and its Hellenistic Background."

________. "The Vocabulary of the New Testament." In *Essays on Religion and the Ancient World*, Vol. I, ed. Zeph Stewart, 341-47. (also in *Journal of Biblical Studies* 52 [1933]), 131-39. Oxford: Clarendon, 1973.

O'Day, Gail R. "Jeremiah 9:22-23 and 1 Corinthians 1:26-31: A Study in Intertextuality." *Journal of Biblical Literature* 109 (1990), 259-267.

Ong, Walter J. "Foreword." In *The Present State of Scholarship in Historical and Contemporary Rhetoric*, ed. Winifred Bryan Horner, 1-9. Columbia: University of Missouri, 1983.

Palmer, Richard E. "Gadamer's Hermeneutics: A Reading of *Truth and Method*." *Philosophy & Rhetoric* 20 (1987): 135-38.

Patton, John H. "Causation and Creativity in Rhetorical Situations: Distinctions and Implications." *The Quarterly Journal of Speech* 65 (1979): 36-55.

Pearson, Birger Albert. *The Pneumatikos-Psychikos Terminology in 1 Cor.* SBL Dissertation Series no. 12. Missoula, MT: Society of Biblical Literature, 1973.

Perelman, Chaim, and L. Olbrechts-Tyteca. *The New Rhetoric: A Treatise on Argumentation.* Notre Dame: University of Notre Dame, 1969.

Perelman, Chaim. *The New Rhetoric and the Humanities: Essays on Rhetoric and Its Applications.* Boston: D. Reidel, 1979.

________. "Address at Ohio State University." In *Practical Reasoning in Human Affairs: Studies in Honor of Chaim Perelman*, eds. James L. Golden and Joseph J. Pilotta. Dordrecht, Holland: D. Reidel, 1986.

________. "Rhetoric." In *The New Encyclopedia Britannica*, Vol. 26, 15th ed., 803-10. Chicago: Encyclopedia Britannica, 1988.

________. *The Realm of Rhetoric.* Tranlated by William Kluback. South Bend, IN: University of Notre Dame Press, 1982.

Petersen, Norman R. *Literary Criticism for New Testament Critics.* Philadelphia: Fortress, 1978.

________. *Rediscovering Paul: Philemon and the Sociology of Paul's Narrative World.* Philadelphia: Fortress, 1985.

Plank, Karl A. *Paul and the Irony of Affliction.* Atlanta: Scholars Press, 1987.

Pomeroy, Ralph S. "'Fitness of Response' in Bitzer's Concept of Rhetorical Discourse." *Georgia Speech Communication Journal* 4 (1972): 42-71.

Pritchard, John Paul. *A Literary Approach to the New Testament.* Norman: University of Oklahoma, 1972.

Quimby, Rollin W. "The Growth of Plato's Perception of Rhetoric." *Philosophy & Rhetoric* 7 (1974): 71-79.

Rackham, H. "Introduction." In *Cicero: De Finibus Bonorum et Malorum*. LCL. Cambridge: Harvard, 1914.

Radermacher, Ludwig. *Neutestamentliche Grammatik: Das Griechische des neuen Testaments im Zusammenhang mit der Volkssprache.* 2nd ed. Handbuch zum Neuen Testament no. 1. Tübingen: J. C. B. Mohr, 1925.

Rengsdorf, Karl Heinrich. "Didasko- etc." In *Theological Dictionary of the New Testament*, ed. and translated by Geoffrey W. Bromiley. Grand Rapids: Eerdmans, 1976.

Rhoads, David M., and Donald Michie. *Mark as Story: An Introduction to the Narrative of a Gospel.* Philadelphia: Fortress, 1982.

Ricoeur, Paul. "Biblical Hermeneutics." *Semeia* 4 (1975), 27-148.

________. *Interpretation Theory: Discourse and the Surplus of Meaning.* Fort Worth: Texas Christian University Press, 1976.

________. *The Rule of Metaphor.* Tranlated by Robert Czerny with Kathleen McGloughlin and John Costello. Toronto: University Press, 1977.

________. *Hermeneutics and the Human Sciences: Essays on Language, Action and Interpretation.* ed. and tranlated by John B. Thompson. Cambridge: Cambridge University Press; Editions de la Maison des Sciences de l'Homme, 1981.

Robbins, Vernon. "Review: *New Testament Interpretation Through Rhetorical Criticism*, by George Kennedy." *Rhetorica* 3 (1985): 145-49.

Robbins, Vernon K. *Jesus the Teacher: A Socio-Rhetorical Interpretation of Mark.* Philadelphia: Fortress, 1984.

Robertson, Archibald, and Alfred Plummer. *A Critical and Exegetical Commentary on the First Epistle of St. Paul to the Corinthians.* 2nd ed. Edinburgh: T. & T. Clark, 1914.

Robinson, James M. "Kerygma and History in the New Testament." In *Trajectories through Early Christianity*, eds. James M. Robinson and Helmut Koester, 20-70. Philadelphia: Fortress, 1971.

Ruef, John. *Paul's First Letter to Corinth.* Baltimore: Penguin, 1971.

Russell, D. A. *Greek Declamation.* Cambridge: Cambridge University, 1983.

Saldarini, Anthony J. *Pharisees, Scribes and Sadducees in Palestinian Society: A Sociological Approach.* Wilmington, DE: Michael Glazier, 1988.

Saller, R. P. *Personal Patronage under the Early Empire.* Cambridge: University Press, 1982.

Sampley, J. Paul. "Paul, His Opponents in 2 Corintians 10-13, and the Rhetorical Handbooks." In *The Social World of Formative Christianity and Judaism*, eds. Jacob Neusner, Peder Borgen, Ernest S. Frerichs, and Richard Horsley, 162-77. Philadelphia: Fortress, 1988.

Sanders, E. P. *Paul and Palestinian Judaism.* Philadelphia: Fortress, 1977.

Sanger, D. "Die *dunatoi* in 1 Kor 1:26." *Zeitschrift für die neutestamentliche Wissenshaft und die Kunde des Urchristentums* 76 (1985): 285-91.

Schmidt, Karl Ludwig. "Die Stellung der Evangelien in der allgemeinen Literaturgeschichte." In *Eucharistarion: Studien zur Religion und Literatur des Alen und Neuen Testaments; Hermann Gunkel zum 60 Geburtstag*, ed. Hans Schmidt, 50-134. Göttingen: Vandenhoeck und Ruprecht, 1923.

Schmithals, Walter. *Gnosticism in Corinth: An Investigation of the Letters to the Corinthians.* Tranlated by J.E. Steely. Nashville: Abingdon, 1971.

Schubert, Paul. *Form and Function of the Pauline Thanksgivings.* Berlin: Töpelmann, 1939.

Schutz, John H. ed. and Tranlated by John. H. Schutz "Introduction." In *The Social Setting of Pauline Christianity: Essays on Corinth by Gerd Theissen*. Philadelphia: Fortress, 1982.

Encylopedia Judaica, s.v. "Scribes." Jerusalem: Keter, 1972.

Scroggs, Robin. "Paul: SOPHOS and PNEUMATIKOS." *New Testament Studies* 14 (1967): 33-35.

________. "The Sociological Interpretation of the New Testament: The Present State of Research." *New Testament Studies* 26 (1980): 164-79.

Sellin, Gerhard. "Das 'Geheimnis' der Weisheit und das Rätsel der 'Christuspartei' (zu 1 Kor 1-4)." *Zeitschrift für die neutestamentliche Wissenshaft und die Kunde des Urchristentums* 73 (1982): 69-96.

________. "Hauptprobleme des Ersten Korintherbrief." In *Augstief und Niedergang der römischen Welt*, Vol. 25:4, eds. Wolfgang Haase and Hildegard Temporini, 2940-3044. Berlin: Walter de Gruyter, 1987.

Shanor, Jay. "Paul as Master Builder: Construction Terms in First Corinthians." *New Testament Studies* 34 (1988): 461-71.

Shuler, Philip L. *A Genre for the Gospels: The Biograpraphical Character of Matthew.* Phildelphia: Fortress, 1982.

Sikes, E. E. "Literature in the Age of Cicero." In *The Cambridge Ancient History*, Vol. IX: The Roman Republic, 133-44 B.C., eds. S. A. Cook, F. E. Adcock, and M. P. Charlesworth. New York: MacMillan, 1932.

Simon, Marcel. "From Greek Hairesis to Christian Heresy." In *Early Christian Literature and the Classical Intellectual Tradition*, eds. William Schoedel and Robert L. Wilken, 101-16. Théologie Historique, no. 53. Paris: Éditions Beauchesne, 1979.

Skehan, Patrick W., and Alexander A. Di Lella. *The Wisdom of Ben Sira.* Anchor Bible, eds. William Foxwell Albright and David Noel Freedman, no. 39. New York: Doubleday, 1987.

Smit, Joop. "The Letter of Paul to the Galatians: A Deliberative Speech." *New Testament Studies* 35 (1989): 1-26.

Smith, Dennis Edwin. "Social Obligation in the Context of Communal Meals: A Study of the Christian Meal in 1 Corinthians in Comparison with Graeco-Roman Communal Meals." Th.D. diss., Harvard, 1980.

________. "Dining and Dining Rooms in the Corinth of 1 Corinthians," unpublished paper delivered at SBL, 1989.

Smith, Robert W. *The Art of Rhetoric in Alexandria: Its Theory and Practice in the Ancient World.* The Hague: Martinus Nijhoff, 1974.

Snyman, A. H. "Style and Rhetorical Situation of Romans 8:31-39." *New Testament Studies* 34 (1988): 218-31.

Stanton, G. L. *Jesus of Nazareth in New Testament Preaching.* Cambridge: University Press, 1974.

Stowers, Stanley Kent. *The Diatribe and Paul's Letter to the Romans.* Chico, CA: Scholars Press, 1981.

________. "Social Status, Public Speaking and Private Teaching: The Circumstances of Paul's Preaching Activity." *Novum Testamentum* 26 (1984): 59-82.

________. *Letter Writing in Greco-Roman Antiquity.* Library of Early Christianity, ed. Wayne A. Meeks, no. 5. Philadelphia: Westminster, 1986.

Sutton, Jane. "The Death of Rhetoric and its Rebirth in Philosophy." *Rhetorica* 4 (1986): 203-26.

Talbert, Charles H. *What is a Gospel? The Genre of the Canonical Gospels.* Philadelphia: Fortress, 1977.

Theissen, Gerd. *The Social Setting of Pauline Christianity.* ed. and Tranlated by John H. Schütz. Philadelphia: Fortress, 1982.

Thistleton, Anthony C. "The New Hermeneutic." In *New Testament Interpretation: Essays on principles and Methods*, ed. I. Howard Marshall, 308-33. Grand Rapids: Eerdmans, 1977.

________. *The Two Horizons: New Testament Hermeneutics and Philosophical Description with Special Reference to Heidegger, Bultmann, Gadamer, and Wittgenstein.* Grand Rapids: Eerdmans, 1980.

Tompkins, Jane P. "An Introduction to Reader-Response Criticism." In *Reader-Response Criticism: From Formalism to Post-Structuralism*, ed. Jane P. Tompkins, ix-xxvi. Baltimore: Johns Hopkins, 1980.

________. "The Reader in History: The Changing Shape of Literary Response." In *Reader-Response Criticism: From Formalism to Post-Structuralism*, ed. Jane P. Tompkins, 201-32. Baltimore: Johns Hopkins, 1980.

Tompkins, Phillip K., John H. Patton, and Lloyd F. Bitzer. "The Forum." *The Quarterly Journal of Speech* 66 (1980): 85-93.

Tracy, David. *Plurality and Ambiguity.* San Francisco: Harper & Row, 1987.

Travis, S. H. "Paul's Boasting in 2 Corinthians 10-12." In *Studia Evangelica*, Vol. 6, ed. Elizabeth A. Livingstone, 527-32. Berlin: Akademie-Verlag, 1973.

Vatz, Richard E. "The Myth of the Rhetorical Situation." *Philosophy & Rhetoric* 6 (1973): 154-61.

Voelz, James W. "The Language of the New Testament." In *ANRW*, Vol. 2.25.2, ed. Wolfgang Haase, 893-977. Berlin: Walter de Gruyter, 1984.

Watson, Duane F. "The New Testament and Greco-Roman Rhetoric: A Bibliography." *Journal of the Evangelical Theological Society* 31 (1988): 465-72.

Weinsheimer, Joel C. *Gadamer's Hermeneutics: A Reading of Truth and Method.* New Haven: Yale, 1985.

Weiss, Johannes. *Der erste Korintherbrief.* 10th ed. Kritisch-exegetischer Kommentar über das Neue Testament no. 5. Göttingen: Vandenhoeck & Ruprecht, 1925.

Welborn, L. L. "A Conciliatory Principle in 1 Cor. 4:6." *Novum Testamentum* 29 (1987): 320-46.

________. "On the Discord in Corinth: 1 Corinthians 1-4 and Ancient Politics." *Journal of Biblical Literature* 106 (1987): 85-111.

White, Eugene E. "Rhetoric as Historical Configuration." In *Rhetoric in Transition: Studies in the Nature and Uses of Rhetoric*, ed. E. E. White, 7-20. University Park and London: Pennsylvania State University Press, 1980.

White, John L. "New Testament Epistolary Literature in the Framework of Ancient Epistolography." In *Aufstieg und Niedergan der*

Römishcen Welt, Vol. 2. 25.2, ed. Wolfgang Haase, 1730-56. Berlin: Walter de Gruyter, 1984.

________. *Light from Ancient Letters.* Philadelphia: Fortress, 1986.

Wilckens, Ulrich. *Weisheit und Torheit.* Tübingen: J.C.B. Mohr, 1959.

________. "Σοφια." In *Theological Dictionary of the New Testament*, Vol. 7, ed. Gerhard Kittel, ed. and tranlated by Geoffrey Bromily, 467-70, 496-528. Grand Rapids: Eerdmans, 1971.

Willis, Wendell. "The 'Mind of Christ' in 1 Corinthians 2:16." *Biblica* 70 (1989): 110-22.

Wilson, Robert McLachlan. *Gnosis and the New Testament.* Philadelphia: Fortress, 1968.

________. "How Gnostic were the Corinthians?" *NTS* 19 (1972): 65-74.

________. "Gnosis at Corinth." In *Paul and Paulinism: Essays in Honour of C.K. Barrett*, eds. Morna D. Hooker and S. G. Wilson. London: Alden, 1982.

Windisch, Hans. s.v., "καπηλευω." In *Theological Dictionary of the New Testament*, ed. G. Kittel, ed. and tranlated by G.W. Bromiley. Grand Rapids, MI: Eerdmans, 1965.

Winterbottom, M. "Introduction." In *The Elder Seneca: Declamations*, vii-xxiv. Cambridge: Harvard, 1974.

Wiseman, J. "Corinth and Rome I: 228 B.C. - A.D. 267." In *Aufstieg und Niedergang der römischen Welt*, Vol. 2.7.1, ed. Hildegard Temporini, 438-548. Berlin: Walter de Gruyter, 1979.

Wright, Wilmer Cave. "Introduction." In *Philostratus and Eunapius: The Lives of the Sophists*, ix-xli. LCL. Cambridge: Harvard, 1921.

Wuellner, Wilhelm. "Haggadic Homily Genre in I Corinthians 1-3." *JBL* 89 (1970): 199-204.

________. "The Sociological Implications of 1 Corinthians 1:26-28 Reconsidered." In *Studia Evangelica*, Vol. 6, ed. Elizabeth A. Livingstone, 666-72. Berlin: Akademie-Verlag, 1973.

________. "Ursprung und Verwendung der σοφός- δυνατός- εὐγενής Formel in 1 Kor. 1,26." In *Donum Gentilicum*, eds. E. Bammel, C. K. Barrett, and W. D. Davies, 165-84. Oxford: University Press, 1978.

________. "Greek Rhetoric and Pauline Argumentation." In *Early Christian Literature and the Classical Intellectual Tradition*, eds. William Schoedel and Robert L. Wilken, 177-88. Théologie Historique, no. 53. Paris: Éditions Beauchesne, 1979.

________. "Where is Rhetorical Criticism Taking Us?" *Catholic Biblical Quarterly* 49 (1987): 448-63.

Young, Norman H. "The Social Setting of the Paidagogos." *Novum Testamentum* 29 (1984): 150-76.

Zuntz, G. *The Text of the Epistles: A Disquisition upon the Corpus Paulinum.* London: Oxford University, 1953.